Longman Dictionary of Common Errors

N D Turton and J B Heaton

Longman

Pearson Education Limited
Edinburgh Gate
Harlow
Essex
CM20 2JE
England
and Associated Companies throughout the world.

Visit our website: http:/ww .longman-elt.com/dictionaries

First published 1987
Second edition 1996
Ninth impression 2000

British Library Cataloguing-in-Publication Data
A catalogue record for this book is available from the British Library

ISBN 0 582 23752 1

Set in Adobe Helvetica

Printed in China
SWTC/09

Contents

Acknowledgements

The authors would like to thank Della Summers, Director – Longman Dictionaries, for granting them permission to use the Longman Learners' Corpus and the British National Corpus as sources of information for this new edition. At the same time, we are deeply indebted to all those who have designed, managed and contributed to these invaluable databanks.

Our sincere thanks are also extended to Judith Aguda for editing the entire manuscript with meticulous care and super-human patience, to Alison Steadman for co-ordinating the production stages, and to Lizzie Warren for overseeing the project from start to finish.

We have not forgotten those who made important contributions to the first edition and we would like to reacknowledge our debt to Sue Maingay, Kelly Davis, Diane Sutton and Mona Scheraga, and to the University of Cambridge Local Examinations Syndicate.

Finally, we must thank the countless foreign students of English who have provided the content of both editions.

Preface

The *Longman Dictionary of Common Errors* provides learners and teachers of English with a practical guide to common errors and their correction. It contains the words and phrases which regularly cause difficulty for foreign learners, regardless of nationality and language background. Arranged alphabetically for ease of use, the entries deal with those errors that regularly appear in the written English of learners at the intermediate level of proficiency and above. Each error is accompanied by a correction and a short, simple explanation.

Since the appearance of the first edition of this dictionary almost a decade ago, dictionary making has been transformed by major developments in information technology. Today's dictionary makers are able to draw upon huge computerized databanks to discover exactly how language is used. This new edition of the *Longman Dictionary of Common Errors* owes its authority to two such databanks: the Longman Learners' Corpus and the British National Corpus.

The Longman Learners' Corpus contains samples of the written English produced by students from over 70 different countries. With this carefully coded corpus of ten million words, it is possible to identify more clearly than ever before the words and phrases which cause problems for particular groups of learners and for learners in general. As a result, this second edition contains a large number of new entries, while first edition entries which are insufficiently supported by the corpus have been removed.

The investigation of common errors sometimes raises questions about usage for which there are no readily available answers. For example, what do native speakers usually say – 'I disagree that heart transplants should be stopped.' or 'I don't agree that heart transplants should be stopped'? According to modern usage, is it usual to say 'She failed her examination.' or 'She failed in her examination'? Is it incorrect to say 'More houses are built yearly.' and, if so, why is yearly unacceptable here? In helping us to answer questions such as these, the British National Corpus has been an indispensable source of information. This large corpus of modern British English usage has been particularly useful in revealing the subtle differences that make one word or phrase exactly right in a particular context, and others unsuitable.

Despite the recognized usefulness of computerized corpora in dictionary making, this application of information technology is still relatively new. Accordingly, while we believe that this new edition is a major advance on the original, we welcome all comments and suggestions.

Guide to the Dictionary

Finding the information you need

The entries in this dictionary are in alphabetical order: **about** is at the front of the book and **youth** is at the back. To help you find an entry quickly, there is a word in heavy type at the top of each page. The word at the top of a left-hand page is the name of the first entry; the word at the top of a right-hand page is the name of the last entry.

To use this dictionary to correct errors, you need to know which word to look up. In many cases, you will find the information you need at the entry for the **keyword.** This is the most important word in a group of words which regularly occur together. For example, to find out why 'a hole on my sock' is incorrect, you should look up the entry for **hole** (not **on**).

To find out what is wrong with 'He'll be here at December', you should turn to the entry for **at** (not **December**). In cases like this, there is no fixed group of words and therefore no keyword.

Sometimes, the keyword is separated from the part of the sentence containing the error. For example, in: 'She never lets the children to go out on their own', your teacher may underline <u>to</u> or <u>to go</u>. In cases like this, the information you need is to be found at the entry for the word or phrase which requires a particular form to be used later on in the sentence. For example, you <u>allow</u> someone <u>to do</u> something, but you <u>let</u> someone <u>do</u> something (not 'to do').

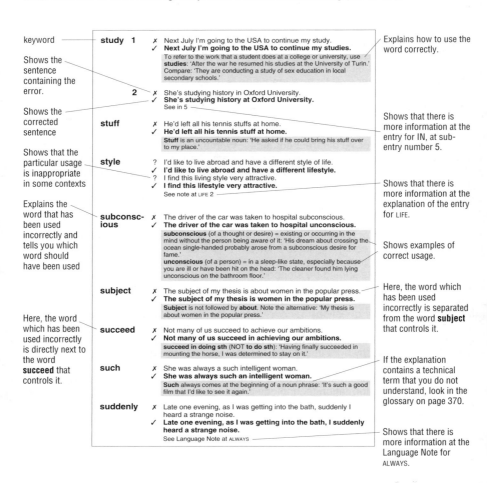

keyword

Shows the sentence containing the error.

Shows the corrected sentence

Shows that the particular usage is inappropriate in some contexts

Explains the word that has been used incorrectly and tells you which word should have been used

Here, the word which has been used incorrectly is directly next to the word **succeed** that controls it.

Explains how to use the word correctly.

Shows that there is more information at the entry for IN, at sub-entry number 5.

Shows that there is more information at the explanation of the entry for LIFE.

Shows examples of correct usage.

Here, the word which has been used incorrectly is separated from the word **subject** that controls it.

If the explanation contains a technical term that you do not understand, look in the glossary on page 370.

Shows that there is more information at the Language Note for ALWAYS.

study 1 ✗ Next July I'm going to the USA to continue my study.
✓ **Next July I'm going to the USA to continue my studies.**
To refer to the work that a student does at a college or university, use **studies**: 'After the war he resumed his studies at the University of Turin.' Compare: 'They are conducting a study of sex education in local secondary schools.'

2 ✗ She's studying history in Oxford University.
✓ **She's studying history at Oxford University.**
See in 5

stuff ✗ He'd left all his tennis stuffs at home.
✓ **He'd left all his tennis stuff at home.**
Stuff is an uncountable noun: 'He asked if he could bring his stuff over to my place.'

style ? I'd like to live abroad and have a different style of life.
✓ **I'd like to live abroad and have a different lifestyle.**
? I find this living style very attractive.
✓ **I find this lifestyle very attractive.**
See note at LIFE 2

subconsc-ious ✗ The driver of the car was taken to hospital subconscious.
✓ **The driver of the car was taken to hospital unconscious.**
subconscious (of a thought or desire) = existing or occurring in the mind without the person being aware of it: 'His dream about crossing the ocean single-handed probably arose from a subconscious desire for fame.'
unconscious (of a person) = in a sleep-like state, especially because you are ill or have been hit on the head: 'The cleaner found him lying unconscious on the bathroom floor.'

subject ✗ The subject of my thesis is about women in the popular press.
✓ **The subject of my thesis is women in the popular press.**
Subject is not followed by **about**. Note the alternative: 'My thesis is about women in the popular press.'

succeed ✗ Not many of us succeed to achieve our ambitions.
✓ **Not many of us succeed in achieving our ambitions.**
succeed in doing sth (NOT to do sth): 'Having finally succeeded in mounting the horse, I was determined to stay on it.'

such ✗ She was always a such intelligent woman.
✓ **She was always such an intelligent woman.**
Such always comes at the beginning of a noun phrase: 'It's such a good film that I'd like to see it again.'

suddenly ✗ Late one evening, as I was getting into the bath, suddenly I heard a strange noise.
✓ **Late one evening, as I was getting into the bath, I suddenly heard a strange noise.**
See Language Note at ALWAYS

Some entries have sub entries, each with their own numbers.
Errors involving vocabulary usually come before errors in grammar, and very common errors come before those which occur less frequently.

will 1

✗ When capital punishment was abolished, people thought that murders will become more numerous.
✓ **When capital punishment was abolished, people thought that murders would become more numerous.**

A reporting verb in the past tense (e.g. 'thought') is usually followed by **would/could** (NOT **will/can**). Compare: 'I think she will accept any job that comes along.' 'I thought she would accept any job that came along.'

2

✗ If a developing country will become a developed country, it has to attract foreign investors.
✓ **If a developing country is to become a developed country, it has to attract foreign investors.**

When you are talking about what must happen in order to make something possible, use **if ... am/is/are to do sth** (NOT **will**): 'If we are to get there by six o'clock, we'll have to get a taxi.'

3

See Language Note below

When there is a lot of information about a group of related errors, this is presented in a Language Note.

Talking about the future

• When you talk about something happening in the future, you often use one of the following conjunctions:

TIME   **after, as soon as, before, immediately, once, the moment, until, when, whenever, while**

CONDITION   **if, whether, as long as, in case, unless**

• To refer to the future after these conjunctions, use the present simple tense (NOT **will/shall**):

I'll phone you as soon as I <u>arrive</u> at the airport.
The plane should be taking off shortly, as long as there <u>aren't</u> any delays.

Note:
1 Sometimes it is possible to use the present perfect tense instead of the present simple. The present perfect expresses a sense of completion:

She doesn't want to buy a car until she's <u>passed</u> her driving test.
Once you'<u>ve made</u> a few friends, you won't feel so lonely.

2 When the clause beginning with **if, whether, when**, etc is the object of the sentence, **will** may be used:

I doubt <u>whether David will still recognize me.</u>
I don't know <u>when they'll be back.</u>

Also, **if ... will** is possible when **will** expresses the idea of willingness:

What are you going to do if she won't help you?
If you'll take a seat for a moment, I'll tell Mr Fox you're here.

a 1

✗ I hope you all have a enjoyable stay.
✓ **I hope you all have an enjoyable stay.**

> Always use **an** (NOT **a**) before a word beginning with a vowel sound: 'an egg' /ən eg/, 'an envelope' /ən ˈenvələʊp/.

2

✗ My husband is doing a MSc in civil engineering.
✓ **My husband is doing an MSc in civil engineering.**

> Use **an** (NOT **a**) before an abbreviation that begins with a vowel sound: 'an MSc' /ən ˌem es ˈsiː/, 'an MP' /ən ˌem ˈpiː/.

3

✗ Sometimes it is difficult to live a honest life.
✓ **Sometimes it is difficult to live an honest life.**

> Use **an** (NOT **a**) before words beginning with **h** when the **h** is not pronounced: 'an honour' /ən ˈɒnə/, 'an hour' /ən aʊə/.

a/an 1

✗ The child had been a deaf since birth.
✓ **The child had been deaf since birth.**
✗ One of the girls I share with is a British.
✓ **One of the girls I share with is British.**

> Do not use **a/an** before an adjective (e.g. 'deaf', 'British') unless the adjective is followed by a noun: 'Her husband is disabled.'
> Compare: 'The footbridge cannot be used by the disabled.' (= all people who are disabled)

2

See ANOTHER 6

abandon 1

✗ Since capital punishment was abandoned, the crime rate has increased.
✓ **Since capital punishment was abolished, the crime rate has increased.**

> **abandon** = give up a plan, activity or attempt to do something, without being successful: 'Bad weather forced them to abandon the search.' 'Without government support, the project will have to be abandoned.'
> **abolish** = remove a law, tradition or system, often by introducing a new law; do away with: 'In which year was slavery abolished in the United States?' 'I'd hate to see the monarchy abolished.'

2

✗ It is difficult to reach abandoned places such as small country villages.
✓ **It is difficult to reach remote places such as small country villages.**

> **abandoned** = left for ever by the owners or occupiers: 'The field was littered with abandoned cars.' 'Some of these old abandoned coal mines could be dangerous.'

remote = far away and difficult to reach: 'The tribe lives in a small remote mountain village.' 'We have now managed to bring famine relief to people in even the most remote areas.'

ability 1   ✗ These machines are destroying our ability of thinking.
✓ **These machines are destroying our ability to think.**
ability to do sth (NOT **of doing**): 'Nobody doubts his ability to get the job done.' 'We need someone with the ability to work under pressure.'

2   ✗ I want to improve my ability of reading.
✓ **I want to improve my reading ability.**
✓ **reading/writing/teaching/acting ability**: 'Her acting ability was recognized at a very early age.'

3   ✗ I want to improve my ability of English.
✓ **I want to improve my ability in English.**
ability in a language or subject: 'Sarah has demonstrated considerable ability in both maths and chemistry.'

able 1   ✗ One man is able to destroy the whole world.
✓ **One man is capable of destroying the whole world.**
If someone is **able to do something,** they can do it and it is not unusual or surprising if they do it: 'The doctor said that after a few days I'd be able to get out of bed.' 'Will you be able to play on Saturday?'
If someone is **capable of (doing) something,** they do not usually do it, but it is possible for them to do it if they want to: 'I'm sure he's quite capable of getting here on time, but he can't be bothered.' 'The power station is capable of generating enough electricity for the whole region.'

2   ✗ There are so many places to visit in London that I'm not able to decide where to go.
✓ **There are so many places to visit in London that I can't decide where to go.**
✗ We weren't able to stop laughing.
✓ **We couldn't stop laughing.**
With verbs of perception (e.g. **see, hear, smell**) and verbs of the mind (e.g. **understand, decide, remember**), we usually use **can, can't,** etc: 'I can't hear you. Could you speak a bit louder, please?' 'I think I can smell something burning.' 'Having met her new boss, I can see why she doesn't like him.' Note also the phrase **can't/couldn't stop doing something**: 'The book was so fascinating I couldn't stop reading it.'
See also COULD 1

3   ✗ In some countries you are not able to drink until you are 21.
✓ **In some countries you can't drink until you are 21.**
For actions that are controlled by laws or rules, use **can, can't,** etc, or **be (not) allowed to**: 'Now that they are both sixteen, they can get married.' 'The goalkeeper can touch the ball, but nobody else can.'

4   ✗ Technology has made them able to grow their own food.
✓ **Technology has enabled them to grow their own food.**
enable = make someone able to do something: 'This scheme is designed to enable young people to find work.'
Note also the phrase can't/couldn't stop doing something: 'The book was so fascinating I couldn't stop reading it.' See also COULD 1

about 1

✗ I am always delighted when I receive a letter from you. About the party on December 26th, I shall be very pleased to attend.

✓ **I am always delighted when I receive a letter from you. With regard to the party on December 26th, I shall be very pleased to attend.**

✗ People usually sleep with the doors and windows closed. About public transport, the bus and train services are excellent.

✓ **People usually sleep with the doors and windows closed. As for public transport, the bus and train services are excellent.**

About may be used to introduce a topic (or change of topic), but only in informal styles: 'About that book you asked for – I'll get you a copy when I go to London.'
In other styles, use **with regard to, regarding, as for, as regards** or **as far as ... is concerned**: 'With regard to the matter of unemployment, I would like to add a few remarks to those of the previous speaker.' 'I regret to inform you that *Language and Culture* is out of print. As regards your second question, I suggest that you write to the British Museum.'

2

✗ It all depends on how different the new country is from your own. About myself, I haven't experienced any culture shock but then this is my second trip to the States.

✓ **It all depends on how different the new country is from your own. In my own case, I haven't experienced any culture shock but then this is my second trip to the States.**

To show that you are going to start talking about your own personal experience or situation, use **in my own case** or (especially in informal styles) **as for me/myself**: 'Many people have benefited from the operation. In my own case, I began to feel better immediately.' 'Most of my friends like school. As for me, I can't wait to leave.'

3

✗ I was about leaving when the telephone rang.

✓ **I was about to leave when the telephone rang.**

be about to do sth (NOT **doing**)
Compare: 'I was just leaving when the telephone rang.'

above 1

✗ There were above a hundred people in the crowd.

✓ **There were over a hundred people in the crowd.**

Do not use **above** with numbers (unless referring to points on a scale): 'He is over eighty years of age.' 'I receive over twenty letters a day.' Compare 'Don't let the temperature get above thirty degrees.'

2

? I like to stay at home on a Sunday, as I've said above.

✓ **I like to stay at home on a Sunday, as I've already said.**

? What do you think of the above suggestion?

✓ **What do you think of my/this suggestion?**

Above is used in formal writing to refer to something that has been mentioned earlier: 'From the above arguments it can be seen that supporters of the dam project fall into two camps.' In informal styles, this use of **above** is inappropriate.

3

? Taking all the above into account, one could say that tourism does more harm than good.

✓ **Taking all the above arguments into account, one could say that tourism does more harm than good.**

Instead of using **the above** as a loose reference to something mentioned earlier, make the reference more precise by using **the above** + noun (or **the** + noun + **above**): 'the above reasons', 'the statement above '.

above all 1 ✗ He likes reading, above all novels.
    ✓ **He likes reading, especially novels.**

Above all means 'most importantly': 'Get plenty of sleep, eat lots of good food, and above all try to relax.' 'There were many qualities that made him a great leader. Above all, he had charisma.'

2 ✗ This year English is above all my most important subject.
    ✓ **This year English is by far my most important subject.**

With a superlative form ('the most important'), use **by far**: 'The riot was by far the most horrific scene I'd ever witnessed.'

3 ✗ Where would you like to go above all?
    ✓ **Where would you like to go most of all?**

When you mean 'more than anywhere/anything/anyone else', use **most of all** or **the most**: 'What worries me most of all is that the car is not roadworthy.' 'The one I liked the most was too expensive.'

above-mentioned ✗ I would be grateful if you would send it to the address above-mentioned.
    ✓ **I would be grateful if you would send it to the above-mentioned address.**

Above-mentioned comes before the noun: 'the above-mentioned person', 'the above-mentioned company'.
Note that **above** may be used before or after the noun: 'the above address', 'the address above'.

abroad ✗ Since I was small, I've always wanted to go to abroad.
    ✓ **Since I was small, I've always wanted to go abroad.**
    ✗ I would like to continue my studies in abroad.
    ✓ **I would like to continue my studies abroad.**

go/live/be abroad (WITHOUT **to, at, in** etc)
The only preposition that is used before **abroad** is **from**: 'She came back from abroad saying how much she had missed her home and family.'

absent ✗ It's a pity that you were absent from the training session.
    ✓ **It's a pity that you missed the training session.**
    ✓ **It's a pity that you weren't at the training session.**

be absent = not be present at something that you are officially supposed to attend: 'Her teacher wanted to know why she'd been absent.'
miss = not be present at something: 'She's missed a lot of classes this term because of illness.' 'I wouldn't miss Sandro's party for the world!' (= I really want to go to it).
be at = be present at something: 'John won't be at the meeting. He's had to fly to Rome on business.'

absolutely ✗ It is absolutely important that you see a doctor immediately.
    ✓ **It is very important that you see a doctor immediately.**
    ✓ **It is absolutely essential that you see a doctor immediately.**
See note at VERY 2

accept 1 ✗ The company will not accept to buy new machines.
  ✓ **The company will not agree to buy new machines.**

You **accept** someone's advice, opinion, or suggestion BUT you **agree** (= say you are willing) to do something. Compare: 'I accepted her suggestion and agreed to see the doctor that evening.'

2 ✗ The driver did not accept me to get on the bus.
  ✓ **The driver did not allow me to get on the bus.**
  ✗ We can't accept a motorway to be built through our town.
  ✓ **We can't allow a motorway to be built through our town.**

You **allow/permit** someone to do something, or **let** them do it: 'Many parents do not allow/permit their children to watch violent films.' 'Many parents do not let their children watch violent films.'

access ✗ Computers give us an easier access to information.
  ✓ **Computers give us easier access to information.**

Access is an uncountable noun: 'The entrance has been widened to provide easier access for disabled people.' 'They have no right to refuse us access to the files.'

accident ✗ Her car was involved in a big accident.
  ✓ **Her car was involved in a serious accident.**

a **bad/dreadful/nasty/serious/fatal accident** (NOT **big**)

accommoda- ✗ Could you help me look for an accommodation?
tion ✓ **Could you help me look for accommodation?**
  ✗ Accommodations in London are very expensive.
  ✓ **Accommodation in London is very expensive.**

In British English **accommodation** (= a place to stay or live in) is always uncountable: 'For the first year we stayed in rented accommodation.' In American English both **accommodation** and **accommodations** (plural) are used.

accomplish ✗ To accomplish world unity, we need peace.
  ✓ **To achieve world unity, we need peace.**
  ✗ A balanced diet is accomplished by eating many different kinds of food.
  ✓ **A balanced diet is achieved by eating many different kinds of food.**

When you **accomplish** something, you manage to do it or complete it, especially something that gives you satisfaction: 'She felt that she could accomplish more through journalism.' 'During his five years as President, he accomplished very little.'
When you **achieve** something, you manage to do or obtain what you have planned to do or obtain, especially after a lot of effort: 'The company intends to achieve all these goals within the next five years.' 'By the age of twenty, she had already achieved her ambition.'
Note that **achieve** is also used to mean 'accomplish': 'By the end of the course, you will feel that you've really achieved something.'

according ✗ According to me, we should spend more money on education.
to 1 ✓ **In my opinion, we should spend more money on education.**

according to + the writer/Dr Owen/her teachers/them etc (NOT **me/us**): 'According to Charles Anderson, the government should pay

closer attention to public opinion.'
To introduce your own opinion, use **in my/our opinion**: 'In my opinion, he didn't deserve a prison sentence.'

2 See OPINION 1, POINT OF VIEW 1

account

✗ We also have to take into account that the schools are overcrowded.
✓ **We also have to take into account the fact that the schools are overcrowded.**

take into account + **the fact** + **that**-clause: 'They should take into account the fact that these archaeological treasures are extremely valuable.'

accurate

✗ I cannot give you the accurate date of my arrival yet.
✓ **I cannot give you the exact date of my arrival yet.**

Accurate is mainly used (1) to describe something said or written that contains no errors: 'Her novels are always historically accurate.' 'These figures can't be accurate, surely.' (2) to describe something that produces no errors: 'Are you sure the bathroom scales are accurate?' When you mean 'correct and as detailed as possible', use **exact**: 'The exact time is three minutes to seven.' 'Do you remember his exact words?' 'They'll be arriving next week – on Friday at three, to be exact.'

accustom 1

✗ I am beginning to accustom to the British way of life.
✓ **I am beginning to get accustomed to the British way of life.**

be/become/get/grow accustomed to sth: 'Within a few minutes, my eyes had grown accustomed to the dark.'
Note that, apart from in formal styles, most people prefer **be/become/get/grow used to**: 'I am beginning to get used to the British way of life.'

2 ✗ Where I come from, we are not accustomed to see so many things in the shops.
✓ **Where I come from, we are not accustomed to seeing so many things in the shops.**

be accustomed to doing sth (NOT **to do**): 'He was accustomed to leading a life of luxury.'

ache

✗ After the run, I had an ache in my legs.
✓ **After the run, my legs were aching.**

Ache is usually used either as a verb or in compounds with **tooth, ear, head, back, stomach**: 'I did some weight training on Monday and my shoulders have been aching ever since.' 'That radio of yours is giving me a headache.'
Compare: 'After the run, I had pains in my legs.'

act 1

✗ I am interested in the way people act towards each other.
✓ **I am interested in the way people behave towards each other.**
✗ It is time that human beings learned how to act properly, without killing each other.
✓ **It is time that human beings learned how to behave properly, without killing each other.**

When you are talking about what someone does on a particular occasion, **act** and **behave** are interchangeable: 'Passengers who left the

flight in Rhodes said that they had seen two men acting/behaving very suspiciously.'
When you are talking generally about what someone does or what people do, use **behave**: 'You can't expect all babies to behave the same.' 'From the way he behaves, anyone would think that he doesn't get paid.'

2 ✗ He refused to accept responsibility for his acts.
✓ **He refused to accept responsibility for his actions.**

The noun **act** is usually used when you want to comment on a particular thing that someone has done: 'It was an act of great courage.' 'These cowardly terrorist acts bring death and suffering to the innocent.'
When you are talking about someone's general behaviour, use **actions**: 'You can't be blamed for your parents' actions.' 'Her words and actions have not gone unnoticed.' See also ACTION 2

action 1 ✗ The actions that we do everyday are made easier by computers.
✓ **The things that we do everyday are made easier by computers.**
✗ If someone has done a wrong action, he should be punished.
✓ **If someone has done something wrong, he should be punished.**

Do and **action** cannot be used together. Use **do** + **things/something/anything** etc: 'She's always doing things for charity.' 'Don't do anything that might upset them.'

2 ✗ It is difficult to forgive those responsible for actions of terrorism.
✓ **It is difficult to forgive those responsible for acts of terrorism.**
✗ Blackmail is the action of trying to obtain money from someone by threatening to expose them.
✓ **Blackmail is the act of trying to obtain money from someone by threatening to expose them.**

an/the act of (doing) sth (NOT **action**): 'Such acts of violence will not be tolerated.' 'For some people, the very act of talking to a doctor can help them to feel better.'

3 ✗ Few people are aware that an urgent action is needed.
✓ **Few people are aware that urgent action is needed.**
✗ The government should take an action to reduce the birth rate.
✓ **The government should take action to reduce the birth rate.**

When you are talking about the idea or process of doing something, **action** is uncountable: 'There is too much talk and not enough action.'
In the phrase **take action**, **action** is always uncountable: 'This illegal trade will continue unless action is taken to stop it.'

actual ✗ We'd like to know more about the actual crisis (Not the economic problems of the past).
✓ **We'd like to know more about the present crisis (Not the economic problems of the past).**
✗ My actual job involves a lot of administration.
✓ **My present job involves a lot of administration.**

actual = real (as opposed what is believed, planned or expected): 'People think he is over fifty but his actual age is forty-eight.' 'Although

buses are supposed to run every fifteen minutes, the actual waiting time can be up to an hour.'
present/current = happening or existing now: 'No one can drive that car in its present condition.' 'Her current boyfriend works for Shell.'

actually 1   ✗   I never get bored by this city. Actually, each time I return I find something new to interest me.
✓   **I never get bored by this city. In fact, each time I return I find something new to interest me.**

When **actually** means 'in fact', it is usually used to correct a misunderstanding: 'People think we've got lots of money, but actually we're quite poor.' 'I'm sorry to have kept you waiting.' - 'Well actually I've only just arrived.'
When you simply want to develop a previous statement, use **in fact** or **as a matter of fact**: 'The winter of 1940 was extremely bad. In fact most people say it was the worst winter in living memory.' 'The company is doing very well. As a matter of fact, our sales have doubled.' See also ACTUAL

2   ✗   We need to produce and export more than we do actually.
✓   **We need to produce and export more than we do at present.**

When you mean 'at the present time', use **at present, at the moment** or **currently** (NOT **actually**) : 'At present the company is very short of staff.' 'At the moment I'm working part-time in a travel agency.'

add   ✗   The other ingredients are then added into the mixture.
✓   **The other ingredients are then added to the mixture.**

add sth to sth (NOT **into**): 'They are demanding that a new clause be added to the contract which will give them a share of the profits.' 'When a prefix is added to a word, you make a new word.'

admire 1   ✗   One hour is not long enough to admire all the exhibits.
✓   **One hour is not long enough to see all the exhibits.**
✗   I enjoyed admiring all the old buildings.
✓   **I enjoyed looking at all the old buildings.**

Do not use **admire** when you just mean 'see' or 'look at'. **Admire** means 'look at someone or something with a strong feeling of pleasure'. This meaning of **admire** is found mainly in novels and tourist brochures: 'Come and admire the magnificence of the Niagara Falls.' 'Rupert was sitting outside on the verandah, admiring the many jewels in the night sky.'

2   ✗   Although it was a sad film, I admired it very much.
✓   **Although it was a sad film, I enjoyed it very much.**
✗   Everybody admired your talk because it was lively and interesting.
✓   **Everybody enjoyed your talk because it was lively and interesting.**

Do not use **admire** when you mean 'enjoy'. **Admire** means 'have a very high opinion of someone': 'I've always admired people who think for themselves.' 'Lewis was probably best known and admired for his work on medieval literature.'

adore   ✗   I adore meeting new people.
✓   **I like/enjoy/love meeting new people.**

    ✗ I adore reading too.
    ✓ **I like/enjoy/love reading too.**

> **Adore** usually expresses a very strong feeling: 'She adores her grandchildren and is always buying them presents.' 'The one singer I absolutely adore is Whitney Houston.' If you use **adore** to mean 'like/enjoy/love', you may sound insincere.

advance   See THANK 3

advan-   ✗ Although the film has its advantages, it also has a serious flaw.
tage **1** ✓ **Although the film has its merits/good points, it also has a serious flaw.**

> **advantage** = something that puts you in a better position than other people: 'A healthier lifestyle is just one of the advantages of living in the country.' 'The main advantage of using word processors is the amount of time you save.'
> **merit** = a good quality; a strength: 'The merits of the new health programme are gradually being recognized.' 'We should judge each application on its own merits.'

  2 ✗ Television provides many advantages.
     ✓ **Television provides many benefits.**

> **benefit** = a good result which improves your life or situation: 'Belonging to a union has a number of important benefits.' 'It's over a month since I got back from holiday, but I still feel the benefit.'

  3 ✗ What are the advantages in studying in the United States?
     ✓ **What are the advantages of studying in the United States?**
     ✗ There are many advantages of having your own computer.
     ✓ **There are many advantages to/in having your own computer.**

> **the advantage/s of (doing/having) sth:** 'He described the advantages of renewing the contract.' 'The advantages of independence soon became clear.'
> **there are (several/many** etc) **advantages to/in (doing/having) sth:** 'There are advantages to working in a supermarket.' 'There are clear advantages to such an approach.' 'Are there any advantages in appointing coordinators?'

advertise- ✗ I have just seen your advertisement about a Chinese cook.
ment   ✓ **I have just seen your advertisement for a Chinese cook.**
     ✗ I am writing in reply to your advertisement of a part-time sales assistant.
     ✓ **I am writing in reply to your advertisement for a part-time sales assistant.**

> **an advertisement for sb/sth**: 'an advertisement for Heinz tomato soup'

advice 1 ✗ I adviced him to tell the police.
     ✓ **I advised him to tell the police.**

> **Advice** /əd'vaɪs/ is a noun. **Advise** /əd'vaɪz/ is a verb.

  2 ✗ She gave me a good advice.
     ✓ **She gave me some good advice.**
     ✗ It is full of good advices on healthy eating.
     ✓ **It is full of good advice on healthy eating.**

> **Advice** is an uncountable noun: 'I could do with some advice.'
> Compare: 'She gave me a good piece of advice.'

advise 1 ✗ I asked my lawyer for her advise.
✓ **I asked my lawyer for her advice.**
See note at ADVICE 1

2 ✗ Nowadays many doctors advise to live in the countryside.
✓ **Nowadays many doctors advise living in the countryside.**
✓ **Nowadays many doctors advise people to live in the countryside.**

> **advise sb to do sth**: 'I advised her to see a lawyer.'
> **advise doing sth** (NOT **to do**): 'I would advise leaving very early. Then you'll miss all the traffic.'

affect 1 ✗ The programme is about computers and their affect on our lives.
✓ **The programme is about computers and their effect on our lives.**

> To **affect** something (verb) is to have an **effect** on it (noun): 'Smoking affects your health.' (= smoking has an effect on your health)

2 ✗ This problem has also affected on the automobile industry.
✓ **This problem has also affected the automobile industry.**

> **affect sb/sth** (WITHOUT **on**): 'Fortunately these new tax laws don't affect us.'
> Compare: 'This problem has also had an effect on the automobile industry.'

afford ✗ My father couldn't afford paying for my education.
✓ **My father couldn't afford to pay for my education.**

> **afford (to do) sth**: 'Not many couples can afford to run two cars nowadays.'

afraid ✗ The road to the airport was very busy and we were afraid to miss the plane.
✓ **The road to the airport was very busy and we were afraid of missing the plane.**

> **be afraid to do sth** = be unwilling to do something because you are frightened about what may happen: 'She was afraid to eat it in case it was poisonous.' 'Don't be afraid to ask for help.'
> **be afraid of doing sth** = be worried or anxious about something which might happen: 'Most criminals are afraid of being caught.' 'He says that he is afraid of losing his job.'

after 1 ✗ After a week we're going to Italy.
✓ **In a week's time we're going to Italy.**
✗ I hope that I'll still be healthy after ten years.
✓ **I hope that I'll still be healthy in ten years' time.**

> When you mention a time in the future that is measured from 'now' (the moment of speaking), use **in a month's time, in three weeks' time**, etc (or just **in a month, in three weeks**): 'She'll be back again in a couple of weeks' time.'

Note the alternatives: 'A week (from) today we're going to Italy.' 'I hope that I'll still be healthy ten years from now.'

2 ✗ I promised to meet Hitomi at the exhibition a week after.
✓ **I promised to meet Hitomi at the exhibition a week later.**
✗ I returned to Germany after two years' time.
✓ **I returned to Germany two years later.**

When you mention a time in the past that is measured from an earlier time in the past, use **a month later, three months later,** etc: 'Six months later they got married.'

3 ✗ After 1961 the consumption of cheese has increased each year.
✓ **Since 1961 the consumption of cheese has increased each year.**

To refer to a period of time that begins in the past and continues up to 'now' (the moment of speaking), use **since** (NOT **after**): 'I've been standing here waiting for you since half past three.' 'She hasn't been to see us since she got married.'

4 ✗ My first aim is to get a master's degree. After I would like to go and work in Canada.
✓ **My first aim is to get a master's degree. Afterwards, I would like to go and work in Canada.**
? A police car arrived within minutes and soon after an ambulance came.
✓ **A police car arrived within minutes and soon afterwards an ambulance came.**

After is used instead of **afterwards** only in informal styles, usually in phrases such as 'soon after', 'not long after' or 'just after'. Careful users generally prefer **afterwards**, especially at the beginning of a sentence: 'Shortly afterwards it was announced that the bank had collapsed.'
In American English **after** is often used instead of **afterwards**.

5 ? A police car arrived within minutes and soon after an ambulance came.
✓ **A police car arrived within minutes and soon afterwards an ambulance came.**

In informal styles, **after** is used in phrases such as 'soon after', 'not long after' and 'just after'. Careful users prefer **afterwards**, especially in formal styles: 'Shortly afterwards it was announced that the bank had collapsed.'
In American English **after** is often used instead of **afterwards**.

6 ? I studied English for 2 years. After that I got a job as a stewardess on an American airline.
✓ **After studying English for 2 years, I got a job as a stewardess on an American airline.**
? We could all meet at my house for lunch. After doing this, we could go to the beach.
✓ **We could all meet at my house for lunch and afterwards we could go to the beach.**

The meaning 'then' can be expressed in a number of ways, e.g. **afterwards, then, later on, subsequently, after** + v-ing. Avoid the repeated use of **after that** and **after doing this/that.**

7   ✗ After you will leave, we will write to you every day.
    ✓ **After you leave/have left, we will write to you every day.**
    See Language Note at WILL .

after all   ✗ First we got stuck in a traffic jam and then our car broke down. After all we decided to cancel the trip and went back home.
    ✓ **First we got stuck in a traffic jam and then our car broke down. In the end, we decided to cancel the trip and went back home.**
    ✗ We stopped for a meal on the way and after all we didn't arrive until midnight.
    ✓ **We stopped for a meal on the way and in the end we didn't arrive until midnight.**
    See Language Note at END

afternoon   ✗ Afternoon we have classes until five o'clock.
    ✓ **In the afternoon we have classes until five o'clock.**
    ✗ School finishes at five in afternoon.
    ✓ **School finishes at five in the afternoon.**
    ✗ The afternoon I met them at the hotel and we went to the beach.
    ✓ **In the afternoon I met them at the hotel and we went to the beach.**
    See Language Note at TIME

afterwards 1 ? We started going out together just to have fun, as friends. Afterwards we both realized that there was more than just friendship.
    ✓ **We started going out together just to have fun, as friends. Later on we both realized that there was more than just friendship.**
    Afterwards suggests that the next thing happens as soon as the last thing has finished: 'On Saturday morning I went to see Adrian in hospital. Afterwards I drove into town to do some shopping.'
    When there is a long interval or delay between two actions or events, use **later on**: 'I couldn't understand why she hadn't answered my letters. Later on I discovered that she had moved to a new address.'

2 ? First you draw a long straight line. Afterwards you draw another line, parallel to the first one.
    ✓ **First you draw a long straight line. Then you draw another line, parallel to the first one.**
    To introduce the next action in a process or series of actions, use **then**: 'Check that the paper is properly loaded. Then press the start button.' Compare: 'We all had lunch together at one o'clock. Afterwards we went to the beach.'

again 1   ✗ It's time I gave you your photographs again.
    ✓ **It's time I gave you your photographs back.**
    ? He'd like to have his bicycle again if you've finished with it.
    ✓ **He'd like to have his bicycle back if you've finished with it.**
    If you give something to the person who gave it to you, you **give** it **back** to them. When you mean 'to the person who had it before', 'to the place where something was before' etc., use **back** (NOT **again**): 'He took the

camera back to the shop and asked for his money back.' 'Shall I put these books back on the shelf?'

2

✗ I'll phone you again in five minutes.
✓ **I'll phone you back in five minutes.**

If you telephone someone after they have telephoned you, you **call/ring/phone** them **back:** 'Put down the receiver and I'll call you back.'

3

✗ I would like to visit again some of these places.
✓ **I would like to visit some of these places again.**
✗ I'll give you again my address.
✓ **I'll give you my address again.**

Again (= a second time) usually comes after the object: 'It's wonderful to see you again.' 'Would you like to watch the film again?'

4

See REPEAT

against

✗ Trying to avoid the sheep, he drove his car against a tree.
✓ **Trying to avoid the sheep, he drove his car into a tree.**

When someone has an accident, they **drive/run/walk/crash/bump into something** (NOT **against**): 'The lorry skidded on the ice and crashed into a wall.'

age 1

✗ I'm at the age of 22.
✓ **I'm 22 (years old).**

be + NUMBER (+ **years old**): 'David is almost twelve (years old).'

2

✗ His age is about fifty-five years old.
✓ **He's about fifty-five (years old).**

Do not use **age** and **years old** together. The usual way of mentioning someone's age is simply **be** + NUMBER: 'She'll be sixteen next August.'

3

✗ Soon you'll be of my age.
✓ **Soon you'll be my age.**
✗ Although we are at the same age, we have different interests.
✓ **Although we are the same age, we have different interests.**

be my/your etc age: 'When I was your age, I was already going out to work.'
be the same age (as sb): 'Most of my friends are the same age as me.'

4

✗ In the age of 15, you are allowed to drive a car.
✓ **At the age of 15, you are allowed to drive a car.**

Phrases with **age** as their main word usually begin with **at** (NOT **in**): 'Keeping fit is very important at your age.' 'Some girls get married at a very young age.' 'She is at the age when she wants to go to school.'

5

✗ A child in the age of seven or eight needs a little push.
✓ **A child of seven or eight needs a little push.**
✗ People in my age spend a lot of time in pubs.
✓ **People of my age spend a lot of time in pubs.**

noun + **of** + NUMBER: 'They have a little girl of three and a boy of five.'
noun + **of** + **my/your etc age**: 'He is very clever for a boy of his age.' 'A girl of her age needs someone to play with.'

Note the alternative with **aged**: 'A child aged seven or eight needs a little push.'

6

✗ They have two children in the age of 8 and 12 years.
✓ **They have two children aged 8 and 12.**
✓ **They have two children, 8 and 12 years of age.**

When you mention two ages after a noun, use either of the following:
aged + NUMBER + **and** + NUMBER: 'two boys aged 12 and 14'
NUMBER + **and** + NUMBER + **years of age**: 'two boys, 12 and 14 years of age'.

7

✗ These books are for children at the age of from 4 to 6 years.
✓ **These books are for children aged 4 to 6.**
✓ **These books are for children between the ages of 4 and 6.**

When you mention an age range after a noun, use either **aged** + NUMBER + **to** + NUMBER: 'suitable for children aged seven to eleven' or **between the ages of** + NUMBER + **and** + NUMBER: 'suitable for children between the ages of seven and eleven'.

8

See MIDDLE AGE

aged 1

? Not all aged parents have children to look after them.
✓ **Not all elderly parents have children to look after them.**

When it means 'very old', **aged** (pronounced / ˈeɪdʒɪd /) is mainly used in formal styles, usually in the phrase **the aged**: 'The poor and the aged are entitled to free health care.'
The usual word for this meaning is **elderly,** which also sounds polite: 'The photograph was of an elderly gentleman with a white moustache.' 'The building has been converted into a retirement home for the elderly.'

2

✗ My father left school at aged fourteen.
✓ **My father left school at (the age of) fourteen.**
✗ At aged 45, farmers are able to retire.
✓ **At (the age of) 45, farmers are able to retire.**

at (the age of) + NUMBER: 'Alan got married at twenty.' 'Sue got divorced at the age of twenty-one.'

agent

✗ I applied for a job at a travel agent.
✓ **I applied for a job at a travel agent's.**

To refer to a shop or company, use the **'s** form: **a greengrocer's, a chemist's, a tailor's, a butcher's.**

ago 1

✗ The accident happened at ten years ago.
✓ **The accident happened ten years ago.**
✗ I came to England in two years ago.
✓ **I came to England two years ago.**
✗ He went to Sydney before five years ago.
✓ **He went to Sydney five years ago.**
✗ I started learning English since two years ago.
✓ **I started learning English two years ago.**

See Language Note at TIME

2

✗ I'm writing in reply to your letter that I've received two days ago.
✓ **I'm writing in reply to your letter that I received two days ago.**

With references to past time such as **yesterday, last week, a year ago**, use a past tense (NOT the present perfect): 'I came to England exactly six months ago.' (NOT 'have come')

3 ✗ The train left at exactly 3 o'clock. Just five minutes ago I had been stuck in a traffic jam.
✓ **The train left at exactly 3 o'clock. Just five minutes before I had been stuck in a traffic jam.**
See note at BEFORE 1

agree 1 ✗ I don't agree the people who say women should stay at home.
✓ **I don't agree with the people who say women should stay at home.**
✗ In many ways I agree to his statement.
✓ **In many ways I agree with his statement.**

agree with sb/sth = have the same opinion as: 'You can't expect everyone to agree with you all the time.' 'I tend to agree with you that the proposal is too risky.'

2 ✗ I don't understand why he doesn't agree the divorce.
✓ **I don't understand why he doesn't agree to the divorce.**
✗ Conservationists will never agree the building of the motorway.
✓ **Conservationists will never agree to the building of the motorway.**

agree to sth = be willing to accept or allow something: 'The bank manager has agreed to our request for a loan.'

3 ✗ I am agree that archaeological treasures should be protected.
✓ **I agree that archaeological treasures should be protected.**
✗ In some ways I am agree with those who want stricter punishments.
✓ **In some ways I agree with those who want stricter punishments.**

Agree is a verb (NOT an adjective).

4 See FACT 4

agreement ✗ The government has made an agreement with the People's Republic of China.
✓ **The government has reached agreement with the People's Republic of China.**

reach agreement or **reach/come to/work out an agreement** (with sb): 'After a week of talks, Britain and Iceland reached agreement on fishing limits.' 'Recent government attempts to work out an agreement have proved unsuccessful.'

agriculture ✗ The country's economy is based on the agriculture.
✓ **The country's economy is based on agriculture.**
See note at THE 4

aid 1 ✗ We must begin to aid ourselves and not wait for other countries.
✓ **We must begin to help ourselves and not wait for other countries.**

✗ Education can aid us to understand our world.
✓ **Education can help us to understand our world.**

> **Aid** is mainly used as a noun: 'Many countries survive on foreign aid from richer neighbours.' 'It is government policy to provide aid to the homeless or the unemployed.'
> As a verb, **aid** is used in formal styles and usually means 'help something recover, develop, grow, etc': 'The country's economic recovery has been aided by the recent peace agreement.'

2

✗ They can learn faster by the aid of computers.
✓ **They can learn faster with the aid of computers.**

> **with the aid of sth** (NOT **by**): 'These bacteria cannot be seen without the aid of a microscope.'

aim 1

✗ Her lifelong aim was to learn how to fly.
✓ **Her lifelong ambition was to learn how to fly.**
See note at AMBITION 1

2

✗ He was aiming a gun against me.
✓ **He was aiming a gun at me.**
✗ These programmes are aimed to a very wide audience.
✓ **These programmes are aimed at a very wide audience.**

> **aim sth at sb/sth**: 'Each ball seemed to be aimed at my head.' 'This new dictionary is aimed at intermediate learners of English.'

3

✗ I started to learn English with the aim to become a teacher.
✓ **I started to learn English with the aim of becoming a teacher.**

> **with the aim of doing sth**: 'I originally went out to the Far East with the aim of setting up my own import-export business.'
> Compare: 'My aim is to become a teacher.'

air 1

✗ It's hard to find a fresh air nowadays.
✓ **It's hard to find any fresh air nowadays.**

> **Air** (= the mixture of gases that we breathe) is an uncountable noun: 'Let's go for a walk and get some air in our lungs.'

2

See PURE

aircraft

✗ All the aircrafts have to be checked and refuelled.
✓ **All the aircraft have to be checked and refuelled.**

> The plural form of **aircraft** is **aircraft** (no change).

alarm

✗ Finally we got really worried and alarmed the local police.
✓ **Finally we got really worried and alerted the local police.**

> **alarm** = make someone feel worried about a possible danger: 'We don't wish to alarm people unnecessarily, but it would be wise to avoid drinking the tap water here.'
> **alert** = inform someone of possible danger so that they can be ready to deal with it: 'When the pilot realized that one engine had failed, he alerted air traffic control.'

alive 1

✗ Every alive creature in the sea is affected by pollution.
✓ **Every living creature in the sea is affected by pollution.**

alive = not dead: 'He was very seriously ill and is lucky to be alive.'
living = (1) alive now: 'He has no living relatives.' (2) used to refer to all creatures and things that live and die: 'Yeast is a living organism and too much heat or cold can kill it.' 'The ants will eat any living thing that comes into their path.'

2   ✗ Our teacher, Mr Collins, is very alive.
    ✓ **Our teacher, Mr Collins, is very lively.**

lively = full of energy: 'The Yorkshire Terrier is a lively breed of dog.'

3   ✗ My reason for being alive had disappeared.
    ✓ **My reason for living had disappeared.**

When you mean 'continue to be alive', use the verb **live**: 'Her grandmother lived to a great age.' 'The baby was four months premature and was not expected to live.'

all 1   ? He spent all the journey talking about accidents.
    ✓ **He spent the whole journey talking about accidents.**
    ✗ This decision changed all of her life.
    ✓ **This decision changed her whole life.**

Before the singular form of a countable noun we usually use **whole** or **entire**: 'We spent the whole lesson singing songs.' 'The entire document will have to be rewritten.' Note that sometimes both **all** and **whole/entire** are possible: 'It rained the whole/all the afternoon.' In these cases, **whole/entire** provides greater emphasis and often expresses a feeling of surprise, disappointment, satisfaction etc: 'I read the whole book in just two evenings.'

2   ✗ People envy her because she is good at all.
    ✓ **People envy her because she is good at everything.**
    ✗ Nobody understands all.
    ✓ **Nobody understands everything.**

Do not use **all** to mean 'everything' unless it is immediately followed by a relative clause: 'Is that all she wanted to know?'

3   ✗ All of us didn't want to go to bed.
    ✓ **None of us wanted to go to bed.**
    ✗ All companies will not tolerate lazy workers.
    ✓ **No company will tolerate lazy workers.**

See Language Note at NOT

4   ✗ We all must try to find a solution to the problem.
    ✓ **We must all try to find a solution to the problem.**
    ✗ We all were delighted when we heard the news.
    ✓ **We were all delighted when we heard the news.**

See Language Note at ALWAYS

5   ✗ As all you know, my name is Mary Smith.
    ✓ **As you all know, my name is Mary Smith.**
    ✗ I've never forgotten how beautiful all it was.
    ✓ **I've never forgotten how beautiful it all was.**

All of is placed immediately before a pronoun, but **all** is placed immediately after. Compare: 'All of them speak French.' 'They all speak French.'

6

✗ I like all the kinds of music.
✓ **I like all kinds of music.**
✗ All of children learn to speak naturally.
✓ **All children learn to speak naturally.**
✗ All of the young couples need a home of their own.
✓ **All young couples need a home of their own.**

For general reference, put **all/most/some etc** immediately in front of the noun: 'In Japan most people use chopsticks.'
For specific reference, use **all/most/some** + **of the/these/their etc** + noun: 'Most of the Americans I met were very friendly.'

7

✗ I didn't like the meal and couldn't eat all.
✓ **I didn't like the meal and couldn't eat it all.**
✓ **I didn't like the meal and couldn't eat all of it.**

Do not use **all** to replace a pronoun. Use **all** (or **all of**) with a pronoun: 'She took six exams and passed them all.' 'She took six exams and passed all of them.'

8

See DURING 2

9

See PEOPLE 1

allow 1

✗ They also allow to the prisoners to keep birds.
✓ **They also allow the prisoners to keep birds.**

allow sb to do sth (NOT **to sb**): 'The principal doesn't allow them to wear jewellery to school.'

2

✗ It's not allowed to talk in the library.
✓ **You aren't allowed to talk in the library.**
✓ **Talking in the library isn't allowed.**

It is not usually used as a preparatory subject before **(not) allowed**, especially in spoken English.

almost 1

✗ I almost have forgotten what she looks like.
✓ **I have almost forgotten what she looks like.**
✗ The suitcase almost was too heavy to lift.
✓ **The suitcase was almost too heavy to lift.**

See Language Note at ALWAYS

2

✗ My job takes me almost to every part of the world.
✓ **My job takes me to almost every part of the world.**

Almost comes immediately before the word it modifies: 'He was working in Hungary for almost ten years.'

3

? Outside Japan, almost nobody speaks Japanese.
✓ **Outside Japan, hardly anybody speaks Japanese.**

Instead of saying **almost no/nobody/never etc**, it is more usual to say **hardly any/anybody/ever etc**: 'It was so early that there was hardly any traffic.' 'I hardly ever go to the cinema nowadays.'

4

✗ She almost couldn't breathe.
✓ **She could hardly breathe.**

Almost is used with a negative verb when something does actually happen although, at the time, there is a strong possibility that it will not happen: 'I was feeling so tired that I almost didn't come.' 'The traffic was so heavy that she almost didn't get here in time.'

> When you mean 'only a little' or 'only with great difficulty', use **hardly**: 'We hardly know each other.' 'She was so tired that she could hardly keep her eyes open.' 'I can hardly hear myself think.'

alone 1

✗ I was very alone at first but then I made some friends.
✓ **I was very lonely at first but then I made some friends.**

> **alone** = without other people around you: 'I've thought about getting married, but I prefer living alone.'
> **lonely** = sad because you are alone and feel that nobody loves you or cares about you: 'I didn't know anyone in Boston and felt very lonely.' 'Sarah hated the long lonely days in the empty house.'

2

✗ Children learn a lot by doing things alone.
✓ **Children learn a lot by doing things on their own.**

> **on your own** = without anyone's help or supervision; independently: 'He built the car all on his own.'

along

✗ Walking along the city after dark is not a good idea.
✓ **Walking through the city after dark is not a good idea.**

> **along** = (moving) next to the side of something long such as a road or river: 'We walked along the Thames as far as Hampton Court.'
> **through** = from one side of an area to another: 'The road goes through all the major towns.'

a lot (of)

See LOT/LOTS

already 1

✗ Next July I'm going back to Hong Kong. I booked the tickets already.
✓ **Next July I'm going back to Hong Kong. I've booked the tickets already.**

> **Already** is usually used with the present perfect tense (NOT the past tense): 'If he's already seen the film, he won't want to see it again.'

2

✗ Most of the food is cold already when you get it.
✓ **Most of the food is already cold when you get it.**
✗ They had already ten children and didn't want any more.
✓ **They already had ten children and didn't want any more.**
✓ **They had ten children already and didn't want any more.**

See Language Note at ALWAYS

3

✗ The war is not over already.
✓ **The war is not over yet.**
✗ The new shop has not been opened already.
✓ **The new shop has not been opened yet.**

> Instead of using **not** + **already**, use **not** + **yet**: 'We haven't been paid yet.' 'The plane hasn't landed yet.'

also 1

✗ We also would like to be given more fresh food.
✓ **We would also like to be given more fresh food.**
✗ The school has also a gymnasium.
✓ **The school also has a gymnasium.**
✗ Besides the nature society, there also is a music society.
✓ **Besides the nature society, there is also a music society.**

See Language Note at ALWAYS

2
    ✗ I don't like your climate and I don't like English food also.
    ✓ **I don't like your climate and I don't like English food either.**
    ✗ He doesn't also recommend winter holidays.
    ✓ **He doesn't recommend winter holidays either.**
    See note at TOO 2

3
    ? Women are often better at negotiating than men. Also, they don't give up so easily.
    ✓ **Women are often better at negotiating than men. What's more, they don't give up so easily.**
    ? A footbridge would take too long to build. Also, it would be of no use to the disabled.
    ✓ **A footbridge would take too long to build. Furthermore, it would be of no use to the disabled.**

When you want to add another reason and give it special emphasis or importance, use **furthermore**, **moreover**, **what's more** or **besides**: 'The drug has powerful side effects. Moreover, it can be addictive.' **Also** is not wrong but does not have the same persuasive force.

alternate
    ✗ We decided to make alternate arrangements in case the hotel was fully booked.
    ✓ **We decided to make alternative arrangements in case the hotel was fully booked.**

In British English **alternate** and **alternative** have different meanings.
alternate = (1) happening in turn, first one then the other: 'alternate periods of sun and rain' (2) every second (day, week, etc): 'Our local football team plays at home on alternate Saturdays.'
alternative = that may be used instead of the usual one or the one you had planned to use: 'In view of the roadworks, motorists are advised to use an alternative route.'
In American English **alternate** is used with the same meaning as **alternative**.

alternatively
    ✗ In Sweden many wives and husbands stay at home alternatively to look after their children.
    ✓ **In Sweden many wives and husbands stay at home alternately to look after their children.**

alternatively = another possibility is: 'I thought we'd stay at home. Alternatively, you might like to go for a walk.'
alternately = in turns, first one then the other: 'The play is alternately sad and happy.'
Note the more common alternative: 'In Sweden many wives and husbands take it in turns to stay at home and look after their children.'

although
    See BUT

altogether
    ✗ Afterwards, we played altogether monopoly.
    ✓ **Afterwards, we all played monopoly.**
    ✗ After dinner, we watch altogether television.
    ✓ **After dinner, we all watch television.**

When you mean 'each person or thing (in a group)', use **all** after the subject (NOT **altogether**): 'The flowers had all died.' 'The children were all tired and hungry.'

always 1 ✗ Come and spend the weekend with me. I live always at the same address in Croydon.
  ✓ **Come and spend the weekend with me. I still live at the same address in Croydon.**
  ✗ He died a long time ago, but his ideas are always alive.
  ✓ **He died a long time ago, but his ideas are still alive.**

> **Always** means 'all the time' or 'every time': 'She has always wanted her own Mercedes.' 'I always go to work by train.'
> To say that a previous situation has not changed and continues 'now' (at the time of speaking), use **still** (NOT **always**): 'Lucy is recovering, but she's still in hospital.' 'The house is still for sale.'

2 ✗ I have always the feeling that she enjoys teaching us.
  ✓ **I always have the feeling that she enjoys teaching us.**
  ✗ You will be always welcome.
  ✓ **You will always be welcome.**
  ✗ During the winter months, they always were in the kitchen.
  ✓ **During the winter months, they were always in the kitchen.**

See Language Note on next page

a.m. See O'CLOCK 2

ambition 1 ✗ My immediate ambition is to find somewhere to live.
  ✓ **My immediate aim is to find somewhere to live.**

> **ambition** = something very important that you have wanted to do or achieve for a very long time: 'Sandro's one ambition is to play for Italy in the World Cup.'
> **aim** = what you hope to achieve when you do something: 'The aim of the course is to develop the students' writing skills.'

2 ✗ Not many people manage to satisfy their ambitions.
  ✓ **Not many people manage to achieve their ambitions.**

> **achieve your ambition** (NOT **satisfy, meet, reach, arrive etc**): 'He has achieved his main ambition – to make a name for himself in politics.'

among 1 ✗ The main purpose of the visit is to develop a closer relationship among the two countries.
  ✓ **The main purpose of the visit is to develop a closer relationship between the two countries.**

> Use **among** when you are talking about three or more people or things. For two people or things, use **between**.

2 ✗ Try to avoid arousing anger and fear among the children.
  ✓ **Try to avoid arousing anger and fear in the children.**
  ✗ He is very popular among the people of Japan.
  ✓ **He is very popular with the people of Japan.**

> Do not use **among** when the preceding verb/noun/adjective requires a different preposition: e.g. **arouse** anger **in** someone.

3 ✗ Among these problems, the most serious is the excessive growth of the world's population.
  ✓ **The most serious of these problems is the excessive growth of the world's population.**

When a phrase beginning with **among** comes at the start of a sentence, it is usually followed by the verb **be** (NOT by the subject of the sentence): 'Among her reasons for resigning is the fact that she wants to move back to her home town.' 'Among those attending the ceremony were the Sultan of Pahang and his wife.' Note also that this structure is not common and is used only in formal styles.

Using 'middle position' adverbs

The words below are common examples of 'middle position' adverbs.

FREQUENCY	**always, usually, normally, often, frequently, sometimes, occasionally, rarely, seldom, hardly ever, never**
TIME	**already, just, soon, still, once**
DEGREE	**almost, nearly, hardly, really**
FOCUS	**even, just, merely, only, really**
OTHER	**also, probably, definitely, suddenly**

• Middle position adverbs usually go immediately in front of the main verb:

I **usually** have a cold shower in the morning.
It was so dark that I could **hardly** see.
You will **always** be welcome.

• When there is more than one auxiliary verb, these adverbs usually go immediately after the first one:

I have **often** been asked why I chose this career.
We will **soon** be taking our examinations.

• When the main verb is **am/is/are/was/were,** these adverbs go immediately after it (NOT in front of it):

He was **soon** fit and well again.
Fortunately, the shops were **still** open.

Note:
1 These rules also apply to **all, both** and **each** when these words are used for emphasis:

These countries **each** have their own traditions.
The rooms on the top floor are **all** being redecorated.
We are **both** fond of music.

2 Adverbs such as **sometimes, usually** and **soon** may also go at the beginning or end of a clause. In these positions they receive more emphasis:

Don't worry. I'm sure they'll be arriving **soon**.
Sometimes the noise keeps us awake at night.
Usually they come home for lunch.

amount 1   ✗ The amount of accidents is steadily increasing.
              ✓ **The number of accidents is steadily increasing.**

✗ Only small amounts of students will be admitted.
✓ **Only small numbers of students will be admitted.**

> **amount of** + uncountable noun
> **number of** + plural countable noun
> Compare: 'an amount of money', 'a number of coins'

2 ✗ I was lucky and won a big amount of money.
✓ **I was lucky and won a large amount of money.**
✗ Cream cheese contains a high amount of fat.
✓ **Cream cheese contains a large amount of fat.**

> **a large amount** (NOT big/high)

3 ✗ The amount of crime have increased.
✓ **The amount of crime has increased.**
✗ A tremendous amount of research have been carried out.
✓ **A tremendous amount of research has been carried out.**

> **amount of** (singular) + uncountable noun + singular verb
> **amounts of** (plural) + uncountable noun + plural verb
> Compare: 'A large amount of money is required.' 'Large amounts of money are required.'

ample ✗ The kitchen is very ample and has a window overlooking the garden.
✓ **The kitchen is very spacious and has a window overlooking the garden.**

> **ample** = (more than) enough; plenty (of): 'The boot contains ample room for two large suitcases.' 'Just one spoonful should be ample.' 'He was given ample opportunity to express his opinion.'
> **spacious** = large, with a lot of space: 'These ideal holiday homes are extremely spacious and within walking distance of the sea.'

amuse ✗ I made a lot of new friends during my stay in England and amused myself a lot.
✓ **I made a lot of new friends during my stay in England and really enjoyed myself.**

> **amuse yourself** = do something to stop yourself from getting bored: 'Can't you find something to do to amuse yourself?' 'With a pencil or two and a few sheets of paper, young children can amuse themselves for hours.'
> **enjoy yourself** = have a pleasant time: 'The party was a huge success and all the guests enjoyed themselves.'

amusing 1 ✗ The last three years have been the most amusing years of my life.
✓ **The last three years have been the most enjoyable years of my life.**

> **amusing** = causing you to laugh or smile: 'The speaker was clearly embarrassed when the microphone stopped working, but the audience found the situation very amusing.' 'I don't see anything amusing about finding a snake in your tent in the middle of the night.'
> **enjoyable** = causing you to feel happy; pleasant: 'It was one of the most enjoyable holidays we've ever had.' 'Exercise may be hard work, but it can also be enjoyable.'

2   ✗   Most visitors find the museum extremely amusing.
  ✓   **Most visitors find the museum extremely interesting.**

Something that holds your attention (and makes you want to know more) is **interesting** (NOT **amusing**): 'The most interesting thing about the dinosaurs is their sudden disappearance.' 'His plan for raising more money sounds interesting but I'm not sure it'll work.'

an   ✗   I had never visited an hospital before.
  ✓   **I had never visited a hospital before.**

Before a word beginning with **h**, use **a** if the **h** is pronounced: 'a house', 'a half', 'a horrible day'. Use **an** if the **h** is silent: 'an hour', 'an honour'. If the **h** is pronounced but the syllable is unstressed, it is possible to use **a** or **an** ('a/an hotel'). However, the use of **an** here is considered old-fashioned and most people use **a**.

and 1   ✗   There is a beautiful and old church in the centre of the town.
  ✓   **There is a beautiful old church in the centre of the town.**

Do not use **and** between two adjectives that come before a noun unless they describe similar qualities, e.g. 'a red and green umbrella' (two colours), 'a gold and silver bracelet' (two materials), 'a hunting and fishing knife' (two functions).

2   See MANY 3

anger 1   ✗   I was surprised and anger that he did not apologize.
  ✓   **I was surprised and angry that he did not apologize.**

Anger is a noun and a verb: 'The workers who lost their jobs expressed anger and resentment.' 'The government's handling of the affair has angered local residents.' The adjective is **angry**: 'Some of the women felt angry about the way they were treated.'

2   ✗   He'll have to learn how to control his anger.
  ✓   **He'll have to learn how to control his temper.**

control/keep/lose your temper (NOT **anger**): 'The problem with George is that he can't control his temper.' (= cannot stop himself from suddenly getting angry)

announce   ✗   The following day their father suddenly announced them that he was leaving.
  ✓   **The following day their father suddenly announced (to them) that he was leaving.**

After **announce**, use **to** before the listener: 'Shortly after losing the heavyweight title, he announced (to the world's press) that he was retiring from the ring.'

announce-ment   ✗   On almost every page there were announcements for cigarettes and tobacco.
  ✓   **On almost every page there were advertisements for cigarettes and tobacco.**

When you want to give people some important information, you make an **announcement**: 'Following the announcement of their marriage, they were pursued by crowds of journalists.'
An **advertisement** is an item in a newspaper, on television, etc, that tries to persuade people to buy something, apply for a job, etc: 'At this time of the year, the papers are full of holiday advertisements.'

annoy/	?	The noise of the traffic outside all day annoys me.
annoyed 1	✓	**The noise of the traffic outside all day irritates me.**
	?	I feel rather annoyed when I see the same advertisement time and time again.
	✓	**I feel rather irritated when I see the same advertisement time and time again.**

> Something unpleasant that happens repeatedly or continuously over a long period of time tends to **irritate** or **frustrate** people, especially because they know that they can do nothing to stop it: 'I felt so tense that even the ticking of the clock began to irritate me.' 'I am constantly frustrated by all the niggling little jobs I have to do.'

2	✗	Some people are annoyed by these violent films.
	✓	**Some people are disturbed by these violent films.**
	✓	**Some people find these violent films disturbing.**

> Someone who is emotionally shocked by something they see or read is **disturbed/upset/distressed/offended** by it, or they find it **disturbing/upsetting/distressing/offensive**: 'Viewers are warned that this documentary contains a number of violent scenes which they may find disturbing.'

3	✗	She annoyed that I hadn't waited for her.
	✓	**She was annoyed that I hadn't waited for her.**

> **be/get annoyed**: 'My boss is always getting annoyed with me for some reason or other.'

annoyed	✗	I felt terribly annoyed with his lack of sensitivity.
	✓	**I felt terribly annoyed at his lack of sensitivity.**

> **annoyed with/at sb**: 'She's annoyed with you for not answering her letters.'
> **annoyed at/about sth**: 'The thing that I'm really annoyed about is that nobody told me.'

another 1	✗	Rio has another important sights such as the famous football stadium.
	✓	**Rio has other important sights such as the famous football stadium.**

> **another** + singular: 'another child'
> **other** + plural: 'other children'

2	✗	He gave the class another homework.
	✓	**He gave the class some more homework.**

> **another** + singular countable noun: 'We need another chair.'
> **(some) more** + uncountable noun: 'We need (some) more furniture.'

3	✗	I hate horror films. Let's watch another.
	✓	**I hate horror films. Let's watch something else.**
	✗	If Henry is busy, get another man to help you.
	✓	**If Henry is busy, get someone else to help you.**
	✗	Can't you use another's computer?
	✓	**Can't you use someone else's computer?**

> When you mean 'a different person/thing/place', use **someone else, something else, somewhere else**: 'I got fed up with the job and decided to do something else.'

4 ✗ There is also another point that is worth mentioning.
  ✓ **There is another point that is worth mentioning.**
  ✗ Also another way to lose weight is to eat less.
  ✓ **Another way to lose weight is to eat less.**

> **another** (NOT **also another**): 'Another problem, of course, is finding a job.'

5 ✗ Families fall into two categories. One is the composite family; another is the nuclear family.
  ✓ **Families fall into two categories. One is the composite family; the other is the nuclear family.**

> When you are talking about two people or things, use **the other** (NOT **another**): 'One of the twins is called Youki and the other is called Azusa.'

6 ✗ Without a car, it takes a long time to get from a place to another.
  ✓ **Without a car, it takes a long time to get from one place to another.**

> **from one ... to another** (NOT **from a/an ... to another**): 'The job involves travelling from one country to another.'

answer 1 ✗ They still can't find an answer for this problem.
  ✓ **They still can't find an answer to this problem.**

> **an answer to** a problem or question (NOT **for**): 'The answer to the second question is Abraham Lincoln.'

2 ✗ It has taken them almost two months to answer to my letter.
  ✓ **It has taken them almost two months to answer my letter.**
  ✗ I couldn't answer to the last two questions.
  ✓ **I couldn't answer the last two questions.**
  ✗ My job involves cooking, cleaning and answering to the door bell.
  ✓ **My job involves cooking, cleaning and answering the door bell.**

> **answer sb/sth** (WITHOUT **to**): 'Have you answered their letter yet?' Note that **answer** also has less common meanings where **to** is necessary: 'Anyone who upsets you will have me to answer to.' 'The dog answers to the name of Zak.'

3 ✗ I rang the number you gave me but nobody answered me.
  ✓ **I rang the number you gave me but nobody answered.**
  ✗ I called her name but nobody answered me.
  ✓ **I called her name but nobody answered.**

> Do not use an object with **answer** unless this adds new meaning to the sentence (meaning which is not obvious from the rest of the sentence). Compare: 'He asked her for an explanation but she didn't answer.' 'I'd like to speak to him but he refuses to answer the phone.' In the first sentence the object 'him' is understood and there is no need to mention it.

antique 1 ✗ There is a beautiful antique church in the centre of the town.
  ✓ **There is a beautiful old church in the centre of the town.**

> **Antique** is used for objects (NOT buildings): 'The upper-middle class have become collectors of antique furniture.'

2   ✗ He has made a lot of money from selling antique things.
       ✓ **He has made a lot of money from selling antiques.**

> **an antique** (NOT **an antique thing**): 'Some of these antiques must be worth a fortune.'

anxious 1   ✗ I always feel anxious when I have to make a speech.
        ✓ **I always feel nervous when I have to make a speech.**

> **anxious** = worried because you fear that something bad may happen or may have happened: 'Their daughter hadn't come home from school and they were anxious about her safety.' 'I knew it was just a minor operation, but I couldn't help feeling anxious.'
> **nervous** = worried because you are in or about to enter a stressful situation: 'I was so nervous about the exam that I couldn't sleep.' 'It was our first television appearance and we were all feeling nervous.'

2   ✗ She is anxious that the hotel rates will be too expensive.
       ✓ **She is worried that the hotel rates will be too expensive.**
       ✗ I was anxious that somebody would see us through the window.
       ✓ **I was worried that somebody would see us through the window.**

> **worried** = unhappy because you have (or expect that you are going to have) a problem: 'The business is losing money and the boss is very worried.'

3   ✗ He obviously isn't anxious about public opinion.
       ✓ **He obviously isn't worried about public opinion.**

> **not worried/concerned/bothered about sth** = feeling that something is not a problem: 'I'm not bothered about how much it will cost.'
> Note the alternative: 'He obviously doesn't care about public opinion.'

4   ✗ I'm anxious to hear about your new boyfriend.
       ✓ **I can't wait to hear about your new boyfriend.**
       ✗ I am anxious to see how British people celebrate Christmas.
       ✓ **I'm longing to see how British people celebrate Christmas.**

> If you are **anxious** to do something, you want to do it in order to improve a (difficult or unpleasant) situation: 'We are anxious that people are informed of the truth of the matter.' 'The police are anxious to speak to anyone who witnessed the accident.'
> If you simply have a strong desire to do something, you are **keen/eager/longing/dying** to do it, or you **cannot wait** to do it: 'I can't wait to get out of these wet clothes.'

5   ✗ Most unemployed people are anxious for finding work.
       ✓ **Most unemployed people are anxious to find work.**

> **anxious to do sth** (NOT **for doing**): 'He was anxious to gain approval.'

any 1   ✗ Any day was the same.
       ✓ **Each day was the same.**
       ✗ Any smoker must remember that the people around him are inhaling the smoke.
       ✓ **Every smoker must remember that the people around him are inhaling the smoke.**
       ✗ Any parents are thrilled when their first baby arrives.
       ✓ **All parents are thrilled when their first baby arrives.**

To refer to all the people or things in a group or category, use **each/every** + singular countable noun OR **all** + plural countable noun (NOT **any**): 'Every house in the street had one or two broken windows.' 'All students are required to register during the first week.'

2

✗ If you have any question, ask your teacher.
✓ **If you have any questions, ask your teacher.**
✗ She doesn't have any friend.
✓ **She doesn't have any friends.**

When **any** is used with a countable noun, the noun is usually plural: 'a question' BUT 'any questions'.

3

✗ Has Atsuko found any job yet?
✓ **Has Atsuko found a job yet?**
✗ If there is any hole in the balloon, the air will escape.
✓ **If there is a hole in the balloon, the air will escape.**

Any is usually used with uncountable nouns and plural countables (NOT with singular countable nouns). Compare: 'Do you have any money?' (**money** is an uncountable noun) 'Do you have any fifty-cent coins?' (**coins** is a plural countable noun) 'Do you have a fifty-cent coin?' (**coin** is a singular countable noun)
Note, however: 'I'll accept any job I'm offered.' (= it does not matter which job)

4

✗ When he asked if he could use the telephone, he was told that the family didn't have any.
✓ **When he asked if he could use the telephone, he was told that the family didn't have one.**

Do not use **any** as a pronoun for a singular countable noun (see last entry). Compare: 'He asked for some help but nobody gave him <u>any</u>.' (**help** is an uncountable noun) 'She wanted to borrow some books but nobody would lend her <u>any</u>.' (**books** is a plural countable noun) 'I need a new computer but I can't afford <u>one</u>.' (**computer** is a singular countable noun)

5

See Language Note at NOT

any more

✗ People go there when they are not able any more to look after themselves.
✓ **People go there when they are not able to look after themselves any more.**
✗ The state does not any more provide a pension for everyone.
✓ **The state does not provide a pension for everyone any more.**

When used in connection with time, **any more** usually comes at the end of the sentence: 'Helen doesn't work here any more.'
Note the alternatives: 'People go there when they are no longer able to look after themselves.' 'The state no longer provides a pension for everyone.'

anybody/ anyone 1

✗ Anyone should speak not just one but several languages.
✓ **Everyone should speak not just one but several languages.**
✗ Anybody else in the class speaks Japanese.
✓ **Everybody else in the class speaks Japanese.**

To refer to all the people in a group, use **everybody/everyone** (NOT **anybody/anyone**).

2   ✗   Please ask your staff if anybody of them has seen my purse.
  ✓   **Please ask your staff if any of them has seen my purse.**
  ✗   He doesn't know anyone of them, but he doesn't care.
  ✓   **He doesn't know any of them, but he doesn't care.**
  Before an **of** phrase, use **any** (NOT **anybody/anyone**).

3   ✗   Anyone are welcome to join us.
  ✓   **Anyone is welcome to join us.**
  ✗   If anybody want one, please write your name on the board.
  ✓   **If anybody wants one, please write your name on the board.**
  anybody/anyone + singular verb: 'If anyone calls, tell them I'll be back after lunch.'

4   ?   If anyone wants to leave now, he may do so.
  ✓   **Anyone who wants to leave now may do so.**
  ?   When anyone reads these lines, he or she will think that the writer is very sad.
  ✓   **Anyone reading these lines will think that the writer is very sad.**
  See Language Note at HE

anyhow/ anyway   ✗   Those students who pass are given an intermediate certificate Anyhow, the examination is far from easy.
  ✓   **Those students who pass are given an intermediate certificate. However, the examination is far from easy.**
  ✗   Unfortunately, the beach is not white and sandy. Anyway, it is seldom crowded and we can enjoy the sea.
  ✓   **Unfortunately, the beach is not white and sandy. On the other hand, it is seldom crowded and we can enjoy the sea.**
  ✗   I'm sorry that I won't be able to attend your wedding. Anyway, I would like to give you something for your new home.
  ✓   **I'm sorry that I won't be able to attend your wedding. Nevertheless, I would like to give you something for your new home.**

  Anyhow and **anyway** are used to connect sentences only in informal styles (NOT in essays, written reports, etc). Their main uses are: (1) to show that you are about to return to the main topic or story line: 'Anyway, as soon as the plane landed he was rushed off to hospital and that was the last I saw of him.' (2) to show that your next point is just as important or relevant as your last one; 'In any case, I'm too busy to play tennis this afternoon. Anyhow, it looks like it's going to rain.' For reasons of style and logic, **anyhow** and **anyway** cannot be used in place of **however, on the other hand** or **nevertheless**.

anyone   See ANYBODY/ANYONE

anyway   See ANYHOW/ANYWAY

anywhere 1   ✗   This is a serious problem for teachers anywhere.
  ✓   **This is a serious problem for teachers everywhere.**

    ✗ Computers will be anywhere we go.
    ✓ **Computers will be everywhere we go.**
    When you mean 'in/to all places', use **everywhere** (NOT **anywhere**).

2 ✗ When it snows, it is difficult to go to anywhere.
    ✓ **When it snows, it is difficult to go anywhere.**
    See note at SOMEWHERE 2

∨apologize 1 ✗ The waiter was made to apologize my father.
    ✓ **The waiter was made to apologize to my father.**
    ✗ He apologized her for the long delay.
    ✓ **He apologized to her for the long delay.**
    apologize to sb: 'The US has apologized to Britain for the accident that cost nine lives.'

2 ✗ She insisted on apologizing her husband's behaviour.
    ✓ **She insisted on apologizing for her husband's behaviour.**
    ✗ I apologize that I can't come to the wedding. ✗
    ✓ **I apologize for not being able to come to the wedding.**
    apologize (to sb) for (doing) sth: 'I'd like to apologize for causing you so much trouble.'

appear 1 ✗ Suddenly, a bright flash of lightning appeared.
    ✓ **Suddenly, there was a bright flash of lightning.**
    ✗ We don't want any more wars to appear.
    ✓ **We don't want there to be any more wars.**
    A simple way of saying that something happens or develops is to use **there + be**: 'Suddenly, there was a loud bang and all the lights went out.' 'There have been several serious accidents along this stretch of the road.' 'This time I don't want there to be any mistakes.'

2 ✗ Unemployment appears in nearly all developed countries.
    ✓ **Unemployment occurs in nearly all developed countries.**
    ✗ Unfortunately, another problem has appeared.
    ✓ **Unfortunately, another problem has occurred.**
    appear = (1) become visible or (suddenly) be seen: 'Small red patches appeared all over the child's back.' 'A minute later the manager appeared and asked what was wrong.'(2) (of something new) become available or be seen for the first time: 'The first edition appeared in 1987.' 'The new model will not appear in the shops until the end of the year.' 'When did dinosaurs first appear?'
    occur = (1) (of unplanned events) happen: 'The crash occurred just minutes after take-off.' 'These storms usually occur in the late afternoon.' (2) exist or be found (in a particular place): 'The Japanese 'f' sound does not occur in European languages.'

3 ✗ If he were alive, he would appear a lot of good films.
    ✓ **If he were alive, he would appear in a lot of good films.**
    ✗ Recently she has appeared on several TV commercials.
    ✓ **Recently she has appeared in several TV commercials.**
    appear on television, a television channel: 'This is the first time that Britt has appeared on television.' 'He is scheduled to appear on Channel 4 next month.'
    appear on/in a television programme: 'He's always appearing on/in BBC

sports programmes.' 'We asked the Home Office to appear on/in this programme, but they refused.'
appear in a film, play, show, television commercial: 'What's the name of that young actor who appeared in *Jurassic Park*?' 'Before that she had appeared in a Broadway production of *West Side Story*.'

4   ✗   There appears a haphazard attitude among the younger generation.
   ✓   **There appears to be a haphazard attitude among the younger generation.**

   there appears/appeared + **to be** + noun phrase (= seem): 'There appears to be a shortage of paper.' 'There appears to have been a breakdown in communication.'

apply 1   ✗   I've applied a one-year course in computer studies.
   ✓   **I've applied for a one-year course in computer studies.**
   ✗   I don't have enough experience to apply to the job.
   ✓   **I don't have enough experience to apply for the job.**

   apply (**to** an organization) **for** a job, course, scholarship etc.: 'She has applied for the post of Senior Lecturer.'

2   ✗   The new tax law applies only on people with large incomes.
   ✓   **The new tax law applies only to people with large incomes.**

   apply to sb/sth (= be aimed at): 'The club's rules and regulations apply to all members.'

appoint- 1
ment   ✗   I was very nervous during the appointment and I'm sure they'll give the job to someone else.
   ✓   **I was very nervous during the interview and I'm sure they'll give the job to someone else.**

   appointment = an arrangement that you have made to see a doctor, dentist, business person, etc at a particular time: 'You can't see the manager without an appointment.' 'My appointment was for ten thirty.'
   interview = a formal meeting at which people ask you questions to see if you are suitable for a particular job, course of study, etc: 'If they're interested in your application, they'll ask you to go for an interview.'

2   ✗   I had an appointment with Takumi, a friend of mine.
   ✓   **I had arranged to meet Takumi, a friend of mine.**

   You make an **appointment** to see a doctor, principal, business person, etc: 'I've got an appointment to see Dr Tanner on Tuesday.'
   You **arrange to meet/see** a friend, relative etc: 'We've arranged to meet Alan at the swimming pool.'

appreciate 1   ✗   I don't appreciate magazines or newspapers that have been censored.
   ✓   **I don't like magazines or newspapers that have been censored.**

   appreciate = like or enjoy something because you have studied it and understand the value of it: 'I've never appreciated modern art.' 'It was during my years in Paris that I learned to appreciate good wine.'

2   ✗   I would greatly appreciate if you could send me Ray's address.
   ✓   **I would greatly appreciate it if you could send me Ray's address.**

appreciate + **it** (+ **if/when** clause): 'I'm sure she'd appreciate it if you could give her a hand.' See also GRANTED

approach

✗ He approached to my table and took a seat opposite me.
✓ **He approached my table and took a seat opposite me.**

approach sb/sth (WITHOUT **to**): 'One of the girls approached our car and held out her hand.'

appro-priate 1

✗ The third paragraph of the essay is not appropriate.
✓ **The third paragraph of the essay is not relevant.**
✗ Will you please send me all the appropriate information?
✓ **Will you please send me all the relevant information?**

appropriate = suitable in a particular situation: 'Once we know more about the cause of the problem, we can take appropriate action.' 'To offer them more money at this stage would not be appropriate.'
relevant = having a clear connection with what you are doing or talking about: 'I'll try to answer any questions, as long as they are relevant.' 'You cannot enter the country unless you have obtained all the relevant documents.'

2

✗ Some bottles are not appropriate for recycling.
✓ **Some bottles are not suitable for recycling.**
✗ She is clearly the most appropriate person for the job.
✓ **She is clearly the most suitable person for the job.**

Appropriate and **suitable** have similar meanings and are sometimes interchangeable: 'We're still waiting for a suitable/an appropriate moment to break the news to them.'
When you mean 'having the necessary qualities, skills etc, the usual word is **suitable**: 'The hotel isn't suitable for families with children.'

approve

✗ Those who approve the death penalty claim that life imprisonment is not effective.
✓ **Those who approve of the death penalty claim that life imprisonment is not effective.**
✗ Some husbands do not approve the idea of their wives having a job.
✓ **Some husbands do not approve of the idea of their wives having a job.**

approve sth (without **of**) = formally accept a plan, proposal or application: 'The use of the new drug has yet to be approved by the Medical Research Council.'
approve of sb/sth = think that someone or something is good: 'I'm sure that most athletes will approve of the new rules on drug testing.' 'I don't approve of sending young children to boarding school.'

approxim-ately

? I arrived in L.A. approximately a month ago.
✓ **I arrived in L.A. about a month ago.**
? The party should end at approximately midnight.
✓ **The party should end at around midnight.**
? The train fare is approximately £20.
✓ **The train fare is roughly £20.**

Approximately is used mainly in formal written styles: 'It is estimated that, during the period in question, approximately 47,000 cars were stolen in the London area alone.'
Unless you wish to sound formal, use **about, around** or **roughly**.

area

? A number of different countries and areas face the same problem.

✓ **A number of different countries and regions face the same problem.**

To refer to one of the very large parts of a country, or to an area which includes more than one country, use **region**: 'This region of France is famous for its wine.' 'We apologize to viewers in the southern region for the poor picture quality.' 'This variety of rice is grown mainly in cool temperate regions.'

argue

✗ In the first class after lunch we usually argue.

✓ **In the first class after lunch we usually have a discussion.**

When people **argue** (or **quarrel**), they disagree strongly about something and are often angry or upset: 'Parents should try not to argue in front of their children.' 'We were always arguing about silly things, like whose turn it was to do the shopping.'

When people consider a subject from several points of view, they **have a discussion** or **have a debate** (= a formal discussion in which two or more groups take it in turns to present their opinions).

argument

✗ There are several good arguments for people preferring to live in the countryside.

✓ **There are several good reasons for people preferring to live in the countryside.**

✗ They don't want children, for purely personal arguments.

✓ **They don't want children, for purely personal reasons.**

argument = a reason that you give to support your opinion, especially when you are trying to persuade someone: 'The writer's main argument is that a better train service will take cars off the road and lead to a healthier environment.' 'The argument against higher taxation is very simple.'

reason = something that explains someone's actions or feelings, or why a particular situation exists: 'My main reason for doing the course is to improve my qualifications.' 'He's got to go back to Mexico, for family reasons.'

arise

✗ These problems have been arised as a result of overpopulation.

✓ **These problems have arisen as a result of overpopulation.**

Arise (arising, arose, arisen) is an intransitive verb, just like **arrive, happen** etc: 'When there is a clear written agreement, these misunderstandings do not arise.' 'The problem first arose when I tried to get a visa.' 'Should the need arise, you could sell the Mercedes and buy something cheaper.'

arithmetic

✗ She comes to see me three times a week for help with her arithmetics.

✓ **She comes to see me three times a week for help with her arithmetic.**

mathematics (WITH **-s**) but **arithmetic** (WITHOUT **-s**): 'Arithemtic isn't difficult if it's taught properly.'

See also MATHEMATICS

arm 1

✗ The plan to reduce the arm forces is strongly opposed.

✓ **The plan to reduce the armed forces is strongly opposed.**

armed = having one or more weapons: 'Both hijackers are believed to be armed.'
the armed forces = (a country's) army, navy, and air force

2

✗ She wouldn't stop crying until I held her on my arms.
✓ **She wouldn't stop crying until I held her in my arms.**
✗ I shall never forget the day he died on my arms.
✓ **I shall never forget the day he died in my arms.**
(hold sb/sth) in your arms (NOT **on**): 'He had a great pile of books in his arms.'

armchair

✗ She was sitting on her favourite armchair.
✓ **She was sitting in her favourite armchair.**
sit (down) in an armchair (NOT **on**): 'He sat down in the armchair and almost immediately fell asleep.'

arrival 1

✗ At his arrival in Vienna, he was surprised not to find his friend.
✓ **On his arrival in Vienna, he was surprised not to find his friend.**
on/upon sb's arrival (NOT **at**): 'On arrival in Addis Ababa I reported immediately to the British High Commission.'

2

✗ The Pope's arrival to the Philippines caused a lot of excitement.
✓ **The Pope's arrival in the Philippines caused a lot of excitement.**
See notes at ARRIVE 1, 2

arrive 1

✗ You'll arrive to London at two in the morning.
✓ **You'll arrive in London at two in the morning.**
✗ When the train arrived at Munich, he was still asleep.
✓ **When the train arrived in Munich, he was still asleep.**
arrive/arrival in a country, city etc: 'I'll be arriving in Hong Kong in time for Chinese New Year.'

2

✗ She arrived the station just in time to catch the train.
✓ **She arrived at the station just in time to catch the train.**
✗ We arrived to the hotel in time for dinner.
✓ **We arrived at the hotel in time for dinner.**
arrive/arrival at a building, station, airport etc: 'Make sure you arrive at the airport with plenty of time to spare.' See also HOME 1

arouse

✗ If your feelings arouse easily, you cannot concentrate.
✓ **If your feelings are easily aroused, you cannot concentrate.**
Arouse is a transitive verb: 'The chairman's resignation is bound to arouse new fears about the company's future.' 'My suspicions were aroused when I noticed that the car had been resprayed.'

art

✗ The college offers both science and art subjects.
✓ **The college offers both science and arts subjects.**
✗ I worked as a tutor in the Faculty of Art and Social Sciences.
✓ **I worked as a tutor in the Faculty of Arts and Social Sciences.**

Subjects of study are divided into **the sciences** (e.g. biology, physics, chemistry) and **the arts** (e.g. history, French, geography): 'If you don't like numbers, you should stick to the arts.'
The noun **arts** (WITH **-s**) is often used in front of another noun: 'I'm studying for an arts degree.'

artificial 1

✗ There are two artificial lakes – one for swimming and one for fishing.
✓ **There are two man-made lakes – one for swimming and one for fishing.**
✗ The city has suffered both natural and artificial disasters.
✓ **The city has suffered both natural and man-made disasters.**

artificial = not made of natural materials: 'I still prefer sugar to all those artificial sweeteners.' 'Most people look better under artificial light.'
man-made = made or caused by people, although sometimes having a natural appearance: 'This canal is the longest man-made waterway in the world.' 'It's hard to believe that these enormous caves are actually man-made.'

2

✗ He managed to lose weight by eating artificial diet foods.
✓ **He managed to lose weight by eating synthetic diet foods.**
✗ I am worried about taking artificial products into the body.
✓ **I am worried about taking synthetic products into the body.**
✗ I never eat artificial foods.
✓ **I never eat synthetic foods/food substitutes.**

synthetic = not natural but made by a chemical process: 'Many old herbal remedies have been replaced by synthetic drugs.'

artistic

✗ The country's artistic treasures should be left where they are.
✓ **The country's art treasures should be left where they are.**
✗ Students coming from artistic schools can join the Academy of Arts.
✓ **Students coming from art schools can join the Academy of Arts.**

artistic = (1) showing the skill or imagination of an artist: 'Both my parents were highly imaginative and artistic.' (2) connected with art or artists: 'His paintings have little artistic merit.'
art = things produced by artists such as paintings and sculptures. This word is used as a noun and to modify another noun: 'The portrait is a fine example of early Renaissance art.' 'She owns one of the finest art collections in Europe.'

as 1

✗ His skin is not as the skin of a young man.
✓ **His skin is not like the skin of a young man.**
✗ It looked very fragile and so I handled it as china.
✓ **It looked very fragile and so I handled it like china.**

In comparisons, the word that is usually used in front of a noun or noun phrase is **like** (NOT **as**): 'James is very tall, just like his father.' 'Their car is like ours - old and full of rust.'
As is used in the patterns **(not) as ... as, not so ... as,** and **the same (...) as**: 'James is as tall as his father.' 'Their car is the same colour as ours.'

2

✗ The book is concerned with important social issues as child abuse and women's rights.

    ✓ **The book is concerned with important social issues such as child abuse and women's rights.**

    ✓ **The book is concerned with important social issues like child abuse and women's rights.**

> Examples of a class or category are introduced by **such as** or **like** (NOT **as**): 'Serious diseases such as AIDS and cancer can cause a great deal of suffering.'

3

    ✗ She looked at everyone as she were their superior.

    ✓ **She looked at everyone as if she were their superior.**

    ✗ I suddenly felt as I was fifteen again.

    ✓ **I suddenly felt as if I was/were fifteen again.**

> To compare a real situation with an imaginary or remembered situation, use **as if** or **as though** (NOT **as**): 'She came straight over and spoke to me as if we had known each other for years.' See also WAS

4

    ✗ As our room was upstairs, so we didn't hear him.

    ✓ **As our room was upstairs, we didn't hear him.**

    ✓ **Our room was upstairs and so we didn't hear him.**

> See note at SO 1

as if

    ✗ I was treated as if an old friend.

    ✓ **I was treated as if I was/were an old friend.**

    ✓ **I was treated like an old friend.**

> Do not use a noun phrase immediately after **as if** and **as though**: 'She looked at me as if/though she'd never seen me before.' 'He walked with difficulty, as if/though (he were) in pain.' See also WAS

as long as

    ✗ I'll go with you as long as I won't have to sing.

    ✓ **I'll go with you as long as I don't have to sing.**

> See Language Note at WILL

as soon as

    ✗ I'll pay you as soon as I will receive the parcel.

    ✓ **I'll pay you as soon as I receive/I've received the parcel.**

as well 1

    ✗ I don't have a car and I don't want one as well.

    ✓ **I don't have a car and I don't want one either.**

> See note at TOO 2

2

    ✗ As good Spaniards, they know as well how to enjoy life.

    ✓ **As good Spaniards, they also know how to enjoy life.**

    ✓ **As good Spaniards, they know how to enjoy life as well/too.**

    ✗ Could you bring as well a tape recorder?

    ✓ **Could you also bring a tape recorder?**

    ✓ **Could you bring a tape recorder as well/too?**

> **As well** usually goes at the end of the clause: 'Do we have to invite their husbands as well?'

3

    ? The book is useful for teachers and pupils as well.

    ✓ **The book is useful for teachers and pupils alike.**

> To emphasize that something is equally true for each of the people, groups or things mentioned, use **alike**: 'This new medical dictionary will serve doctors and nurses alike.'

as well as

✗ Each week he wrote her three letters, as well as telephoned her.
✓ **Each week he wrote her three letters, as well as telephoning her.**

> **as well as** + v-ing: 'Did you realize that, as well as being a dress designer, she manages a chain of health food shops?'

ashamed

✗ I always feel ashamed when I have to speak in public.
✓ **I always feel embarrassed when I have to speak in public.**

> **ashamed** = guilty and disgusted with yourself because of something (bad) that you have done: 'Anyone who steals from the poor should be ashamed of themselves.'
> **embarrassed** = feeling socially uncomfortable or anxious: 'You can imagine how embarrassed I felt when I couldn't pay the bill.'

ask 1

✗ We have to ask to ourselves whether such films should be censored.
✓ **We have to ask ourselves whether such films should be censored.**
✗ She asked to me to tell her a story.
✓ **She asked me to tell her a story.**

> **ask sb** (NOT **to sb**): 'He asked me if I could give him a lift to the station.'

2

✗ She asked me what was the time.
✓ **She asked me what the time was.**
✗ They asked him what would he like to do.
✓ **They asked him what he would like to do.**

> When the object of the sentence is a **wh-** clause, the subject and the verb in the **wh-** clause do not change places. Compare: 'How old are you?' 'She asked me how old I was.'

aspect 1

✗ From a biological aspect, the two plants are very similar.
✓ **From a biological point of view, the two plants are very similar.**
✗ History can be studied in many different aspects.
✓ **History can be studied from many different points of view.**

> **aspect** = one of the parts or features of a situation, idea, problem, etc: 'Modern technology affects all aspects of our daily lives.' 'The book concentrates on the cruel aspects of war.'
> **point of view** = a particular way of looking at a situation, event, problem, etc: 'From a vegetarian's point of view, these new controls on meat preparation are of little interest.' 'What does the process of getting old mean from a medical point of view?' 'I wish you'd try and see things from my point of view for a change.'

2

✗ Another function of newspapers is to shape public opinion and in this aspect the Guardian is very influential indeed.
✓ **Another function of newspapers is to shape public opinion and in this respect the Guardian is very influential indeed.**

> To refer back to something that you have just said, use **in this respect** (NOT **in this aspect**): 'Mr Jones has far more experience than the other applicants, and in this respect I'd say that he is the strongest candidate.'

3

✗ At one time it seemed as if men were stronger than women in every aspect.

✓ **At one time it seemed as if men were stronger than women in every respect.**

> When you wish to control the strength of a statement, use **in some/several/certain/many/all respects** or **in one/this/every respect**: 'In many respects she is the best teacher I've ever had.' 'In some respects the two cultures are very similar.'

assassinate ✗ He was charged with assassinating a taxi-driver.

✓ **He was charged with murdering a taxi-driver.**

> See Language Note at KILL

assassin

✗ The prison is full of crooks, thieves and assassins.

✓ **The prison is full of crooks, thieves and murderers.**

> See Language Note at KILL

assist 1

✗ All members are required to assist to the meeting.

✓ **All members are required to attend the meeting.**

✗ The school where I am going to assist is in Cambridge.

✓ **The school that I am going to attend is in Cambridge.**

> **assist** = (formal) help: 'Should you have difficulty in finding a book, the library staff will be pleased to assist you.'
> **attend** = (formal) (1) be present at a meeting or event; go to: 'He's had to cancel the trip in order to attend his mother's funeral.' (2) be a member of something that has regular meetings, such as a school or class; go to: 'The couples who attended the prenatal classes found childbirth much easier, especially the wives.' See also ATTEND 1

2

✗ One of the prison guards assisted them to escape.

✓ **One of the prison guards assisted them in their escape.**

✓ **One of the prison guards assisted them in escaping.**

> **assist (sb) in/with sth**: 'A Swiss rescue team is being flown in to assist in the search for survivors.' 'I've been asked to assist with the wedding arrangements.'
> **assist (sb) in doing sth** (NOT **to do**): 'Our main job is to assist foreign governments in developing their economies.'

3

✗ Ask Susie to assist you.

✓ **Ask Susie to help you.**

> **Assist** is used only in formal styles. See note at ASSIST 1.

assure

✗ I can assure that your name will not be mentioned.

✓ **I can assure you that your name will not be mentioned.**

✗ I assure that the meeting will not last very long.

✓ **I assure you that the meeting will not last very long.**

> **assure sb that**: 'I assure you that we are doing everything we can to avoid further delays.'

asylum

✗ Asylums are typically seen as places where people go to die.

✓ **Hospices are typically seen as places where people go to die.**

> **asylum** = (old-fashioned) a hospital for the mentally ill, nowadays known as a **psychiatric hospital**
> **hospice** = a special type of hospital for people who are dying
> Note also the term **old people's home** = a place where old people go to live when they need someone to look after them: 'She'd rather stay in an old people's home than be a burden to her family.'

at 1   ✗ I always have a good breakfast at the morning.
✓ **I always have a good breakfast in the morning.**
✗ At afternoon I visited the Fitzwilliam Museum.
✓ **In the afternoon I visited the Fitzwilliam Museum.**
See Language Note at TIME

2   ✗ In Germany we have a lot of snow at wintertime.
✓ **In Germany we have a lot of snow in wintertime.**
✗ I was married at 1989 and have two children, a boy and a girl.
✓ **I was married in 1989 and have two children, a boy and a girl.**
See Language Note at TIME

3   ✗ I bought the tape just a week ago, at 4th December.
✓ **I bought the tape just a week ago, on 4th December.**
✗ We were all very tired at the last day of our journey.
✓ **We were all very tired on the last day of our journey.**
See Language Note at TIME

athletic   ✗ A lot of athletic reporters write for the magazine.
✓ **A lot of athletics reporters write for the magazine.**
✗ The race was organized by the National Athletic Association.
✓ **The race was organized by the National Athletics Association.**

athletic = physically strong and good at running, jumping, etc: 'I've never been very athletic.'
athletics = sports such as running, jumping, and throwing the javelin: 'I've never been very good at athletics.'
The noun **athletics** (WITH **-s**) is often used in front of another noun: 'He's been selected for the athletics team.'

attempt   ✗ His attempt of seizing power was defeated by the army.
✓ **His attempt to seize power was defeated by the army.**

(make) an attempt to do/at doing sth: 'The government's attempts to control inflation have failed miserably.' 'He made several unsuccessful attempts at getting the car started.'

attend 1   ? I'm sorry that I won't be able to attend your wedding.
✓ **I'm sorry that I won't be able to be at your wedding.**
? I'm afraid that I can't attend your party.
✓ **I'm afraid that I can't make it to your party.**

Attend is used mainly in formal styles: 'All committee members are expected to attend the meeting.' In other styles use **be at, come/go (to)** or (informal) **make it (to)**: 'Apart from John and Sue, who else will be at the party?' 'Did you go to the match on Saturday?' 'We hope you can come but don't worry if you can't make it.'

2   ✗ It's very important to attend to all the classes.
✓ **It's very important to attend all the classes.**
✗ I won't be able to attend at the meeting.
✓ **I won't be able to attend the meeting.**

attend a meeting, class, school, etc (WITHOUT **to** or **at**)

attention 1 ✗ Everyone should pay attention to avoiding stressful situations.
✓ **Everyone should take care to avoid stressful situations.**
✗ Pay attention when refuelling and try not to spill any petrol.
✓ **Be careful when refuelling and try not to spill any petrol.**
When talking about a situation that could be dangerous or harmful, use **be careful** or **take care** (NOT **pay attention**): 'When the road surface is wet, drivers should take extra care.' 'Be careful to keep all medicines out of the reach of children.'

2 ✗ People should pay more attention on what they eat.
✓ **People should pay more attention to what they eat.**
pay attention to sb/sth (NOT **on/in/at**): 'This part of the course pays special attention to the spoken language.'

3 ✗ When driving, you must give your best attention to what you are doing.
✓ **When driving, you must give your full attention to what you are doing.**
full/undivided attention: 'I assure you that this matter will receive our undivided attention.'

4 ✗ The attention is a bit slow, but the waiters are always polite.
✓ **The service is a bit slow, but the waiters are always polite.**
service = the help and attention that you get from the people who work in a shop or restaurant: 'We complained about the poor service.'

5 ✗ To the attention of: Mrs H. Greaves, Principal.
✓ **For the attention of: Mrs H. Greaves, Principal.**
for the attention of (NOT **to/at**)

audience ✗ The priest stands in front of the bride and groom, facing the audience.
✓ **The priest stands in front of the bride and groom, facing the congregation.**
audience = the people who go to watch/listen to a film, play, concert, public lecture, etc: 'The group has played to vast audiences all over the world.' 'At the end of the talk, members of the audience were invited to ask questions.'
congregation = the people who attend a church service: 'The vicar is always pleased to see new faces in the congregation.'

authority ✗ Those who bend the rules are reported to the authority.
✓ **Those who bend the rules are reported to the authorities.**
✗ The authority had refused them even their basic civil rights.
✓ **The authorities had refused them even their basic civil rights.**
To refer in a general way to the officials who make all the important decisions in a country, use **the authorities**: 'The authorities estimate that nearly 100,000 immigrants have entered the country illegally.'
As a countable noun, **authority** refers to an official group or organization that controls an area or activity: 'You can claim housing benefit from your local authority.'

average 1 ✗ The article was about average British people and their reluctance to learn foreign languages.
✓ **The article was about typical British people and their reluctance to learn foreign languages.**
✗ The Los Angeles Medical Centre announced that the average AIDS patient requires about two to three months of hospitalization.
✓ **The Los Angeles Medical Centre announced that the typical AIDS patient requires about two to three months of hospitalization.**

average = not special or unusual in any way; of the usual standard or level: 'Anyone of average intelligence knows that drugs are dangerous.' 'The average student takes about two hours to complete the test.'
typical = having the same appearance, behaviour or characteristics as a particular type of person or thing: 'McGarron looked like a typical American car salesman.' 'John's wife is a typical teacher.'

2 ✗ The average of hours spent watching television has increased.
✓ **The average number of hours spent watching television has increased.**
✓ **The average hours spent watching television have increased.**

an/the average of + NUMBER: 'The average of 3, 4 and 8 is 5.' 'The test results produced an average of 65 per cent.'
the average number/amount/level/age of + NOUN: 'The average age of the children is five years and seven months.'
an/the average + NOUN: 'The average salary is $2100 a month.'

avoid 1 ✗ He put his hand over my mouth to avoid me to scream.
✓ **He put his hand over my mouth to prevent me from screaming.**
✗ These new measures are intended to avoid the spread of the disease.
✓ **These new measures are intended to prevent the spread of the disease.**
✓ **These new measures are intended to prevent the disease from spreading.**

avoid (doing) sth = be careful not to do something: 'The best way to lose weight is to avoid eating fatty foods.' 'These drugs are dangerous and should be avoided.' 'Try to avoid subjects that can cause offence.'
prevent sb/sth (from doing sth) = stop someone or something from doing something; stop something from happening: 'The wall is supposed to prevent dogs from getting into the garden.' 'It is hoped that the new speed limit will help to prevent accidents.'

2 ✗ He is such a nice man that you can't avoid liking him.
✓ **He is such a nice man that you can't help liking him.**
✗ I couldn't avoid falling in love with her.
✓ **I couldn't help falling in love with her.**

can't help doing sth = cannot stop yourself from doing something: 'Whenever he tries to sing, I just can't help laughing.'

3

✗ I told him that we would be grateful if he would kindly avoid ringing our doorbell after midnight.
✓ **I told him that we would be grateful if he would kindly refrain from ringing our doorbell after midnight.**

> **refrain from doing sth** = (formal) stop yourself from doing something because other people do not like it: 'Hotel guests are asked to refrain from smoking in the restaurants.'

4

✗ I avoid to use a computer for personal letters.
✓ **I avoid using a computer for personal letters.**

> **avoid doing sth** (NOT **to do**): 'He obviously wants to avoid getting involved in the dispute.'

await

✗ We await for your reply and apologize for any inconvenience.
✓ **We await your reply and apologize for any inconvenience.**

> **await sb/sth** (WITHOUT **for**): 'The committee is awaiting a decision from head office.'

awake

✗ I get up at seven o'clock but I awake an hour earlier.
✓ **I get up at seven o'clock but I wake up an hour earlier.**
✗ The next morning we awoke up at 7 o'clock to catch the train.
✓ **The next morning we woke up at 7 o'clock to catch the train.**

> **Awake** is used mainly as an adjective: 'It's gone ten o'clock and the children are still awake.' As a verb, **awake** (WITHOUT **up**) is used only in literary styles: 'I awoke to the sound of church bells.'
> The usual verb is **wake up**: 'She told me that she keeps waking up in the middle of the night.' 'I was woken up by a loud whistling noise.'

award

✗ The insurance company has offered an award to anyone who can provide information about the theft.
✓ **The insurance company has offered a reward to anyone who can provide information about the theft.**

> **award** = (1) a prize, certificate, or medal that is given for doing something very well: 'The award for this year's best actor went to Harry Cohen.' (2) a sum of money that someone wins in a court of law: 'Each survivor of the disaster received an award of $20,000.'
> **reward** = (1) something that you are given by someone who is pleased by what you have done: 'As a reward for eating all her dinner, she was given an ice cream.' (2) a sum of money that someone promises to pay to the person who provides useful information, usually in connection with a crime that has been committed or something that has been lost: 'A reward of $5,000 has been offered for information leading to the recovery of the necklace.'

B*b*

baby

? Sitting in the next seat was a young woman who was having a baby.

✓ **Sitting in the next seat was a young woman who was expecting a baby.**

> **have a baby** = give birth to a baby: 'She's worried about having the baby at home in case there are complications.'
> **be expecting a baby** = be pregnant: 'Janet is expecting another baby.'
> Note that **be having a baby** can be used to mean 'be pregnant' but this should be avoided when there is a danger of confusion.

back

See RETURN 1

bad 1

✗ I'm afraid I speak English very bad.

✓ **I'm afraid I speak English very badly.**

> **Bad** is an adjective: 'I tried to ignore the child's bad behaviour.'
> **Badly** is an adverb: 'The child behaved very badly indeed.'

2

? Of course, there are also bad things about living in a city.

✓ **Of course, there are also disadvantages to living in a city.**

? It's a bad thing that the population is increasing so quickly.

✓ **It's unfortunate that the population is increasing so quickly.**

> The phrase **bad thing/s** is generally over-used and often sounds unnatural.

See also THING

badly 1

✗ My shoulders were sunburnt badly.

✓ **My shoulders were badly sunburnt.**

✗ Some were killed and others were injured badly.

✓ **Some were killed and others were badly injured.**

> **badly** + past participle: 'The other car was badly damaged.'

2

See ILL 2

baggage

✗ All the passengers carried their own baggages.

✓ **All the passengers carried their own baggage.**

> **Baggage** is an uncountable noun: 'Baggage must not be left unattended in the terminal building.' 'How many pieces of baggage do you have?'

band

See MUSIC 2

barely

✗ Although I am a member of the club, I barely go there.

✓ **Although I am a member of the club, I rarely go there.**

> **barely** = almost not; only just: 'His handwriting is barely legible.' (= you can only just read it) 'The fog was so bad that we barely made it to the motel.'

rarely/seldom/hardly ever = almost never: 'He rarely makes any serious mistakes.'

base 1

  ✗ Political stability provides the base for economic development.
  ✓ **Political stability provides the basis for economic development.**

base = (1) the main part of something: 'Most of the paints we produce have an oil base.' (2) the lowest part of something: 'The base of the column is made of marble.'
basis = the very important thing from which something else develops or is made possible: 'The basis of a successful marriage is mutual respect.' 'Newton's discoveries provided the basis for future research.'

2

  ✗ The first role play base on a conversation at a hotel reception desk.
  ✓ **The first role play was based on a conversation at a hotel reception desk.**

be based on/upon = be developed from: 'Republican policy is based on the idea that people should compete with each other.' 'The film is based on a popular Bengali novel.'

basis

  ✗ The course is for students with a basis knowledge of English.
  ✓ **The course is for students with a basic knowledge of English.**

Basis is a noun. See note at BASE 1
Basic is an adjective: 'basic computer skills', 'basic principles'

bath 1

  ✗ We decided to have a bath in the hotel pool.
  ✓ **We decided to have a swim in the hotel pool.**

have a bath = wash yourself in a bath: 'I always have a bath or shower before going to bed.'
When you are talking about swimming, use **have a swim, have a dip** or (in formal styles of British English) **have a bathe.** See note at BATHE

2

  ✗ I always take a bath before going to bed.
  ✓ **I always have a bath before going to bed.**

In British English the phrase is **have a bath** (NOT **take**): 'There isn't enough water to have a bath.' **Take a bath** is used in American English.

3

  See *SUNBATH

bathe

  ✗ Most nights when I come home, I'm too tired to bathe.
  ✓ **Most nights when I come home, I'm too tired to have a bath.**

In British English, **bathe, have/go for a bathe** and **go bathing** mean 'swim, play or just relax in the water' (NOT 'get clean in a bath'): 'It was the first time I'd bathed in the Red Sea.' Nowadays most people use **swim, have/go for a swim** or **go swimming** for this meaning.
In American English, **bathe** means 'get clean in a bath'.

battle

  ✗ Many young Americans refused to battle in Vietnam.
  ✓ **Many young Americans refused to fight in Vietnam.**

battle = struggle to do or get something: 'Doctors are still battling to save the child's life.'
fight = use violence to hurt or kill people: 'My grandfather fought in the Spanish Civil War.'

be 1 ✗ Meanwhile, Sarah was beginning to be upset.
✓ **Meanwhile, Sarah was beginning to get upset.**
✗ When she didn't arrive, I started to be anxious.
✓ **When she didn't arrive, I started to become anxious.**
When talking about a change in state, use **get/become/grow** + adjective (NOT **be**): 'I've put a couple of apples in your bag in case you get hungry.' 'The children were growing impatient.'

2 ✗ After six months he was the general manager.
✓ **After six months he became the general manager.**
When talking about a change in state, use **become** + noun phrase (NOT **be**): 'In 1975 she became leader of the Conservative Party.'

3 ✗ Nowadays is very difficult to get a job.
✓ **Nowadays it is very difficult to get a job.**
See IT 1

4 ✗ On Saturdays is usually a party at someone's house.
✓ **On Saturdays there is usually a party at someone's house.**
See THERE 1

bear 1 ✗ The government also controls the number of children that a couple can bear.
✓ **The government also controls the number of children that a couple can have.**
✗ I want to get married and bear children.
✓ **I want to get married and have children.**
Bear (sb) a child is used only in formal styles and refers to the physical process of giving birth: 'She bore her husband two daughters and one son.' The subject of **bear** is always a woman.
When you are talking about beginning a family or the number of children in a family, use **have** (NOT **bear**): 'We'd like to have children while we're still young.'

2 ✗ 'I can't bear any longer,' he said. 'I'm ready to resign.'
✓ **'I can't bear it any longer,' he said. 'I'm ready to resign.'**
✗ I can't bear if someone starts cracking their knuckles.
✓ **I can't bear it if someone starts cracking their knuckles.**
can't bear + **it** (+ **if/when** clause): 'I can't bear it when people start complaining about nothing.'

beautiful ? Thank you for your beautiful letter.
✓ **Thank you for your interesting/newsy letter.**
See Language Note at KILL

because 1 See REASON 3, 4

2 See note at SO 1

become 1 ✗ Eventually I became to like Singapore.
✓ **Eventually I came to like Singapore.**
Become means 'start to be' and is followed by an adjective or noun (NOT a verb): 'We didn't meet again until after she had become famous.'

'Brunei became an independent member of the Commonwealth in 1984.'
When talking about a gradual change in the way a person feels or thinks about someone or something, use **come/grow** + to-v (NOT **become**):
'Although she had come to dislike her boss, she tried not to let it show.'
'As the months passed, I actually grew to enjoy his company.'

2 ✗ When my first child was born, I became to think seriously about my future.
✓ **When my first child was born, I began to think seriously about my future.**

begin/start to do sth (NOT **become**): 'My evenings were free and so I began to learn German.'

3 ✗ The housing problem in Hong Kong becomes more serious.
✓ **The housing problem in Hong Kong is becoming more serious.**

To refer to something that is still happening or taking place, use the present progressive tense of **become**: 'It's becoming difficult to find somewhere to park.'

4 See BLIND, DARK, MAD 1, TRUE

bed 1 ✗ Every morning I have to get up from my bed very early.
✓ **Every morning I have to get up very early.**
✗ I left my bed at 8 a.m. and had a shower.
✓ **I got up at 8 a.m. and had a shower.**

get up = get out of bed and start your day: 'I've got to get up early in the morning to catch the 7.00 train.'

2 ✗ I decided to stay in my bed this morning.
✓ **I decided to stay in bed this morning.**
✗ I never go to my bed before 11 p.m.
✓ **I never go to bed before 11 p.m.**

stay in bed, go to bed, get out of bed, lie in bed, be in bed (WITHOUT **my, his, the,** etc)
Compare: 'Who's been sleeping in my bed?' asked Daddy Bear.

been 1 ✗ I hadn't been in Scotland before.
✓ **I hadn't been to Scotland before.**
✗ Have you ever been in California?
✓ **Have you ever been to California?**

been in = been living or staying in: 'I've been in Paris since the beginning of June.' 'How long has Wendy been in hospital?'
been to = gone to and come back from; visited: 'I've been to Paris three times.' 'I've been to the hospital to see Wendy.'

2 ✗ Last year I've been to England for a month.
✓ **Last year I went to England for a month.**
✗ First of all we've been to UCLA to see Ray's brother.
✓ **First of all we went to UCLA to see Ray's brother.**

When you are talking about a specific visit or trip that you made in the past, use **went to** (NOT **have been to**). Compare: 'I've been to England and Italy, but I haven't been to France.' 'I went to England in 1993 and to Italy in 1994.'

before 1   ✗   Before forty years the journey took twice as long.
    ✓   **Forty years ago the journey took twice as long.**
    ✗   Not so long before we used animals for transportation.
    ✓   **Not so long ago we used animals for transportation.**

> **ago** = before 'now', the moment of speaking: 'Her plane landed ten minutes ago. In fact, here she comes now.' 'I saw him just five minutes ago.' (= five minutes before now)
> **before** = before 'then', a time in the past: 'I went to the airport last Monday to meet Sue. I hadn't been to the airport before.' (= before last Monday). 'I saw him last Friday in London and two days before in Leeds.' (= last Wednesday)

2   ✗   My parents first came here before 40 years ago.
   ✓   **My parents first came here 40 years ago.**

See Language Note at TIME

3   See EVER 2

beg 1   ✗   I beg you to send me the information as soon as possible.
   ✓   **I should be grateful if you would send me the information as soon as possible.**

> When **beg** means 'ask someone to do something', it is nearly always used as a reporting verb. Compare: 'Please forgive me.' 'He begged her to forgive him.'
> To make a request in a formal letter, use **I/we should/would be grateful if ...** (NOT **I/we beg you ...**): 'I would be grateful if you could raise this question at the next meeting.'

2   See PARDON 2

beginning 1 ✗   In the beginning of the century people travelled from Britain to Egypt by sea.
   ✓   **At the beginning of the century people travelled from Britain to Egypt by sea.**

See Language Note at FIRST

2 ✗   At the beginning I thought that the switch was broken but then I discovered it was a fuse.
  ✓   **At first I thought that the switch was broken but then I discovered it was a fuse.**

See Language Note at FIRST

behave   ✗   The magazine teaches parents how to behave with their children.
   ✓   **The magazine teaches parents how to behave towards their children.**

> **behave towards sb** (NOT **with**): 'I've been noting the way he behaves towards you and I'm not impressed.'

behaviour 1 ✗   We were surprised by their peculiar behaviours.
   ✓   **We were surprised by their peculiar behaviour.**
   ✗   Such a behaviour can easily cause offence.
   ✓   **Such behaviour can easily cause offence.**

> **Behaviour** is an uncountable noun.

2 ✗ Sometimes Juan has a very strange behaviour.
 ✓ **Sometimes Juan behaves very strangely.**
 ✓ **Sometimes Juan's behaviour is very strange.**
 ✗ There are very few people having such a behaviour.
 ✓ **Very few people behave in such a way.**

> Instead of using **have** + **behaviour**, use **behaviour** + **be** or use the verb **behave** + adverb: 'His behaviour is atrocious.' 'He behaves atrociously.'

behind ✗ At night I keep my wallet behind my pillow.
 ✓ **At night I keep my wallet under my pillow.**

> **behind** = at the back of something: 'Lizzie ran and hid behind a tree.'
> **under** (or **beneath/underneath**) = directly below something, and sometimes touching or covered by it: 'Come and stand under my umbrella.' 'I eventually found the letter under a pile of old newspapers.'

believe 1 ✗ You should not believe in everything you hear.
 ✓ **You should not believe everything you hear.**
 ✗ She couldn't believe in what was happening to her.
 ✓ **She couldn't believe what was happening to her.**

> **believe in sth** = (1) accept that something exists: 'Do you believe in ghosts?' 'James still believes in Father Christmas.'
> (2) think that something is good: 'I don't believe in capital punishment.' 'I believe in getting a good night's sleep before an examination.'
> **believe sth** = accept that something is true or real: 'I believe every word she said.' 'I couldn't believe what I was seeing.'

2 ✗ I could hardly believe in my eyes.
 ✓ **I could hardly believe my eyes.**

> **could not/hardly believe your ears/eyes** (WITHOUT **in**)

3 ✗ I deeply believe that tourists will stop coming here.
 ✓ **I firmly believe that tourists will stop coming here.**
 ✗ My brother deeply believes in freedom of speech.
 ✓ **My brother strongly believes in freedom of speech.**

> **firmly/strongly/fervently/sincerely/truly believe** (NOT **deeply**): 'I sincerely believe that he had no connection with the crime.'

belong 1 ✗ 'Are these gloves belonging to you?' she asked.
 ✓ **'Do these gloves belong to you?' she asked.**
 See Language Note at INCLUDE

2 ✗ The Toyota is belong to my wife.
 ✓ **The Toyota belongs to my wife.**
 ✗ Patreze is belong to the Williams team.
 ✓ **Patreze belongs to the Williams team.**

> **Belong** is a verb (NOT an adjective).

beloved ✗ He spends as much time as he can with his beloved children.
 ✓ **He spends as much time as he can with his children.**

> **Beloved** is used only in literary and humorous styles: 'There were many regrets in her life, but her beloved son was not one of them.' 'He wants to move closer to his beloved football team, Chester City.' It is particularly common on gravestones and old-fashioned birthday cards: 'To the memory of Alice Holt, beloved wife of Thomas Holt.'

below 1

✗ Below the table there were some empty wine bottles.
✓ **Under the table there were some empty wine bottles.**

> **below** = at or to a lower level than something: 'My room is on the third floor, and John's is on the floor below.' 'Our helicopter hovered just below the summit so that we could film the rescue.'
> **under** (or **beneath/underneath**) = directly below something, and sometimes touching or covered by it: 'Come and stand under my umbrella.' 'I eventually found the letter under a pile of old newspapers.'

2

✗ The below report describes my recent stay at the Hotel Grove.
✓ **The report below describes my recent stay at the Hotel Grove.**

> When **below** refers to the position of something on a page, it comes after the noun: 'Last month's sales figures are set out in the table below.'
> Note that **above** can go before or after the noun: 'the table above', 'the above table'.

3

✗ The room rates are much below average for hotels in this area.
✓ **The room rates are far below average for hotels in this area.**

> **far below** (NOT **much**): 'The cost of the trip was far below what we had expected.'
> Compare: 'The room rates were much/far lower than we had expected.'

benefit 1

✗ This new service should benefit to all our customers.
✓ **This new service should benefit all our customers.**
✗ The trade agreement will benefit for both parties.
✓ **The trade agreement will benefit both parties.**

> **benefit sb** (WITHOUT **to/for**): 'The new tax laws will not benefit the unemployed.'

2

✗ It is not true that only businessmen are benefited by tourism.
✓ **It is not true that only businessmen benefit from tourism.**

> Instead of using **be benefited by** (passive), use **benefit from/by**. The subject of **benefit from/by** is the receiver of the benefit: 'Do you think she has benefited from going to extra classes?' 'The room would benefit by altering the size of the window.'

beside/ besides 1

✗ We need to discover another source of income, beside oil.
✓ **We need to discover another source of income, besides oil.**
✗ We went swimming in the river besides my house.
✓ **We went swimming in the river beside my house.**

> **beside** = next to: 'She walked over and sat down beside me.'
> **besides** = in addition to; also: 'Who did you invite besides Tom and Mary?' 'Besides tennis, what other games do you play?' 'I'm too old to apply for the job. Besides, it would mean moving house.'

2

✗ Beside of the traditional ceremonies, there are also foreign weddings.
✓ **Besides the traditional ceremonies, there are also foreign weddings.**
✗ Besides of this problem, her husband had lost his job.
✓ **Besides this problem, her husband had lost his job.**

> When you mean 'in addition to', use **besides** (WITHOUT **of**): 'Who did you speak to, besides Alice?' **Beside/s of** does not exist.

3   ✗ Beside the reduction of unemployment, the government has achieved very little.
     ✓ **Apart from the reduction of unemployment, the government has achieved very little.**
     ✗ Besides the goalkeeper, who was a disaster, the team played very well.
     ✓ **Apart from the goalkeeper, who was a disaster, the team played very well.**

> When you want to say that someone or something is not included in your main statement, use **apart from** (NOT **beside/s**): 'Apart from Peter, everyone had a good time.'

4   ✗ I'd like to have two children. Besides, I hope that the first one will be a girl.
     ✓ **I'd like to have two children and I hope that the first one will be a girl.**

> Use **besides** only when you give an additional reason for something: 'If you're too busy, I'll go and post the letter myself. Besides, I think the walk will do me good.'

best 1   ✗ He is the best surgeon of the hospital.
     ✓ **He is the best surgeon in the hospital.**
     ✗ It is one of the best theatres of Spain.
     ✓ **It is one of the best theatres in Spain.**

> The phrase that follows **the best** (+ noun) usually begins with **in** (NOT **of**): 'one of the best restaurants in London', 'the best team in the league', 'some of the best students in the class'.

2   ✗ We all made our best to see that they enjoyed themselves.
     ✓ **We all did our best to see that they enjoyed themselves.**
> See Language Note at DO

better 1   ✗ German cars are more expensive but they are more better.
     ✓ **German cars are more expensive but they are better.**

> **good, better, best**

2   ✗ You better make sure you're not late again.
     ✓ **You'd better make sure you're not late again.**
     ✗ My friends warned me that I should better be careful.
     ✓ **My friends warned me that I had better be careful.**

> **had better (not)**: 'If the phone rings again, you'd better answer it.' 'If it's a secret, you'd better not tell me.'
> Note that **had** is usually shortened to **d** and sometimes may not be heard at all.

3   ✗ 'You'd better to hurry up,' she shouted.
     ✓ **'You'd better hurry up,' she shouted.**

> **had better (not) do sth** (NOT **to do**): 'You'd better not leave all that money on the table.'

4   ✗ Instead of using a dictionary all the time, you had better try to guess the meaning of the words.

✓ **Instead of using a dictionary all the time, you should try to guess the meanings of the words.**

✗ If people want to be healthy, they had better be more careful about what they eat.

✓ **If people want to be healthy, they should be more careful about what they eat.**

Had better is used in informal styles when you give someone strong advice about what to do in a particular situation. The situation usually exists at the moment of speaking and so there is usually a sense of urgency in the advice: 'You'd better hurry or you'll miss the bus.' 'You'd better ring your parents - just in case they're worrying about you.'

To give advice on a general situation or to say that one course of action is better than another one, use **should, ought to** or **it would be better to:** 'Parents should teach their children to be kind to animals.' 'Rather than complain and risk upsetting her, it would be better to say nothing.'

between 1

✗ Between all the magazines on the shelves, only one was of any interest.

✓ **Among all the magazines on the shelves, only one was of any interest.**

✗ He wandered silently between the passengers on the boat.

✓ **He wandered silently among the passengers on the boat.**

Between is used when there are people or things on either side of someone or something: 'The ball went straight between the goalkeeper's legs.' 'The teacher walked up and down between the rows of desks.' 'Give me a number between 4 and 14.'

Among (or **amongst**) is used when (at least three) people or things are considered as a group or mass: 'I eventually found the photograph among a pile of old letters.'

2

✗ Children between three to five go to kindergarten.

✓ **Children between three and five go to kindergarten.**

✗ Between June 1987 to March 1990 I was in France.

✓ **From June 1987 to March 1990 I was in France.**

✗ It will take them between six to eight weeks to finish it.

✓ **It will take them between six and eight weeks to finish it.**

Use **between ... and** or **from ... to** (NOT **between ... to**).

bicycle

? I enjoy riding a bicycle and playing badminton.

✓ **I enjoy cycling and playing badminton.**

? In the evenings we usually ride our bicycles.

✓ **In the evenings we usually go cycling.**

cycling = riding a bicycle as a sport or leisure activity: 'In the summer I do a lot of cycling.'

Compare: 'He learned to ride a bicycle at the age of four.'

big

✗ The party was big fun and we all enjoyed ourselves.

✓ **The party was great fun and we all enjoyed ourselves.**

✗ There is a big possibility that they may not come.

✓ **There is a strong possibility that they may not come.**

See Language Note on next page

Choosing the right word: WORD COMBINATIONS

As well as knowing what a word means, you need to know how to use it and this includes knowing which words it usually goes with. For example, **possibility** is often used with **strong** but not with **big**. The phrases 'a big possibility' and 'a strong possibility' have the same meaning and both will be understood. However, 'a big possibility' is unnatural and is generally regarded as an error. The rule that is broken by putting **big** and **possibility** together is one of word combination or 'collocation'.

Big and **strong** belong to a group of adjectives that are commonly used with abstract nouns (e.g. **change, risk, possibility, effect, difficulty**). It is important to know which adjectives go with which nouns. The table below shows which combinations are acceptable.

	big	deep	great	high	serious	strong
accident					✓	
attempt					✓	
change	✓		✓			
concern		✓	✓		✓	
cost			✓	✓		
crime					✓	
damage					✓	
danger			✓		✓	
difference	✓		✓			
difficulty			✓		✓	
effect	✓		✓		✓	✓
fun			✓			
impression		✓				✓
improvement	✓		✓			
income				✓		
influence	✓		✓		✓	✓
interest					✓	✓
mistake	✓		✓		✓	
possibility						✓
price				✓		
pride			✓			
problem	✓		✓		✓	
risk	✓		✓	✓	✓	
shock	✓		✓			
skill			✓			
speed			✓	✓		
surprise	✓		✓			
threat					✓	
trouble	✓	✓			✓	

bit 1
    ?   'An' is a bit problematic.
    ✓   **'An' is slightly problematic.**
    ?   The instructions were a little bit confusing.
    ✓   **The instructions were a little confusing.**
    ?   My diet is a little bit different nowadays.
    ✓   **My diet is slightly different nowadays.**
    ✗   Thank you very much for giving us a bit of your free time.
    ✓   **Thank you very much for giving us a little of your free time.**

> **A bit** and **a little bit** are used mainly in informal styles. In other styles, it is better to use **a little, slightly, rather, quite** or **somewhat**: 'His brother was somewhat older than we had expected.'

2
    ✗   I watched a little bit television and went to bed.
    ✓   **I watched a little television and went to bed.**
    ✓   **I watched a bit of television and went to bed.**

> Use **a (little) bit** before adjectives: 'She looked a bit tired.'
> Before nouns, use **a little** or (in informal styles) **a (little) bit of**: 'He could do with a little help.' 'He's been a bit of a nuisance recently.'

3
    ✗   He is a little bit too short to be a policeman.
    ✓   **He is a bit/little too short to be a policeman.**
    ✓   **He is slightly too short to be a policeman.**
    ✗   The speech was a little bit too formal.
    ✓   **The speech was a bit/little too formal.**
    ✓   **The speech was slightly too formal.**

> Use **a bit/little too** or **slightly/rather/somewhat too** (NOT **a little bit too**): 'She is still a bit too young.' 'The pears were a little too hard.' 'The basic salary is rather too low.'

blame
    ✗   I wasn't even there so you can't blame on me.
    ✓   **I wasn't even there so you can't blame me.**
    ✓   **I wasn't even there so you can't blame it on me.**
    ✗   Who is to be blamed about this?
    ✓   **Who is to be blamed for this?**

> **blame sb** (**for sth**): 'Nobody can blame you for telling the truth.'
> **blame sth on sb/sth**: 'Whenever children behave badly, people blame it on the teachers.'
> Compare: 'He always tries to put the blame on me.'

blind 1
    ✗   Some people become blind with the disease.
    ✓   **Some people go blind with the disease.**

> **go blind** (**not become**): 'When I couldn't see anything, I thought I'd gone blind.'

2
    ✗   Usually he just keeps a blind eye and lets them carry on.
    ✓   **Usually he just turns a blind eye and lets them carry on.**

> **turn a blind eye** (**to sth**) = pretend not to notice something: 'The government prefers to turn a blind eye to these activities.'

board
    ✗   Within a week, I found myself on board of an aeroplane.
    ✓   **Within a week, I found myself on board an aeroplane.**

> **on board** an aircraft, ship, etc (WITHOUT **of**): 'How the child managed to get on board the plane remains a mystery.'

body   ?   His dead body was flown back home for burial.
           ✓   **His body was flown back home for burial.**

> When it is clear from the context that the person referred to is dead, use **body** (WITHOUT **dead**): 'The police found his body floating in the river.'

book   ✗   I'm afraid that we're out of stock but I can book one for you.
           ✓   **I'm afraid that we're out of stock but I can order one for you.**

> **book** = reserve a seat on a plane, a room in a hotel, a table at a restaurant, etc: 'The train was packed and I wished I'd booked a seat.' **order** = ask for certain goods to be sent to a shop, especially because a customer wants to buy them: 'If you want to be sure of getting a daily newspaper, it's best to order one.'

bored 1   ✗   My job at the bank was very bored.
             ✓   **My job at the bank was very boring.**

> See note at BORING

2   ✗   I don't think I'll ever get bored of the book.
        ✓   **I don't think I'll ever get bored with the book.**
        ✗   She soon got bored of talking to him.
        ✓   **She soon got bored with talking to him.**

> **be/get bored with (doing) sth**: 'I'm bored with pasta and tomatoes – I want something different.' 'I got bored with lying on the beach and went off to explore the town.'

boring   ✗   We get very boring with the same food every day.
             ✓   **We get very bored with the same food every day.**
             ✗   You'll be boring with nothing to do.
             ✓   **You'll be bored with nothing to do.**

> If someone or something is **boring/exciting/frightening/interesting** (-ING), you feel **bored/excited/frightened/interested** (-ED): 'The lecture was terribly boring. Some of us were so bored that we fell asleep.'

born 1   ✗   My name is Ali Sariat and I born in Tehran.
             ✓   **My name is Ali Sariat and I was born in Tehran.**

> **be born**: 'Do you realize that a child is born every few seconds.' 'The baby was born in the middle of the night.' 'It was the first time I'd actually watched a child being born.'

2   ✗   I have been born in a town just outside Paris.
        ✓   **I was born in a town just outside Paris.**

> Use 'I was born', 'They were born', etc (NOT 'I have been born' or 'I am born'): 'I'll never forget the day when the seven puppies were born.'

3   ✗   He was born in a Catholic family.
        ✓   **He was born into a Catholic family.**

> **be born into** a particular type of family, world, etc (NOT **in**): 'She was born into a world that was on the brink of war.'

borrow   ✗   I asked my friend to borrow me some money.
             ✓   **I asked my friend to lend me some money.**
             ✗   He borrowed me some of his books.
             ✓   **He lent me some of his books.**

✓ **I borrowed some of his books.**

When you **borrow** something (**from** someone), you are allowed to use it: 'Can I borrow one of your pencils?'
When you **lend** something (**to** someone), you let them use it: 'He asked me to lend him one of my pencils.'

boss

? My father is the boss of a small shipping company.
✓ **My father is the manager of a small shipping company.**

Boss is usually used in informal styles: 'From the way he acts, you'd think that he was the boss.'

both 1

✗ Both of them have not apologized yet.
✓ **Neither of them has apologized yet.**
✗ Both the husband and the wife aren't reliable.
✓ **Neither the husband nor the wife is reliable.**
See Language Note at NOT

2

✗ Anne and John both are scientists.
✓ **Anne and John are both scientists.**
✗ Two of the biggest firms are Apple and IBM, which both are in the computer business.
✓ **Two of the biggest firms are Apple and IBM, which are both in the computer business.**
See Language Note at ALWAYS

bottom

See note at TOP

boundary

✗ The country shares boundaries with Ruanda and Burundi.
✓ **The country shares borders with Ruanda and Burundi.**

Use **boundary** when you are talking about an area of land within a country: 'The Mississippi River forms a natural boundary between Tennessee and Arkansas.' 'Their farm is just inside the boundary of the National Park.'
The place where two countries meet is the **border**: 'We're about to cross the border between Austria and Switzerland.'

bread

✗ He's gone to buy a fresh bread.
✓ **He's gone to buy some fresh bread.**
See Language Note at SCENERY

break 1

✗ The family broke just after he was born.
✓ **The family broke up just after he was born.**

break up = stop being together as a couple or group: 'Did you know that Carol and Richard have broken up?' 'Can you remember when the Beatles broke up?'

2

? The police had to break the door to get in.
✓ **The police had to break down the door to get in.**

In an emergency situation, policemen, firemen, etc **break down** the door of a room or building: 'If the door's locked, you'll just have to break it down.'

3

See BROKEN

breakfast 1   ✗   After the breakfast, we went shopping.
     ✓   **After breakfast, we went shopping.**
     ✗   Before my breakfast I usually go for a run.
     ✓   **Before breakfast I usually go for a run.**

> When **breakfast/lunch/dinner** etc refer to an event (rather than to the meal itself), they are used without **a/the/this/my** etc: 'What shall we do after lunch?' 'Pam and Simon have invited us to dinner.' 'What time do you have breakfast?'
> You use **a/the/this/my** etc when you refer to the meal itself: 'We enjoyed the evening, even though the dinner was cold.' 'I don't usually have time for a cooked breakfast.'

2   ✗   Before I have a breakfast, I usually make my bed.
   ✓   **Before I have (my) breakfast, I usually make my bed.**
   ✗   Every morning my first job is to prepare a breakfast.
   ✓   **Every morning my first job is to prepare (the) breakfast.**

> **have (your) breakfast/lunch/dinner** etc (NOT **a**): 'Have you had (your) breakfast yet?'
> **make/prepare (the/your) breakfast/lunch/dinner** etc (NOT **a**): 'Whose turn is it to make the dinner tonight?'
> Use **a/an** with **breakfast/lunch/dinner** etc only when you describe the meal: 'a cooked breakfast', 'a big breakfast', 'an American breakfast'.

3   ✗   There wasn't enough time to eat breakfast.
   ✓   **There wasn't enough time to have breakfast.**
   ✗   While I am taking breakfast, I listen to the radio.
   ✓   **While I am having breakfast, I listen to the radio.**

> **have (your) breakfast/lunch/dinner** etc (NOT **eat/take**): 'We had dinner in the hotel restaurant.'
> **have sth for breakfast/lunch/dinner** etc: 'What did you have for lunch?'
> Do not use **eat** unless you wish to emphasize the activity of eating. Compare: 'We prefer to have dinner in the evening.' 'James always takes a long time to eat his dinner.'

breath   ✗   She had a very bad cold and couldn't breath properly.
     ✓   **She had a very bad cold and couldn't breathe properly.**

> **Breath** / breθ / is a noun. **Breathe** / briːð / is a verb.
> The verb is longer than the noun both in its spelling and in its vowel sound.

bribe   ✗   He was accused of accepting bribe money.
    ✓   **He was accused of accepting a bribe.**

> **a bribe** (NOT **bribe money**) = money or something valuable that is given to someone in an official position to persuade them to do something dishonest: 'As a police officer, what would you do if someone offered you a bribe?'

bring 1   ✗   Would you like me to bring you home?
     ✓   **Would you like me to take you home?**
     ✗   Whenever I go sightseeing, I bring my camera with me.
     ✓   **Whenever I go sightseeing, I take my camera with me.**

> See Language Note at TAKE

2 ✗ I went back into the house to bring my sunglasses.
  ✓ **I went back into the house to fetch my sunglasses.**
  See Language Note at TAKE

3 ✗ Global warming is bringing changes in the weather.
  ✓ **Global warming is bringing about changes in the weather.**
  ✗ Nuclear power could bring the destruction of our planet.
  ✓ **Nuclear power could bring about the destruction of our planet.**

  When you mean 'finally cause something to happen or exist', use **bring about**: 'These new manufacturing methods brought about an increase in production.' 'The company's poor performance was brought about by factors beyond its control.'

4 ✗ Our tourist industry brings a lot of foreign exchange.
  ✓ **Our tourist industry brings in a lot of foreign exchange.**

  bring in = make or earn (money): 'The job keeps me busy and brings in a little extra cash.'

bring up 1 ✗ I'm not working now because I'm bringing up my baby.
  ✓ **I'm not working now because I'm looking after my baby.**

  bring up a child: 'Our parents brought us up to believe in the power of truth.'
  look after/take care of a baby: 'Who looks after the baby while you're at work?'

2 ✗ I shall never forget the place where I brought up.
  ✓ **I shall never forget the place where I was brought up.**

  be brought up (**by sb**): 'I was brought up to believe that people were basically kind.'

British 1 ✗ I would prefer to study in America or British.
  ✓ **I would prefer to study in America or Britain.**

  The name of the country is **Britain** (or **Great Britain**).
  British is an adjective: 'British industry', 'British Airways'.

2 See THE 12

British Council 1 ✗ I am learning English at British Council.
  ✓ **I am learning English at the British Council.**

  the British Council: 'Professor Sinclair's visit was organized by the British Council.'

2 ✗ I am a student in the British Council.
  ✓ **I am a student at the British Council.**
  See IN 5

broken ✗ The car could not stop because its brakes were broken.
  ✓ **The car could not stop because its brakes were not working.**
  ✗ I turned on the radio but it was broken.
  ✓ **I turned on the radio but it wasn't working.**

  broken = physically damaged: 'a broken windscreen'
  not working = not functioning properly: 'I can't ring him because his phone's not working.'

bus	✗	The best way to see London is to get in a bus.
	✓	**The best way to see London is to get on a bus.**
	✗	She said I was in the wrong bus.
	✓	**She said I was on the wrong bus.**

be/get on a bus (NOT **in**): 'During the rush hour, it's quicker to walk than get on a bus.'

business	✗	I often have to go abroad for business.
	✓	**I often have to go abroad on business.**
	✗	My father is now in Paris on his business.
	✓	**My father is now in Paris on business.**

(be/go somewhere) on business: 'I'm off to Amsterdam tomorrow, on business as usual.'

busy	✗	I was busy with cooking the dinner.
	✓	**I was busy cooking the dinner.**

be busy doing sth: 'She's busy trying to finish her thesis.'
Compare: 'I was busy with the housework.' 'I was busy doing the housework.'

but	✗	Although I enjoyed my stay in the USA, but I was still glad to come home.
	✓	**Although I enjoyed my stay in the USA, I was still glad to come home.**
	✓	**I enjoyed my stay in the USA, but I was still glad to come home.**

If the first clause begins with **although** or **(even) though,** do not begin the second clause with **but** or **yet**.
See also SO 1

by 1	✗	He managed to open the lid by a screwdriver.
	✓	**He managed to open the lid with a screwdriver.**

You do something **with** a tool, instrument, etc (NOT **by**): 'He opened the envelope with a chopstick.' 'You can't eat spaghetti with a spoon.'

2	✗	I am staying in a small town by Oxford.
	✓	**I am staying in a small town near Oxford.**

by = next to or very close to something: 'I've been sitting by the phone all morning waiting for her to ring.' 'I'll meet you on the corner, by the bank.'
When talking about the position of towns, cities, countries etc, use **near**: 'I spent the first month in a little village called Farchant, near Garmen-Partenkirchen.'

3	✗	We can gain a lot of knowledge by these books.
	✓	**We can gain a lot of knowledge from these books.**

You get information **from** a source: 'You can learn a great deal from a good dictionary.' 'I obtained their new number from directory enquiries.'

4	✗	Being locked up is a punishment by itself.
	✓	**Being locked up is a punishment in itself.**
	✗	Money by itself is of no interest to me.
	✓	**Money in itself is of no interest to me.**

in itself = without anything added: 'His offer to pay for the repairs is in itself an admission of guilt.'

5   See MADE, REASON 5, REPLACE, SEE 2

Cc

call 1

✗ Last night I tried to call to my father back home in Turkey.
✓ **Last night I tried to call my father back home in Turkey.**
✗ Please call to 945 8026.
✓ **Please call 945 8026.**

> **call/ring/telephone** a person, place or number (WITHOUT **to**): 'Call me tonight and we'll make arrangements for the morning.' 'If you're sure that it's been stolen, you'd better call the police.'

2

✗ If you receive this note, please phone call me.
✓ **If you receive this note, please call/ring me.**
✓ **If you receive this note, please give me a call/ring.**

> The verb is **call/ring/phone/telephone** (NOT **phone call**).
> **Phone call** is a noun: 'I need to make one or two phone calls.'

3

✗ Please call me with number 0248 312689.
✓ **Please call me on 0248 312689.**

> **call sb on** a particular number (British English)
> **call sb at** a particular number (American English)

4

✗ Koreans call this room as 'anbang'.
✓ **Koreans call this room 'anbang'.**
✗ This process is called as nitrogen fixation.
✓ **This process is called nitrogen fixation.**

> **call sb/sth** + name (WITHOUT **as**): 'People call her the Queen of Rock.'
> 'The big apples are called Red Delicious.'

calm 1

✗ If you prefer a calm environment, try the countryside.
✓ **If you prefer a peaceful environment, try the countryside.**
✗ Go and find somewhere calm and get some rest.
✓ **Go and find somewhere quiet and get some rest.**
✗ What you need is a calm holiday somewhere.
✓ **What you need is a quiet and relaxing holiday somewhere.**

> **Calm** is usually used to describe situations where there has recently been violence or noisy activity: 'After yesterday's fighting, the streets of Jerusalem are reported to be calm again this morning.'

2

✗ You need calm and quiet to digest your lunch properly.
✓ **You need peace and quiet to digest your lunch properly.**

> **Peace and quiet** is a fixed phrase: 'It's impossible to find peace and quiet in a house full of children.'

3

? My best friend Nick is very calm and never gets upset.
✓ **My best friend Nick is very easygoing and never gets upset.**

Calm is usually used to describe how someone behaves in a difficult situation: 'The boat was being tossed by the waves but we managed to stay calm.'
To describe someone who has a relaxed attitude to life, use words such as **easygoing, placid, laid-back** (informal), **patient, tolerant.**

4 ? I fastened my seat belt and tried to be calm.
✓ **I fastened my seat belt and tried to stay calm.**

When you are talking about someone's behaviour in an emergency or unpleasant situation, use **keep/stay/remain calm**: 'In the event of fire, leave the building by the nearest exit and remain calm.'
Compare: 'For the first two days the sea was perfectly calm.'

calm down ✗ He had calmed down his anger, but he was still annoyed.
✓ **He had calmed down, but he was still annoyed.**

Calm down (intransitive) means 'to become less angry, less excited, etc': 'Once everyone had calmed down, the meeting continued.'
The object of **calm down** (transitive) is always a person: 'The doctor gave him a tranquillizer to calm him down.' 'In the end I agreed to go with her, just to calm her down.'

cameraman ✗ Shotaro Akiyama is a famous Japanese cameraman.
✓ **Shotaro Akiyama is a famous Japanese photographer.**

cameraman = a person who is employed by a television or film company to operate a camera: 'The cameraman had never shot a car chase before and needed the director's advice.'
photographer = a person who takes (or whose job is to take) photographs: 'She is one of the world's leading fashion photographers.'

camping See GO 3

can 1 ? Can you possibly send me an application form?
✓ **Could you possibly send me an application form?**
? I'd be grateful if you can confirm whether you are coming.
✓ **I'd be grateful if you could confirm whether you are coming.**

To make a polite request, use **could**: 'Could you pass the butter, please?'

2 ✗ The next generation can fly to the moon for their holidays.
✓ **The next generation will be able to fly to the moon for their holidays.**

Use **can** to talk about someone's present ability: 'All our children can swim.'
Use **be able to** to predict someone's future ability: 'You'll never be able to swim if you don't try.'

3 See REMEMBER

4 See COULD

cancel ✗ The meeting has been cancelled until next Thursday.
✓ **The meeting has been postponed until next Thursday.**

cancel = arrange for a planned event not to take place after all: 'Five of their players were either ill or injured, and so the match had to be cancelled.'

postpone = arrange for a planned event to take place at a later time or date: 'We've decided to postpone the wedding until Steve has found a job.'

cancer

✗ Her husband died 10 years ago of a lung cancer.
✓ **Her husband died 10 years ago of lung cancer.**

cancer (uncountable) = a type of serious disease: 'It is generally believed that diet plays an important role in the prevention of cancer.' 'Skin cancer is related to prolonged exposure to sunlight.'
a cancer (countable) = an abnormal growth in someone's body which is caused by this disease; tumour: 'Some small cancers may be destroyed by the body's defence mechanisms.'

capable

✗ She is no longer capable to do her job properly.
✓ **She is no longer capable of doing her job properly.**

able to do sth: 'I hope you'll be able to come.'
capable of doing sth: 'She is quite capable of passing the exam, provided that she does some work.'

capacity 1

✗ This type of job requires special capacities.
✓ **This type of job requires special skills.**
✗ I wish to improve my speaking and listening capacities.
✓ **I wish to improve my speaking and listening skills.**

capacity = the power or quality that makes someone able to do, experience, give or receive something: 'These children display an extraordinary capacity for learning.' 'Man's capacity for love and generosity is unlimited.'
skill = what someone needs to have learned before they can actually do a particular job or activity: 'Being a good manager requires a number of highly specialized skills.' 'This course is designed to develop the student's reading and writing skills.'

2

✗ The atomic bomb has given man the capacity of self-destruction.
✓ **The atomic bomb has given man the capacity for self-destruction.**

capacity for sth: 'He has an enormous capacity for hard work.'
capacity to do sth: 'The human race shows an extraordinary capacity to change with the times.'

capture

✗ Her blue eyes and long blond hair captured him.
✓ **Her blue eyes and long blond hair captivated him.**

capture = make someone a prisoner: 'That day they captured twenty enemy soldiers.' 'The leader of the resistance group was captured and executed.'
captivate = strongly attract and impress someone: 'From the day she met him, she was captivated by his charm.'

car 1

✗ I went into the car and turned on the engine.
✓ **I got into the car and turned on the engine.**
✗ I went out of the car and waited outside the shop.
✓ **I got out of the car and waited outside the shop.**
✗ She got out from the car and apologized.
✓ **She got out of the car and apologized.**

get in/into or **get out of** a car, taxi, etc: 'She got in the car and drove away.' 'I got out of the car to see what was happening.'

2

✗ He brought me back to Cambridge with his car.
✓ **He brought me back to Cambridge in his car.**
✗ We went to the party by a friend's car.
✓ **We went to the party in a friend's car.**

> You go somewhere **by car** or **in someone's car** (NOT with): 'If you'd rather go by car, we can go in mine.'

care 1

✗ These children need a special care and attention.
✓ **These children need special care and attention.**
✗ My host family took a good care of me.
✓ **My host family took good care of me.**

> **Care** is nearly always an uncountable noun: 'Care of the environment has become a priority in government thinking.' 'Would you like me to take care of the plants while you're away?'

2

✗ The only thing they cared for was how to make money.
✓ **The only thing they cared about was how to make money.**
✗ It encourages readers to care for what they buy.
✓ **It encourages readers to care about what they buy.**
✗ Some criminals simply don't care of being caught.
✓ **Some criminals simply don't care about being caught.**
✗ They don't take care about religion.
✓ **They don't care about religion.**

> **care for** = (1) (formal) like: 'Would you care for another drink?'
> (2) = (usually adjectival or passive) look after: 'Don't worry. The child is being well cared for.'
> **care (about)** = think that something is important: 'I don't care (about) how much it costs.' 'I don't care about the cost.'

3

✗ Take care of not catching a cold.
✓ **Take care not to catch a cold.**
✗ You'd better take care of not offending her.
✓ **You'd better take care not to offend her.**

> **Take care of** means 'look after': 'Who's going to take care of the dog while you're away?'
> When you mean 'be careful to avoid something', use **take care not to** or **take care that you don't**: 'He took great care not to let anyone know his intentions.'

4

✗ Some women stay at home to take care after the children.
✓ **Some women stay at home to take care of the children.**
✗ The government must take care for the teachers.
✓ **The government must take care of the teachers.**
✗ Who will take care about the shop?
✓ **Who will take care of the shop?**

> **take care of** or **look after sb/sth**: 'After his mother died, there was nobody to take care of him.'

career 1

✗ After ten years as a taxi driver, he decided it was time to change his career.
✓ **After ten years as a taxi driver, he decided it was time to change his job/occupation.**

See Language Note at OCCUPATION

2 ✗ I'd like to be a doctor or something related to that career.
✓ **I'd like to be a doctor or something related to that profession.**
See Language Note at OCCUPATION

careful ✗ Be careful to water the African violets regularly.
✓ **Make sure (that) you water the African violets regularly.**
✗ Be careful to fix any oil leaks.
✓ **Make sure (that) you fix any oil leaks.**

Use **be careful** when you want someone to pay special attention to something so that they do not have an accident, make a mistake, or do something that will cause damage: 'Be careful! You're about to spill your coffee.' 'You should be careful about what you say to her. She is easily offended.'
To tell someone that they must not forget to do or check something, use **make sure**: 'Before you set off, make sure that you have enough petrol.' 'Make sure that you don't leave the key in the car.'

careless ✗ How wonderful it would be to be young and careless again!
✓ **How wonderful it would be to be young and carefree again!**

careless = paying too little attention to something: 'If you're careless, you're bound to make mistakes.'
carefree = happy because you have no worries or responsibilities: 'Some children never know what it means to be carefree.'

carry ✗ An ambulance arrived and the man was carried to hospital.
✓ **An ambulance arrived and the man was taken to hospital.**
✗ He said he would carry me home and told me to get in the car.
✓ **He said he would take me home and told me to get in the car.**
See Language Note at TAKE

carry out ✗ I shall now describe how wedding ceremonies are carried out in Iran.
✓ **I shall now describe how wedding ceremonies are conducted in Iran.**

conduct/perform a ceremony or ritual (NOT **carry out**): 'The funeral ceremony was conducted according to ancient traditions.'

case 1 ✗ Switzerland has very little unemployment and in this case we are very lucky.
✓ **Switzerland has very little unemployment and in this respect we are very lucky.**

in this/that case = in these/those circumstances: 'What shall I do if there are no trains?' 'In that case you'll have to go by bus.'
in this/that respect = with regard to this/that point or detail: 'The film is full of violence and in this respect is unsuitable for children.'

2 ✗ I advise you to eat something now in case there won't be any food when we get there.
✓ **I advise you to eat something now in case there isn't any food when we get there.**
See Language Note at WILL

3   ✗ In case a woman goes out to work, she shouldn't have to do all
          the housework.
       ✓ **If a woman goes out to work, she shouldn't have to do all
          the housework.**

> In British English **in case** is used only when you talk about something
> that is done as a precaution: 'Let's wait for another five minutes, just in
> case he shows up.'
> In American English **in case** is sometimes used like **if** at the beginning of
> a conditional clause.

cash 1   ✗ I prefer to pay by cash.
          ✓ **I prefer to pay in cash.**
          ✓ **I prefer to pay cash.**

> **pay by cheque**, **pay by credit card** BUT **pay in cash** or just **pay cash**:
> 'If you pay (in) cash, you might get a discount.'

2   ✗ The purse contained about $200 cash.
       ✓ **The purse contained about $200 in cash.**

> amount of money + **in cash**: '£550 in cash', '$190 in cash'

catch   ✗ The dialogue in this video is very difficult to catch.
          ✓ **The dialogue in this video is very difficult to understand.**
          ✗ At that time I couldn't speak or catch English at all.
          ✓ **At that time I couldn't speak or understand English at all.**

> **Catch** (= hear and/or understand) is used only in connection with what
> someone has just said: 'I'm afraid I didn't quite catch the last point.
> Could you go over it again?' 'Did either of you manage to catch her
> name?'

catch up 1 ✗ I have to catch up all the lessons I missed.
          ✓ **I have to catch up on all the lessons I missed.**

> **catch up (on/with sth)** = do the things that you should have done before
> so that your work is up to date: 'Why don't you stay at home tonight and
> catch up on some of your homework?'
> Compare: 'Don't get too far behind with your homework or you'll never be
> able to catch up.'

2   ✗ New job opportunities will never catch up the rapid growth in
          population.
       ✓ **New job opportunities will never catch up with the rapid
          growth in population.**

> **catch up (with sb/sth)** = draw level with: 'Let's stop here for a few
> minutes so that the others can catch up with us.' 'In schools up and down
> the country, girls have not only caught up with boys but they're now in
> the lead.'

cause 1   ✗ The cause why I want to change my job is as follows.
          ✓ **The reason why I want to change my job is as follows.**
          ✗ For this cause the journey took a long time.
          ✓ **For this reason the journey took a long time.**

> **cause** = an action, event, situation etc that makes something happen:
> 'The cause of the fire is still being investigated.' 'These outbreaks of
> violence will continue to occur until the causes have been eliminated.'
> **reason** = something that provides an explanation: 'I'm sure that they

must have good reasons for wanting to live abroad.' 'The reason why there is only one applicant is that the job wasn't advertised.'

2   ✗ The police wanted to know the cause for the accident.
   ✓ **The police wanted to know the cause of the accident.**

   reason for sth BUT **cause of sth**: 'The underlying causes of the present dispute date back to 1987.'
   Note however: **cause for concern/alarm/complaint/hope etc**: 'The new rise in unemployment has given the government cause for concern.'

3   ✗ This causes that the children look for affection elsewhere.
   ✓ **This causes the children to look for affection elsewhere.**

   cause sb to do sth (NOT **cause that**): 'A week-long power failure caused the whole computer network to shut down.'

4   ✗ Smoking is one of the most important causes of lung cancer.
   ✓ **Smoking is one of the major causes of lung cancer.**

   a major/chief/primary cause (NOT **important**)

5   ✗ Acid rain is caused by several reasons.
   ✓ **Acid rain has several causes.**

   Do not use **reason** after **be caused by**: 'The autopsy showed that her death was caused by liver failure.'

celebrate   See PARTY 1

centre   See CITY CENTRE

ceremony   See CARRY OUT

certain 1   ✗ Just suppose, for a certain reason, that there was suddenly a shortage of oil.
   ✓ **Just suppose, for some reason, that there was suddenly a shortage of oil.**
   ✗ Every creature must have a certain way of protecting itself.
   ✓ **Every creature must have some way of protecting itself.**
   ✗ He's working in London for a certain travel company.
   ✓ **He's working in London for some travel company or other.**

   Use **certain** + noun when you continue (or could continue) by giving details: 'There are certain advantages to living in the countryside, the most important being the fresh air.' 'I'm not allowed to eat certain types of seafood, especially squid and octopus.'
   Use **some** + noun (+ **or other**) when you cannot or do not wish to give details: 'In the end, he sold it to some second-hand car dealer.' 'If the factory is shut down for some reason, what will happen to all the workers?'
   The phrase **some** + noun + **or other** is often used in informal styles to suggest that the person or thing is completely unknown to you and not worth thinking about: 'Apparently, their daughter has got engaged to some shop assistant or other.'

2   ✗ Under some certain circumstances, such as war, food has to be rationed.
   ✓ **Under certain circumstances, such as war, food has to be rationed.**

Do not use a determiner (e.g. **some, the, their**) before **certain** when it means 'particular' (see the note at **certain 1** above): 'Each member of the committee has certain duties to perform.'

certainly 1 ✗ All of a sudden the engine started to make a strange noise. Certainly, I stopped the car at once to see what had happened.
✓ **All of a sudden the engine started to make a strange noise. Naturally, I stopped the car at once to see what had happened.**

Certainly is mainly used to emphasize that something is really true, really happened, etc: 'I'm sorry if I upset you. I certainly didn't mean to.' 'The file certainly wasn't given to me or it would be on my desk.' When you mean 'as anyone would expect', use **naturally** or **of course**: 'It was the first time the little boy had seen an elephant and naturally he was a little scared.'

2 ✗ Are you sure that you certainly don't want to go?
✓ **Are you sure that you definitely don't want to go?**
✗ If they certainly can't find a job, they should be given further training.
✓ **If they definitely can't find a job, they should be given further training.**

When you mean 'absolutely certain and without even the slightest doubt', use **definitely**. This word gives very strong emphasis and is often used in connection with intentions and future events: 'He definitely wants to be a vet.' 'Do you think that you'll definitely be able to come?'

3 ✗ Certainly I think so.
✓ **I certainly think so.**
✗ The car can be repaired certainly.
✓ **The car can certainly be repaired.**
✗ Certainly, it was a pleasant surprise.
✓ **It was certainly a pleasant surprise.**
✓ **It certainly was a pleasant surprise.**

Certainly is usually used like a middle position adverb (see Language Note at ALWAYS): 'She certainly likes you.' 'His work has certainly improved this year.'
For extra emphasis, however, **certainly** may be placed before the first auxiliary verb and before **be** when this is the main verb: 'His work certainly has improved this year.' 'She certainly is one of the best teachers on the staff.'

certificate ✗ The other day I was given a gift certificate, but it was only worth two thousand yen.
✓ **The other day I was given a gift voucher, but it was only worth two thousand yen.**

certificate = an official document that states certain facts about someone: 'a birth/marriage/death certificate', 'a certificate of health'
voucher = a kind of ticket that can be used instead of money: 'a gift/luncheon/travel voucher'.

chair 1 ✗ During the flight she sat on the chair behind me.
✓ **During the flight she sat in the seat behind me.**

seat = a place to sit, as found in a cinema, train, bus etc: 'To be on the safe side, you'd better reserve a seat.'
chair = a movable seat for one person: 'Before the children go home, they have to put all the chairs on top of the desks.'

2   See ARMCHAIR

chance   ✗ The higher your qualifications, the better your chances to find a job.
    ✓ **The higher your qualifications, the better your chances of finding a job.**
chances of doing sth (= degree of probability): 'What are the chances of finding them alive?'

change 1   ✗ We can reduce the unemployment rate with a change of the economy.
    ✓ **We can reduce the unemployment rate with a change in the economy.**
    ✗ I'm disappointed by all the changes of London.
    ✓ **I'm disappointed by all the changes in London.**
Use **change of** when you mean that someone or something has been replaced: 'What the country needs is a change of government.' (= a completely new government)
When you mean that someone or something is now different in some way, use **change in**: 'The Prime Minister has made several changes in the government.'

2   ✗ I took the camera back to the shop and changed it with another one.
    ✓ **I took the camera back to the shop and changed it for another one.**
change/exchange sth for sth: 'I'd like to change this shirt for a smaller size.'

character   ✗ She has that rare character – the ability to listen to people.
    ✓ **She has that rare characteristic – the ability to listen to people.**
    ✗ However, the Japanese also have a lot of good characters.
    ✓ **However, the Japanese also have a lot of good points.**
When you mean 'a feature of someone's character', use **characteristic** or **quality**: 'All great leaders share certain mean characteristics.' 'What qualities do you need to be a good parent?' In contrast with qualities that you do not like, you can also talk about someone's **good points.**

cheap 1   ✗ The wages in Taiwan are very cheap.
    ✓ **The wages in Taiwan are very low.**
    ✗ The monthly payments were cheaper than I'd expected.
    ✓ **The monthly payments were lower/less than I'd expected.**
When you talk about costs, payments, rents, wages, salaries, incomes, expenses, taxes, fees etc, use **low/high** (NOT **cheap/ expensive**): 'During the recession, prices stayed low.' 'People on low incomes have been severely hit.' 'Rents in Helsinki are very high compared to the rest of Finland.'
Note that **price** is sometimes used with **cheap/expensive**, but not in formal styles.

2   ? The train fare is very cheap.
    ✓ **The train fare is very reasonable.**
    ? It's difficult to find a cheap flat in Tokyo.
    ✓ **It's difficult to find an affordable flat in Tokyo.**
       See Language Note at KILL

checking ✗ Once inside the airport, I made my way to the checking.
    ✓ **Once inside the airport, I made my way to the check-in.**

> **check-in** = the place at an airport (or hotel) where you check in: 'There's bound to be a long queue at the check-in.' 'The girl at the check-in desk asked if we had a reservation.'
> **check in** = show your ticket, passport and luggage at a counter in an airport and receive a boarding card: 'Once you've checked in, you have to go through customs.'

cheque   ✗ I am enclosing a cheque of £49.
    ✓ **I am enclosing a cheque for £49.**
    ✗ He gave me a cheque £5.
    ✓ **He gave me a cheque for £5.**

> **a cheque for** an amount of money: 'He wrote me a cheque for $50.'

children ✗ Some couples prefer NOT to make children.
    ✓ **Some couples prefer not to have children.**

> **have children** (NOT **make**): 'We'd like to settle down and have children while we're still young.'

choice   ✗ In my new job I have to make a lot of important choices.
    ✓ **In my new job I have to make a lot of important decisions.**
    ✗ Please will you let us know your choice by the end of the month.
    ✓ **Please will you let us know your decision by the end of the month.**

> When you pick the person/thing that you want (from a range of possibilities), you make a **choice**: 'Her parents are not happy about her choice of husband.' 'Oxford was my first choice, but I didn't get the grades.'
> When you make a judgement about something, especially after thinking carefully about it, you make a **decision**: 'Although the job offer is attractive, I'd like more time to make a decision.' 'My decision to leave school at 15 was the biggest mistake I ever made.'

choose 1 ✗ If you choose to see a film, we can go to the cinema instead.
    ✓ **If you prefer to see a film, we can go to the cinema instead.**
    ✗ I choose the first story because it's more exciting.
    ✓ **I prefer the first story because it's more exciting.**

> **prefer** = like something more than something else: 'Which do you prefer, black coffee or white coffee?' 'Peter prefers classical music to rock.' 'I'd prefer to stay here, if you don't mind.'

2   ✗ There are over forty different courses to choose between.
    ✓ **There are over forty different courses to choose from.**
    ✗ There is also a library where you can choose among a wide range of books.
    ✓ **There is also a library where you can choose from a wide range of books.**

choose between two (or a few) possibilities: 'You have to choose between a beginner's course and a more advanced course.' 'If I had to choose between staying here and living abroad, I'd stay here.'
choose from a large number of possibilities: 'When it comes to wallpaper, there are hundreds of different patterns to choose from.'

3   ✗ Hilde chose for sources of energy as her topic.
   ✓ **Hilde chose sources of energy as her topic.**

choose sb/sth (WITHOUT **for**): 'The roses were too expensive so I chose the daffodils.' 'The team chose Alan as their captain.'
Compare: 'Tests have shown that girls opt for languages whereas boys choose science or maths.'

church   ✗ Not so long ago nearly everybody used to go to the church.
   ✓ **Not so long ago nearly everybody used to go to church.**
   See note at SCHOOL 1

cinema   ✗ We went to cinema to see 'Who framed Roger Rabbit?'
   ✓ **We went to the cinema to see 'Who framed Roger Rabbit?'**

go to the cinema (WITH **the**): 'Before the baby was born, we used to go to the cinema about once a week.'
See also SCHOOL 1

circulate   ✗ The story circulates around his career in the army.
   ✓ **The story revolves around his career in the army.**

Circulate = (of news, stories, rumours etc) spread by being passed from one person to another: 'One of the rumours circulating at the moment is that the company is about to go bankrupt.'
revolve around = (of a novel, film, story etc) be about: 'His latest film revolves around the difficulties of being a single parent.'

circum-   ✗ I believe that in this circumstance students should be allowed to
stance   have a part-time job.
   ✓ **I believe that in these circumstances students should be allowed to have a part-time job.**

Circumstances is nearly always used as a plural noun (WITH **s**): 'The police are investigating the circumstances surrounding his death.' 'Under normal circumstances, I would never have left my passport with a stranger.'

city centre   ✗ Most people work in city centre.
   ✓ **Most people work in the city centre.**

the city centre (WITH **the**): 'It's only five minutes by bus to the city centre.'

civilization   ✗ Each country has its own civilization and ideology.
   ✓ **Each country has its own culture and ideology.**
   ✗ American civilization is very different from that of Japan.
   ✓ **American culture is very different from that of Japan.**

civilization = (a society or group of societies having) a way of life that is considered to be advanced in terms of culture and social organization: 'The remote mountain villages are still untouched by modern civilization.' 'The film examines the ancient civilizations of Greece and Rome, and their contributions to Western society.'

> **culture** = art, music, literature, etc especially that which is produced by a particular society or group of societies: 'Visitors to Singapore discover a happy marriage of western and oriental cultures.' 'The Samba is an important part of Brazilian culture.'

claim 1   ✗   The public are claiming stricter laws.
         ✓   **The public are demanding stricter laws.**

> **claim** = ask to be given something that belongs to you or that you think you are entitled to: 'People on a low income are able to claim legal aid.'
> **demand** = ask strongly for something: 'The laboratory was surrounded by demonstrators demanding an end to animal experiments.'
> Note also **clamour for** = repeatedly ask for something in a noisy or angry way: 'In response to the increase in domestic violence, people are clamouring for stricter laws that will help to protect wives and children.'

2   ✗   At the end of World War II there was a claim for a 'United Europe'.
   ✓   **At the end of World War II there was a demand/clamour for a 'United Europe'.**

> See note at CLAIM 1

classic 1   ✗   I prefer classic music to pop.
         ✓   **I prefer classical music to pop.**

> **classic** = being among the best or most typical of its class; serving as a standard or model: 'The painting is a classic example of sixteenth-century Venetian art.'
> **classical music** = the music of Mozart, Beethoven, etc

2   ✗   I love the sound of a classic guitar.
   ✓   **I love the sound of a classical guitar.**

> **a classical guitar** = a guitar that is used to play classical music

clean   ✗   The local residents would like to clean the neighbourhood.
      ✓   **The local residents would like to clean up the neighbourhood.**

> **clean up** = (1) clean a place, especially by taking away all the things which make it look dirty, untidy or unattractive: 'You can play in your bedroom as long as you promise to clean it up afterwards.' (2) make an area or organization a better place for people to live or work in, especially by removing criminals, corrupt officials, etc: 'It's time someone cleaned up this city; we have one of the highest crime rates in the country.'

clear   ✗   I should like to make clear that the accommodation is far from luxurious.
      ✓   **I should like to make it clear that the accommodation is far from luxurious.**

> **make it clear** + **that**-clause (WITH **it**): 'She made it quite clear (to him) that she wasn't interested in getting married.'

climate   ✗   While I was driving to the airport, the climate was still wet and foggy.
        ✓   **While I was driving to the airport, the weather was still wet and foggy.**

✗ Before going off in the boat, you should check the climate conditions.
✓ **Before going off in the boat, you should check the weather conditions.**

climate = the typical weather conditions that exist in a country or region; the place where these weather conditions exist: 'Northern Europe has a mild climate and a high rainfall.' 'These flowers will not grow in cold climates.'

clock See O'CLOCK

close 1 ✗ They closed the man in a room until the police came.
✓ **They locked the man in a room until the police came.**

lock/shut sb in a room, house, etc (NOT **close**): 'He was picked up by the police and locked in a cell for the night.'
Compare: 'She closed the door and then locked it so he couldn't escape.'

2 ✗ I always close the television when there is a storm.
✓ **I always turn/switch the television off when there is a storm.**
See note at OPEN 1

cloth 1 ✗ I bought some cheap cloth to make some curtains.
✓ **I bought some cheap material to make some curtains.**

Cloth (uncountable) usually refers to material made of cotton, wool etc that is used for making clothes: 'The tailor took my measurements and then showed me several rolls of cloth.'
Material (and **fabric**) have a more general meaning and may be used in connection with clothes, curtains, sheets, etc: 'The cushion covers and the curtains were made from the same material.' 'They specialize in the manufacture of elasticated fabric.'

2 ✗ He likes fast cars and expensive cloths.
✓ **He likes fast cars and expensive clothes.**
✗ None of the cloth shops had any pink socks.
✓ **None of the clothes shops had any pink socks.**

A cloth (pronounced /klɒθ/) is a piece of material made of cotton, wool, etc, usually used for cleaning or drying something: 'I'm afraid I've spilled some milk. Have you got a cloth?' 'I need a new face cloth.'
Clothes (pronounced /kləʊðz/) are the things people wear, such as trousers, sweaters, etc: 'I spend half my salary on clothes.'

clothes 1 ✗ The dancers were dressed in their national clothes.
✓ **The dancers were dressed in their national costume.**

costume = (1) (countable) a set of clothes worn during a performance by an actor, clown, etc: 'She used to work for a theatre company, designing and making costumes.' (2) (uncountable) a set of clothes that are typical of a particular country or historical period: 'The castle guides were dressed up in Elizabethan costume.' 'A group of Hungarian folk dancers came on stage, all wearing national costume.'

2 ✗ Don't go out and buy a special clothes.
✓ **Don't go out and buy any special clothes.**

Clothes is a plural noun: 'I need some new clothes.' (NOT 'a new clothes')

clothing 1   ✗ As soon as I arrived, I unpacked my clothing.
✓ **As soon as I arrived, I unpacked my clothes.**
✗ He had grown so much that his clothing didn't fit him.
✓ **He had grown so much that his clothes didn't fit him.**

Use **clothing** when you are thinking about clothes in general:
'The population is in desperate need of foreign aid - especially food, medicine and clothing.' 'She works in the clothing industry.'
To refer to the things that you wear, use **clothes**: 'You'd better take off those wet clothes or you'll catch a cold.'

2   ✗ Those who work with pesticides are given protective clothings.
✓ **Those who work with pesticides are given protective clothing.**

Clothing is an uncountable noun: 'The population is in desperate need of foreign aid, especially food, medicine and clothing.'

club   See PART 6

coin   See FACE 5

collabor-   ✗ The police were grateful to the public for their collaboration.
ation   ✓ **The police were grateful to the public for their co-operation.**

Collaboration comes from the verb **collaborate** (= work in partnership with someone on the same task, especially one of a scientific, artistic or industrial nature): 'He was one of the scientists who had collaborated with Oppenheimer to produce the first atomic bomb.'
Co-operation comes from the verb **co-operate** (= be willing to help someone to achieve something; be helpful): 'Faced with the threat of a full-scale military invasion, the general had no choice but to co-operate.'

college   ✗ By going to the college or university, you become more mature.
✓ **By going to college or university, you become more mature.**
See note at SCHOOL 1

colour 1   ✗ The belt has the same colour as the coat.
✓ **The belt is the same colour as the coat.**

When you describe or enquire about the colour of something, use **be** (NOT **have**): 'What colour was the dress she was wearing?'

2   ✗ I bought a blue colour shirt and a pair of socks.
✓ **I bought a blue shirt and a pair of socks.**
✗ I have never liked black colour.
✓ **I have never liked black.**

The noun **colour** is not usually used with the name of a colour (**red, green, blue** etc). **Colour** is used only when the colour of something is not pure or is difficult to describe exactly: 'It's an unusual bluish-grey colour'. See note at COLOURED 1
Note however that the name of a colour can be used with **in colour**: 'It's brown in colour with white buttons down the front.'

3   ✗ The purse is made of leather and is dark brown colour.
✓ **The purse is made of leather and is a dark brown colour.**

When describing a colour that is not pure, use **a/an**: 'The dress is a reddish-green colour.'

4   ✗   My wallet colour is black.
       ✓   **The colour of my wallet is black.**
       the colour of sth: 'Do you remember the colour of their kitchen?'

5   ✗   At Hari Raya we hang colour lights around the house.
       ✓   **At Hari Raya we hang coloured lights around the house.**
       colour = showing people and things in their natural colours: 'a colour television', 'a colour photograph'
       coloured = having one or more colours (not white or black), especially in order to look attractive: 'Do you want plain envelopes or coloured ones?' 'Each book is full of brightly-coloured full-page illustrations.'

coloured 1   ?   The cardigan is pink-coloured and is made of wool.
       ✓   **The cardigan is pink and is made of wool.**
       When you describe the colour of something, you usually just say that it is **red, blue, green etc** (WITHOUT **-coloured**): 'Her new dress is pale blue with red buttons down the front.'
       Adjectives ending with **-coloured** are quite rare. They are mainly used when the colour of something is difficult to describe exactly ('pink-coloured' = not exactly pink) and usually come before the noun: 'a cream-coloured dressing gown' See note at COLOUR 2

2   ✗   He showed me the coloured photographs he had taken.
       ✓   **He showed me the colour photographs he had taken.**
       See note at COLOUR 5

come 1   ✗   He was afraid of his father and didn't want to come back home.
       ✓   **He was afraid of his father and didn't want to go back home.**
       Come is used for movement towards the place where the speaker is, was, or intends to be, or towards the person being talked about: 'Come and look at this.' 'Why didn't he come to see me?' 'He was just about to go out when his wife came into the office in tears.'
       Go is used for movement in other directions: 'I wish those noisy children would go away.' 'Let's go to London for a few days.'

2   ✗   The students who are coming from Japan are hard-working.
       ✓   **The students who come from Japan are hard-working.**
       When you mention someone's country or where something was made or grown, use the present simple tense. Compare: 'She comes from Germany.' (= she was born in Germany) 'She is coming from Germany.' (= she is travelling from Germany)

common 1   ✗   I think that people in common have good sides and bad sides.
       ✓   **I think that people in general have good sides and bad sides.**
       If you have the same background, interests, tastes etc as someone, the two of you have a lot **in common**: 'I'm sure the marriage won't last. They've got nothing in common.'
       When you mean that something happens or is true 'in most situations', use **in general**: 'In general, parents care more about their children's health than about their own.' 'Students in general have very little money to spend on luxuries.'

2 ✗ There are so many things in common between us.
✓ **We have so many things in common.**

> Two or more people **have (got)** something **in common**: 'We've moved in the same circles over the last ten years and so we have a great deal in common.'

3 ✗ In Spain it is common that people turn up at your house without warning.
✓ **In Spain it is common for people to turn up at your house without warning.**

> **it is common + for sb to do sth** (NOT **that**): 'It's quite common for new fathers to feel jealous for the first few weeks.'

company ✗ For those who live by themselves, television provides a good company.
✓ **For those who live by themselves, television provides good company.**

> When **company** means 'someone or something that stops you from feeling lonely or bored; companionship', it is uncountable: 'Whenever he goes off on a long trip, he takes his radio with him for company.'

compare ✗ The teachers will be able to visit our schools and compare our teaching methods to their own.
✓ **The teachers will be able to visit our schools and compare our teaching methods with their own.**

> **compare to** = describe (someone or something) as being similar to (someone or something else); liken: 'She compared the child to a noisy monkey.'
> **compare with** = examine two or more people/things/ideas etc to discover similarities and/or differences: 'Having compared the new dictionary with the old one, she found the new one more helpful.'

complain ✗ It is childish to complain against rules.
✓ **It is childish to complain about rules.**
✗ They are always complaining for something.
✓ **They are always complaining about something.**

> **complain about sth**: 'Residents living near the airport have a lot to complain about.'

complaint ✗ There have been several complaints for the service in the canteen.
✓ **There have been several complaints about the service in the canteen.**

> **(make) a complaint about sth** (NOT **for**): 'If you have any complaints about the service, you should write to the manager.'

completely ✗ Then the lights went out and we were completely scared.
✓ **Then the lights went out and we were very scared.**
> See note at VERY 2

composed ✗ The committee is composed by six teachers and a student representative.
✓ **The committee is composed of six teachers and a student representative.**

be composed of (NOT **by**): 'The human body is composed of billions of tiny cells.'

**comprehen-
sion**

✗ There is not enough comprehension between our two countries.
✓ **There is not enough understanding between our two countries.**

Comprehension refers to the ability to understand the meaning of something, especially something that is spoken or written: 'I'd like to develop my vocabulary and improve my listening comprehension.'
When you mean 'an attitude of sympathy', use **understanding**: 'When it comes to the employees' personal problems, the management shows a complete lack of understanding.'

**comprehen-
sive**

✗ The teachers are very kind and comprehensive.
✓ **The teachers are very kind and understanding.**

comprehensive = including everything or almost everything: 'The witness provided a comprehensive account of the accident.'
understanding = feeling sympathy for someone: 'As people grow older, they tend to be a bit more understanding and easier to live with.'

comprise

✗ The former Soviet Union comprised of fifteen union republics.
✓ **The former Soviet Union comprised fifteen union republics.**
See Language Note at INCLUDE

**concen-
trate 1**

✗ I am concentrated on both speaking and writing.
✓ **I am concentrating on both speaking and writing.**
✗ A bus driver has to be concentrated and should not speak to the passengers.
✓ **A bus driver has to concentrate and should not speak to the passengers.**

concentrate (on sth) NOT **be concentrated**: 'How can children concentrate on their homework when they have one eye on the television?'
Compare: 'The juice is then concentrated by a process of evaporation.'

2

✗ The teaching tends to concentrate in grammar.
✓ **The teaching tends to concentrate on grammar.**
✗ I try to concentrate in one subject at a time.
✓ **I try to concentrate on one subject at a time.**

concentrate on sth (NOT **in**): 'She gave up teaching so that she could concentrate on research.'

3

✗ I couldn't concentrate myself as there was someone talking.
✓ **I couldn't concentrate as there was someone talking.**
See Language Note at MYSELF

concern 1

✗ As far as I concern, the cost of the repair is not my responsibility.
✓ **As far as I'm concerned, the cost of the repair is not my responsibility.**

as far as sb/sth is concerned: 'As far as my parents are concerned, I'm free to come whenever I like.' 'As far as the law is concerned, you are innocent until proven guilty.' 'As far as your grammar is concerned, you seem to be having a problem with tenses.'

2 ✗ You should concern more about your health.
 ✓ **You should be more concerned about your health.**
 ✗ There are far more serious things to concern about.
 ✓ **There are far more serious things to be concerned about.**

> **be concerned about sth** (= be worried or anxious): 'The government is becoming increasingly concerned about the rising level of unemployment.' 'The manager is naturally very concerned about the recent spate of injuries.'

3 ✗ The first chapter is concerned about the disposal of nuclear waste.
 ✓ **The first chapter is concerned with the disposal of nuclear waste.**
 ✓ **The first chapter concerns the disposal of nuclear waste.**

> **be concerned with sth** OR **concern sth** = (of a book, film, essay etc) be about a particular subject: 'The article is concerned with recent developments in primary education.'

4 ✗ Some dentists are more concerned in earning money than doing a good job.
 ✓ **Some dentists are more concerned with earning money than doing a good job.**

> **be concerned with (doing) sth** = be interested in: 'We should be more concerned with re-educating criminals than punishing them.'

concerning ✗ Concerning your accommodation, there are several possibilities.
 ✓ **With regard to your accommodation, there are several possibilities.**

> To introduce a new topic, use **with regard to, regarding, as regards, as far as ... is concerned** (NOT **concerning**): 'As far as food is concerned, the college has its own canteen.'
> Compare: 'He was then asked several questions concerning his banking activities.' 'We got into an interesting discussion concerning the need for censorship.'

conclusion ✗ As a conclusion, I'd like to say that everyone should be able to work if they want to.
 ✓ **In conclusion, I'd like to say that everyone should be able to work if they want to.**
 ✗ To come to the conclusion, I would like to say that everyone should read the book.
 ✓ **To conclude, I would like to say that everyone should read the book.**

> To introduce a concluding statement, use **in conclusion, by way of conclusion,** or **to conclude**: 'By way of conclusion, I'd just like to add that the answers to the questions I have raised would still appear to be a long way off.'

condition 1 ✗ You should try to keep the car in a good condition.
 ✓ **You should try to keep the car in good condition.**

> **in good/excellent/perfect/bad/terrible ... condition** (WITHOUT **a/an**): 'Most of the CDs were still in excellent condition.' 'What sort of condition is the car in?'

2 ✗ They are forced to live in a terrible condition.
  ✓ **They are forced to live in terrible conditions.**

> When you describe the situation in which someone lives or works, use **conditions**: 'Latest reports from the capital suggest that the conditions there are getting worse.' 'How do they manage to survive in such dreadful conditions?'

3 ✗ How are you? I hope you're in good condition.
  ✓ **How are you? I hope you're keeping fit and well.**

> **in good condition/shape** = physically fit and strong because you do exercises: 'Most of the team had kept themselves in good condition during the summer months.'
> To enquire about or refer to someone's general state of health, use **well** or **fit and well**: 'Sarah has a bit of a cold but apart from that we're all well and looking forward to the summer holiday.'

confidence ✗ She has no confidence for what the future has to offer.
  ✓ **She has no confidence in what the future has to offer.**

> **confidence in sb/sth**: 'The trouble is she lacks confidence in her own ability.' 'It seems that investors have lost confidence in the major stock markets.'

confident 1 ✗ I feel quite confident with my English.
  ✓ **I feel quite confident about my English.**

> **confident about sth**: 'The more familiar you are with the machine, the more confident you will be about using it.'

2 ✗ I began to feel more confident of myself.
  ✓ **I began to feel more self-confident.**

> If you have confidence in your own abilities, you feel **self-confident**: 'Even as a child he was surprisingly self-confident and didn't mind being left with strangers.'

confirm ✗ Could you please confirm me whether you have received my order.
  ✓ **Could you please confirm whether you have received my order.**

> **confirm** + direct object (WITHOUT **me, us, them** etc): 'I am pleased to confirm that your application has been approved.'

confront ✗ Almost every day we confront with some new environmental problem.
  ✓ **Almost every day we confront some new environmental problem.**
  ✓ **Almost every day we are confronted with some new environmental problem.**

> **confront sb/sth** (WITHOUT **with**): 'Sooner or later the management will have to confront these issues.'
> **confront sb with sth**: 'She continued to deny the charge until the prosecution finally confronted her with the evidence.'
> **be confronted with/by sth**: 'She continued to deny the charge until she was finally confronted with the evidence.'

congrat-
ulate

✗ First of all I'd like to congratulate you both for your wedding.
✓ **First of all I'd like to congratulate you both on your wedding.**

congratulate sb on (doing) sth: 'The President was among the first to congratulate the crew on the success of their mission.' 'On behalf of the school, I'd like to congratulate the first eleven on getting through to the final.'

congratula-
tions 1

✗ Congratulation! You must be feeling very proud.
✓ **Congratulations! You must be feeling very proud.**

Congratulations is a plural noun: 'Many congratulations to you both. I'm sure you'll be very happy together.' 'Give them our congratulations and say that we'll be getting in touch soon.'

2

✗ Congratulations for your splendid examination results!
✓ **Congratulations on your splendid examination results!**

congratulations on (doing) sth (NOT **for**): 'Congratulations on your promotion. You certainly deserve it.'

conscious

✗ People today are more conscious about the importance of health care.
✓ **People today are more conscious of the importance of health care.**

be conscious of sth: 'I was very conscious of the fact that my every move was being watched.'

consider

✗ We're considering to visit Switzerland next year.
✓ **We're considering visiting Switzerland next year.**

consider doing sth (= think about something that you might do in the future): 'To save money, we even considered repairing the roof ourselves.'

consist of 1 ✗ The house was consisting of three bedrooms, a kitchen, and a bathroom.
✓ **The house consisted of three bedrooms, a kitchen, and a bathroom.**

See Language Note at INCLUDE

2 ✗ The group was consisted of ten people.
✓ **The group consisted of ten people.**
✗ An extended family is consisted of at least two generations.
✓ **An extended family consists of at least two generations.**

See Language Note at INCLUDE

3 ✗ The school consists on four large buildings.
✓ **The school consists of four large buildings.**

consist of (NOT **on**): 'Spain consists of 51 different provinces.'

constantly

? He constantly got into trouble.
✓ **He was constantly getting into trouble.**

When **constantly** means 'again and again', the verb is usually a progressive form: 'The old computer was constantly breaking down.'

contact   ✗ You can contact with me any evening after six.
              ✓ **You can contact me any evening after six.**

> **contact sb** (WITHOUT **with**): 'Unless we have an address or phone number, we can't contact them.'
> Compare: 'Mrs Lewis phoned and would like you to get in touch with her.'

contain   ✗ The wallet was containing about $25.
              ✓ **The wallet contained about $25.**
              See Language Note opposite.

content   ✗ The content of the latest peace talks is still a secret.
              ✓ **The contents of the latest peace talks are still a secret.**
              ✗ The cover page tells you about the magazine's content.
              ✓ **The cover page tells you about the magazine's contents.**

> **content** (WITHOUT **s**) = the (interesting) facts, ideas or opinions expressed in a book, film, essay, speech etc: 'His letters tend to have very little content.'
> **contents** (WITH **s**) = (1) all the (interesting and uninteresting) things that are inside something: 'The customs officer opened my suitcase and examined the contents.' (2) all the things that are written or talked about in a book, report, letter, discussion etc: 'The contents of the diary are strictly confidential.', (3) a list at the front of a book, report, thesis, etc, saying what each chapter or section is about: 'If you want to know which chapters to read, just look at the contents.'

contents ✗ I didn't find the contents of the novel very interesting.
              ✓ **I didn't find the content of the novel very interesting.**
              See note at CONTENT

continual ✗ The canals join to form one continual waterway.
              ✓ **The canals join to form one continuous waterway.**
              ✗ A line of cars stretched continually down the motorway.
              ✓ **A line of cars stretched continuously down the motorway.**

> **continual** = happening repeatedly over a long period of time, especially in a way that you find annoying: 'That telephone has been ringing continually.'
> **continuous** = without any break or interruption: 'Gas central heating provides a continuous supply of hot water.'

continuous ✗ I grew tired of his continuous moaning.
               ✓ **I grew tired of his continual moaning.**
               ✗ The meeting was continuously interrupted.
               ✓ **The meeting was continually interrupted.**
               See note at CONTINUAL

contrary ✗ It is impossible to tell whether a man is married or NOT. On the contrary, women usually have 'Mrs' or 'Miss' before their name.
              ✓ **It is impossible to tell whether a man is married or not. On the other hand, women usually have 'Mrs' or 'Miss' before their name.**
              ✗ I've never been able to cook. My sister on the contrary can bake wonderful biscuits and cakes.
              ✓ **I've never been able to cook. My sister on the other hand can bake wonderful biscuits and cakes.**

Using progressive tenses

- Progressive tenses are used to talk about things that are happening at a particular point in time:

  Progressive tenses are NOT used to talk about states (i.e. the way things are or the way things feel):

  > Bill **was painting** the kitchen when I arrived.
  > What **are** you **eating**?

  > My brother **belongs** to a boxing club. (NOT 'is belonging')
  > Each envelope **contained** twenty dollars. (NOT 'was containing')
  > The cat **sensed** danger so it turned and ran away (NOT 'was sensing')

- Verbs with 'state' meanings which are NOT used in progressive tenses include:

LIKES and DISLIKES	**admire, adore, like/dislike, love, prefer, hate**
NEEDS and WANTS	**need, lack, want**
SENSES	**feel, hear, wish, see, notice, smell, taste, sound, sense**
KNOWLEDGE	**forget, know, realize, remember, understand**
OPINIONS	**believe, doubt, feel, imagine, suppose, suspect, think**
COMPOSITION	**comprise, consist of, contain, include**
APPEARANCE	**appear, be, seem, look, resemble**
POSSESSION	**have, belong to, own, possess, owe**
RELATIONSHIPS	**come from, concern, involve, depend, fit, suit**
EXISTENCE	**be, exist**

- Remember that many verbs have both 'action' and 'state' meanings.

  Compare:
  > George **is having** a bath.
  > George **has** two sisters and one brother. (NOT 'is having')

  > I**'m thinking** about where to go for my next holiday.
  > I **think** history lessons are boring. (NOT 'am thinking')

- Remember that the progressive form of a verb (**be** + **-ing**) is not the same as the **-ing** form.

  Compare:
  > ✗ I was not having a watch and so I didn't know the time.
  > ✓ **I didn't have a watch and so I didn't know the time.**
  > ✓ **Not having a watch, I didn't know the time.**

  When a verb is used to describe a state, the simple form and the **-ing** form may be used, but not the progressive form.

> Use **on the contrary** to show that you strongly disagree with a previous statement and believe that the opposite is true: 'Your parents didn't want you to go abroad, did they?' 'On the contrary, they were all for it.'
> To introduce a statement that is in sharp contrast with a previous statement, use **on the other hand**: 'These new XJ100 computers are amazingly fast. On the other hand, they're very expensive.'

contribute　✗ Oxfam and Save the Children have contributed a lot of money for the relief work.
　✓ **Oxfam and Save the Children have contributed a lot of money to the relief work.**
　✗ When I return home, I hope to contribute my country's economic development.
　✓ **When I return home, I hope to contribute to my country's economic development.**

> **contribute** (money or some other form of assistance) **to sth**: 'In recent years a number of major corporations have contributed large sums of money to the President's campaign funds.'

control 1　✗ I was surprised that nobody wanted to control my luggage.
　✓ **I was surprised that nobody wanted to inspect my luggage.**
　✗ After controlling his fingerprints, the police arrested him.
　✓ **After inspecting his fingerprints, the police arrested him.**
　✗ At this stage in the process, every mould is controlled again.
　✓ **At this stage in the process, every mould is inspected again.**

> **control** = make people or machines do what you want them to do: 'Who will control the aircraft if the pilot has a heart attack?' 'The police were unable to control the crowd.'
> **inspect** = carefully check or examine something: 'The building is regularly inspected by fire-safety officers.' 'I got out of the car to inspect the damage.'

2　✗ These people want to control over our lives.
　✓ **These people want to control our lives.**
　✓ **These people want control over our lives.**

> **control sth** (verb) WITHOUT **of/over**: 'It's usually the editor who controls what goes into a newspaper.' 'The security forces are no longer able to control the situation.'
> **control of/over sth** (noun): 'It's usually the editor who has control over what goes into a newspaper.' 'The security forces have lost control of the situation.'

3　✗ My boat had lost control.
　✓ **My boat had gone out of control.**
　✗ There was a loud bang and my car became out of control.
　✓ **There was a loud bang and my car went out of control.**
　✗ The ferry was not under control and collided with a sampan.
　✓ **The ferry was out of control and collided with a sampan.**

> People **lose control of** vehicles, machines etc: 'The pilot lost control of the aircraft and it plummeted to the ground.'
> Vehicles and machines **are/go out of control**: 'The aircraft went out of control and plummeted to the ground.'

4　✗ I had lost my control and crashed into a tree.
　✓ **I had lost control and crashed into a tree.**

✗ He lost the control of the car and hit a wall.
✓ **He lost control of the car and hit a wall.**

> **lose control (of sth)**, WITHOUT **the, his, my,** etc: 'In 1993 Roseberg lost control of the company after a surprise takeover bid.'

convince   ✗ We all tried to convince her to sing.
✓ **We all tried to persuade her to sing.**

> **convince** = make someone feel completely certain that something is true: 'Somehow the party will have to convince the voters that it is capable of governing the country.' 'She failed to convince the jury of her innocence.'
> **persuade** = make someone agree to do something (or believe that something is true): 'Her parents have persuaded her to stop seeing him.' 'Despite our efforts to persuade them, they still haven't signed the contract.'

cooker   ✗ The cooker puts too much salt in the food.
✓ **The cook/chef puts too much salt in the food.**

> **cooker** (AmE **stove**) = a piece of equipment that you use for cooking food: 'I've never used a gas cooker before.'
> **cook** = a person who cooks: 'My sister is a superb cook.'
> **chef** = a cook who works in a restaurant: 'Jean-Paul is training to be a chef.'

corner   ✗ I have written my address on the top right-hand corner.
✓ **I have written my address in the top right-hand corner.**
✗ I'd rather sit on the corner, near the door.
✓ **I'd rather sit in the corner, near the door.**

> **in the corner** of an area or room (NOT **on** or **at**): 'I suggest that we put the piano in the corner where it won't get in the way.'
> Compare: 'The bank is on the corner, next to the launderette.' 'I'll meet you at the corner in half an hour.'

cost 1   ✗ That shop is always empty because the costs are too high.
✓ **That shop is always empty because the prices are too high.**
See Language Note at PRICE

2   ✗ I'll be happy to pay the costs of the postage.
✓ **I'll be happy to pay the cost of the postage.**
See Language Note at PRICE

3   ✗ They agreed to repair the damage free of cost.
✓ **They agreed to repair the damage free of charge.**
See Language Note at PRICE

4   ✗ In London the cost of life is very high.
✓ **In London the cost of living is very high.**
✗ The costs of living are always higher in city areas.
✓ **The cost of living is always higher in city areas.**
See Language Note at PRICE

5   See VERY MUCH 2

could 1 ✗ As I've already mentioned, I could learn a great deal during the two years I spent in England.
✓ **As I've already mentioned, I was able to learn a great deal during the two years I spent in England.**
✗ By reading quickly, I could finish the book before the library closed.
✓ **By reading quickly, I managed to finish the book before the library closed.**

When talking about a skill or general ability in the past, use **could** or **be able to**: 'By the time she was four, she could/was able to swim the whole length of the pool.'
When talking about a single event in the past, we usually use **be able to** or **manage** (NOT **could**): 'Luckily, we managed to get there before the shops closed.' 'Were you able to start the car?'
Note however that **could** is used in negative contexts and before verbs such as **see, hear, smell** etc: 'We looked everywhere for the cassette, but we couldn't find it.' 'Couldn't you start the car?' 'From where I was standing, I could hear everything they said.' See also ABLE 2

2 SEE POSSIBLE 2

country-side ? Some of us did our teaching practice in the countryside.
✓ **Some of us did our teaching practice in rural areas.**

Use **countryside** when you are thinking about the beauty or lifestyle of this type of area: 'We have to act now to save the countryside for future generations.' 'We enjoy walking in the countryside around Bristol.'
To refer to areas that do not have cities or towns, use **rural/country areas**: 'Housing tends to be more affordable in rural areas.'

course 1 ✗ I'm taking an intermediate course of English.
✓ **I'm taking an intermediate course in English.**

a course in/on sth (NOT **of**): 'I've been attending an evening course in business studies.' 'I'm interested in doing a correspondence course in English and Maths.' 'There is also a two-day course on new technology for teachers.'

2 ✗ The boys and girls in my English course come from all over the world.
✓ **The boys and girls on my English course come from all over the world.**

In British English you say that someone is **on a course**: 'Some of the people on the course came to a few classes and then dropped out.'
Note that **in a course** is used in American English.

3 ? We'll probably go to the cinema or to a discotheque. Of course, since Fiona is my guest, I'll let her decide.
✓ **We'll probably go to the cinema or to a discotheque. Naturally, since Fiona is my guest, I'll let her decide.**
? The construction of a new motorway is totally unnecessary and of course the local residents are completely against the idea.
✓ **The construction of a new motorway is totally unnecessary and, as one would expect, the local residents are completely against the idea.**

Of course is generally over-used. Common words and phrases that may be used as alternatives include: **naturally, obviously, clearly, certainly, evidently, predictably, as you/one would expect, as is to be expected, as you know, it is clear/obvious that.**

crash

✗ The train couldn't stop in time and crashed with the truck.
✓ **The train couldn't stop in time and crashed into the truck.**
✗ I lost control of the car and crashed a palm tree.
✓ **I lost control of the car and crashed into a palm tree.**

crash into sth: 'The aircraft had crashed into the mountainside, leaving no survivors.'

crazy

See note at MAD 2

crime 1

✗ We need to understand why people do these crimes.
✓ **We need to understand why people commit these crimes.**
✗ Somehow we must stop people from making these crimes.
✓ **Somehow we must stop people from committing these crimes.**

commit a crime (NOT **do, make, perform**): 'Women commit far fewer crimes than men.'

2

✗ All the prisoners had committed heavy crimes.
✓ **All the prisoners had committed serious crimes.**

a serious crime (NOT **heavy**): 'The public are alarmed by the increase in serious crimes.'

criminal

✗ The criminal rate among juveniles is still increasing.
✓ **The crime rate among juveniles is still increasing.**
✗ What makes them choose a criminal life?
✓ **What makes them choose a life of crime?**

'criminal activity', 'a criminal offence', 'a criminal record', 'criminal law', BUT 'crime prevention', 'the crime rate', 'crime statistics', 'a life of crime'

criteria

✗ These decisions should not be based on purely financial criterias.
✓ **These decisions should not be based on purely financial criteria.**

Criteria is the plural of **criterion**: 'The company's sole criterion of success is high sales.' 'These new criteria make it easier to get a visa.'

critic

✗ The entertainment page usually contains one or two critics on films being shown in local cinemas.
✓ **The entertainment page usually contains one or two reviews of films being shown in local cinemas.**

critic = a person who writes reviews of new books, films etc: 'For five years she was theatre critic for the New Yorker.'
review = a short article in a newspaper or magazine which describes the good and bad qualities of a new book, film, play etc: 'According to the reviews, the film is definitely worth seeing.'
Compare **critique** = an article, book, speech etc which carefully explains the weaknesses of a theory, policy, philosophy etc: 'The speech was a devastating critique of Reagan's economic policy.'

critical   ✗ The article is highly critical on the government's refugee policy.
    ✓ **The article is highly critical of the government's refugee policy.**

> critical of sth: 'Miller was critical of the way in which the company conducted its business.'

criticism 1   ✗ The writer who did that criticism was unaware of the facts.
    ✓ **The writer who made that criticism was unaware of the facts.**

> make a criticism (of sth): 'The committee has made four specific criticisms of the government's transport policy.'

    2   ✗ My criticism on this type of journalism is that it is totally irresponsible.
    ✓ **My criticism of this type of journalism is that it is totally irresponsible.**

> criticism of sth: 'The most common criticism of the magazine is that it is poorly illustrated.'

cry 1   ✗ The children got very excited and began to cry.
    ✓ **The children got very excited and began to scream.**

> cry = shout something: ' "Help! Help!" she cried.'
> cry out = make a sudden loud noise when you are frightened, shocked, hurt, etc: 'When they tried to move him, he cried out in pain.'
> scream = make a loud, high, continuous noise, especially when you are very frightened, very excited or in great pain: 'One of the firemen thought he heard someone screaming inside the building.' 'The fans didn't stop screaming until the group had left the stage.'

    2   ✗ Even when she is angry, she never cries.
    ✓ **Even when she is angry, she never shouts.**

> shout = speak in a very loud voice, especially because you want someone to hear you or because you are angry: 'There's no need to shout. I'm not deaf, you know.' 'The demonstrators marched through the streets shouting:No more war! No more war!'

    3   ? When he reached the point in his story when his friends were arrested and tortured, he began to cry.
    ✓ **When he reached the point in his story when his friends were arrested and tortured, he began to weep.**

> cry = the opposite of laugh: 'As the child was running towards me, she fell over and began to cry.' 'Babies always cry when they're hungry.'
> weep = cry quietly, usually because of great sadness. This word is mainly used in literary styles: 'He knelt down by his son's small grave and wept.'

    4   ✗ I didn't know whether to cry or laugh.
    ✓ **I didn't know whether to laugh or cry.**

> **Laugh or cry** is a fixed phrase: 'His jokes are so awful that you don't know whether to laugh or cry.'

culture   ✗ The year in Boston taught me a lot about the American culture.
    ✓ **The year in Boston taught me a lot about American culture.**

American culture, British culture, etc (WITHOUT **the**): 'The lecture this afternoon is on the history of French culture and institutions.'

cure 1   ✗ The wound took several weeks to cure.
　　　　✓ **The wound took several weeks to heal.**

Cuts, wounds, injuries, etc **heal**: 'Cuts generally take longer to heal in humid climates.'

2   ✗ I was the doctor who cured your head injury.
　　✓ **I was the doctor who treated your head injury.**

Doctors and nurses **treat** an injury, disease, sick person, etc: 'Serious burns must be treated as soon as possible.' 'The usual way of treating malaria is to give the patient large doses of quinine.' 'Some hospitals refuse to treat people who don't have medical insurance.'

3   ✗ Those who are seriously ill take a long time to cure.
　　✓ **Those who are seriously ill take a long time to recover.**

When people who have been ill or injured return to their normal state of health, they **recover** or **get better**: 'Some of the flood victims are still recovering in hospital.' 'It takes a long time to recover from glandular fever.' 'Within a month of the heart attack, he had fully recovered.'

4   ✗ As yet, nobody has found a cure to AIDS or cancer.
　　✓ **As yet, nobody has found a cure for AIDS or cancer.**
　　✗ The best cure of a cold is a good night's sleep.
　　✓ **The best cure for a cold is a good night's sleep.**

a cure for a disease: 'Is there a cure for tuberculosis?'

curiosity 1   ✗ It was this film that first aroused my curiosity on Korean culture.
　　　　　✓ **It was this film that first aroused my curiosity about Korean culture.**

curiosity about sth: 'The article was inspired by her curiosity about plants and medicine.'

2   ✗ Several passers-by stopped to look at the strange bicycle from curiosity.
　　✓ **Several passers-by stopped to look at the strange bicycle out of curiosity.**

You do or ask something **out of curiosity** (NOT **from**): 'Just out of curiosity, what made you decide to marry him after all?'

curious   ✗ I was curious what she would look like.
　　　　✓ **I was curious to know what she would look like.**
　　　　✗ I'm very curious of the country and its inhabitants.
　　　　✓ **I'm very curious about the country and its inhabitants.**

curious about/as to: 'I'm curious as to how he knows our address.'
curious to see/know etc: 'We're all curious to see what his new girlfriend is like.'

current   ✗ The current world encourages creativity.
　　　　✓ **The modern world encourages creativity.**
　　　　✗ We need to know current English, not the language of Shakespeare.

✓ **We need to know modern English, not the language of Shakespeare.**

> **current** = happening or existing now, but not likely to last for a long time: 'How long has she been going out with her current boyfriend?' 'The current boom in long-haul travel has led to fierce competition among the major airlines.'
> **modern** = used or existing in the period of history that we live in now, and not in an earlier period: 'What do you think of modern architecture?' 'Even by modern standards, the pyramids are a remarkable piece of engineering.'

custom 1 ✗ I went there hoping to learn something about Indian culture and custom.
✓ **I went there hoping to learn something about Indian culture and customs.**

> You talk about a country's **customs** (WITH **s**): 'In Hong Kong I learned a lot about Chinese customs.'
> See also Language Note at MANNER

2 ✗ He has a custom of coughing before he speaks.
✓ **He has a habit of coughing before he speaks.**
✗ It's very difficult for people to change their customs.
✓ **It's very difficult for people to change their habits.**

> See Language Note at MANNER

3 ✗ Will I have to pay custom duty?
✓ **Will I have to pay customs duty?**

> **customs** (WITH **s**) = the place where your bags are examined when you enter a country: 'We got held up at the customs while they went through our suitcases.'
> **customs duty** (WITH **s**) = taxes that you have to pay to bring certain goods into a country: 'The customs duty on electrical goods is twenty percent of the retail price.'

cut 1 ✗ He cut the strip of photographs and gave one to me.
✓ **He cut up the strip of photographs and gave one to me.**
✗ Then you cut the carrots and put them into the saucepan.
✓ **Then you cut up the carrots and put them into the saucepan.**

> **cut up** = cut something into small pieces: 'Two-year-olds can't eat meat unless you cut it up for them.'

2 ✗ I cut the picture and stuck it on a sheet of paper.
✓ **I cut out the picture and stuck it on a sheet of paper.**

> **cut out** = remove a part of something by cutting all around it: 'Each child had to draw a face and then cut it out.'

3 ✗ To build the motorway, they will have to cut a lot of trees.
✓ **To build the motorway, they will have to cut down a lot of trees.**

> **cut down** = make something tall (such as a tree) fall down by cutting through it close to the ground: 'All the elms were diseased and had to be cut down.'

4   ✗ In the summer I cut my hair very short.
     ✓ **In the summer I have my hair cut very short.**

> **have/get your hair cut:** 'When was the last time you had your hair cut?'

cut down   ✗ Through rationalization they were able to cut down the cost of production.
       ✓ **Through rationalization they were able to cut the cost of production.**

> **cut** (WITHOUT **down**) = reduce the cost, price, size etc of something: 'In the last twelve months the size of the workforce has been cut by fifty percent.'

cut out   ✗ Without a car, you are virtually cut out from society.
      ✓ **Without a car, you are virtually cut off from society.**

> When you are **cut off from** a group of people, you are separated from them (and feel lonely): 'It's easy to feel cut off from your loved ones when you first go overseas.'

cutlery   ✗ All the cutleries are in the top drawer.
      ✓ **All the cutlery is in the top drawer.**

> **Cutlery** (= knives, forks, spoons etc) is an uncountable noun: 'You'll find some clean cutlery in the top drawer.'

D*d*

damage 1 ✗ The driver was very lucky and was only slightly damaged.
  ✓ **The driver was very lucky and was only slightly hurt.**
  ✗ During the protests, some students were killed and others were seriously damaged.
  ✓ **During the protests, some students were killed and others were seriously injured/wounded.**

> **Damaged** is used in connection with things or parts of your body (NOT people): 'The engine was too badly damaged to be repaired.' 'The cause of the oil leak was a damaged pipeline.'
> People are **hurt** or **injured** (badly hurt) in an accident, earthquake, hurricane etc: 'The scaffolding collapsed, killing one of the construction workers and injuring two passers-by.'
> Someone who is injured by a weapon, such as a gun or knife, is **wounded**: 'He is accused of wounding a fellow prisoner.' 'The wounded soldiers were sent home for medical treatment.'

2 ✗ The fire caused a lot of damages.
  ✓ **The fire caused a lot of damage.**
  ✗ The car crashed into a tree and suffered a severe damage.
  ✓ **The car crashed into a tree and suffered severe damage.**

> In its usual meaning, **damage** is an uncountable noun: 'The insurance company will pay for any damage.' 'The ceiling had suffered a great deal of damage.'
> **damages** (plural noun) = a sum of money that someone is awarded in a court of law: 'She was awarded $3000 in damages.' 'She claimed damages of £2000 for wrongful dismissal.'

3 ✗ The floods made a lot of damage.
  ✓ **The floods did/caused a lot of damage.**
  ✗ Most of the damage has been produced by acid rain.
  ✓ **Most of the damage has been caused by acid rain.**

> **do/cause damage** (NOT **make** or **produce**): 'According to local farmers, the rabbits do a lot of damage to the crops.' 'It's the gas from fridges that causes most of the damage.'
> See Language Note at DO

4 ✗ The bomb caused extensive damage of the surrounding buildings.
  ✓ **The bomb caused extensive damage to the surrounding buildings.**
  ✗ We all know about the damage that smoking can do in our health.
  ✓ **We all know about the damage that smoking can do to our health.**

(cause/do) damage to sth: 'Lack of oxygen can cause serious damage to the brain.' 'The scandal did a great deal of damage to his reputation.'

damp

✗ The summer in Japan is very hot and damp.
✓ **The summer in Japan is very hot and humid.**

damp = slightly wet, especially in a cold and unpleasant way: 'Our hotel room felt cold and damp.' 'On damp days, we have to dry the washing indoors.'
humid = warm and full of water vapour: 'The air in tropical forests is extremely humid.' 'I didn't expect Singapore to be so humid.'

dance

✗ There were lots of young boys and girls dancing pop music.
✓ **There were lots of young boys and girls dancing to pop music.**
✗ Then we danced with the music of 'Grease'.
✓ **Then we danced to the music of 'Grease'.**

dance to a particular type/piece of music: 'What type of music do you prefer dancing to?'

dare 1

✗ I dare to say that the book is worth reading.
✓ **I daresay that the book is worth reading.**

I daresay (also written **I dare say**) is a fixed phrase: 'I dare say that we'll be hearing from them again.' 'The team will put up a good performance, I daresay, but I don't think they'll win.'

2

✗ 'How dare you to come in without knocking!' he shouted.
✓ **'How dare you come in without knocking!' he shouted.**

When **dare** comes in front of the subject, use an infinitive WITHOUT **to**: 'How dare you say such a thing!' 'Dare I mention it to her? She'll be furious.'

3

✗ He dares to die rather than break his promise.
✓ **He is prepared to die rather than break his promise.**
✗ I didn't enjoy the drink but I dared to try it again.
✓ **I didn't enjoy the drink but I was ready to try it again.**

Dare (= have enough courage) is used mainly in negative sentences and questions: 'I wouldn't dare to take the car without permission.' 'She stood at the edge of the cliff, not daring to look down.'
In affirmative sentences, use **be ready/prepared/willing**: 'Some people are prepared to do anything for money.' 'Despite the threat on his life, he's ready to testify.'

4

✗ His mother thinks that somebody must have dared him steal the bicycle.
✓ **His mother thinks that somebody must have dared him to steal the bicycle.**

dare sb to do sth: 'I dare you to drink it.' 'They dared me to do it again.'

daren't

✗ I daren't to ask her for any more money.
✓ **I daren't ask her for any more money.**

daren't do sth (WITHOUT to): 'I daren't tell George what happened or he'll be furious.'
Compare: 'I don't dare tell/to tell George what happened ... .'

dark

✗ Soon it began to become dark and it was time to go home.
✓ **Soon it began to get dark and it was time to go home.**
✗ The last candle went out and everything became dark.
✓ **The last candle went out and everything went dark.**

> To refer to the time in the evening or at night when the daylight disappears, use **get dark** or (in formal styles) **grow dark**: 'In the winter it gets dark by five o'clock.' 'It began to grow dark and so we headed back to the shore.'
> To describe what happens when all the lights in a room, building, etc suddenly go out, use **go dark** or (especially in formal styles) **be plunged into darkness**: 'During the last storm the whole town was plunged into darkness.'

date 1

✗ On the date of your wedding, I shall be in England.
✓ **On the day of your wedding, I shall be in England.**
✗ I have to pay the rent on the first date of the month.
✓ **I have to pay the rent on the first day of the month.**

> **on the day of sth** (NOT **on the date of**): 'On the day of my departure, I woke up very early.'

2

✗ I have an interview at the same date.
✓ **I have an interview on the same date/day.**

> **on** a specific **date/day** (NOT **at/in**): 'I'm afraid we have no rooms available on that date.' See Language Note at TIME
> Note, however, the phrases **at a later date** and **at some future date**: 'The rest of the money can be paid at a later date.'

3

✗ Up to date, they still haven't answered our letter.
✓ **To date, they still haven't answered our letter.**

> **to date** or **up to/until now** (NOT **up to date**): 'To date there are no signs that the situation is likely to improve.'

4

See UP-TO-DATE

day 1

✗ It was fine autumn day.
✓ **It was a fine autumn day.**
✗ It was very long day for the children.
✓ **It was a very long day for the children.**

> **a/an** + adjective + **day**: 'It was a perfect day for a picnic.' 'It's a beautiful day, isn't it?' 'What a terrible day I've had!'

2

✗ Some people watch television all the day.
✓ **Some people watch television all day.**

> **all day** (WITHOUT **the**): 'What have you been doing all day?'

3

✗ I'm afraid that I can't come at that day.
✓ **I'm afraid that I can't come on that day.**
✗ In the first day, my sunglasses disappeared.
✓ **On the first day, my sunglasses disappeared.**

> See Language Note at TIME

4

✗ My travel agent had arranged a 6 days coach tour.
✓ **My travel agent had arranged a 6-day coach tour.**

5   ✗ Day after day the world is becoming a better place.
✓ **Day by day the world is becoming a better place.**
✗ Men and women have to work in overcrowded offices day by day.
✓ **Men and women have to work in overcrowded offices day after day.**

> **day after day** = repeatedly or continuously, especially in a boring or unpleasant way: 'I get fed up with listening to their complaints day after day.' 'I'm not prepared to sit here day after day doing nothing.'
> **day by day** = gradually: 'Day by day the weather is getting warmer.' 'Their love grew day by day.'

days 1   ✗ In these days many children have their own computer.
✓ **These days many children have their own computer.**

> **these days** (WITHOUT **in/during** etc): 'He's very busy these days.'
> Note however: 'In those days cigarettes were much cheaper.'

2   ✗ In our days we know more about the causes of pollution.
✓ **Nowadays we know more about the causes of pollution.**

> The phrase 'in our days' does not exist. For this meaning, use **nowadays, these days,** or **today**: 'I get the feeling that some people nowadays cannot live without television.'

3   See SOME 4

dead 1   ✗ My father is dead when I was still a baby.
✓ **My father died when I was still a baby.**
✗ The doctor said that she dead because the wound became infected.
✓ **The doctor said that she died because the wound became infected.**

> **Dead** is an adjective and describes a state: 'I can't tell whether that plant is dead or alive.' 'Some of the fish were dead and were floating on the surface.'
> **Died** is the past tense and past participle of **die**: 'I think she died from a heart attack.' 'He died on the way to hospital.'
> See also note at DIED

2   ✗ The purpose of this ceremony is to honour the dead people.
✓ **The purpose of this ceremony is to honour the dead.**

> When you mean 'dead people', use **the dead**: 'At this time of the year the villages make offerings to the spirits of the dead.'

3   See BODY

deal 1   ✗ We have received a great deal of complaints.
✓ **We have received a large number of complaints.**
✗ English contains a great deal of words.
✓ **English contains a great many words.**
✗ A great deal of countries have already signed the agreement.
✓ **Many countries have already signed the agreement.**

> **a great/good deal of** + uncountable noun: 'a great deal of money/time/pleasure'

> **a large number of** + plural count noun: 'a large number of coins/cars/tourists'
> **a great/good many** + plural count noun: 'This operation has already saved the lives of a great many people.'
> When there is no need to emphasize the size of the number, use **many** or (especially in informal styles) **a lot of**: 'Many people have stopped smoking.'

2
  ✗ We have to find a new way of dealing crime.
  ✓ **We have to find a new way of dealing with crime.**
  ✗ I don't have enough time to deal all the questions.
  ✓ **I don't have enough time to deal with all the questions.**

> **deal with** a problem or situation that requires action or attention: 'Customer complaints are dealt with by Mr Adams.' 'How should the government deal with the AIDS crisis?'

deal in
  ✗ The play deals in the struggle of a married couple to live their own lives.
  ✓ **The play deals with the struggle of a married couple to live their own lives.**

> **deal in** = buy and sell: 'The company deals in textiles.' 'Her husband deals in used cars.'
> **deal with** = (of books, articles etc) be about: 'The last chapter deals with economic issues.' 'Her first book dealt with social discrimination against women.'

deal with
  ✗ These days even young schoolchildren know how to deal with computers.
  ✓ **These days even young schoolchildren know how to use computers.**

> **use/operate/handle** a piece of equipment that requires special skill (= make it work): 'Do you know how to operate a video camera?'

death 1
  ✗ In the United States, there were over 17000 deaths of AIDS in 1991.
  ✓ **In the United States, there were over 17000 deaths from AIDS in 1991.**

> **deaths from** a disease: 'The increase in the number of deaths from malaria was causing concern.'

2
See THE 4

3
See SHOOT 1

deeply
See BELIEVE 3, HOPE 3, KNOW 3, RELATED 2, THINK 4, UNDERSTAND 2

defect
  ✗ Any products that are found to be defect will be replaced.
  ✓ **Any products that are found to be defective will be replaced.**

> **Defect** is a noun: 'The test flight revealed a number of small defects in the navigation system.'
> The adjective is **defective**: 'Nowadays defective software is quite unusual.'

degree 1   ✗ I have a Master degree in international journalism.
           ✓ **I have a Master's degree in international journalism.**

                a Master's degree (or **a Master's**), **a bachelor's degree** (WITH **'s**): 'I'm studying for a Master's degree in fuel science.'

2   ✗ I have the degree in economics.
           ✓ **I have a degree in economics.**

                a degree (NOT **the**): 'She is studying for a postgraduate degree.'

3   ✗ He is studying for a degree of computer science
           ✓ **He is studying for a degree in computer science**

                a degree in a particular subject (NOT **of**): 'a degree in law'.
                Note the alternative structure: 'a computer science degree,' 'a law degree'

4   ? I've come here to obtain a Master's degree in International Journalism.
           ✓ **I've come here to do a Master's degree in International Journalism.**

                do/take/get a degree (**in** a particular subject area): 'I'm thinking about doing a Master's degree in business administration.'

delighted   ✗ When they knew that they had won, they were very delighted.
           ✓ **When they knew that they had won, they were absolutely delighted.**

                See note at VERY 2

delightful   ✗ I know that Dad will be delightful if you can come.
           ✓ **I know that Dad will be delighted if you can come.**

                delightful = (fairly formal) giving great pleasure: 'Thank you for such a delightful evening. George and I thoroughly enjoyed ourselves.'
                delighted = extremely pleased: 'I'm delighted to hear that you are feeling better.'

demand 1   ✗ In my new job I am demanded to work overtime.
           ✓ **In my new job I am required to work overtime.**

                If you have to do something because of a rule, law etc, you are **required** to do it: 'Under the law the President is required to notify Congress when US troops face imminent hostilities.'

2   ✗ The demand of butter has decreased in recent years.
           ✓ **The demand for butter has decreased in recent years.**

                a demand for sth (NOT **of**): 'Ford has increased production to meet the demand for its new range of cars.'

demonstra-   ✗ Many demonstrations have been made in recent years in protest
tion   against the level of pollution.
           ✓ **Many demonstrations have been held in recent years in protest against the level of pollution.**

                hold/stage a demonstration (NOT **make**): 'In London, students and lecturers staged a mass demonstration against the proposed education cuts.'

deny 1   ✗ He asked his parents to help him, but they denied.
    ✓ **He asked his parents to help him, but they refused.**
    ✗ When she denied to wear the uniform, she was dismissed.
    ✓ **When she refused to wear the uniform, she was dismissed.**

deny sth = say that it is not true: 'He has been accused of stealing a car, but he denies it.' 'Both companies denied that they had been discharging toxic waste.'
refuse (to do sth) = say that you will not do it: 'Employers are refusing to discuss a pay settlement until the staff return to work.' 'The students were told to leave the building, but they refused.'

2   ✗ She asked him if he had seen a little boy but he denied.
    ✓ **She asked him if he had seen a little boy but he said he hadn't.**

You **deny** an accusation or claim (NOT a question): 'The accused denied both charges.' 'He denied being anywhere near the scene of the crime.'

3   ✗ She accused him of cheating but he denied.
    ✓ **She accused him of cheating but he denied it.**

Deny is a transitive verb: 'He denied that he forged the signature.' 'He denied having forged the signature.' 'He denied it.'

depart   ✗ The next ferry will depart the pier at 9.30 a.m.
    ✓ **The next ferry will depart from the pier at 9.30 a.m.**

depart from a place (= leave): 'The 12.15 shuttle service to Atlanta will depart from platform seven.'

depend 1   ✗ The number of hours he worked was depend on the number of absentees.
    ✓ **The number of hours he worked depended on the number of absentees.**
    ✗ The insurance payment is depends on the value of the goods.
    ✓ **The insurance payment depends on the value of the goods.**

Do not confuse **depend on/upon** and the more formal phrase **be dependent on/upon**. Compare: 'The speed of a car depends on the size of the engine.' 'The speed of a car is dependent on the size of the engine.'

2   ✗ Whether or not she passes is depending upon how hard she works.
    ✓ **Whether or not she passes depends upon how hard she works.**

When **depend on/upon** means 'be shaped or determined by', it is not used in progressive tenses. See Language Note at CONTAIN

3   ✗ It depends on if you've got enough money.
    ✓ **It depends on whether you've got enough money.**

it depends on whether (NOT **if**): 'We don't know yet. It all depends on whether the car is fixed in time.'

describe   ✗ He described me his sister in great detail.
    ✓ **He described his sister (to me) in great detail.**
    ✗ Let me describe you a typical day in Brazil and then you'll understand why I live here.

✓ **Let me describe (to you) a typical day in Brazil and then you'll understand why I live here.**

describe sth (to sb): 'I described my symptoms to the doctor at the hospital.'

description ✗ They needed a description about the stolen car.
✓ **They needed a description of the stolen car.**
✗ I'll send you some English food and a description on how to prepare it.
✓ **I'll send you some English food and a description of how to prepare it.**

description of sb/sth: 'The police now have a full description of the suspects.'

desert ✗ I was miles from anywhere, stuck on a desert country road.
✓ **I was miles from anywhere, stuck on a deserted country road.**

desert = a large area of land, where there is usually nothing but sand: 'the Sahara Desert'
deserted = empty and quiet, especially because the people who are usually there have all left: 'I came back to find the house dark and deserted.' 'At night, the city streets are deserted.'

desire 1 ✗ Despite all my money, I desired to live in an ordinary house.
✓ **Despite all my money, I wanted to live in an ordinary house.**
✗ I desire that world peace will continue for ever.
✓ **I hope that world peace will continue for ever.**

In the meaning 'want/wish', **desire** is usually used as a noun (NOT as a verb): 'His one desire was to live to see his three grandchildren again.' 'I have no desire to go there again. Once is enough.' Note however that this usage is fairly formal.
As a verb meaning 'want/wish', **desire** is used mainly in literary styles: 'For the first time in her life, she had everything her heart desired.' In other styles, use verbs such as **want, would like, hope, wish, intend,** etc.

2 ✗ My desire is to become a successful business manager.
✓ **My ambition is to become a successful business manager.**

When you are talking about something very important that you want to achieve, use **aim** or **ambition**: 'Her ambition is to represent her country in the Olympic Games.' 'Our ultimate aim is to find a cure for the disease.'

3 ✗ I have always had a strong desire of becoming somebody.
✓ **I have always had a strong desire to become somebody.**

a desire to do sth (NOT **of doing**): 'She has no desire to travel and prefers to stay at home.'

despite 1 ✗ Despite the train was empty, he came and sat in front of me.
✓ **Although the train was empty, he came and sat in front of me.**
✓ **Despite the train being empty, he came and sat in front of me.**

Despite and **in spite of** are prepositions (NOT conjunctions). Unlike **although** (a conjunction), they cannot introduce a clause that has a finite verb ('was'). Compare: 'In spite of/Despite owning two cars, he can't drive.' 'Although he owns two cars, he can't drive.'

2   ✗ Despite of my qualifications, I couldn't get a job.
   ✓ **Despite my qualifications, I couldn't get a job.**
   ✓ **In spite of my qualifications, I couldn't get a job.**

> **despite sth** (WITHOUT **of**): 'Despite the heat, she wouldn't take her coat off.'
> **in spite of sth** (WITH **of**): 'In spite of the heat, she wouldn't take her coat off.'

destroy 1

   ✗ This unpleasant man with his endless complaints destroyed my journey.
   ✓ **This unpleasant man with his endless complaints spoilt my journey.**

> When you mean 'remove the pleasure or enjoyment from', use **spoil** or **ruin** (= spoil completely): 'The trip was spoilt by bad weather.' 'I've spent weeks planning this surprise party for Dad, and now you've ruined it by telling him.'

2   ✗ The water had been much too hot and most of the clothes were destroyed.
   ✓ **The water had been much too hot and most of the clothes were ruined.**

> When you mean 'make something less attractive, effective or useful', use **spoil** or **ruin** (= spoil completely): 'I didn't join them on their walk because I didn't want to spoil my new shoes.' 'If you open the camera, you'll ruin the film.'

3   ✗ The bus wasn't badly damaged, but the car was completely destroyed.
   ✓ **The bus wasn't badly damaged, but the car was a write-off.**

> A vehicle that cannot be used again after being damaged in a road accident is **wrecked** or (especially in spoken English) is a **write-off**: 'I was stupid enough to lend him my car, and now it's a write-off!' 'Wrecked vehicles lay abandoned along the roadside.'

detail

   ✗ With a zoom lens, I can study the image in details.
   ✓ **With a zoom lens, I can study the image in detail.**

> **in (great/more/some) detail** (WITHOUT **-s**): 'The victim was able to describe her attacker in detail.' 'Having actually stayed at the hotel, he was able to describe it in greater detail.'

deter

   ✗ How can we deter our leaders to use the atomic bomb?
   ✓ **How can we deter our leaders from using the atomic bomb?**

> **deter sb (from doing sth)** = persuade them not to do it: 'The common assumption is that imprisonment deters them from returning to a life of crime.'

die

   ✗ People say she died with pneumonia.
   ✓ **People say she died of pneumonia.**

> **die of/from** a disease, heart attack, hunger etc (NOT **with**): 'Of these, one in ten will die of lung cancer.' 'Her husband died of a heart attack.' 'Each year over a million children die from diarrhoea.'
> **die of shame/embarrassment/grief/despair/shock** etc: 'When he told

me the price, I nearly died of shock.' 'The poor girl almost died of fright.'
die from the effects of violence, pollution etc: 'He died from a bullet
wound in the chest.' 'Police predict that more people will die from their
injuries.'

died
   ✗ Her husband was died two years earlier.
   ✓ **Her husband had died two years earlier.**

When you are talking about an event, use **die** (**dying, died, died**).
When you are talking about a state, use **be dead**. Compare: 'He died in
an ambulance on the way to hospital.' 'By the time the ambulance
reached the hospital, he was dead.'
See also note at DEAD 1

difference 1
   ✗ You have to make a difference between women who have to
work and women who choose to work.
   ✓ **You have to make a distinction between women who have to
work and women who choose to work.**

make/draw a distinction (between A and B) = not regard or treat A and
B in the same way: 'Sometimes it is difficult to make a clear distinction
between qualifications and experience.' 'Most societies draw a distinction
between the status of an unmarried woman and a married one.'

2
   ✗ As soon as I arrived in the USA, I noticed a big difference of
social behaviour.
   ✓ **As soon as I arrived in the USA, I noticed a big difference in
social behaviour.**

difference in a particular shared feature, practice or quality: 'Since there
was very little difference in price, we bought the large packet.'
'Differences in eating habits can cause considerable embarrassment.'

different 1
   ✗ London is different of Hong Kong.
   ✓ **London is different from/to Hong Kong.**
   ✗ In Argentina, Christmas celebrations are completely different as
the ones in England.
   ✓ **In Argentina, Christmas celebrations are completely
different from/to the ones in England.**

A is **different from/to** B: 'Alex was different from all the other boys she
knew.' Note that most teachers and careful users prefer **from**.

2
   ? My new school is very different than the old one.
   ✓ **My new school is very different from/to the old one.**

Different than is used in American English but is rarely used in British
English.

difficulty 1
   ✗ She had a difficulty in obtaining a visa.
   ✓ **She had difficulty (in) obtaining a visa.**

have difficulty/difficulties (in) doing sth (NOT **a difficulty**):
'Sometimes he has difficulty in making himself understood.'

2
   ✗ I have great difficulty to understand him.
   ✓ **I have great difficulty (in) understanding him.**

have difficulty/difficulties (in) doing sth (NOT **to do**): 'You should
have no difficulty in passing the exam.'

dinner   See BREAKFAST

disagree 1 ✗ Those who disagreed to join the army were put in prison.
              ✓ **Those who refused to join the army were put in prison.**

> **disagree** = not have the same opinion: 'He disagreed with nearly
> everything I said.' 'Why did she disagree with you?' 'We tended to
> disagree about politics, but we were still good friends.'
> **refuse (to do sth)** = say that you will not do something that someone
> has asked you to do: 'The students were asked to leave the building but
> they refused.' 'If anyone refuses to pay their bill, send for the manager.'

2 ? As a conservationist, I strongly disagree with the removal of
        these trees.
     ✓ **As a conservationist, I strongly object to the removal of
        these trees.**

> **object (to sth)** = say that you are against something' 'No member of the
> Council has ever objected to this principle.' 'He objects to being treated
> like a child.'

3 ✗ She disagreed totally to what I said.
     ✓ **She disagreed totally with what I said.**
     ✗ Some people disagree to the death penalty.
     ✓ **Some people disagree with the death penalty.**

> **disagree with sb/sth**: 'I disagreed with their interpretation of the statistics.'

4 ? I disagree that heart transplants should be stopped.
     ✓ **I don't agree that heart transplants should be stopped.**

> When the subject is a particular person, use **not agree** to introduce a
> **that** clause: 'I don't agree that the people there are repressed.' 'She
> cannot agree that farmers should be an exception.'
> In more general statements, **disagree** is usually used with **not, nobody
> etc** before a **that** clause, to give an affirmative meaning; 'No one can
> disagree that these crimes must be stopped.' (=everyone must agree
> that ...) 'Few would disagree that she has served her country well.'
> (=most would agree that ...)

5 ✗ I am disagree with the statement.
     ✓ **I disagree with the statement.**

> **Disagree** is used only as a verb (NOT as an adjective): 'She always
> disagrees with me.'

disappeared ✗ The next morning, the snowman was disappeared.
              ✓ **The next morning, the snowman had disappeared.**
              ✗ One day these problems will be disappeared.
              ✓ **One day these problems will disappear.**

> **Disappeared** (from the verb **disappear**) is not used like an adjective:
> 'His wife has disappeared with the children.' 'Suddenly, the pain in my
> back just disappeared.'
> Compare: 'The next morning, the snowman was gone.' Unlike
> **disappeared, gone** (from the verb **go**) may be used like an adjective.

discourage ✗ Somehow we have to discourage people to commit crimes.
             ✓ **Somehow we have to discourage people from committing
             crimes.**

discourage sb from doing sth: 'We always leave the lights on at night to discourage people from breaking in.'
Compare: 'You should try and encourage her to take more exercise.'

discriminate ✗ Society discriminates old people by denying them the chance to work.
✓ **Society discriminates against old people by denying them the chance to work.**
✗ Women have been discriminated for far too long.
✓ **Women have been discriminated against for far too long.**

discriminate against a group of people: 'The court has ruled that UK employment laws discriminate against part-time workers.'

discrimin- ✗ It is time that sexual discrimination on women was eliminated.
ation ✓ **It is time that sexual discrimination against women was eliminated.**

discrimination against a group of people (NOT **on/about/for** etc): 'Feminist groups see this practice as a form of discrimination against women.'

discuss 1 ✗ When I discuss with them, I cannot say the things that I want to say because of my English.
✓ **When I talk to them, I cannot say the things that I want to say because of my English.**
✗ Some people were discussing; some listening to the radio.
✓ **Some people were talking; some listening to the radio.**

Discuss is a transitive verb and needs an object: 'I'd like to discuss my homework with you.' 'The two sides will discuss further arms reductions.'

2 ✗ They'd like to discuss about what to do next.
✓ **They'd like to discuss what to do next.**

discuss sth (WITHOUT **about/on**): 'He simply refuses to discuss the matter.' 'There is nothing to discuss.'
Compare **talk about, a discussion about/on**: 'They want to talk about what to do next.' 'They want a discussion about/on what to do next.'

discussion ✗ He ran away from home after a discussion with his father.
✓ **He ran away from home after an argument with his father.**
✗ They had a discussion and Dusty killed him.
✓ **They had an argument and Dusty killed him.**

discussion = a talk about something, especially one which allows different points of view to be expressed: 'After further discussion, the government has decided to reject the American offer.'
argument = a quarrel or disagreement: 'The couple next door are always having arguments.' 'I hate arguments. They upset me.'

disguise ✗ To get into the building, I'll disguise as a reporter.
✓ **To get into the building, I'll disguise myself as a reporter.**
See Language Note at MYSELF

dish 1 ✗ Dinner usually consists of three dishes.
✓ **Dinner usually consists of three courses.**
✗ The main dish was roast beef with fresh vegetables.

✓ **The main course was roast beef with fresh vegetables.**
See Language Note at PLATE

2   ✗ Some children have to prepare their own dishes.
✓ **Some children have to prepare their own meals.**
✗ Dinner is the main dish of the day.
✓ **Dinner is the main meal of the day.**
See Language Note at PLATE

dispose   ✗ Jumble sales provide people with a good opportunity to dispose all their unwanted goods.
✓ **Jumble sales provide people with a good opportunity to dispose of all their unwanted goods.**

dispose of sth (= get rid of): 'The quickest way to dispose of the rubbish is to burn it.'

distance 1   ✗ It was a long distance between the hotel and the beach.
✓ **It was a long way from the hotel to the beach.**

When you want to say that two places are far apart, use **a long way** (NOT **a long distance**): 'My flat is quite a long way from the university.' 'We're nearly half-way there, but there's still a long way to go.'
Compare: 'I hate driving long distances.' 'Computers can talk to each other, even over long distances.' 'Trains are excellent for long distance travel.'

2   ✗ The nearest town is in a distance of ten miles.
✓ **The nearest town is ten miles away.**

One place is a number of miles/kilometres/yards etc **away** from another place: 'She was offered a job in Sheffield, about thirty miles away.' 'The secondary school is about five miles away.'

district   ✗ We will be touring the famous fruit-growing districts.
✓ **We will be touring the famous fruit-growing regions.**
✗ The original inhabitants of the district were probably Chinese.
✓ **The original inhabitants of the region/area were probably Chinese.**

district = (1) one of the official divisions of a city or country: 'the London postal district', 'the South Cambridgeshire District', 'the Liverpool 8 district of Merseyside', 'Last winter several London health districts faced a cash crisis.' (2) an area in a city (or sometimes in a country) that has a particular quality or feature: 'a very wealthy district', 'one of the most deprived districts in the inner city', 'an old slum district where the gangs operate'.
A **region** is usually a large area of a country and has no official boundaries: 'The President has declared the region a disaster area.' 'Such expansion would most likely occur in the Amazon region.' 'The people who live in this region have a strong accent.'
When you are unsure about which word to choose, use **area**. An **area** can be large or small and has a very general meaning.

divide   ✗ For lunch and dinner we were divided in groups of ten.
✓ **For lunch and dinner we were divided into groups of ten.**
✗ The university is divided in five different faculties.
✓ **The university is divided into five different faculties.**

divide sth into two or more parts (NOT **in**): 'Some of these big old houses have been divided into separate apartments.'

divorce 1 ✗ Sally told me she was going to divorce.
  ✓ **Sally told me she was going to get a divorce.**
  ✗ When there are children involved, it is difficult to divorce.
  ✓ **When there are children involved, it is difficult to get divorced.**

get a divorce or **get divorced** (= end one's marriage by taking legal action): 'I had just turned ten when my parents got divorced.' 'It took my sister almost a year to get a divorce.'

  2 ✗ It's bad enough when you get divorce, but far worse when you lose your children as well.
  ✓ **It's bad enough when you get divorced, but far worse when you lose your children as well.**
  ✗ If we were divorce, who would look after the children?
  ✓ **If we were divorced, who would look after the children?**

be/get divorced (WITH **'d'**): 'They got divorced in 1993, just twelve months after they were married.' 'It seems as if getting divorced has become fashionable nowadays.'

  3 ✗ The fact that your wife crashed the Ferrari is not a good reason to divorce to her.
  ✓ **The fact that your wife crashed the Ferrari is not a good reason to divorce her.**
  ✗ For some reason, she didn't want to divorce with him.
  ✓ **For some reason, she didn't want to divorce him.**

divorce sb (WITHOUT **to/with**): 'She'd divorced her husband six months before and had gone back to live with her parents.'
Note that **get divorced** is far more common than **divorce** someone: 'For some reason, she didn't want to get divorced.'

do 1 See Language Note on next page

  2 See THAT 8

doubt 1 ✗ Whenever I doubt about the meaning of a word, I look in my dictionary.
  ✓ **Whenever I am in doubt about the meaning of a word, I look in my dictionary.**
  ✗ If ever you have any kind of doubt, come and see me or one of the other teachers.
  ✓ **If ever you are in any doubt about anything, come and see me or one of the other teachers.**

(be) in doubt about sth (= feel unsure): 'Is anyone in doubt about what they're supposed to be doing?' 'If you're in any doubt about your child's safety, talk to your doctor.'
Note that this meaning is more commonly expressed by **be unsure/uncertain** (or **not be sure/certain**): 'Whenever I'm not sure about the meaning of a word, I look in my dictionary.'

Verb + Noun Combinations:
DO • HAVE • MAKE • TAKE

Many phrases begin with a very common verb such as **do, make, have** or **take**:
'I felt very nervous about **taking** the **test** but, after **having** a long **talk** with Mrs Fisher, I decided I would just **do my best** and try not to **make** too many silly **mistakes.**'
These verbs can be combined with some nouns but not with others and since they do not have a clear meaning of their own, choosing the right combination can be a problem. Phrases which tend to cause difficulty are shown in the table below.

HAVE

have a <u>bath</u> (or esp. AmE **take**)	'She's probably upstairs having a bath.'
have (your) <u>breakfast</u>	'We usually have breakfast in the kitchen.'
have (your) <u>dinner</u>	'We had dinner and then went for a walk.'
have a <u>drink</u>	'I'll collapse if I don't have a drink soon.'
have (an) <u>experience</u>	'He has no experience of running a large company.'
have <u>fun</u>	'You can't stop people from having fun.'
have a <u>holiday</u>	'It's almost a year since we had a real holiday.'
have an <u>interview</u>	'I've had six interviews but no one has offered me a job.'
have a <u>lesson</u>	'Every morning we have three fifty-minute lessons.'
have (your) <u>lunch</u>	'Isn't it about time we had lunch?'
have an <u>operation</u>	'Before I had the operation I could hardly walk.'
have a <u>party</u>	'On Saturday we're having a party.'
have a <u>picnic</u>	'If it's sunny we could have a picnic.'
have a <u>shower</u>	(or esp. AmE **take**) 'It only takes me a minute to have a shower.'

TAKE

take/do an <u>examination</u>	'Why do we have to take so many tests?'
take (your) <u>medicine</u>	'Don't forget to take your medicine.'
take a <u>pill</u>	'He refuses to take sleeping pills'.
take/do a <u>test</u>	'The last test I took was a disaster.'

MAKE

make an <u>effort</u>	'I had to make a big effort not to laugh.'
make a <u>journey</u>	'It was the first journey he'd made all on his own.'
make a <u>mistake</u>	'He has made a serious mistake.'
make a <u>noise</u>	'How can one small child make so much noise?'
make <u>progress</u>	'I made very little progress at the start of the course.'

DO

do your <u>best</u>	'Don't worry, Tim. Just do your best.'
do (or **cause**) <u>damage</u>	'The storm did a lot of damage to the crops.'
do an <u>exercise</u>	'Have you done your exercises today?'
do an <u>experiment</u>	'To do this experiment, you'll need two eggs.'
do (sb) <u>good</u>	'The holiday has done him a lot of good.'
do <u>harm</u>	'A scandal would do his reputation a lot of harm.'
do your <u>homework</u>	'Have you done your homework yet?'
do a <u>job</u>	'I've got one or two jobs to do this evening.'
do the/some <u>shopping</u>	'Jake has gone into town to do some shopping.'
do <u>research</u>	'We need to do a lot more research.'
do <u>things</u>	'We've done lots of different things today.'
do your <u>training</u>	'Where did you do your training?'

Note also: **do something/anything** etc: 'I can't come now – I'm doing something.' 'He hasn't done anything wrong.'

2 ✗ That is why we still doubt about beings existing in outer space.
    ✓ **That is why we still have doubts about beings existing in outer space.**

> **have (your) doubts about (doing) sth** = feel unsure whether something is true or the right thing to do: 'We have our doubts about sending Kevin to a boarding school.' 'Any doubts she'd had about marrying him soon disappeared.'

3 ? I doubt that she is telling the truth.
    ✓ **I doubt whether she is telling the truth.**

> When **doubt** is used to express certainty or near certainty, it is usually followed by a **that**-clause: 'There's no doubt that he's innocent.' 'I've no doubt that he's innocent.' 'I'm in little doubt that he's innocent.' 'I don't doubt that he's innocent.' In this meaning, **doubt** is used with a negative word, e.g. **not/no/little/not much.**
> When **doubt** means 'think that something is unlikely', it is usually followed by **if/whether**: 'I doubt whether he's innocent.' (= I think that he is probably guilty) 'She doubts whether she'll be able to come on Sunday.'
> Note that some people may also say 'I doubt that he's innocent', but careful users regard this as incorrect.

4 ? There is no doubt that she doesn't want the job.
    ✓ **She obviously doesn't want the job.**
    ? There is no doubt that most parents are willing to spend a lot of money on their child's education.
    ✓ **Most parents are willing to spend a lot of money on their child's education.**

> **There is no doubt that** is usually used in formal styles when you want to persuade someone that what you are saying is true: 'There is no doubt that the present government has lost a great deal of support.'
> This phrase is sometimes used when a 'lighter' expression (e.g. **of course, obviously, clearly, certainly, needless to say**) or nothing at all would be more natural.

5 ✗ It is no doubt that the rich have a great advantage.
    ✓ **There is no doubt that the rich have a great advantage.**

> **there is no doubt that** (NOT **it is ...**): 'There is no doubt that the number of casualties would have escalated had it not been for UN intervention.'

6 ✗ Without doubt you're tired after your journey.
    ✓ **No doubt you're tired after your journey.**
    ✗ The recovery of the Mary Rose is, no doubt, a great scientific achievement.
    ✓ **The recovery of the Mary Rose is, without doubt, a great scientific achievement.**

> **without doubt** = 'I firmly believe this to be true': 'He is without doubt one of the greatest composers the world has ever known.'
> **no doubt** = 'I expect' or 'I suppose': 'No doubt you could do with a drink.' 'They will no doubt be writing to us again.'

7 ✗ Another reason for getting married is without doubt to have children.

✓ **Another reason for getting married of course is to have children.**

Use **without doubt** with opinions and judgements: 'She is without doubt one of the kindest women you'll ever meet.'
When you mention a fact or something that is generally agreed, use **of course**: 'Mrs Thatcher is no longer in charge, of course.'

downstairs   ✗ I ran to downstairs and picked up the telephone.
✓ **I ran downstairs and picked up the telephone.**
✗ The dining room and kitchen are in the downstairs.
✓ **The dining room and kitchen are downstairs.**

Downstairs and **upstairs** are usually adverbs and are not used with **to/in/at** etc: 'The bathroom is upstairs.' 'I ran upstairs to see what all the noise was about.'

dozen   See Language Note at HUNDRED

drama   ✗ After the meal, we went to see a drama at the Cambridge Theatre.
✓ **After the meal, we went to see a play at the Cambridge Theatre.**

drama (uncountable) = a type of literature consisting of plays in general, or a particular group of plays: 'She has always been interested in music and drama.' 'Elizabethan drama is too bloodthirsty for my liking.'
play (countable) = a dramatic performance by actors in a theatre or on the radio/television; a piece of literature that has been written for actors to perform in a theatre etc: 'The film is a clever adaptation of Alan Ayckbourn's popular play.' 'The critics have generally been surprised by this play, which was written to be performed without props or scenery.'
Note that **drama** is sometimes used as a countable noun to refer to a specific type of play: 'We were expecting to see a comedy, not a serious drama.' When you simply mean 'a dramatic performance' (as opposed to a musical/ballet/opera etc), use **play**.

dream   ✗ I have always dreamed to visit America.
✓ **I have always dreamed of visiting America.**

dream of doing sth = think about something pleasant that you would like to happen: 'As a child, I used to dream of becoming a famous actress and living in a big house in Hollywood.'

dress 1   ✗ It took me half an hour to dress the kimono.
✓ **It took me half an hour to put on the kimono.**
See Language Note at WEAR

2   ✗ I had a shower and began to dress myself.
✓ **I had a shower and began to get dressed.**
See Language Note at WEAR

3   ✗ At work I have to dress a dark blue suit.
✓ **At work I have to wear a dark blue suit.**
See Language Note at WEAR

4   ✗ You should see the children's faces when we dress ourselves as clowns.

✓ **You should see the children's faces when we dress up as clowns.**
See Language Note at WEAR

5 ✗ She was dressed with a white blouse and blue skirt.
✓ **She was dressed in a white blouse and blue skirt.**
✗ Everybody was dressed with their smartest clothes.
✓ **Everybody was (dressed) in their smartest clothes.**
See Language Note at WEAR

dress up 1 ✗ I dressed up quickly and rushed out of the house.
✓ **I got dressed quickly and rushed out of the house.**
See Language Note at WEAR

2 ✗ Even though they don't have much money, their children are always dressed up smartly.
✓ **Even though they don't have much money, their children are always smartly dressed.**
See Language Note at WEAR

drive See AGAINST

drown 1 ✗ Nobody knows why the ship drowned.
✓ **Nobody know why the ship sank.**
See note at SINK

2 ✗ The boy was nearly drown.
✓ **The boy was drowning.**
✗ A man jumped into the river to save her from being drown.
✓ **A man jumped into the river to save her from drowning.**

> **drown** (verb) = die by being under the water and unable to breathe: 'Help him! He's drowning!' 'The lifeguard got to him too late. He had already drowned.' 'She keeps away from the water because she's afraid of drowning.'

drunken ✗ The man was obviously drunken.
✓ **The man was obviously drunk.**
✗ One of the two drunken men shouted at me.
✓ **One of the two drunks shouted at me.**

> **Drunken** is rarely used to describe a person. It usually describes an action or event: 'drunken driving', 'drunken laughter', 'a drunken brawl', 'a drunken orgy'. The exception is 'drunken drivers' (usually **drunk drivers** in AmE). **Drunken** always comes before a noun.
> To describe a person, use **drunk** (NOT **drunken**): 'I think he wanted to get us all drunk.' 'One of the students was always getting drunk.' **Drunk** is not used before a noun.
> When you mean 'a person who is drunk', use **a drunk**: 'A couple of drunks were causing a disturbance.'

dull ✗ If I did the same thing every day, I would be dull.
✓ **If I did the same thing every day, I would be bored.**
? It was such a dull job that I decided to leave.
✓ **It was such a boring job that I decided to leave.**

When **dull** is used to describe a person, it means 'slow to learn or understand': 'He was one of the dullest students I'd ever taught.'
Both **dull** and **boring** can mean 'uninteresting' but in this sense **dull** usually describes a lecture, book, film etc: 'The lecture was so dull that some of the students got up and left.'
bored = tired and uninterested: 'bored students'
boring = causing someone to be tired and uninterested: 'a boring lesson'

during 1
✗ After the accident, I had to stay in hospital during three months.
✓ **After the accident, I had to stay in hospital for three months.**
✗ It is difficult to concentrate during such a long time.
✓ **It is difficult to concentrate for such a long time.**

During answers the question 'When?': 'During her stay here, she made a lot of good friends.'
For answers the question 'How long?': 'I've been learning English for two years.' 'We've been waiting here for almost an hour.'

2
✗ My uncle has known me during all my life.
✓ **My uncle has known me all my life.**
✗ The baby cried during all night long.
✓ **The baby cried all night long.**

When a phrase saying 'how long' begins with **all**, there is no preposition: 'It rained all night.' 'He's been in bed all day.'

3
✗ During waiting for the train, I met an old friend of mine.
✓ **While waiting for the train, I met an old friend of mine.**
✗ This was my biggest problem during I was living in the United States.
✓ **This was my biggest problem while I was living in the United States.**

See note at WHILE 1

dust
✗ People eventually get ill from breathing in all the dusts and smoke.
✓ **People eventually get ill from breathing in all the dust and smoke.**

Dust is an uncountable noun: 'The house hadn't been lived in for a long time and the furniture was covered in dust.'

E*e*

each 1   ✗ We had to answer each questions on a new page.
         ✓ **We had to answer each question on a new page.**
         each + singular noun: 'Each child was given a balloon.'

2   ✗ Each of the nurses were very kind.
      ✓ **Each of the nurses was very kind.**
      ✗ Each of us have a room on the top floor.
      ✓ **Each of us has a room on the top floor.**
      each of + plural noun/pronoun + singular verb: 'Each of the three
      children was given a balloon.'

3   ✗ Each of us did not have an umbrella.
      ✓ **None/Neither of us had an umbrella.**
      See Language Note at NOT

4   ✗ They have each their own problems.
      ✓ **They each have their own problems.**
      See Language Note at ALWAYS

**each
other 1**   ✗ I hope that you will both write to each others.
          ✓ **I hope that you will both write to each other.**
          Each other has no plural form: 'We've been writing letters to each other
          for the last two years.'

2   ✗ We had to describe the pictures each other.
      ✓ **We had to describe the pictures to each other.**
      ✗ They live a long way each other.
      ✓ **They live a long way from each other.**
      You use prepositions in front of **each other** (pronoun) in the same way
      as you use prepositions in front of **him, her, us** etc. Compare: 'We talked
      to her.' 'We talked to each other.'
      See also ONE ANOTHER

earn   ✗ He earned a lot of money on the lottery.
         ✓ **He won a lot of money on the lottery.**
         You **earn** money by doing work for which you are paid: 'She earns
         $4,000 a month.'
         You **win** money by being lucky in a competition etc: 'The last time he
         played roulette, he won about $50,000.'

earnest   ✗ The earnest students never missed a class.
            ✓ **The serious students never missed a class.**

Earnest is used to describe someone who takes life too seriously, often failing to see things that are humorous: 'He's one of those very earnest types that go around looking for problems to solve.'
Serious is used to describe someone who is fully committed to something: 'I see her at the karate club once a week, but I don't think she's serious.'

earth 1
  ✗ I have friends in different parts of the earth.
  ✓ **I have friends in different parts of the world.**
  ✗ We must all work together to protect the earth.
  ✓ **We must all work together to protect the planet.**

earth/Earth = the ball-shaped object that we live on, usually seen as a planet in space: 'The earth moves round the sun every 365 days.' 'On the journey back to Earth, one of the spaceship's computers failed.'
world = the ball-shaped object that we live on, usually seen in terms of people, countries, cities etc: 'Tuberculosis is still common in some parts of the world.' 'It's one of the largest countries in the world.' 'You'll be seeing some of the world's leading golfers.'
Note the expression **all over the world** (= everywhere in the world): 'I have friends all over the world.'
planet = the ball-shaped object that we live on, usually seen in terms of the natural environment: 'This disaster could affect the whole planet.' 'The planet is gradually getting warmer.'

2
  ✗ The aliens were fascinated by life in earth.
  ✓ **The aliens were fascinated by life on earth.**
  ✗ Mankind has lived in the earth for thousands of years.
  ✓ **Mankind has lived on the earth for thousands of years.**

on (the) earth (NOT **in (the) earth**): 'Australia has some of the strangest animals to be found anywhere on earth.' 'Peace on earth is still just a dream.'

easily 1
  ✗ These computers can be used easily.
  ✓ **These computers are easy to use.**

subject + **be easy to use/make/read** etc: 'Her English is very easy to understand.' 'The old manager was much easier to get along with.'

2
  ✗ In London you easily get from one place to another.
  ✓ **In London it's easy to get from one place to another.**

It's easy (for sb) to do sth: 'It's easy to get lost in London.' 'It's easy to see why everyone likes him.'

3
  ✗ The next morning I didn't get up easily.
  ✓ **The next morning I found it difficult to get up.**
  ✓ **The next morning I had difficulty (in) getting up.**

Instead of using a negative verb with **easily,** use an affirmative verb with **difficult/difficulty**: 'I find Carl's handwriting very difficult to read.' 'Sometimes it's difficult to know what to do.'

East
  See NORTH

eat 1
  ✗ Instead of having a proper meal, he just eats a few pills.
  ✓ **Instead of having a proper meal, he just takes a few pills.**

take a pill, tablet, aspirin, medicine, etc (NOT **eat**): 'Why do you take sleeping pills every night?'

2   See BREAKFAST 3

economic 1 ✗ The main aim is to develop the country's economic.
     ✓ **The main aim is to develop the country's economy.**
       See Language Note below

2 ✗ Travelling around Spain is easy and economic.
   ✓ **Travelling around Spain is easy and inexpensive.**
     See Language Note below

ECONOMIC • ECONOMICAL • ECONOMICS • ECONOMIST • ECONOMY • INEXPENSIVE • SAVINGS

economic	**Economic** means connected with the economy of a country or region: 'The country's economic growth is considered to be too slow.'
economical	**Economical** describes something that is cheaper to use or operate than something similar: 'The house has a very economical heating system.' 'Gas or electricity? Which is more economical?' 'The large size is more economical.'
economics	**Economics** is (1) the study of how money is earned, spent and controlled within a country: 'He's now in his second year at Oxford, studying economics.' 'an economics graduate' (2) the financial aspects of something: 'the economics of dairy farming'
economist	An **economist** is an expert in economics: 'Economists remain undecided about what action should be taken.'
economy	**Economy** means (1) the financial and business system that exists in a country, which aims to produce wealth: 'The government's management of the economy has been severely criticized.' (2) a way of reducing the amount of money that is spent: 'The first economy to be introduced by the new government involved the reduction of fuel consumption.' (3) (used as a modifier) money-saving: 'Buy the giant economy size and save money!'
inexpensive	If something is **inexpensive**, it costs less than you might expect: 'This excellent but inexpensive hotel can be thoroughly recommended.' 'Denmark is famous for its friendly people and inexpensive accommodation.'
savings	**Savings** is money saved over a period of time, usually by a person or family: 'I'm paying for the course out of my own savings.' 'She invested her life savings in the new business.'

economical ✗ The undeveloped countries need economical support.
✓ **The undeveloped countries need economic support.**
✗ The economical crisis was caused by a sudden increase in the size of the population.
✓ **The economic crisis was caused by a sudden increase in the size of the population.**
See Language Note at ECONOMIC

economics1 ✗ My country has serious economics problems.
✓ **My country has serious economic problems.**
See Language Note at ECONOMIC

2 ✗ The Brazilian economics seem to be improving.
✓ **The Brazilian economy seems to be improving.**
See Language Note at ECONOMIC

edit ✗ I have never seen the magazine before – I think it's only just been edited.
✓ **I have never seen the magazine before – I think it's only just been published.**
✗ For the last three years I've been working for a French editing company.
✓ **For the last three years I've been working for a French publishing company.**

edit = examine and make changes and corrections to a manuscript in preparation for printing: 'The text was still full of mistakes and obviously hadn't been edited.'
publish = produce (a book, magazine, newspaper, etc) for sale to the public: 'The book was first published in 1987.'

education ✗ The education has changed my country a lot.
✓ **Education has changed my country a lot.**
✗ The goal is to provide the free education for every girl and boy.
✓ **The goal is to provide free education for every girl and boy.**
See THE 4

effect 1 ✗ I thought that the long illness would effect my chances of passing the exam.
✓ **I thought that the long illness would affect my chances of passing the exam.**

affect sth (verb) ≘ **have an effect on sth** (noun)
Compare: 'There is no doubt that smoking affects people's health.'
'There is no doubt that smoking has an effect on people's health.'
When used as a verb, **effect** means 'bring about': 'The new president effected several major changes.'

2 ✗ Many women stop smoking during pregnancy because of the effects to the baby.
✓ **Many women stop smoking during pregnancy because of the effects on the baby.**
effect on sb/sth: 'These rays can have a harmful effect on the skin.'

effective 1 ✗ British farmers receive only a little aid since their farms are relatively effective.
✓ **British farmers receive only a little aid since their farms are relatively efficient.**
See note at EFFICIENT

2 ✗ Aspirin is very effective to relieve pain.
✓ **Aspirin is very effective in relieving pain.**

be effective in doing sth: 'Doctors soon realized that this drug was also effective in relieving the symptoms of arthritis.'

effectively ✗ We finally got to see the secretary who confirmed that there was effectively a young man being held in prison.
✓ **We finally got to see the secretary who confirmed that there was indeed a young man being held in prison.**

Effectively is used to show that you are describing what a particular situation is really like, especially when this is not obvious: 'At that time, free elections in Zambia were unknown, and Kaunda had, effectively, made himself life-president.'
Indeed is used to confirm that something is true, especially something that a person suspects but is unsure about: 'I imagined that Rupert had gone back to the hotel and indeed it was there that I found him, splashing around in the pool.'

efficient ✗ The medicine proved very efficient.
✓ **The medicine proved very effective.**
✗ We need more efficient ways of dealing with pollution or the problem will get worse.
✓ **We need more effective ways of dealing with pollution or the problem will get worse.**

efficient = working quickly and without waste: 'The more efficient the engine, the less petrol it uses.' 'Since the new software was installed, library services have become much more efficient.'
effective = having the desired effect: 'There are many effective ways of using computers for training purposes.' 'The advertisement was simple, but remarkably effective.'

effort 1 ✗ The authorities have put a lot of efforts into making the streets cleaner.
✓ **The authorities have put a lot of effort into making the streets cleaner.**

When you mean 'the energy or hard work that is needed to do something', use **effort** (uncountable): 'Digging the tunnel demanded a great deal of effort.'
Compare: 'All our efforts to persuade Wendell to stay have failed.'

2 ✗ In my opinion, a holiday is a hopeless effort to relax.
✓ **In my opinion, a holiday is a hopeless attempt to relax.**

When someone tries to do something, especially without being sure of success, they make an **attempt** to do it: 'Having failed to reach the summit last October, the climbers are now getting ready to make a second attempt.' 'All attempts to control inflation have failed.'

3   ✗ Little effort has been done to solve the problem.
✓ **Little effort has been made to solve the problem.**
✗ Sometimes I have to do a great effort not to cry.
✓ **Sometimes I have to make a great effort not to cry.**

> **make an effort** (NOT **do**): 'The manager would like to see the whole team making more of an effort.' See Language Note at DO

either 1   ✗ I shall either go home to Brazil or my family will come to England.
✓ **Either I shall go home to Brazil or my family will come to England.**
✗ We either can go by bus or by car.
✓ **We can go either by bus or by car.**

> The position of **either** should be the same as the position of **or** (i.e. immediately before a subject, immediately before a main verb, immediately after a verb, etc): 'Either stay or go.' 'You should either stay or go.' 'You should stay either here or at home.' 'You should stay with either me or your uncle.'
> Note that this rule applies mainly in formal styles. In everyday conversation, **either** often goes immediately before the main verb: 'We can either go by bus or by car.'

2   ✗ In fact, a motorway wouldn't either disturb the animals because they are used to cars.
✓ **In fact, a motorway wouldn't disturb the animals either because they are used to cars.**

> When **either** is used after **not/never** etc, it goes at the end of the clause: 'John isn't going to the party, and Ray doesn't want to go either.'

elder 1   ✗ The restaurant seems to be more popular with elder people.
✓ **The restaurant seems to be more popular with older people.**
✗ The young man was unhurt but the elder one was taken to hospital in an ambulance.
✓ **The young man was unhurt but the older one was taken to hospital in an ambulance.**

> Do not use **elder** unless you are talking about the members of a family: 'her elder brother', 'my elder son'.

2   ✗ My sister is just two years elder than me.
✓ **My sister is just two years older than me.**

> Someone/something is **older** (**than** someone/something else): 'Their children are older than ours.' 'Her husband is five years older.'
> **Elder** is mainly used in front of a noun ('my elder sister') and as a pronoun ('Which of the two sisters is the elder?')

elderly   ✗ John, her elderly son, is still at university.
✓ **John, her elder son, is still at university.**

> **elderly** = old: 'an elderly man with white hair and a stick'
> **elder** = (of brothers, daughters etc) older: 'our elder daughter'

elect   ✗ Some people elect marriage partners who are totally unsuitable.
✓ **Some people choose marriage partners who are totally unsuitable.**

elect = choose (someone) by voting for them: 'The committee has elected a new chairman.'
choose = decide which one you want: 'We chose Greece because we hadn't been there before.'

ELECTRIC • ELECTRICAL • ELECTRONIC • ELECTRONICS

electric	**Electric** means carrying, producing, produced by, powered by, or charged with electricity: 'an electric wire', 'an electric generator', 'an electric shock', 'an electric current', 'an electric light bulb', 'an electric toaster' For machines and devices that are powered by electricity but do not have transistors, microchips, valves, etc, use **electric** (NOT **electronic**): 'an electric guitar', 'an electric train set', 'an electric razor'
electrical	**Electrical** means associated with electricity: 'electrical systems', 'a course in electrical engineering', 'an electrical engineer' To refer to the general class of things that are powered by electricity, use **electrical** (NOT **electric**): 'electrical equipment', 'We stock all the latest electrical kitchen appliances.'
electronic	**Electronic** is used to refer to equipment which is designed to work by means of an electric current passing through a large number of transistors, microchips, valves etc, and components of this equipment: 'an electronic calculator', 'tiny electronic components' Compare: 'an electronic calculator' BUT 'an electric oven' An **electronic** system is one that uses equipment of this type: 'electronic surveillance', 'e-mail' (= electronic mail, a system for sending messages very quickly by means of computers)
electronics	**Electronics** (WITH **s**) refers to (1) the branch of science and technology concerned with the study, design or use of electronic equipment: 'a student of electronics' (2) (used as a modifier) anything that is connected with this branch: 'the electronics industry'

electric   ✗   My father's company imports electric goods.
               ✓   **My father's company imports electrical goods.**
                  See Language Note above

electricity   ✗   Our lives depend on the electricity.
               ✓   **Our lives depend on electricity.**
                  See note at THE 4

electronic 1   ✗   I studied electronic and computers for three years.
                 ✓   **I studied electronics and computers for three years.**
                 ✗   I work for an electronic company.
                 ✓   **I work for an electronics company.**
                  See Language Note above

2 ✗ An electronic razor is fine until there is a power cut.
   ✓ **An electric razor is fine until there is a power cut.**
   See Language Note at ELECTRIC

else ✗ She said that she hadn't told anybody else than her husband.
   ✓ **She said that she hadn't told anybody other than her husband.**

> **other than** = apart from; except for (NOT **else than**): 'The two of us had nothing that was worth stealing other than my watch.'
> Compare: 'I'm tired of this programme; let's watch something else.'

emergency ✗ We were shown what to do if there was an emergency event.
   ✓ **We were shown what to do in an emergency (situation).**
   ✗ A basic understanding of car engines can be very useful, especially in emergency cases.
   ✓ **A basic understanding of car engines can be very useful, especially in emergencies.**

> **emergency** or **emergency situation**: 'Should you ever have to deal with an emergency, just stay calm and try not to panic.'

emphasis ✗ Both philosophies emphasis the individual.
   ✓ **Both philosophies emphasize the individual.**

> **Emphasis** is a noun: 'Modern society places emphasis on achievement.'
> The verb is **emphasize**: 'Modern society emphasizes achievement.'

emphasize ✗ My previous teacher emphasized on the importance of grammar.
   ✓ **My previous teacher emphasized the importance of grammar.**

> **emphasize sth** (verb) WITHOUT **on**: 'The candidate made a short speech emphasizing the need for solidarity.'
> **emphasis on sth** (noun): 'In all our courses there is an emphasis on student-centred learning.'

end 1 ✗ At the end I decided not to go.
   ✓ **In the end I decided not to go.**
   ✗ In the end of the dinner someone made a speech.
   ✓ **At the end of the dinner someone made a speech.**
   See Language Note opposite

2 ✗ In the end, I would like to wish you all a very interesting and enjoyable stay.
   ✓ **Finally, I would like to wish you all a very interesting and enjoyable stay.**
   See Language Note opposite

3 ✗ The film was ended at eight-thirty.
   ✓ **The film ended at eight-thirty.**

> The verb **end** is usually intransitive: 'The war ended in 1975.' 'When does the next programme end?' 'Just as the film was ending, the baby woke up.'
> When **end** is transitive, it means 'finish or stop something': 'I couldn't decide how to end the letter.' 'To end the meal we had some coffee and an ice-cream.'

4

✗ Since nobody would lend me the money, I ended asking my father for it.
✓ **Since nobody would lend me the money, I ended up asking my father for it.**
✗ The trouble with smoking is that you end with making a habit of it.
✓ **The trouble with smoking is that you end up making a habit of it.**
✗ Nowadays very few criminals end in jail.
✓ **Nowadays very few criminals end up in jail.**

FINALLY • IN THE END • EVENTUALLY • AT LAST AFTER ALL • AT THE END

finally/lastly	**Finally** and **lastly** are used (1) (at the beginning of a sentence) to introduce the last point in a speech, reply, essay, etc: 'Finally, I'd like to consider the economic arguments.' 'Lastly, I'd like to thank you all for coming and wish you a safe journey home.' (2) to introduce the last action in a sequence of actions or the last thing in a list: 'Finally, as soon as you hear a beep, press the start button.' 'She showed us the new dress, then the blouse, and lastly the shoes.
finally/eventually	**Finally** and **eventually** are used to show that something happens after a long time or delay: 'When the bus finally arrived it was full up.' 'Eventually the baby stopped crying and we managed to get some sleep.'
eventually/in the end	**Eventually** and **in the end** are used to introduce the result or outcome of something: 'In the end United won by three goals to two.' 'It seems more and more likely that the human race will eventually destroy itself.'
at last	**At last** means 'after a long period of waiting or trying to do something': 'I'm pleased to hear that you are out of hospital at last.' Unlike **eventually, at last** is often used in connection with the present situation, and expresses a sense of relief: 'I can't believe that we're actually getting on the plane at last.' 'Do you mean that you've really stopped smoking at last?'
after all	**After all** means 'despite what was planned, expected or believed': 'We stayed at home after all and watched the match on television.' 'I'm sorry to hear that you won't be coming to London after all.' **After all** is also used to remind someone of a fact which they should consider: 'I'm not surprised you're tired. After all, you didn't get any sleep last night.' 'Why are you so upset about losing? After all, it's only a game.'
at the end	**At the end** refers to the point where something finishes: 'Their house is at the end of the road.' 'Do you remember what happens at the end of the film?' Unlike **in the end, at the end** is usually followed by **of**: ' at the end of the lesson/course/road/year'.
	See also Language Note at FIRST

end = finish or cause (something) to finish: 'The lessons usually end at five o'clock but some teachers end their lessons early.'
end up = (1) be forced to do something (after everything else has failed): 'For months she refused to pay us any rent, so we ended up taking her to court.' (2) eventually find yourself in a particular place or condition: 'If you don't stop smoking, you'll end up in hospital.'

end up

✗ The talk was followed by a film which ended up at midnight.
✓ **The talk was followed by a film which ended at midnight.**
✗ I shall have to end up my letter here.
✓ **I shall have to end my letter here.**

See note at END 4

endure 1

✗ More than 160 million people endure malaria.
✓ **More than 160 million people suffer from malaria.**

endure a painful or very unpleasant situation: 'The people in this country have had to endure almost a decade of economic hardship.'
suffer from/with a disease or medical condition: 'My youngest son suffers from asthma.'

2

✗ Some people cannot endure the idea of devoting themselves to children.
✓ **Some people cannot bear the idea of devoting themselves to children.**

When you mean 'strongly dislike' or 'be unable to accept', use **can't bear/stand**: 'He used to like cricket, but now he can't stand it.' 'He couldn't bear the thought of his wife leaving him.'

energetic

✗ Our main energetic source is nuclear power.
✓ **Our main energy source is nuclear power.**

energetic = active and able to work or play for a long time: 'Does anyone feel energetic enough to go for another swim?' 'My mother was a bustling energetic woman, always in a hurry, always busy.'
energy = the power obtained from oil, coal, the sun, etc: 'Oil is not only an expensive source of energy, it's running out.' 'There should be more research into solar energy.'

engage

✗ Simon gave me the ring when we engaged.
✓ **Simon gave me the ring when we got engaged.**

be/get engaged: 'When did you get engaged?' 'We were engaged for almost a year before we finally got married.'

engaged

✗ Why did you get engaged with Paul if you don't want to marry him?
✓ **Why did you get engaged to Paul if you don't want to marry him?**

be/get engaged to sb: 'When we first met, she was already engaged to an airline pilot.'

engine

✗ I was amazed that such a small engine could hold so much information.
✓ **I was amazed that such a small machine could hold so much information.**

See note at MACHINE

English   ✗ She's going to get married to an English.
          ✓ **She's going to get married to an Englishman.**

          an Englishman, an Englishwoman (NOT **an English**): 'She was the very first Englishwoman to set foot on the moon.'

enjoy 1   ✗ I enjoy to speak foreign languages.
          ✓ **I enjoy speaking foreign languages.**

          enjoy doing sth: 'I wouldn't enjoy sitting at a desk all day.'

2   ✗ During the Christmas holidays I really enjoyed.
          ✓ **During the Christmas holidays I really enjoyed myself.**
          See Language Note at MYSELF

enough   ✗ The car parking facilities are not enough.
          ✓ **There are not enough car parking facilities.**
          ✗ The time isn't enough for us to catch the next train.
          ✓ **There isn't enough time for us to catch the next train.**

          Enough usually goes in front of the noun it refers to: 'Do you have enough money?' 'There aren't enough teachers.' For this reason, the sentence often begins with **there is/are** etc: 'Is there enough hot water for a bath?'

enquiry   See note at INQUIRY

ensure   ✗ We ensure you that we will do our best.
          ✓ **We assure you that we will do our best.**

          ensure = make certain (that something will happen or exist): 'We need to ensure that our prices remain competitive.' 'Measures are being taken to ensure public safety.'
          assure = tell someone that something will definitely happen or is definitely true, especially to make them feel less worried: 'I assure you that the report will be on your desk by tomorrow lunchtime at the latest.' 'The doctor assured me that there was no need for alarm.'

enter 1   ✗ The number of foreign workers that are allowed to enter into Japan has increased.
          ✓ **The number of foreign workers that are allowed to enter Japan has increased.**

          enter a room, building, country etc (WITHOUT **into**): 'Whenever a teacher entered the room, the children had to stand up.'

2   ✗ I entered the train in Oslo.
          ✓ **I got on the train in Oslo.**
          ✓ **I boarded the train in Oslo.**

          get on/board a train/plane/ship: 'The ticket inspector wanted to know where I had got on.' 'There's still time for some duty-free shopping before we have to board the plane.'

3   ✗ Unfortunately, some of my classmates didn't enter university.
          ✓ **Unfortunately, some of my classmates didn't get into university.**

          get into (a) college, university etc (= be admitted to): 'What qualifications do you need to get into medical school?'

entertain- ment

✗ The town offers all sorts of entertainments.
✓ **The town offers all sorts of entertainment.**

Entertainment (= all the things that provide amusement) is an uncountable noun: 'As far as entertainment is concerned, we usually go to the discotheque.'

equipment

✗ They were not satisfied with the new equipments.
✓ **They were not satisfied with the new equipment.**
✗ It's a useful equipment and I intend to have it repaired.
✓ **It's a useful piece of equipment and I intend to have it repaired.**

Equipment is an uncountable noun: 'The school is trying to raise funds to buy some new sports equipment.'

especially 1 ✗ The course has been especially designed for students preparing for the First Certificate examination.
✓ **The course has been specially designed for students preparing for the First Certificate examination.**

See note at SPECIALLY 1

2 ✗ In the south of Germany there is a different mentality. Especially the Bavarians are very lively and cheerful.
✓ **In the south of Germany there is a different mentality. The Bavarians especially are very lively and cheerful.**
✗ Looking after children can be very tiring. Especially young children need a lot of attention.
✓ **Looking after children can be very tiring. Young children especially need a lot of attention.**

Especially cannot come at the beginning of a sentence. Put it after the subject (NOT in front of the subject): 'This year's examination results are surprisingly good. The girls especially have done better than we expected.'

establish

✗ I want to establish a cooperative store.
✓ **I want to open a cooperative store.**

You **establish** a major company or organization that will probably run forever or for a very long time: 'As soon as Rwanda became independent, it established its own national bank.' 'Most of the money is to be used to establish local industries and mobilize the workforce.'
You **start** or **start up** a small company or organization: 'They intend to use the money to start up their own taxi business.'
You **open** a new shop, restaurant, shopping mall etc: 'They're planning to open a small hotel just outside town.'

estimate 1 ✗ Her master's thesis was highly estimated and is now being prepared for publication.
✓ **Her master's thesis was highly esteemed and is now being prepared for publication.**

estimate = calculate an amount or price without being exact: 'The police department estimates that the number of crimes will increase this year by about 15%.' 'At that point, the public sector deficit was estimated to be around £45 billion.' 'The population of Adelaide is estimated at 917,000.'
be highly esteemed/thought of = be greatly admired, especially by a large number of people: 'In the world of fashion, his work is highly thought of.'

2   ✗ Each of us gave a short talk and then we had to estimate each other's performance.

     ✓ **Each of us gave a short talk and then we had to assess each other's performance.**

> **assess** = consider something carefully and give an opinion about how good or bad it is: 'Parents should be shown how to assess the quality of a school.' 'This test provides a simple means of assessing an applicant's suitability.'

even 1   ✗ Even I go to bed early, I'm still tired in the morning.

     ✓ **Even when I go to bed early, I'm still tired in the morning.**

> To introduce a subordinate clause, use **even if, even though** or **even when** (NOT **even** on its own): 'You'll have to accept the invitation, even though you don't want to.' 'Even when my father is angry, he never raises his voice.'

2   ✗ Even though I paid her for the room, but I knew she would prefer to live alone.

     ✓ **Even though I paid her for the room, I knew she would prefer to live alone.**

> See note at BUT

3   ? Many people think that it even snows in Norway in the summer.

     ✓ **Many people think that it snows in Norway even in the summer.**

> When there is a danger of confusion, put **even** immediately before the word or phrase that you want to emphasize (the 'surprising' part of the sentence).

4   ✗ In the future it even might be possible to work only thirty-five hours a week.

     ✓ **In the future it might even be possible to work only thirty-five hours a week.**

> See Language Note at ALWAYS

evening   See Language Note at TIME

eventually 1   ✗ I am pleased to be able to write to you eventually.

     ✓ **I am pleased to be able to write to you at (long) last.**

> See Language Note at END

2   ✗ You will be informed of the committee's decision eventually.

     ✓ **You will be informed of the committee's decision in due course.**

> When you mean that something will be done at the appropriate time (remembering that other things have to be done first), use **in due course**: 'The 300 new computers have now been received and arrangements for their distribution will be made in due course.'

etc   ✗ They make televisions, radios, and etc.

     ✓ **They make televisions, radios, etc.**

> **And** is not used with **etc**: 'On the first floor they sell washing machines, dishwashers, spin driers, etc.'

ever 1

✗ He has ever been my hero.
✓ **He has always been my hero.**

> **ever** = at any time: 'Have you ever been to Paris?'
> **always** = from the beginning until now; every time: 'He's always been very generous.' 'She always arrives late.'

2

✗ She was the most unpleasant person that I had ever met before.
✓ **She was the most unpleasant person that I had ever met.**

> **ever** (used with a verb in the present perfect or past perfect tense) = at any time before now/then: 'It's one of nicest houses I've ever seen.'

3

✗ I'm surprised that nobody ever has thought of it.
✓ **I'm surprised that nobody has ever thought of it.**

See Language Note at ALWAYS

every 1

✗ There was a representative from every countries.
✓ **There was a representative from every country.**
✗ Every mornings I give him his breakfast.
✓ **Every morning I give him his breakfast.**

> **every** + singular count noun: 'I understood every word.'

2

✗ Every job have its good points.
✓ **Every job has its good points.**

> **every** + noun + singular verb: 'Every child was given a red balloon.'

3

✗ I have to visit the hospital every six week.
✓ **I have to visit the hospital every six weeks.**

> 'every day', 'every week' BUT 'every two days', 'every six weeks'

4

✗ On every Saturday afternoon I play tennis.
✓ **Every Saturday afternoon I play tennis.**

See Language Note at TIME

5

See PERSON 1, PEOPLE 1

6

See TIME 6

7

✗ The shop sells every thing, from toothbrushes to radios.
✓ **The shop sells everything, from toothbrushes to radios.**

> **Every thing** (two words) is not common and is used only when things are considered as separate items: 'She worries about every silly little thing.'

8

✗ This example shows how computers affect our every day life.
✓ **This example shows how computers affect our everyday life.**

See note at EVERYBODY

9

✗ Every one was tired of listening to her voice.
✓ **Everyone was tired of listening to her voice.**

See note at EVERYONE 1

10   ✗   There aren't enough jobs for every body.
         ✓   **There aren't enough jobs for everybody.**

> **everybody** (one word) = each person; everyone: 'One day everybody will be able to travel to the moon.'
> **every body** (two words) = each (dead) body: 'Every body was collected from the battlefield and given a proper burial.'

everybody 1   ✗   Everybody have to work.
            ✓   **Everybody has to work.**

> **Everybody, everyone** and **everything** are used with a singular verb: 'Everybody was tired of waiting.' 'During the first few days, everything was new to me.'

2   ✗   Everybody does not like studying when they are that age.
     ✓   **Nobody likes studying when they are that age.**
       See Language Note at NOT

everyday   ✗   The sun shines here everyday.
         ✓   **The sun shines here every day.**

> **everyday** (one word) = not special or unusual in any way: 'A good photographer can make everyday objects look rare and special.'
> **every day** (two words) = each day: 'Every day I try to learn ten new words.'

everyone 1   ✗   This problem affects each and everyone of us.
          ✓   **This problem affects each and every one of us.**

> **everyone** = all the people: 'Hurry up! Everyone is waiting for you.'
> **every one** = each single one (of a group or number): 'When we examined the books we found that every one of them had a page missing.'

2   See EVERYBODY

everything   See EVERYBODY

evidence   ✗   There are no reliable evidences to suggest that the situation is improving.
        ✓   **There is no reliable evidence to suggest that the situation is improving.**
        ✗   This true story provides an evidence of the power of advertising.
        ✓   **This true story provides evidence of the power of advertising.**

> **Evidence** is an uncountable noun: 'Medical evidence suggests that men are more likely to have heart attacks than women.'

exam/examination 1   ✗   It happened a few years ago when I was making my university entrance exams.
        ✓   **It happened a few years ago when I was taking my university entrance exams.**

> **take/sit (for)/have/do an examination** (NOT **make**): 'Of all the students who took the exam, only 45% passed.' 'I sit my final exams next July. Note that **sit (for)** an examination is not used in American English.

2 ✗ Unfortunately, I didn't pass in the exam.
　 ✓ **Unfortunately, I didn't pass the exam.**

> **pass/fail an examination** (WITHOUT **in**): 'She passed all six examinations at the first attempt.'
> Compare: 'I passed the written paper but failed (on) the oral test.' 'She did well in chemistry but failed (in) maths.'

example 1 ✗ Medicine is a good example for something that we pass from one generation to the next.
　 ✓ **Medicine is a good example of something that we pass from one generation to the next.**

> **an example of sth** (NOT **for**): 'He is a classic example of a man who cannot control his ambition.'

2 ✗ A manager is supposed to give a good example.
　 ✓ **A manager is supposed to set a good example.**

> **set an example** or **set a good example** = behave correctly so that the people who copy you will behave correctly: 'The school captain is expected to set a good example.'
> Compare: 'Instead of trying to explain the theory, he just gave us a few good examples.'

except 1 ✗ Except smoke and traffic fumes, there are several other types of pollution.
　 ✓ **Besides smoke and traffic fumes, there are several other types of pollution.**

> **except** = not including; but not: 'She eats everything except fish.'
> **besides** = in addition to: 'Besides football, he also plays tennis and badminton.'

2 ✗ The old lady never spoke to anyone except someone came to visit her.
　 ✓ **The old lady never spoke to anyone unless someone came to visit her.**
　 ✓ **The old lady never spoke to anyone except when someone came to visit her.**

> **Except** (a preposition) cannot be followed by a clause that has a finite verb ('came'). Use **unless** (a conjunction) or **except when, except while, except if, except that**: 'Americans are just like any other people in the world, except that they are more tolerant.' 'He tends to ignore me except when he needs something.'

3 ✗ I had never really spoken to him except saying hello.
　 ✓ **I had never really spoken to him except to say hello.**

> When you are talking about purpose, use **except** + to-v: 'I rarely go the market, except to buy vegetables.'

4 ✗ They want nothing except seeing that the children are happy.
　 ✓ **They want nothing except to see that the children are happy.**
　 ✗ My brother is good at everything except to wash the dishes.
　 ✓ **My brother is good at everything except washing the dishes.**

> The choice of verb form after **except** is sometimes determined by a word that comes earlier in the sentence, e.g. **want** + to-v, **good at** + v-ing.

5   ✗   In their free time they do nothing except going from one cafeteria to another.
     ✓   **In their free time they do nothing except go from one cafeteria to another.**
     ✗   She was willing to do anything except to tell me her name.
     ✓   **She was willing to do anything except tell me her name.**

> **do** (anything/nothing/what you like etc) + **except** + bare infinitive: 'There was nothing I could do except sit and wait.'

exception   ✗   Every major city keeps changing and Lisbon is not an exception.
     ✓   **Every major city keeps changing and Lisbon is no exception.**

> **Be no exception** is a fixed phrase: 'I never go out on Sundays, and this Sunday is no exception.'

exchange   ✗   Is it possible to exchange the camera with a new one?
     ✓   **Is it possible to exchange the camera for a new one?**

> **exchange sth for sth** (NOT **with**): 'The government is issuing coupons that can be exchanged for food.'

exciting   ✗   It is wonderful to be in London at last. I feel so exciting.
     ✓   **It is wonderful to be in London at last. I feel so excited.**

> See note at BORING

excuse 1   ✗   Excuse me. I didn't know that you wanted to speak to me.
     ✓   **I'm sorry. I didn't know that you wanted to speak to me.**
     ✗   Excuse me. I didn't mean to hurt you.
     ✓   **I'm sorry. I didn't mean to hurt you.**

> Use **excuse me** (1) when you interrupt someone (2) when you are trying to get past someone (3) when you speak to someone you don't know: 'Excuse me but there's a long distance phone call for you.' 'Excuse me. Do you happen to know the way to the station?'
> To apologize to someone, use **I'm sorry** (or just **sorry**): 'I'm terribly sorry. I forgot we'd arranged a meeting.'

2   ✗   When he got back home he excused himself and promised that he would never run away again.
     ✓   **When he got back home he apologized and promised that he would never run away again.**

> **excuse oneself** = give a reason for one's actions: 'She excused herself from the meeting, saying that she wasn't feeling well.'
> **apologize** = say you are sorry for (doing) something: 'The bank wrote to apologize for overcharging me.'

3   ✗   He was sorry that he had lied to her and asked her to excuse him.
     ✓   **He was sorry that he had lied to her and asked her to forgive him.**

> **Excuse** is used only for minor faults and offences: 'I hope you'll excuse my untidy handwriting. I'm trying to write this letter on a train.'
> **Forgive** is used for all faults and offences, both minor and major: 'I don't think he'll ever forgive me for calling off the wedding.' 'Don't forget her birthday or she'll never forgive you.'

exercise 1 ✗ Before breakfast I do exercise and then have a shower.
✓ **Before breakfast I do some exercises and then have a shower.**
✗ I advise you to take as many exercises as you can.
✓ **I advise you to take as much exercise as you can.**
✓ **I advise you to exercise as much as you can.**

exercise (countable noun) = a movement or set of movements that you do regularly to keep or make (a part of) your body strong and healthy: 'These exercises will help to develop your calf muscles.' 'Sometimes he forgets to do his exercises.'
exercise (uncountable noun) = physical activity such as walking, swimming etc: 'The doctor says I don't get enough exercise.'
exercise (verb) = walk, jog, swim etc to stay healthy: 'Just because you're on a diet, it doesn't mean that you don't need to exercise.'

2 ✗ Make sure that you eat properly and don't forget to make your exercises.
✓ **Make sure that you eat properly and don't forget to do your exercises.**

do your exercises (NOT **make**): 'Always warm up before you start doing these exercises.' See Language Note at DO

3 ✗ You will never be able to speak fluently unless you do exercise.
✓ **You will never be able to speak fluently unless you practise.**

practise = do something regularly in order to develop a skill: 'Your driving will never improve if you don't practise.' 'If we're planning to go to Montreal next summer, I'll have to practise my French.' 'Whenever I start practising the violin, everyone leaves the room.'

exhausting ✗ An exhausting investigation finally revealed the cause of the accident.
✓ **An exhaustive investigation finally revealed the cause of the accident.**

exhausting = causing tiredness: 'Pushing the car uphill was exhausting.'
exhaustive = so thorough or complete that not even the smallest detail or possibility is missed: 'Following exhaustive inquiries, the police are at last able to issue a description of the suspects.'

exist ✗ The problem of hunger has been existing for centuries.
✓ **The problem of hunger has existed for centuries.**

See Language Note at CONTAIN

expand 1 ✗ I'm doing the course to expand my job opportunities.
✓ **I'm doing the course to increase my job opportunities.**

expand = become (or make something become) larger in size, area or activity: 'Metals expand when they are heated.' 'Within three years this small business had expanded into a chain of department stores.'
increase = become (or make something become) larger in number, amount, cost, etc: 'Sales of new cars increased from 1.2 million in 1993 to 1.8 million in 1994.' 'By the year 2020 the government aims to increase the number of secondary schools by 50%.'

2 ✗ The epidemic began to expand rapidly.
✓ **The epidemic began to spread rapidly.**

> When you are talking about a disease, fire, war, social problem, feeling, etc, use **spread**: 'The army was called in to stop the riots from spreading.' 'Dissatisfaction with the present government seems to be spreading.'

3 ✗ The newspapers are not allowed to expand political ideas.
✓ **The newspapers are not allowed to spread political ideas.**

> When you are talking about news, information, ideas, etc, use **spread**: 'Within hours the news of the bank's collapse had spread all over the world.' 'I hope you haven't been spreading rumours.'

expect 1 ✗ After a few minutes he stopped speaking and expected their reaction.
✓ **After a few minutes he stopped speaking and waited for their reaction.**
✗ She was standing by the reception desk, expecting a taxi.
✓ **She was standing by the reception desk, waiting for a taxi.**

> Use **expect** when you are talking about what someone thinks: 'We expected that the hotels in London would be very expensive, and we were right.' 'No one expected the President to resign.'
> Use **wait for** when you are talking about what someone does: 'How long do you usually have to wait for a bus?' 'I sat down and waited for my name to be called.'

2 ✗ I expect that you will be able to come to the party.
✓ **I hope that you will be able to come to the party.**

> Use **expect** when you have a reason for thinking that something is going to happen: 'Her husband doesn't like travelling so I expect she'll come on her own.'
> Use **hope** to express a wish: 'I hope you have a safe journey.'

3 ✗ I expect your visit and hope that you will be writing soon with the details.
✓ **I'm looking forward to your visit and hope that you will be writing soon with the details.**

> To say that you feel happy or excited about a future event, use **look forward to**: 'I'm really looking forward to this trip to Japan.' 'I look forward to meeting you at the Frankfurt Book Fair.'
> Note that **look forward to** (NOT **expect**) is often used at the end of a letter: 'I look forward to hearing from you.'

4 ✗ You can expect that you won't be put in the same class as Helga.
✓ **You can't expect to be put in the same class as Helga.**
See Language Note at NOT

expensive ✗ Prices in Britain are not as expensive as in Japan.
✓ **Prices in Britain are not as high as in Japan.**
✗ The disadvantage is that the cost is very expensive.
✓ **The disadvantage is that the cost is very high.**
See note at CHEAP 1

experience ✗ I made my first teaching experience in Scotland.
1 ✓ **I had my first teaching experience in Scotland.**
✗ While I was going home, I made a bad experience.

✓ **While I was going home, I had a bad experience.**

have an experience (NOT **make**): 'The streets were full of beggars and we had one or two very unpleasant experiences.'
See Language Note at DO

2 ✗ If I go to England, I'll have a lot of experiences.
✓ **If I go to England, I'll have a lot of new experiences.**

When **experience** means 'something that happens to you', it is usually modified: 'The book is based on her experiences as a reporter in El Salvador.' 'Don't give up just because of one bad experience.' 'The trip to Niagara Falls was an unforgettable experience.'

3 ✗ I hadn't made any experience of changing a car wheel.
✓ **I hadn't had any experience of changing a car wheel.**

have no/little/some/considerable etc **experience** (NOT **make**): 'Most of the school inspectors had at least ten years' teaching experience.'
See Language Note at DO

4 ✗ I knew that he had no experience driving in the dark.
✓ **I knew that he had no experience of driving in the dark.**
✗ Older people have had more experience in life.
✓ **Older people have had more experience of life.**

have no/little/some/considerable etc **experience of (doing)** sth
'Do you have any previous experience of looking after children?'

5 ✗ Many of us have had experiences of living overseas.
✓ **Many of us have had experience of living overseas.**

When you are talking about someone's life as a whole, **experience** is uncountable: 'Salary will depend upon qualifications and experience.'

experi-
ment 1 ✗ They shouldn't be allowed to make these experiments.
✓ **They shouldn't be allowed to perform these experiments.**

perform/conduct/carry out/do an experiment (NOT **make**): 'Further experiments will have to be conducted before the drug can be tested on humans.'
See Language Note at DO

2 ✗ I agree that it is wrong to experiment with animals.
✓ **I agree that it is wrong to experiment on animals.**

experiment on a person or animal: 'Experiments on twins have shown that the human mind has mysterious powers.'
Compare: 'Doctors are experimenting with a new drug that, they hope, will provide a cure for the common cold.'

explain ✗ Your teachers will explain you where you are going to stay.
✓ **Your teachers will explain to you where you are going to stay.**

If you mention a person after **explain**, you always use **to**: 'Let me explain the problem (to you) again.' 'She then explained (to me) how I could make my own shampoo.'

explode ✗ The hijackers threatened to explode the plane.
✓ **The hijackers threatened to blow up the plane.**

People **blow up** buildings, planes etc. Bombs, fuel tanks etc **explode**. Compare: 'They had planned to blow up the bridge but their bombs failed to explode.'

expose   ✗ His paintings have been exposed in art galleries all over the world.
         ✓ **His paintings have been exhibited in art galleries all over the world.**

expose = let something be seen, especially something that is usually hidden: 'He undid his shirt to expose a white hairless chest.'
display/exhibit a work of art: 'The gallery exhibits mainly contemporary sculpture and photography.'

extinguish   ✗ Many species are becoming extinguished.
            ✓ **Many species are becoming extinct.**

extinguish = make something stop burning: 'Before entering the factory, please make sure that all cigarettes have been properly extinguished.'
extinct = (of a type of animal or plant) completely non-existent, because every single one has died or been killed: 'If nothing is done to save the whales now, the species will soon become extinct.'

extreme   ✗ Since he stopped smoking, there has been an extreme improvement in his health.
          ✓ **Since he stopped smoking, there has been a dramatic improvement in his health.**
          ✗ Doctors have to keep up with all the extreme new medical developments.
          ✓ **Doctors have to keep up with all the major new medical developments.**

Extreme is mainly used to describe situations, behaviour, opinions and beliefs: 'extreme poverty', 'extreme caution', 'extreme views', 'extreme disappointment'.
When you are talking about a change or development, use words such as **great/major/important/considerable/dramatic**: 'Without these major changes, the company would have collapsed.'

extremely   ✗ I'm extremely convinced that there will not be another war.
            ✓ **I'm absolutely convinced that there will not be another war.**
            See note at VERY 2

face 1   ✗ The house faces to a very busy road.
　　　　　✓ **The house faces a very busy road.**
　　　　　✗ It faces to the Gulf of Mexico.
　　　　　✓ **It faces the Gulf of Mexico.**

> **face sb/sth** (WITHOUT **to**): 'The apartments facing the sea are more expensive.' 'They stood facing each other, but neither of them spoke.'

2　　　✗ We now face with a totally different situation.
　　　　　✓ **We now face a totally different situation.**
　　　　　✓ **We are now faced with a totally different situation.**

> **face** a fact, problem or situation (WITHOUT **with/up**): 'You'll have to face the problem sooner or later.' 'As a result of the drought, the people will face food shortages.' 'If found guilty, he faces life imprisonment.'
> **be faced with/by**: 'As a police officer, I'm often faced with the task of breaking bad news to relatives.'

3　　　✗ I didn't like the silly smile in his face.
　　　　　✓ **I didn't like the silly smile on his face.**
　　　　　✗ She always wears a lot of make-up in her face.
　　　　　✓ **She always wears a lot of make-up on her face.**

> Someone has something **on** their **face** (NOT **in**): 'You look like a ghost with all that powder on your face.' 'I could see from the look on her face that she wasn't interested.'

4　　　✗ These problems are just two faces of the same coin.
　　　　　✓ **These problems are just two sides of the same coin.**

> **two sides of the same coin** (= two ways of looking at the same situation): 'Unemployment and social unrest are basically two sides of the same coin.'

fact 1   ✗ In my own country, Saudi Arabia, in fact the government faces many problems.
　　　　　✓ **In my own country, Saudi Arabia, the government faces many problems.**

> See Language Note opposite

2　　　✗ 'Is the operation really necessary?' – 'Well, in fact, if he doesn't have it, he could die.'
　　　　　✓ **'Is the operation really necessary?' – 'Well, the fact is (that) if he doesn't have it, he could die.'**

> See Language Note opposite

3　　　✗ These advertisements are misleading. As a matter of fact, you have to pay for everything in the end.

IN FACT • AS A MATTER OF FACT
• THE FACT IS (THAT) • ACTUALLY

- To develop a previous statement, you usually use **in fact** or **as a matter of fact**:

  The winter of 1940 was very bad. <u>In fact</u>, most people say it was the worst winter they had ever experienced.
  Martin doesn't like his new job. <u>As a matter of fact</u>, he's thinking of leaving.

- Do not use **in fact** or **as a matter of fact** in general or introductory statements:

  In the last two decades advances in technology have changed the face of industry. (NOT 'have in fact changed')

- To correct what someone thinks or supposes, use **in fact**, **as a matter of fact** or **actually**:

  'He's a friend of yours, isn't he?' 'No, he isn't. <u>As a matter of fact</u>, I've just met him.'
  People think they've got lots of money, but <u>in fact</u> they're quite poor.'
  'I'm sorry to have kept you waiting.' 'Well <u>actually</u> I've only just arrived.'

- Use **the fact is (that)** to introduce your main point, especially when this explains the real truth about a particular situation:

  'I'm not surprised that he's looking worried. <u>The fact is (that)</u> he's been spending more than he earns.'
  'We don't really want to go but <u>the fact is (that)</u> we don't have any choice.'

    ✓ **These advertisements are misleading. The fact is (that) you have to pay for everything in the end.**
    ✗ Even if you feel nervous, don't show it. As a matter of fact, the horse will soon sense it if you are afraid.
    ✓ **Even if you feel nervous, don't show it. The fact is (that) the horse will soon sense it if you are afraid.**
    See Language Note above

4   ✗ On the other hand, I agree to the fact that laws are necessary.
    ✓ **On the other hand, I accept the fact that laws are necessary.**
    ✗ I agree with the fact that politics and ecology will never go hand in hand.
    ✓ **I accept the fact that politics and ecology will never go hand in hand.**

    accept/appreciate the fact that ... (NOT **agree to/with the fact that ...**): 'I appreciate the fact that funds are limited.'

factory 1   ✗ The wheat is collected and sent to the flour factory.
    ✓ **The wheat is collected and sent to the flour mill.**
    ✗ The brick factory was closed down during the recession.
    ✓ **The brick works was closed down during the recession.**
    ✗ Just outside the town there is a large chemical factory.
    ✓ **Just outside the town there is a large chemical plant.**
    See Language Note at INDUSTRY

2   ✗ They intend to build either a sports centre or a factory of shoes.
    ✓ **They intend to build either a sports centre or a shoe factory.**
    Put **factory** after the thing that is produced: 'a bottle factory', 'a clothing factory'.

fail   See note at EXAM/EXAMINATION 2

faithfully   See YOURS

fall 1   ✗ This problem has been caused by a fall of the birth rate.
      ✓ **This problem has been caused by a fall in the birth rate.**

   a fall in an amount, rate, level, standard etc: 'Sharp falls in house prices have renewed the interest of the first-time buyer.'

2   See GROUND 6

fall down 1   ✗ She looked at me with tears falling down from her eyes.
      ✓ **She looked at me with tears falling from her eyes.**
      ✗ We sat there watching the leaves falling down from the trees.
      ✓ **We sat there watching the leaves falling from the trees.**

   To refer to the natural downward movement of rain, snow, tears, leaves etc, use **fall** (WITHOUT **down**): 'The rain began to fall more heavily.'

2   ✗ One of the horses suddenly stopped and the rider fell down.
      ✓ **One of the horses suddenly stopped and the rider fell off.**

   fall off a chair, ladder, bicycle, horse, etc: 'One minute she was sitting on the edge of the chair and the next minute she'd fallen off.' 'If you fall off the ladder, try not to spill the paint.'

familiarize   ✗ I would like to familiarize with the latest teaching methods.
      ✓ **I would like to familiarize myself with the latest teaching methods.**

   See Language Note at MYSELF

fantastic   ✗ The shops in London are very fantastic.
      ✓ **The shops in London are absolutely fantastic.**

   See note at VERY 2

fantasy   ✗ Were the voices real or just products of his fantasy?
      ✓ **Were the voices real or just products of his imagination?**

   fantasy = a picture in the mind produced by the imagination, especially one which is very different from reality: 'He lived in a world of fantasy.'
   imagination = (the part of the mind with) the ability to produce mental pictures: 'Unlike adults, young children are usually full of imagination.' 'His paintings show great technical skill but a lack of imagination.'

far 1   ✗ Singapore is far from London.
      ✓ **Singapore is a long way from London.**
      ✗ 'It's far to the nearest garage,' she said.
      ✓ **'It's a long way to the nearest garage,' she said.**

   Far is mainly used in questions and negative sentences: 'How far is it to the station?' 'Oxford isn't far from London.' 'It's not far.'
   In affirmative sentences, people usually say **a long way**: 'Their house is a long way from the town centre.'
   Far is used in affirmative sentences only when it appears in phrases such as **too far, quite far** or **far away**: 'I suggest you take the bus - it's too far to walk.'

2 ✗ When the bomb exploded, everyone tried to get as far as possible.
✓ **When the bomb exploded, everyone tried to get as far away as possible.**

A place that is a long distance from another place is **far away**: 'Her children all live far away, but they still manage to visit her.'

3 ✗ My village is about 10 minutes far away from Ayia Napa.
✓ **My village is about 10 minutes (away) from Ayia Napa.**

Far cannot be used after a unit of distance. Compare: 'The house is rather far from the school.' (WITHOUT unit of distance) 'The house is about two kilometres (away) from the school.' (WITH unit of distance)

Far East See MIDDLE EAST

farm ✗ I'd like to stay in a farm where you can eat homemade food.
✓ **I'd like to stay on a farm where you can eat homemade food.**

You live/work/stay **on a farm** (NOT **in**): 'I wouldn't like to work on a farm during the winter.'

fascinated ✗ I was very fascinated by the speed with which they worked.
✓ **I was (absolutely) fascinated by the speed with which they worked.**

See note at VERY 2

fat ? His wife is a little bit too fat.
✓ **His wife is slightly overweight.**
? He's got very fat since we last saw each other.
✓ **He's put on a lot of weight since we last saw each other.**

In western society being fat is considered to be unattractive. The word **fat** is common but it is not polite. To say the same thing in a less direct way, use words such as **overweight** (weighing more than is normal), **plump** (having a pleasantly rounded shape), **chubby** (to describe babies and children), **stout** (short and rather fat), or **large/big** : 'Large people sometimes have difficulty finding fashionable clothes to fit them.' Another way to avoid **fat** is to use a phrase such as **put on weight** or **(have) a weight problem:** 'He's worried about his weight problem.'

fault 1 ✗ I apologize for our fault and will send you a full refund.
✓ **I apologize for our mistake and will send you a full refund.**
✗ If you have time, could you correct the faults in this letter for me?
✓ **If you have time, could you correct the mistakes in this letter for me?**

Use **fault** in connection with machines, electrical equipment, and someone's character: 'It sounds like there's a fault in one of the loudspeakers.' 'The secret of a successful relationship is to accept each other's faults.'
In connection with spellings, essays, calculations, decisions, etc, use **mistake**: 'There are always a lot of mistakes in Ivan's work.' 'We all make mistakes.'

2 ✗ Since we have the fault, we will not charge you for the dress.
✓ **Since it is our fault, we will not charge you for the dress.**
✓ **Since we are to blame, we will not charge you for the dress.**

If you are responsible for something bad that has happened, it is **your fault** or **you are to blame**: 'It's not my fault that the car ran out of petrol.' 'The inquiry will try to establish who is to blame for the disaster.'

favour

✗ I am totally in favour with the proposal.
✓ **I am totally in favour of the proposal.**
✗ We are going to vote in favour to its construction.
✓ **We are going to vote in favour of its construction.**

in favour of: 'Even the producer argued in favour of an 18 rating for the film.'

favourable

✗ We are not favourable to nuclear weapons.
✓ **We are not in favour of nuclear weapons.**

favourable = expressing approval or encouragement, or saying what someone wants to hear: 'a favourable report', 'a favourable reply'
be in favour of = support or approve of: 'Most UN delegates are in favour of the new peace plan.'

favourite

✗ My most favourite drink is lemonade.
✓ **My favourite drink is lemonade.**

An adjective which contains the sense 'most' as part of its meaning cannot be used with **most**. **Favourite** means 'most preferred'.

fear 1

✗ Then I heard the voice again and I had fear.
✓ **Then I heard the voice again and I was afraid.**
✗ I had fear of being alone.
✓ **I was afraid of being alone.**
✗ She suddenly felt fear.
✓ **She suddenly felt afraid.**

be/feel afraid/frightened/scared (NOT **feel/have fear**): 'Don't be afraid. The dog won't hurt you.' 'There's nothing to be scared of.'
Compare: **have a fear of sth** (= be afraid of something for a long time or all your life): 'I've always had a fear of heights.'

2

✗ I don't go swimming because I fear of the water.
✓ **I don't go swimming because I am afraid of the water.**
✓ **I don't go swimming because of my fear of the water.**
✗ He fears to lose his job.
✓ **He is afraid of losing his job.**
✓ **His fear is that he may lose his job.**
✓ **He fears that he may lose his job.**

Fear is used mainly as a noun: 'My worst fear is that I won't be able to have children.' 'The whole of his life has been dominated by fear of failure.'
As a verb, **fear** is used mainly in formal styles to mean 'be frightened about what may happen if you do something': 'Government officials fear that if they put up taxes, they may lose the election.' 'The rescuers feared that the remains of the building might collapse on top of them.'

3

✗ All these problems make me fear about the children's future.
✓ **All these problems make me fear for the children's future.**

fear for = be worried about the safety or well-being of someone: 'The parents of the kidnapped child did not inform the police because they feared for her safety.'

4　✗ It took me a long time to overcome my fear to fly.
　　✓ **It took me a long time to overcome my fear of flying.**
　　　fear of (doing) sth: 'I have never been able to get over my fear of heights.'

fee 1　✗ I didn't know that there would be a delivery fee.
　　✓ **I didn't know that there would be a delivery charge.**
　　　See Language Note at PRICE

2　✗ We'd like some information about the types of room available and the hotel fees.
　　✓ **We'd like some information about the types of room available and the hotel rates.**
　　　See Language Note at PRICE

3　✗ If you hire a television, there is a monthly fee to pay.
　　✓ **If you hire a television, there is a monthly rental to pay.**
　　　See Language Note at PRICE

feel 1　✗ He is feeling that they have made a big mistake.
　　✓ **He feels that they have made a big mistake.**
　　　See Language Note at CONTAIN

2　✗ I woke up the next day feeling terribly.
　　✓ **I woke up the next day feeling terrible.**
　　　Feel is followed by an adjective (NOT an adverb): 'Does anyone feel hungry?' 'We all felt disappointed.'
　　　Other verbs that are followed by an adjective include **be, look, seem, smell, sound, taste**: 'You look cold.' 'That piano sounds terrible.'

3　✗ She says that she feels herself trapped in the job.
　　✓ **She says that she feels trapped in the job.**
　　　See Language Note at MYSELF

feel like 1　✗ In some places you feel like in a jungle.
　　✓ **In some places you feel like you are in a jungle.**
　　　Feel like (and **feel as if/though**) are followed by a clause: 'I felt as if everyone was staring at me.' (= It seemed as if ...)

2　See HOW 1

feeling 1　✗ The meeting provided a good opportunity for her to express her feeling.
　　✓ **The meeting provided a good opportunity for her to express her feelings.**
　　　feelings (plural) = what you think or feel about something: 'My own feelings are that the marriage won't last more than a year.' 'Why does he always try to hide his feelings?'

2　✗ As it got colder, my fingers lost feeling.
　　✓ **As it got colder, my fingers went numb.**
　　　go numb = (of a part of your body) lose the ability to feel anything: 'While we were waiting for my jaw to go numb, the dentist told me about his holiday.'

feet 1

    ✗ In front of them was a six-feet wall.
    ✓ **In front of them was a six-foot wall.**
    See Language Note at HUNDRED

2

    ✗ It shouldn't take more than ten minutes by feet to reach the underground.
    ✓ **It shouldn't take more than ten minutes on foot to reach the underground.**
    See FOOT

fellow 1

    ✗ That afternoon my fellows and I were at a swimming pool where there was a party going on.
    ✓ **That afternoon my friends and I were at a swimming pool where there was a party going on.**

> **fellow** = (informal) a man or person: 'The new manager seems a pleasant enough sort of fellow.'
> **your fellow students/workers** = the people that you study or work with: 'I soon got to know my fellow students and made one or two good friends.'
> **friend** = a person that you like and enjoy being with: 'I'm having lunch with a friend of mine.'

2

    ✗ My boss started to shout at me in front of all my fellows.
    ✓ **My boss started to shout at me in front of all my workmates.**

> To refer to someone you know because you work at the same place, use **workmate** or (especially of people in professional jobs) **colleague**: 'The police are questioning the missing woman's relatives and workmates.' 'I'd like you to meet a colleague of mine, Jean Armstrong.'

female

    ✗ Most females want to continue their careers after marriage.
    ✓ **Most women want to continue their careers after marriage.**
    ✗ In 1992 she won the female marathon in Athens.
    ✓ **In 1992 she won the women's marathon in Athens.**

> **Female** is used mainly in scientific or technical styles: 'The male birds are usually more colourful than the females.' 'The female butterfly does not require additional salts.'
> **Female** is sometimes used to refer to a woman or girl, but many people find this use of the word offensive.

fetch 1

    ✗ She has already packed all her belongings and I just have to fetch them to her new flat.
    ✓ **She has already packed all her belongings and I just have to take them to her new flat.**
    See Language Note at TAKE

2

    ✗ I'll come and fetch you at the airport.
    ✓ **I'll come and fetch/collect you from the airport.**
    ✓ **I'll come and pick you up at the airport.**
    See Language Note at TAKE

fever

    ✗ I'd caught a cold and had a high fever.
    ✓ **I'd caught a cold and had a high temperature.**

> When someone feels rather ill and their body is hotter than usual, they have **a (high) temperature**: 'I feel as if I've got a temperature.' 'She's in bed with a high temperature.'

A **fever** usually refers to a (dangerously) high body temperature, or the disease that produces this: 'In the steaming jungle he had contracted a fever.' 'It seemed as if the fever would shake him to pieces.'

few 1

✗ With the few money he had been given, he bought an apple and some cheese.
✓ **With the little money he had been given, he bought an apple and some cheese.**

Few is used with plural countable nouns: 'very few cars'.
Little is used with uncountable nouns: 'very little traffic'.
Compare: 'He had very little money, just a few coins.'

2

✗ Few minutes later the sales manager arrived.
✓ **A few minutes later the sales manager arrived.**

a few = not many: 'I saw her just a few days ago.'
few = hardly any: 'Few people die of smallpox nowadays.'

fight

✗ They spent the whole night fighting against the fire.
✓ **They spent the whole night fighting the fire.**
✗ Why were the boys fighting against each other?
✓ **Why were the boys fighting each other?**

When you are talking about an event or something that lasts only a short time, use **fight sb/sth** (WITHOUT **against**): 'He said he would fight anyone who tried to stop him.' 'The best way to fight a cold is to get plenty of sleep.'
You can use either **fight sb/sth** or **fight against sb/sth** when you are talking about a long struggle to overcome things such as poverty, disease, injustice or oppression: 'The ANC has spent half a century fighting (against) racism.' 'The group was founded in 1983 to fight (against) the military regime.'

fill

✗ You'll have to fill an application form.
✓ **You'll have to fill in an application form.**

fill in/out a form, coupon etc: 'To open a new account, you have to fill in an application form.' 'Remember to fill out the counterfoil.'
fill in an empty space on a form, coupon etc: 'Just fill in Section A.'
fill in details on a form: 'Fill in your name and address and then sign the form at the bottom.'
Note that **fill out** is more common in American English.

filled with

✗ My shoes were filled with water so I took them off.
✓ **My shoes were full of water so I took them off.**
✗ The eight o'clock train is usually filled with office workers.
✓ **The eight o'clock train is usually full of office workers.**

be filled with = containing so many or so much that there is no empty space left: 'The first drawer was filled with neat piles of shirts.' 'The front page is filled with the most important news items.'
be full of = (1) containing a large number or amount: 'The kitchen was full of flies.' 'The essay was full of mistakes.' (2) be filled with: 'The kettle was full of boiling water.'

finally

? It was difficult to understand people for a long time but finally I got used to their accent.
✓ **It was difficult to understand people for a long time but eventually I got used to their accent.**

See Language Note at END

find 1

✗ I'd like to find why nobody likes me.
✓ **I'd like to find out why nobody likes me.**
✗ The doctors are trying to find what is wrong with him.
✓ **The doctors are trying to find out what is wrong with him.**

> **find** = discover something by chance or by looking for it: 'Did you ever find the sunglasses you lost?' 'I can't find my comb. Have you seen it anywhere?'
> **find out** = get information about something that you want to know: 'He's gone to find out which gate the plane leaves from.' 'I think we should find out exactly what's missing before we start accusing people.'

2

✗ Nurses find very difficult to start a family while they are working.
✓ **Nurses find it very difficult to start a family while they are working.**

> **find + it + easy/difficult/impossible to do sth**: 'I find it hard to concentrate when I'm hungry.' 'You might find it interesting to spend a few hours at the museum.'

find out

✗ Looking through the magazine, I found out several interesting articles.
✓ **Looking through the magazine, I came across several interesting articles.**
✗ If you find out her address, would you please send it to me?
✓ **If you come across her address, would you please send it to me?**

> **find out** = see note at FIND 1
> **come across** = find or meet someone or something by chance: 'While cleaning out the drawers I came across my old school tie.' 'You'll never guess who I came across in the high street today.'

fine

✗ 'Hello, John. How are you?' 'Very fine, thank you.'
✓ **'Hello, John. How are you?' 'Fine, thank you.'**

> When **fine** means 'very well', it is not used with **very** or **extremely**. See note at VERY 2

fire 1

✗ If there is a gas leak, the house could go on fire.
✓ **If there is a gas leak, the house could catch fire.**
✗ One of the curtains became on fire.
✓ **One of the curtains caught fire.**

> **catch fire**: 'One of the engines had overheated and caught fire.'

2

✗ Eventually, the fire went off and the room got colder.
✓ **Eventually, the fire went out and the room got colder.**

> **go out** = (of a coal fire, cigarette, candle etc) stop burning: 'The problem with cigars is that they keep going out.'

first

✗ At first, I would like to introduce myself.
✓ **First of all, I would like to introduce myself.**
✗ There are four points that I would like to make about the college. At first, there are not enough club activities...
✓ **There are four points that I would like to make about the college. Firstly, there are not enough club activities...**

> See Language Note opposite

FIRST • FIRST OF ALL • AT FIRST • IN/AT THE BEGINNING

first, firstly and first of all	**first** First, **firstly** and **first of all** introduce the first item in a list or sequence. The next item is normally introduced by **then** or **first of all second/secondly**: 'First, open all the windows. Then turn off the gas and, if necessary, call an ambulance.' 'These new computers have several advantages. First of all, they're faster than the older machines. Secondly, they're far easier to use. And thirdly, they're more reliable.' **at first** At first introduces a situation which is in contrast with a later situation (after a change has taken place): 'At first I didn't like the climate, but after two years I got used to it.'
in the beginning	Like **at first, in the beginning** introduces a situation which is in contrast with a later situation. However, **in the beginning** is less common and suggests that the speaker is looking a long way back into the past to the period of time immediately after something began: 'In the beginning, when the first settlers arrived, law and order didn't exist.'
at the beginning	**At the beginning** refers to (1) the point in time when something begins: 'At the beginning of each lesson there is usually a revision exercise.' (2) the place where something begins: 'At the beginning of the novel there is a long description of the farm where Daniel was born and grew up.' Unlike **in the beginning,** at the beginning is usually followed by **of**: 'at the beginning of the week/holiday/film'. See also Language Note at END

firstly

✗ I went and sat next to him. Firstly, I didn't speak. I just sat there wondering what I could say. Then I said, 'Nice day, isn't it?'
✓ **I went and sat next to him. At first, I didn't speak. I just sat there wondering what I could say. Then I said, 'Nice day, isn't it?'**
✗ Firstly, I couldn't understand the local people at all.
✓ **At first, I couldn't understand the local people at all.**
See Language Note above

fish

✗ I had never seen such brightly coloured fishes before.
✓ **I had never seen such brightly coloured fish before.**
The plural form of **fish** is usually **fish**: 'Did you catch any fish?' 'The fish in the market are always fresh.'
The plural form **fishes** is used mainly in stories for small children and in scientific or technical styles (to refer to different species of fish).

fit 1

✗ You should see a doctor or specialist to find out which type of diet will fit you.
✓ **You should see a doctor or specialist to find out which type of diet will suit you.**

✗ A school like Summerhill will not fit for everybody.
✓ **A school like Summerhill will not suit everybody.**

> **fit** = (of clothes, shoes, rings etc) be the correct size and shape for you: 'These trousers don't fit me any more.' 'The next size up should fit.'
> **suit** = be suitable: 'Try and choose a career that suits you.' 'You should buy a dictionary that suits your needs, not just any one.'

2

✗ Of course you will need some old paintings to fit the furniture.
✓ **Of course you will need some old paintings to match the furniture.**

> **match** (or **go with**) = (of clothes, soft furnishings etc) look good when seen together: 'We chose a dark green carpet to go with our yellow curtains.' 'I can't wear blue shoes with a black skirt - they don't match.'

3

✗ A little exercise will help you to keep in fit.
✓ **A little exercise will help you to keep fit.**

> **keep fit** (WITHOUT **in**): 'She keeps fit by jogging five miles every day.' Compare: 'Cycling to work helps me to keep in shape.'

floor 1

✗ I was just about to enter the station when someone grabbed me by the shoulders and threw me to the floor.
✓ **I was just about to enter the station when someone grabbed me by the shoulders and threw me to the ground.**

See Language Note at GROUND

2

✗ The fire started at the seventh floor.
✓ **The fire started on the seventh floor.**
✗ Room 229 was in the second floor.
✓ **Room 229 was on the second floor.**

> **on the ground/first/second** etc **floor** (NOT **in/at**): 'The canteen is downstairs, on the ground floor.'

flu

✗ I think I have caught a flu.
✓ **I think I have caught (the) flu.**

> **flu** or **the flu** (NOT **a flu**): 'They are both off work with flu.' 'Even our doctor is down with the flu.'

follow

✗ You can go in your own car or follow me.
✓ **You can go in your own car or come with me.**

> **Follow** means 'move in the same direction as someone or something that is moving in front of you': 'I have a feeling that the car behind is following us.'

food

✗ The child was caught stealing foods.
✓ **The child was caught stealing food.**
✗ It is a disgrace to serve such a poor food.
✓ **It is a disgrace to serve such poor food.**

> **Food** is nearly always uncountable: 'We need to go out and buy some food.' It is countable only when it refers to a particular kind of food: 'baby foods', 'health foods'.

fool

✗ I was fool to believe him.
✓ **I was a fool to believe him.**
✓ **I was foolish to believe him.**

> **Fool** is a countable noun and refers to a person: 'She thinks I'm a fool for lending him the money.'
> The adjective is **foolish**: 'You were right. It was foolish of me to lend him the money.' 'This foolish idea could ruin everything.'

foot

✗ Whenever there is a strike, we have to go to work by foot.
✓ **Whenever there is a strike, we have to go to work on foot.**

> **go/travel** (somewhere) **by car/bus/train/air** BUT **on foot**: 'We left the car at the bridge and travelled the rest of the way on foot.'

for 1

✗ I have come to London for learning English.
✓ **I have come to London to learn English.**

> To explain 'why' someone does something, use a **to**-infinitive (NOT **for**): 'She opened the door to let the cat out.' In formal styles, **in order to** is also possible: 'UN troops have been sent to the trouble spot in order to restore peace.'

2

✗ I studied in Freiburg for to be a kindergarden teacher.
✓ **I studied in Freiburg to be a kindergarden teacher.**
✗ Being married makes it easier for to answer this question.
✓ **Being married makes it easier to answer this question.**

> **For** never comes immediately in front of a **to**-infinitive. Compare: 'It will be difficult for John to say no.' 'The suitcase is too heavy for anyone to carry all that way.' (**for + sb/sth + to**-infinitive).

3

✗ Unemployment has become a serious problem for the last few years.
✓ **Unemployment has become a serious problem over the last few years.**

> Use **for** to say 'how long': 'He was with the company for forty years.' 'He hasn't eaten anything for the last two days.'
> Use **over/during/in** to say 'when', especially when this is a long period of time: 'She's been a great help to me in recent months.' 'During the next ten years he worked his way up from office boy to general manager.'

4

✗ I'm waiting here for almost an hour.
✓ **I've been waiting here for almost an hour.**
✗ I didn't do any travelling for the last two years.
✓ **I haven't done any travelling for the last two years.**

> For actions and situations which began in the past and continue up to 'now' (the moment of speaking), use the present perfect tense: 'I've been working part-time for the last six months.' 'We haven't seen each other for the past eight months.'
> Note that in informal American English the past tense is also used for this purpose.
> See also SINCE 1

5

✗ I do badly in tests for I am lazy.
✓ **I do badly in tests because I am lazy.**

> Do not use **for** to mean 'because'. This usage has almost disappeared and is found only in very formal styles.

forbid 1

? The government should forbid cigarette advertising.
✓ **The government should ban cigarette advertising.**

> **ban** (or **prohibit**) = forbid someone from doing something by making it illegal: 'The proposed treaty banning all nuclear testing has received widespread approval.' 'International Law prohibits the use of chemical weapons.'

2

✗ There should be a law which forbids to have more than two children.
✓ **There should be a law which forbids couples to have/from having more than two children.**

> **forbid + sb + to do/from doing sth**: 'My parents have forbidden me to stay out after ten o'clock.' 'Her father ought to forbid her from seeing the boy again.'

force

✗ We must not forget Japan's economic force.
✓ **We must not forget Japan's economic power.**
✗ The sovereign has very little force nowadays.
✓ **The sovereign has very little power nowadays.**

> **force** = the use of power or strength: 'The demonstrators were made to leave the building by force.'
> **power** = the ability to control people and events: 'I think the police have too much power.'

foreigner

✗ Some foreigner students feel homesick.
✓ **Some foreign students feel homesick.**
✗ In my job I have to speak foreigner languages.
✓ **In my job I have to speak foreign languages.**

> **Foreigner** is a noun and refers to a person: 'As a foreigner who had only just arrived in England, I found the phrase 'car boot sale' very confusing.' The adjective is **foreign**: 'I enjoy visiting foreign countries.' 'His wife teaches English as a foreign language.'

forever

✗ Nobody lives forever.
✓ **Nobody lives for ever.**

> **forever** = continually; all the time: 'He is forever asking me for more pocket money.'
> **for ever** = for always: 'He promised that he would love me for ever and a day.'

forget

✗ Would you please check whether I have forgotten a black handbag in Room 21.
✓ **Would you please check whether I have left a black handbag in Room 21.**

> If you forget to take something with you, you **leave** it somewhere. Do not use **forget** if you mention a place: 'If the keys aren't in your jacket, you must have left them in the restaurant.' 'I've left all my money at home.'

fortune

✗ It was a good fortune that the driver was able to stop in time.
✓ **It was fortunate/lucky that the driver was able to stop in time.**

> **Good fortune** is quite rare. It occurs mainly in the phrase **have the good fortune to do sth**: 'He had the good fortune to marry a woman who was both kind and understanding.'

friendly 1   ✗   I look forward to hearing from you. Friendly, Leine.
     ✓   **I look forward to hearing from you. Yours, Leine.**

> To end a letter to a friend, use **Yours** or **With best wishes** (NOT **friendly**). See also YOURS 1

2   ✗   Although I was a stranger, they treated me very friendly.
     ✓   **Although I was a stranger, the treatment I received was very friendly.**
     ✓   **Although I was a stranger, they treated me in a very friendly way.**

> **Friendly** is an adjective (NOT an adverb): 'Our new neighbours are very friendly.' 'She gave me a friendly smile.'

frightened   ✗   When I heard the thunder I frightened for a moment.
     ✓   **When I heard the thunder I was frightened for a moment.**

> **frighten** (transitive) = make someone afraid: 'Take that silly mask off – you're frightening the baby.'
> **be frightened** = be afraid: 'Don't be frightened. It's only thunder.'

from 1   ✗   I have been living in England from last September.
     ✓   **I have been living in England since last September.**

> Use **from ... to ...** when you mean 'from one time in the past to another': 'I lived in England from 1986 to 1989.'
> Use **since** when you mean 'from a time in the past until now': 'I've been standing here since 9 o'clock and not one bus has come along.'

2   ✗   She asked if I'd seen any plays from Shakespeare.
     ✓   **She asked if I'd seen any plays by Shakespeare.**

> a play, novel, painting, etc **by** a writer or artist (NOT **from**): 'The reading passage was from a novel by Anita Brookner.'

3   ✗   It's a short, knee-length coat from white wool.
     ✓   **It's a short, knee-length coat made of white wool.**

> See note at MADE

4   See NOW 1

front   ✗   The bus stop is outside the post office, in front of the library.
     ✓   **The bus stop is outside the post office, opposite the library.**

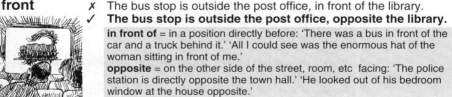

> **in front of** = in a position directly before: 'There was a bus in front of the car and a truck behind it.' 'All I could see was the enormous hat of the woman sitting in front of me.'
> **opposite** = on the other side of the street, room, etc facing: 'The police station is directly opposite the town hall.' 'He looked out of his bedroom window at the house opposite.'

fruit   ✗   The shop sells fruits and vegetables.
     ✓   **The shop sells fruit and vegetables.**
     ✗   I never buy tinned fruits.
     ✓   **I never buy tinned fruit.**

> **Fruit** (= fruit in general) is an uncountable noun: 'We eat lots of fruit in our family.' 'Would anyone care for a piece of fruit?' (= an orange, apple, pear etc)
> **Fruits** (= particular types of fruit) is rarely used in British English.

fully 1   ✗ The editor said that my letter was too long to be fully published.
              ✓ **The editor said that my letter was too long to be published in full.**

> **fully** = completely: 'a fully equipped kitchen', 'a fully furnished apartment', 'The next three flights to Chicago are fully booked.'
> **in full** = without any part missing or removed: 'Your $100 deposit will be refunded in full.'

fun 1   ? A good novel can give you a lot of fun.
            ✓ **A good novel can give you a lot of pleasure.**

> When you are talking about something that provides intellectual or spiritual satisfaction, such as a piano concert or a visit to an art gallery, use **enjoyment/enjoyable** or **pleasure/pleasurable**: 'Reading is her one source of pleasure.' 'We spent an enjoyable afternoon at the art gallery.'
> **Fun** is usually used in connection with light-hearted events and activities such as games, picnics, or children's parties: 'John's parties are always great fun.' 'Let's go to the beach and have some fun.'

2   ✗ The game we played was very fun.
        ✓ **The game we played was a lot of fun.**
        ✗ College life is not very fun.
        ✓ **College life is not much fun.**

> **Fun** is a noun (NOT an adjective): 'a lot of fun', 'not much fun', 'great fun'

3   ✗ On my birthday I had a good fun with my friends.
        ✓ **On my birthday I had some good fun with my friends.**
        ✗ It would be a great fun if we could go together.
        ✓ **It would be great fun if we could go together.**

> See Language Note at SCENERY

4   ✗ While on holiday I made lots of fun.
        ✓ **While on holiday I had lots of fun.**
        ✗ I'm sure that you will get a lot of fun here.
        ✓ **I'm sure that you will have a lot of fun here.**

> **have fun**: 'Everyone needs to have a little fun now and again.'
> See Language Note at DO

funny 1   ✗ It will be more funny to go by bus.
              ✓ **It will be more fun to go by bus.**
              ✗ We've organized lots of funny activities, including a picnic and a trip to the zoo.

              ✓ **We've organized lots of fun activities, including a picnic and a trip to the zoo.**

> Someone or something that is **funny** makes you laugh: 'I always laugh at Jenny's jokes - they're really funny.' 'The funniest part was when her father-in-law sat on the wedding cake.'
> Someone or something that is **fun** gives you pleasure or enjoyment: 'The Disneyland trip sounds like a lot of fun.'

2   ✗ The carnival is held once a year and everyone has a funny time.
        ✓ **The carnival is held once a year and everyone has a good time.**

> **have a good time** = enjoy yourself: 'Everyone was dancing and having a good time.'

furniture ✗ The room was so full of furnitures it was difficult to move.
  ✓ **The room was so full of furniture it was difficult to move.**

Furniture is an uncountable noun: 'We need some new furniture for the lounge.' 'Our showrooms up and down the country stock the latest ideas in bedroom furniture.'

future ✗ In future, when my youngest child has started school, I'd like to get a job.
  ✓ **In the future, when my youngest child has started school, I'd like to get a job.**

in future = from now on (commonly used in announcements and warnings): 'In future anyone arriving late for class will not be admitted.'
in the future = at some time in the future: 'In the future it is quite possible that a new source of energy will be discovered.'

Gg

gain 1

  ✗ For two weeks' work, I gain about 700,000 yen.
  ✓ **For two weeks' work, I earn about 700,000 yen.**
  ✗ Without a job it's impossible to gain any money.
  ✓ **Without a job it's impossible to earn any money.**

> **earn** or (especially in informal styles) **get/make** (a sum of) money by going to work, from investments, etc (NOT **gain**): 'She earns $4,000 a month.'

2

  See PROFIT

gentle

  ? My father was a very gentle man, always helping people.
  ✓ **My father was a very kind man, always helping people.**

> **gentle** = (1) used to describe someone who never shows anger or impatience in what they say or do: 'His brother was always ready for a fight, but Tim was quiet and gentle.'
> (2) not loud, forceful or rough: 'He spoke to the child in a quiet, gentle voice so as not to frighten her.' 'She found the doctor's gentle manner very reassuring.'

gently 1

  ✗ The shop assistant asked me gently what I wanted.
  ✓ **The shop assistant asked me politely what I wanted.**

> **gently** = in a way that will not hurt or damage anything: 'She held the little bird very gently.'
> **politely** = in a way that shows good manners: 'He politely refused her offer, saying that he didn't want to trouble her.'

2

  ✗ I wonder if you would gently lend us a room for one of the monthly meetings.
  ✓ **I wonder if you would kindly lend us a room for one of the monthly meetings.**

> In polite formal requests, use **if you would/could kindly** (or **if you would be so kind as to**): 'I would be very grateful if you would kindly allow Julian to leave school early on Tuesday.'

get off

  ✗ I got off my car to inspect the damage.
  ✓ **I got out of my car to inspect the damage.**

> **get off** a bus, train, plane, boat, ship, bicycle: 'The bus driver will tell you where to get off.' 'I got off the train at the wrong station.'
> **get out of** a car, taxi, boat, train, lift: 'Getting out of a boat can be quite tricky.'

get up

  See BED 1

give

✗ She gave to him some cheese sandwiches.
✓ **She gave him some cheese sandwiches.**
✗ They always give to the new students a warm welcome.
✓ **They always give the new students a warm welcome.**

give sth to sb BUT **give sb sth** (WITHOUT **to**)
Compare: 'They gave a medal to each member of the team.' 'They gave each member of the team a medal.'

glad 1

✗ I would be glad if you could send me an application form.
✓ **I would be grateful if you could send me an application form.**

To make a formal request, use **would be grateful if** (NOT **glad**): 'We would be grateful if you could consider this matter at your earliest convenience.'

2

✗ She was a very glad person, and very intelligent.
✓ **She was a very happy person, and very intelligent.**
✗ We hope that you will like this school and be glad here.
✓ **We hope that you will like this school and be happy here.**

glad (not used in front of a noun) = pleased and happy about something in particular: 'I'm so glad your wife is feeling better.' 'I'm glad it wasn't my turn to pay.'
happy = enjoying life: 'She's a lot happier now that the examinations are over.'

glass

✗ I have to vacuum the floors and clean the glasses of the windows.
✓ **I have to vacuum the floors and clean the windows.**
✗ The sunlight poured in through the glasses of the bedroom window.
✓ **The sunlight poured in through (the panes of) the bedroom window.**

pane (or **window-pane**) = a sheet of glass used in a window: 'The two cracked panes will have to be replaced.'
Note that **pane** and **window-pane** are rarely used. Their meaning is usually expressed by **window**.

glasses 1

✗ He wears an old-fashioned glasses which make him look intelligent.
✓ **He wears old-fashioned glasses which make him look intelligent.**

Glasses (= spectacles) is a plural noun: 'I wear glasses just for reading.' 'Have you seen my glasses?'

2

See PAIR 2

go 1

✗ The next morning she went to see us at the hotel.
✓ **The next morning she came to see us at the hotel.**

Come is used for movement towards the speaker/listener: 'Come in and sit down for a few minutes.' 'When can I come and see you?'
Go is used for movement in other directions: 'Could you go upstairs and turn the lights off?'

2

  ✗ How do I go to the Holiday Inn?
  ✓ **How do I get to the Holiday Inn?**
  ✗ He was lost and didn't know how to go back home.
  ✓ **He was lost and didn't know how to get back home.**

> When you mean 'arrive', use **get (to)**: 'I got to the classroom five minutes late.' 'When does the train get there?'

3

  ✗ We go to swim every day on holiday.
  ✓ **We go swimming every day on holiday.**
  ✗ They've gone for camping on Lantau Island.
  ✓ **They've gone camping on Lantau Island.**

> **go swimming/sightseeing/shopping** etc: 'They've probably gone fishing.'

4

  ✗ That evening my boyfriend and I went out to walk.
  ✓ **That evening my boyfriend and I went for a walk.**

> **go for a walk/swim/jog** etc: 'Would anyone like to go for a drive?'

5   See TO 2

6   See CAR

7   See FIRE 1, 3

go ahead

  ✗ Without additional qualifications, it will be impossible for me to go ahead in my career.
  ✓ **Without additional qualifications, it will be impossible for me to get ahead in my career.**

> If you are successful in your career, studies etc, you **get ahead** (NOT **go ahead**): 'The old education system favoured boys, and girls found it difficult to get ahead.'

go down

  ✗ Culture shock begins as soon as you go down from the plane.
  ✓ **Culture shock begins as soon as you get off the plane.**

> See note at GET OFF

go out

  ✗ As soon as the bus stopped, he went out.
  ✓ **As soon as the bus stopped, he got off.**
  ✗ I went out of the car and waited for someone to stop and help me.
  ✓ **I got out of the car and waited for someone to stop and help me.**

> See note at GET OFF

goal

  ✗ We reached our goal just after three o'clock.
  ✓ **We reached our destination just after three o'clock.**

> **goal** = something that you hope to achieve: 'The company's goal is to double its share of the personal computer market.'
> **destination** = the place that you are travelling to: 'The immigration officer wanted to know my destination and how long I was planning to stay.'

golden

  ✗ It's a navy blue coat with golden buttons.
  ✓ **It's a navy blue coat with gold buttons.**
  ✗ The purse contained six golden coins.
  ✓ **The purse contained six gold coins.**

Golden is used in idiomatic expressions such as 'a golden opportunity', 'a golden handshake', 'a golden wedding anniversary', and in the phrase 'golden hair' (used mainly in literary styles).

To describe something that is made of gold or is the colour of gold, use **gold**: 'a gold bracelet', 'a black dress with red and gold stripes down the front'.

gone

✗ 'Have you ever gone to France?' she asked.
✓ **'Have you ever been to France?' she asked.**

In British English, **been** is used when someone has visited a place and returned. **Gone** is used when the person is still in the place they are visiting. Compare: 'Peter has gone to Paris.' (= he has not yet returned) 'Peter has been to Paris.' (= he has visited Paris and returned)

In American English **gone** can be used instead of **been**.

gonna

✗ Do you know when the plane is gonna land?
✓ **Do you know when the plane is going to land?**
✗ The principal is gonna give a talk in the morning.
✓ **The principal is going to give a talk in the morning.**

Do not use **gonna** (= going to) or **wanna** (= want to) unless you are trying to represent informal conversation.

good 1

✗ I don't speak English very good.
✓ **I don't speak English very well.**

Good is an adjective: 'She is a very good singer.'
Well is an adverb: 'She sings very well.'

2

✗ I hope I'll do good in tomorrow's test.
✓ **I hope I'll do well in tomorrow's test.**

If you are successful (in a test, interview etc), you **do well** (**in** it): 'I did quite well in maths and chemistry but my physics result was very disappointing.'

3

✗ My sister is very good in squash.
✓ **My sister is very good at squash.**
✗ I'm not very good in writing essays.
✓ **I'm not very good at writing essays.**

be good at (**doing**) **sth**: 'He's good at all science subjects.' 'Are you any good at chess?'

4

✗ There's no good putting a very young child in a kindergarten.
✓ **It's no good putting a very young child in a kindergarten.**
✗ It's no good to want to help the poor if you don't do anything about it.
✓ **It's no good wanting to help the poor if you don't do anything about it.**

it is no good/use (**doing sth**) = it is pointless: 'It's no good having a car if you can't drive.'

5

See Language Note at DO

goods

✗ He had very little money and very few goods.
✓ **He had very little money and very few possessions.**

goods = things that are made to be sold: 'The supermarket has a wide variety of frozen goods.' 'The average family's weekly expenditure on goods and services has risen by 20%.'
possessions = all the things that a person owns: 'After his mother died, Andrew had the unpleasant task of sorting through her possessions.'

gossip

✗ She told me gossips about all her relations.
✓ **She told me a lot of gossip about all her relations.**
See Language Note at SCENERY

got

✗ I got several friends who don't want children.
✓ **I have (got) several friends who don't want children.**
Got is not used to replace **have**: 'I have two sisters.' 'I've got two sisters.' (NOT 'I got two sisters.')

grade

✗ By the end of the war he had been promoted to the grade of captain.
✓ **By the end of the war he had been promoted to the rank of captain.**
Soldiers, sailors, police officers etc have different **ranks** (NOT **grades**): 'She joined the police force in 1990 and quickly rose to the rank of sergeant.'

graduate

✗ I graduated at Seoul National University with a degree in politics.
✓ **I graduated from Seoul National University with a degree in politics.**
You **graduate from** a university: 'She graduated from Hull University in 1994 with a first class honours degree in chemistry.'

granted

✗ We cannot take for granted that a computer system will never fail.
✓ **We cannot take it for granted that a computer system will never fail.**
take it for granted (that ...) WITH **it** = assume that something is true or will happen: 'She didn't ask me if I wanted to go. She just took it for granted.'
See also APPRECIATE 2

grave 1

✗ I don't have any grave problems.
✓ **I don't have any serious problems.**
✗ Blackmail is a grave crime.
✓ **Blackmail is a serious crime.**
grave = extremely serious and worrying, especially because someone's life or happiness is in danger: 'The situation has become increasingly grave and war now seems inevitable.' 'The shortage of food and medical supplies is giving rise to grave concern.'

2

✗ We went to see the 'Valley of the Kings', where the grave of Tut-mah-Amun was found.
✓ **We went to see the 'Valley of the Kings', where the tomb of Tut-mah-Amun was found.**
grave = a place in the ground where a dead person is put: 'The coffin was slowly lowered into the grave.'
tomb (pronounced /tuːm/) = a place where a dead person is put. A tomb

is usually made of stone and is above the ground: 'Our first stop was the Tomb of the Unknown Soldier.'

greatly

✗ Living standards have improved greatly.
✓ **Living standards have greatly improved.**
✓ **Living standards have improved enormously.**
✗ The children greatly cheered me up.
✓ **The children cheered me up a lot.**

Greatly is usually placed in front of a main verb, especially in passive structures: 'Your kind offer is greatly appreciated.' 'Stories of panic on Wall Street have been greatly exaggerated.'
To emphasize the meaning of an active verb, use **enormously, tremendously** or (in informal styles) **a lot** at the end of the clause: 'In the last forty years education in China has changed enormously.'

group

✗ The people of each group have to guess the word.
✓ **The people in each group have to guess the word.**

the + noun + **in a group:** 'The girls in my group all come from Italy.'
Note however **member** + **of a group**: 'The members of my group took it in turns to take notes.'

ground 1

✗ Turkey occupies about 40 per cent of our ground.
✓ **Turkey occupies about 40 per cent of our land/territory.**
See Language Note on next page

2

✗ They do not have enough food or ground to grow it on.
✓ **They do not have enough food or land to grow it on.**
See Language Note on next page

3

✗ Gradually the ground loses the ability to hold water.
✓ **Gradually the soil loses the ability to hold water.**
✗ My job is to analyse samples of ground.
✓ **My job is to analyse samples of soil.**
See Language Note on next page

4

✗ People who suffer from backache often sleep on the ground.
✓ **People who suffer from backache often sleep on the floor.**
See Language Note on next page

5

✗ The school building is very old and the ground is very small.
✓ **The school building is very old and the grounds are very small.**
See Language Note on next page

6

✗ A shot rang out and one of the men fell on the ground.
✓ **A shot rang out and one of the men fell to the ground.**
✗ I fell on the ground, hoping that nobody had seen me.
✓ **I fell to the ground, hoping that nobody had seen me.**

Use **on the ground** when you are thinking about position: 'Someone had dropped one of their gloves on the ground.' 'We sat down on the ground just outside the cage.'
When you are thinking about downward movement or (violent) movement from a standing position, use **to the ground**: 'The parachute failed to open and he plummeted to the ground.' 'The impact knocked

him spinning to the ground.' 'They pushed him to the ground and grabbed his wallet.'

FLOOR • GROUND • GROUNDS • LAND • TERRITORY • SOIL

floor	The **floor** is the surface that you walk on when you are <u>indoors</u>: 'Our cat likes to sit on the floor under my desk.' 'It's about time someone cleaned the kitchen floor.'
ground	The **ground** is the surface that you walk on when you are <u>outdoors</u>: 'The ground was covered with snow.' 'In the middle of the forest was a bare patch of marshy ground.'
grounds	**Grounds** refers to the area surrounding and belonging to a school, hospital, hotel, stately home, etc, usually enclosed by a wall or fence: 'Parking within the hospital grounds is strictly prohibited.'
land	**Land** refers to (1) an area of ground that is owned or used by someone, or that is controlled by a particular country: 'All the land from here to the stream belongs to the Pattersons.' 'Disagreements about land have led to many wars.' (2) (also **the land**) the part of the Earth's surface that is not covered by water: 'After three days at sea, I was looking forward to being on land again.'
territory	**Territory** is the area that is controlled by a particular country, army or power: 'One of the results of losing the war was that the country had to give up almost half its territory.' 'They had wandered by mistake into enemy territory.'
soil	**Soil** is the material in which plants and trees grow: 'This plant needs rich soil to grow well.'

grow 1　✗　Many of these children grow in an atmosphere of violence.
✓　**Many of these children grow up in an atmosphere of violence.**

grow = (1) (of children, animals, plants etc) develop or get bigger as part of a natural process: 'Mary's little boy grew four centimetres last year.' 'Orchids don't grow in cold climates.' (2) cause plants, vegetables etc to do this by taking care of them: 'In the back garden we grow onions, potatoes and carrots.'
grow up = (of children) pass from childhood into maturity: 'Of course I know him - we grew up together in New York.' 'Tom wants to be a scientist when he grows up.'

2　✗　Some parents need to be taught how to grow their children.
✓　**Some parents need to be taught how to bring up their children.**

bring up (or **raise**) = look after children until they are old enough to leave home, teaching them how to behave and what to think about the world: 'He was brought up to believe that men and women are equal.'

grow up 1 ✗ The country's GNP is growing up very quickly.
✓ **The country's GNP is growing very quickly.**

> **grow** = increase (in number, volume, cost etc): 'The population is expected to grow by 20% over the next ten years.'

2 ✗ Calcium helps your bones to grow up.
✓ **Calcium helps your bones to grow.**
✗ With a garden you can grow up your own vegetables.
✓ **With a garden you can grow your own vegetables.**

> See note at GROW 1

grown-up ✗ These films are too violent not only for children but also for grown-up people.
✓ **These films are too violent not only for children but also for grown-ups.**

> Instead of using **grown-up person/people**, use **grown-up** as a noun: 'Grown-ups are so boring! All they want to do is talk!' Note that **grown-up** is used mainly by children. The more common word is **adult**.

guarantee ✗ May I remind you that the cassette recorder is still in guarantee.
✓ **May I remind you that the cassette recorder is still under guarantee.**

> **under guarantee** (NOT **in**): 'The watch was still under guarantee so they repaired it free of charge.'

guidance ✗ I greatly appreciate all your help and guidances.
✓ **I greatly appreciate all your help and guidance.**

> **Guidance** is an uncountable noun: 'The council provides guidance and support for students wishing to study abroad.'

guilty 1 ✗ The jury charged the defendant guilty.
✓ **The jury found the defendant guilty.**
✗ He was tried and judged guilty of murder.
✓ **He was tried and found guilty of murder.**

> **find sb guilty/innocent**: 'Despite the flimsy evidence, the jury found her guilty.' 'The accused was found guilty and sentenced to five years' imprisonment.'

2 ✗ They feel guilty of neglecting their duty.
✓ **They feel guilty about neglecting their duty.**
✗ A lot of women feel guilty to leave their children alone or with another person.
✓ **A lot of women feel guilty about leaving their children alone or with another person.**

> **(be) guilty of** a crime or doing something wrong: 'The jury found the defendant guilty of murder.' 'He was guilty of driving without a licence or insurance.'
> **(feel) guilty about (doing) sth** = ashamed: 'I still feel guilty about not visiting her while she was in hospital.'

guitar 1 See PLAY 3

2 See CLASSIC 2

gun See SHOOT 2

gymnastic ✗ I took up gymnastic when I was at school.
✓ **I took up gymnastics when I was at school.**

Gymnastic (WITHOUT **-s**) is an adjective: 'Her gymnastic ability was recognized at a very early age.'
The noun is **gymnastics** (WITH **-s**): 'Her career in international gymnastics began at the age of twelve.'

habit 1

   ✗ It is a habit in Japan to take off your shoes before entering a house.
   ✓ **It is a custom in Japan to take off your shoes before entering a house.**
   See Language Note at MANNER

2

   ✗ Once one has taken the habit, smoking is very difficult to give up.
   ✓ **Once one has acquired the habit, smoking is very difficult to give up.**
   acquire/adopt/develop/get into a habit (NOT **take**): 'He's developed the unfortunate habit of biting his fingernails.'

hair 1

   ✗ He had a black hair and very clear eyes.
   ✓ **He had black hair and very clear eyes.**
   ✗ Her beautiful blond hairs were shining in the sun.
   ✓ **Her beautiful blond hair was shining in the sun.**
   When you mean 'a single hair' or 'several individual hairs', **hair** is a countable noun: 'There was a long black hair in my soup.' 'Stand still and I'll brush the hairs off your jacket.'
   When you mean 'all the hair on a person's head', **hair** is uncountable: 'Where do you go to have your hair cut?'

2

   See CUT 4

half 1

   ✗ He agreed to give her the half of the money.
   ✓ **He agreed to give her half of the money.**
   Do not use **the** before **half** except when talking about a particular half. Compare: 'He spends half the week playing golf.' 'During the second half of the concert I could hardly stay awake.'

2

   ✗ We will stay in Bangkok for two and half days.
   ✓ **We will stay in Bangkok for two and a half days.**
   number + **and a half** (NOT **and half**): 'She can swim two lengths of the pool in four and a half minutes.'

3

   ✗ We have a break of one and a half hour for lunch.
   ✓ **We have a break of one and a half hours for lunch.**
   number greater than one + plural form: 'three and a half minutes', 'twelve and a half miles'
   Note the alternative: 'We have a one and a half hour break for lunch.'

halt

   ✗ Don't stand up until the bus gets to a halt.
   ✓ **Don't stand up until the bus comes to a halt.**

come to a halt (NOT **get**): 'The car that we'd been following came to a sudden halt outside the bank.'

hand 1

✗ In the other hand, many women choose to go out to work.
✓ **On the other hand, many women choose to go out to work.**

on the one hand ... , on the other hand ... , (NOT **in, at**): 'On the other hand, don't forget that these machines are expensive.'

2

✗ The future of millions of people should not be in the hand of one man.
✓ **The future of millions of people should not be in the hands of one man.**

in the hands of (plural) = controlled by: 'All the political power is in the hands of the government.'

3

✗ He came out of the bathroom with a towel in the hand.
✓ **He came out of the bathroom with a towel in his hand.**

in my/her/their etc **hand/s** (NOT **the**): 'You can't argue when someone has a gun in their hand.'

handle

✗ I learned how to run a house and handle with small children.
✓ **I learned how to run a house and handle small children.**
✗ That is surely not the way to handle with something so fragile.
✓ **That is surely not the way to handle something so fragile.**

handle sb/sth (WITHOUT **with**): 'We've decided to let our lawyer handle the matter.' 'Be careful how you handle the vase - it's worth a small fortune.'
Compare: 'This is a highly sensitive issue and needs to be handled with tact and diplomacy.' 'FRAGILE – HANDLE WITH CARE.'

happen 1

✗ It happened something very strange.
✓ **Something very strange happened.**
✗ I was afraid it might happen to me something terrible.
✓ **I was afraid that something terrible might happen to me.**
✗ It didn't happen what the teacher had predicted.
✓ **What the teacher had predicted didn't happen.**

The subject of **happen** comes in front of the verb, in the usual way: 'Accidents happen every day along this stretch of the road.' 'Something unforeseen has happened.'
When you use **it** (preparatory subject) before **happen**, the sentence continues with a **that** clause: 'It happened that we had both booked seats on the same flight.' (= By chance we had both booked ...)

2

✗ One day happened something very sad.
✓ **One day something very sad happened.**
✗ Then happened something that made me very angry.
✓ **Then something happened that made me very angry.**

The subject of the sentence comes in front of **happen** (NOT after it): 'Something unexpected has happened.' 'Something has happened that I think you ought to know about.'

3

✗ I don't know what's happened with him. He should be here by now.
✓ **I don't know what's happened to him. He should be here by now.**

Something **happens to** someone/something (NOT **with**): 'What's happened to the clock? It's not working.'

4 See PROBLEM 3

hardly 1 ✗ I tried hardly to remember where I had parked the car.
✓ **I tried hard to remember where I had parked the car.**
✗ It was raining hardly and we all got wet.
✓ **It was raining hard and we all got wet.**
✗ Society shouldn't punish these people too hardly.
✓ **Society shouldn't punish these people too hard/severely.**

hardly = scarcely; almost not: 'It was hardly raining at all.' 'I could hardly believe my eyes.'
hard = (1) with a lot of effort: 'If you work hard, you're bound to pass.' (2) heavily or severely: 'The authorities are coming down hard on tax evasion.' Before a past participle, use **severely** for this meaning: 'If they are caught, they will be severely punished.'

2 ✗ It was so dark that we hardly could see.
✓ **It was so dark that we could hardly see.**
See Language Note at ALWAYS

3 ✗ There were hardly no trees left, just bare rocky land.
✓ **There were hardly any trees left, just bare rocky land.**
✗ When we arrived at the hotel, we couldn't hardly believe our eyes.
✓ **When we arrived at the hotel, we could hardly believe our eyes.**
See Language Note at NOT

harm See Language Note at DO

have 1 ✗ After buying the food, he had not any money left.
✓ **After buying the food, he didn't have any money left.**

When **have** is used as a main verb, the negative and question forms are made with **do**: 'I didn't have any breakfast this morning.'
Note the alternative: 'After buying the food, he hadn't got any money left.'

2 ✗ I stayed at home yesterday because I was having a bad cold.
✓ **I stayed at home yesterday because I had a bad cold.**
See Language Note at CONTAIN

3 ✗ I don't think that I have to say anything more, so I'll stop now and take this letter to the post office.
✓ **I don't think that I have anything more to say, so I'll stop now and take this letter to the post office.**

have to do sth = must do something: 'My train leaves in ten minutes so I'll have to go now.'
have sth to do = have something that you need or intend to do: 'I have two more letters to write.'

4 See AGO 2

5   See COLOUR 1, SIZE

have got 1   ? He has got white hair, big ears and blue eyes.
✓ **He's got white hair, big ears and blue eyes.**
? I have not got a van and so I can't move my things by myself.
✓ **I haven't got a van and so I can't move my things by myself.**

> The different forms of **have got** are nearly always contracted when they are spoken or written: 'I've got two sisters.' 'She's got big brown eyes.' 'He wanted to know if I'd got any money.'

2   ? It all depends on whether the applicant has got suitable qualifications.
✓ **It all depends on whether the applicant has suitable qualifications.**

> **Have got** is used only in informal styles (mainly in British English). In other styles, use **have**.

have to   ✗ Some wives earn a lot of money and so their husbands haven't to work.
✓ **Some wives earn a lot of money and so their husbands don't have to work.**
✗ He was pleased that he had not to look after the baby.
✓ **He was pleased that he didn't have to look after the baby.**

> The negative and question forms of **have to** are usually made with **do**: 'I don't have to leave just yet.' 'Do you really have to go now?'

he   ? A child is bound to suffer if he thinks that no one loves him.
✓ **Children are bound to suffer if they think that no one loves them.**

See Language Note opposite

he or she,   ? When anyone reads these lines, he or she will think that the
he/she   writer is very sad.
✓ **Anyone reading these lines will think that the writer is very sad.**
? A criminal should be punished when he/she is caught.
✓ **Criminals should be punished when they are caught.**
? If a friend came to stay with me, I would give him or her a souvenir of Barcelona so that he or she would have something to remember his or her visit.
✓ **If a friend came to stay with me, I would give them a souvenir of Barcelona so that they would have something to remember their visit.**

See Language Note opposite

headache   ✗ If I drink coffee, I get headache.
✓ **If I drink coffee, I get a headache.**

> **Headache** is a countable noun: 'I woke up with a terrible headache.' 'My wife suffers from headaches.'

health   ✗ I hope this letter finds you in a good health.
✓ **I hope this letter finds you in good health.**

Avoiding sexism in your writing

In the past, when people referred to a member of a group containing both men and women (or boys and girls), they used the pronouns **he/him/his**:

> A good <u>doctor</u> listens carefully to <u>his</u> patients.
> <u>Anyone</u> who wants to join should give <u>his</u> name to the secretary.

Nowadays, many people feel that this usage is unfair to women. If you want to avoid the danger of seeming sexist, you can use one of the following alternatives.

- **Use They/Them/Their** to refer back to an indefinite pronoun **(anyone, somebody etc):**

> <u>Anyone</u> who wants to join should give <u>their</u> name to the secretary.

Some people object to this usage in formal styles, insisting that **they** (plural) does not agree in number with **anyone** (singular). This usage is nevertheless very common.

- Make all the forms plural:

> Good <u>doctors</u> listen carefully to <u>their</u> patients.
> <u>Those</u> who want to join should give <u>their</u> name to the secretary.

- Design the sentence in such a way that a personal pronoun is not needed. For example, instead of saying 'If <u>anyone</u> wants to go now, <u>he</u> may do so', just say 'Anyone who wants to go now may do so.'

- Use **he or she, his or her, etc**:

> A good <u>doctor</u> listens carefully to <u>his or her</u> patients.

This alternative is found in formal writing, and so is the use of **he/she, his/her, s/he, etc**. However, they are generally felt to produce awkward and unnatural sentences, especially when they are repeated, as in:

> If a <u>doctor</u> listens to <u>his or her</u> patients, <u>he or she</u> will be in a better position to help them.

Health is an uncountable noun: 'Worry can affect your health.' 'Nothing in life is more important than good health.'

hear 1   ✗ They all sat down and heard my story.
✓ **They all sat down and listened to my story.**
✗ I like hearing tapes and watching English films.
✓ **I like listening to tapes and watching English films.**

listen (to) = hear and pay attention (to): 'He listened carefully to every word I said.' Compare: 'I could hear two people talking but I didn't listen to what they were saying.'

2   See LOOK FORWARD TO 2

heavy
  - ✗ Her car was involved in a heavy accident.
  - ✓ **Her car was involved in a serious accident.**
  - ✗ All the prisoners had committed heavy crimes.
  - ✓ **All the prisoners had committed serious crimes.**

  a serious accident/crime/illness etc (NOT **heavy**)

height
  - ✗ She is a medium-height smartly-dressed woman.
  - ✓ **She is a smartly-dressed woman of medium height.**
  - ✗ The police wish to interview an average height man with long black hair.
  - ✓ **The police wish to interview a man of average height with long black hair.**

  of medium/average height: 'The escaped prisoner is of medium-height and was last seen wearing a green tracksuit.'

help 1
  - ✗ The girl's parents couldn't help to worry about her.
  - ✓ **The girl's parents couldn't help worrying about her.**

  can't/couldn't help doing sth: 'I couldn't help laughing when I saw what he was doing.'

2
  - ✗ Remember to call me if you need a help.
  - ✓ **Remember to call me if you need help.**

  Help is usually an uncountable noun: 'Do you want some help?' 'He doesn't like asking for help.'
  Note however the phrase **be a (great/tremendous) help**: 'Thanks for coming and looking after the children. You've been a great help.' 'It would be a great help if you could just address all the envelopes.'

here 1
  - ✗ The weather in here is very cold.
  - ✓ **The weather here is very cold.**
  - ✗ The people in here believe in Hinduism.
  - ✓ **The people here believe in Hinduism.**

  Do not use **in** before **here/there** when you mean 'in this country or region': 'I'm having a problem with the food here.' 'Groceries here are much cheaper than in Japan.'
  You use **in here** when you mean 'in this building/room/container etc': 'Nobody is allowed to come in here except authorized personnel.' 'I leave most of my books in here'.

2
  - x She comes to here every afternoon to feed the birds.
  - ✓ **She comes here every afternoon to feed the birds.**

  Do not use **to** before **here/there** unless you are indicating or pointing to something: 'When the tide comes in, the water reaches right up to here.'

3
  - ✗ You do not need to bring a coat because here is warm.
  - ✓ **You do not need to bring a coat because it's warm here.**
  - ✗ Here is very different.
  - ✓ **It's very different here.**

  When you are describing a situation, begin the clause with **it** (NOT **here**): 'It's raining here.'

high
  - ✗ Beauvais is very proud of having the highest cathedral in Europe.

✓ **Beauvais is very proud of having the tallest cathedral in Europe.**

✗ Smoke pours out of the high chimneys all day long.

✓ **Smoke pours out of the tall chimneys all day long**

> Use **high** to describe something that is a long way above the ground (or whose top is a long way above the ground): 'The rooms on the ground floor have very high ceilings.' 'The top shelf was too high for me to reach.' 'The high wall made it impossible for prisoners to escape.'
> Use **tall** (NOT **high**) to describe people, animals, trees, plants and things which are narrow and above average height: 'Most of the tall trees had been cut down.' 'I'd like to marry someone tall with a sense of humour.' 'He's almost six feet tall.'

hinder 1

✗ His health hindered him to do any hard work.

✓ **His health prevented him from doing any hard work.**

✗ Nobody can hinder people having fun.

✓ **Nobody can prevent people from having fun.**

> **hinder sth** = cause progress, development, growth etc to slow down or stop: 'Higher interest rates could hinder economic growth.' 'Heavy rains hindered the expedition's progress.'
> **prevent** (or **stop**) **sb from doing sth** = make it impossible for someone to do something: 'He removed the ignition key to prevent them from leaving.'

2

✗ Capital punishment aims to hinder people from committing such crimes.

✓ **Capital punishment aims to deter people from committing such crimes.**

> **deter sb (from doing sth)** = persuade someone not to do something: 'The threat of imprisonment has failed to deter these young offenders.'

hire

✗ I'm hiring a small house near the university.

✓ **I'm renting a small house near the university.**

> In British English you **hire** a suit, meeting hall, bicycle, fishing rod etc. You obtain the use of these things, usually for a short period, by making a single payment: 'Why buy a wedding dress when you can hire one?' 'Herr Platzer showed us where we could hire bicycles.'
> You **rent** a house, shop, apartment, television etc, usually for a longer period, by making a series of payments: 'There are plenty of offices to rent in the town centre.' When talking about cars, you can use **rent** or **hire**: 'There's usually a place at the airport where you can hire/rent a car.'
> In American English you always **rent** something (not **hire**), regardless of what it is or the length of the arrangement.

historic 1

✗ She likes reading historic novels.

✓ **She likes reading historical novels.**

> **historic** = (1) very important in history: 'a historic voyage', 'a historic decision' (2) having a long history: 'a historic tradition', 'a historic building'
> **historical** = (1) about or based upon people who actually lived or events that actually happened: 'Historical records suggest that the prince was fully aware of the murders.' (2) connected with or found in history: 'a diary of great historical interest', 'a historical document', 'for historical reasons'.

2   ✗ He likes reading historic books.
       ✓ **He likes reading history books.**
       ✗ We spent the afternoon at the historic museum.
       ✓ **We spent the afternoon at the history museum.**

> **a history book/lesson/museum** etc = a book/lesson/museum etc that deals with the subject of history: 'Our history teacher next term is Mr Young.'

historical   ✗ We shall be taking you to see several interesting historical places.
             ✓ **We shall be taking you to see several interesting historic places.**

> See note at HISTORIC 1

hit 1   ✗ Turning round, I hit a vase which broke into several pieces.
         ✓ **Turning round, I knocked over a vase which broke into several pieces.**

> **knock over** = hit something by accident so that it falls from a standing position: 'The cat jumped up onto the table and knocked over a full glass of red wine.'

2   ✗ I was so terrified that I hit and kicked them with all my might.
       ✓ **I was so terrified that I punched and kicked them with all my might.**

> **punch and kick** (NOT **hit and kick**): 'The boy on the ground was punching and kicking to defend himself.'

hold   ✗ One of the men walked over to me and held my bag.
        ✓ **One of the men walked over to me and took hold of my bag.**
        ✗ As soon as she saw the mouse, she held a knife.
        ✓ **As soon as she saw the mouse, she picked up a knife.**

> **hold** = have something in your hand/hands/arms etc: 'I'd been holding the baby for nearly an hour and my right arm was getting tired.'
> **get/take hold of** = put your fingers or hands around something and hold it: 'Quick! Get hold of the rope! The boat's drifting away.'
> **pick up** = put your fingers around something and take it: 'He bent down to pick up the glove that she'd dropped.'

hole   ✗ He didn't want us to see the hole on his sock.
        ✓ **He didn't want us to see the hole in his sock.**
        ✗ The yacht hit the side of the ferry and made a hole in it.
        ✓ **The yacht hit the side of the ferry and made a hole in it.**

> **(make) a hole in sth** (NOT **on**): 'The bucket had a hole in the bottom.'

holiday 1   ✗ She said she was going on holidays to France.
             ✓ **She said she was going on holiday to France.**
             ✗ I've just got back from holidays.
             ✓ **I've just got back from holiday.**

> Speakers of British English use **(be/go) on holiday, (return/get back) from holiday** (WITHOUT **–s**): 'I met her while I was on holiday in Switzerland.' 'We're supposed to be going on holiday with them.'
> The plural form **holidays** is usually used with **the/my/your** etc: 'Where are you going for your holiday/s this year?' 'During the long summer holiday/s some students get a part-time job.'

Speakers of American Engish use **(be/go) on vacation** etc.

2 ✗ The children stay up late when they are in their holidays.
✓ **The children stay up late when they are on holiday.**
✗ In those days we couldn't afford to go in holidays.
✓ **In those days we couldn't afford to go on holiday.**
(be/go) on holiday (NOT **in (your) holidays**): 'Mark's on holiday this week.' 'On holiday I just like to relax and read a book or two.'

3 ✗ It's time you made a holiday.
✓ **It's time you had a holiday.**
✗ At Easter a lot of pensioners go to Lugano to make a holiday.
✓ **At Easter a lot of pensioners go to Lugano to have a holiday.**
See Language Note at DO

4 See PASS1

home 1 ✗ As soon as I arrived at home, I knew that something was wrong.
✓ **As soon as I arrived home, I knew that something was wrong.**
✗ When the examinations are over, I'm going to home.
✓ **When the examinations are over, I'm going home.**
arrive/go/return home (WITHOUT **at/to**): 'Let's go home and have something to eat.' 'We arrived home at six o'clock.'
Compare: 'We arrived at their house at six o'clock.'

2 ✗ I have to stay in my home to look after our baby.
✓ **I have to stay at home to look after our baby.**
✗ We decided to spend the weekend in our home.
✓ **We decided to spend the weekend at home.**
at home (NOT **in my/our** etc **home**): 'I'm fed up with being at home all the time.'

3 ✗ We left my uncle's home at ten o'clock.
✓ **We left my uncle's house at ten o'clock.**
✗ Why don't you stay in Joan's home?
✓ **Why don't you stay at Joan's house?**
leave/stay at/go home BUT **leave/stay at/go to sb's house**
Compare: 'Shall we go home or shall we go to your house?'

4 ✗ If they want to go outside the home, they have to ask their husbands.
✓ **If they want to go out, they have to ask their husbands.**
When someone leaves their house for a short while, they **go out**: 'I'd like to go out but I'm too tired.'

5 ✗ Saudi women were not allowed to work outside their home.
✓ **Saudi women were not allowed to go out to work.**
See Language Note at OCCUPATION

6 ✗ My parents don't want me to live out of home.
✓ **My parents don't want me to live away from home.**

(live/move) away from home (NOT **out of home**): 'I've been living away from home for almost two years.'

homework 1 ✗ In my opinion, women who go out to work don't have enough time to do the homework.

✓ **In my opinion, women who go out to work don't have enough time to do the housework.**

homework = work that a teacher gives a pupil to do at home
housework = all the jobs that have to be done regularly to keep a house or flat clean and tidy

housework

2 ✗ Have you done your homeworks?

✓ **Have you done your homework?**

Homework is an uncountable noun: 'We're given a lot of homework at the weekend.'

3 ✗ Our teacher wanted to know why we hadn't made our homework.

Our teacher wanted to know why we hadn't done our homework.

homework

See Language Note at DO

honestly 1 ✗ Honestly, we didn't play very well in the final.

✓ **To be honest, we didn't play very well in the final.**

✗ Honestly, I don't really like her husband.

✓ **To tell you the truth, I don't really like her husband.**

Use **honestly** when you want someone to believe that what you are saying is really true: 'I honestly don't mind where we go, as long as we go somewhere.' 'I was going to give it back to you, honestly.'
To show someone that you are about to tell them your own true feelings about something (especially feelings that you usually keep secret), use **to be honest (with you), in all honesty, to tell (you) the truth, (quite) frankly** or **to be frank**: 'In all honesty, I'll be glad when the children are back at school.' 'To tell you the truth, I don't think that the marriage will last long.'

2 ✗ I honestly say that I haven't seen anyone work so hard.

✓ **I can honestly say that I haven't seen anyone work so hard.**

I can honestly say (WITH **can**): 'I can honestly say this is the worst film I've ever seen.'

hope 1 ✗ I hope that one day things would change.

✓ **I hope that one day things will change.**

✗ I hope that you would think seriously about this matter.

✓ **I hope that you will think seriously about this matter.**

You **hope** that someone **will** do something or that something **will** happen (NOT **would**): 'I hope that you won't be offended if I don't come.'

2 ✗ I hope you to have a good time at the party.

✓ **I hope you have a good time at the party.**

When there is a change of subject after **hope**, use **hope** + **that** clause (NOT **hope** + **to-v**): 'She hopes (that) you'll come again.' 'We hope (that) your parents enjoyed their stay.'
When there is no change of subject, use **hope** + **to-v** (or **hope** + **that**

clause): 'She hopes to come again.' (= <u>she</u> hopes that <u>she</u> will come again) 'They hope to visit the Istana.' (=<u>they</u> hope (that) <u>they</u> will visit the Istana)

3 ✗ I deeply hope that there will never be another war.
  ✓ **I sincerely hope that there will never be another war.**
  sincerely hope (NOT **deeply**): 'I sincerely hope that you will understand why we cannot come after all.'

4 ✗ Are you still unhappy? I don't hope so.
  ✓ **Are you still unhappy? I hope not.**
  When you wish that something previously mentioned is not true, use **I hope not**: 'Do you have to have another medical examination?' 'I hope not.'

hopeless ✗ I think the students will feel hopeless because they have already tried their best and failed.
  ✓ **I think the students will feel disheartened because they have already tried their best and failed.**
  Hopeless is usually used to describe a situation, not a person: 'The firemen tried to get the blaze under control, but it was hopeless.' When you say that a person is **hopeless,** you mean that they are very bad at something: 'He's hopeless at remembering names.'
  To describe someone who feels that they have little or no chance of success, especially because they have already experienced failure or disappointment, use **dispirited, dejected, disheartened, discouraged, despondent** or **demoralized**: 'Having lost ten matches in a row, the team felt completely demoralized.'

horizon 1 ✗ The tiny light looked like a star in the horizon.
  ✓ **The tiny light looked like a star on the horizon.**
  on the horizon (NOT **in**): 'The sun was setting on the horizon.'

2 ✗ Further education enables you to broaden your horizon.
  ✓ **Further education enables you to broaden your horizons.**
  your horizons (WITH − s) = the range of things that you are involved or interested in: 'As a politician, his horizons extend no further than the next election.'

hospital 1 ✗ I've been in the hospital for the last five weeks.
  ✓ **I've been in hospital for the last five weeks.**
  See note at SCHOOL 1

2 ✗ I want to go and see my grandmother who is ill at hospital.
  ✓ **I want to go and see my grandmother who is ill in hospital.**
  ✗ It gave me the opportunity to work at a hospital.
  ✓ **It gave me the opportunity to work in a hospital.**
  in (a) hospital (NOT **at**): 'I didn't like being in hospital.'

hour ✗ It was a twelve hours trip.
  ✓ **It was a twelve-hour trip.**
  See Language Note at HUNDRED

household ✗ At the weekend they have to do all the household.
  ✓ **At the weekend they have to do all the housework.**

✗ Some women get no help with the household work.
✓ **Some women get no help with the housework.**

> **household** = all the people living together in a house or flat: 'Be quiet or you'll wake the whole household.'
> **housework** = all the jobs that have to be done regularly to keep a house or flat clean and tidy: 'My husband and I share all the housework between us.'

housekeeper ✗ Most Korean women are housekeepers.
✓ **Most Korean women are housewives.**

> **housekeeper** = a person who does the cooking and keeps a house clean, usually paid by the owners of the house: 'We can't afford to employ a housekeeper.'
> **housewife** = a married woman who does not have a full-time job outside the house: 'She doesn't want to give up her job and become a housewife.'

housework ✗ I do all the houseworks myself.
✓ **I do all the housework myself.**

> **Housework** is an uncountable noun: 'There's always lots of housework to be done.'

how 1 ✗ Could you describe how the driver looks like?
✓ **Could you describe what the driver looks like?**
✗ How is Christmas in France?
✓ **What is Christmas like in France?**
✗ How do the new shoes feel like?
✓ **What do the new shoes feel like?**

> When you ask for or give a description of someone or something, use **what ... like** (NOT **how**): 'What's your new English teacher like?' 'This drawing gives you an idea of what the new shopping complex will look like.' 'What does it feel like to win an Olympic gold medal?' 'What do the apples taste like?'

2 ✗ How do you think of the hotel?
✓ **What do you think of the hotel?**
✗ Should I tell him the truth? How do you think?
✓ **Should I tell him the truth? What do you think?**

> When you ask someone for their opinion, use **what ... think** (NOT **how**): 'What do you think of Ann's new car?'

3 ✗ Their decision will depend on how good is your offer.
✓ **Their decision will depend on how good your offer is.**
✗ Please let me know how much is the postage.
✓ **Please let me know how much the postage is.**

> In a subordinate clause, the subject and verb do NOT change places. Compare: 'How much did she pay for it?' 'Do you know how much she paid for it?'

4 ✗ I must tell you how I was pleased to receive a letter from you.
✓ **I must tell you how pleased I was to receive a letter from you.**
✗ I keep telling myself how I am lucky to have such wonderful children.

✓ **I keep telling myself how lucky I am to have such wonderful children.**

how + adjective/adverb + subject + verb: 'I can't describe how sad I felt.' 'How clumsy you are!' 'I was amazed at how fast she was driving.'

5 ✗ We all know how terrible disease AIDS is.
✓ **We all know what a terrible disease AIDS is.**

what + noun phrase (NOT **how**): 'I've been told what a fine chess player you are.' 'What a stupid thing to say!'

how do you do

✗ Dear Mary ... Hi! How do you do?
✓ **Dear Mary ... Hi! How are you?**

How do you do? is used in spoken English as a polite way of greeting a stranger or someone you do not know very well. It is not used in written English.
How are you? is used in spoken and written English as an informal greeting.

how much

✗ I realized how much different everybody's personality is.
✓ **I realized how different everybody's personality is.**
✗ I just can't tell you how much I'm sorry.
✓ **I just can't tell you how sorry I am.**

how + adjective/adverb (WITHOUT **much**): 'Did you notice how sad he looked?'

however

✗ I don't like shopping however I'll come with you.
✓ **I don't like shopping but I'll come with you.**

Unlike **but, however** is an adverb (NOT a conjunction) and is used only in formal styles: 'I was hoping to deal with this matter quickly. However, the situation is more complicated than I thought.' 'The newspapers always carried stories of new advances and glorious victories. In reality, however, the war was not going well.'
See also NEVERTHELESS, THEREFORE 1

huge

✗ Meno Park in Central Tokyo is very huge.
✓ **Meno Park in Central Tokyo is (absolutely) huge.**
See note at VERY 2

human

✗ The human's brain works better in the morning.
✓ **The human brain works better in the morning.**

Human is mainly used as an adjective: 'We should accept the fact that human judgement is fallible.'
Compare: 'A person's brain works better in the morning.'

humid

✗ He was living in a cold basement flat which had humid walls and almost no furniture.
✓ **He was living in a cold basement flat which had damp walls and almost no furniture.**
See note at DAMP

humour

? Bill looks angry. Is he in a bad humour?
✓ **Bill looks angry. Is he in a bad mood?**
? Sometimes when I'm in a good humour, I like to cook something special.

✓ **Sometimes when I'm in a good mood, I like to cook something special.**

Your **mood** is the way you feel (about life) at a particular time: 'Doctors believe that tiredness affects your mood and behaviour.' 'George is in a bad mood this morning. Has someone upset him?'
Humour is used with a similar meaning, but only in formal or literary styles: 'Steven was deep in bad humour.'

hundred   See Language Note opposite

hurry   ✗ I was in hurry to catch the train.
✓ **I was in a hurry to catch the train.**

(be) in a hurry (to do sth): 'I was in such a hurry that I nearly knocked him over.'

Using numbers

- **Day, month, minute, mile, kilo etc** are always SINGULAR when used (with a number) immediately before a noun: 'a six-minute wait', 'a ten-second silence', 'a five-mile race'.

  > My travel agent had arranged a 6-day coach tour.
  > The company provides a three-month training course.

  Compare: 'We waited for thirty minutes.' 'We had a thirty-minute wait.'

- When you say **100, 1000, etc,** or write these numbers in words, use **a hundred, a thousand** (WITH **a**):

  > The palace was built a thousand years ago.

  Compare: 'The palace was built 1000 years ago.'

  For emphasis or to be exact, it is possible to use **one** instead of **a**:

  > I am one hundred percent against the idea.

- After **a/one/five/twelve etc,** the words **hundred, thousand, etc** are always SINGULAR and are NOT followed by **of**:

  > Five hundred children are born in the city every day.
  > More than three thousand people were there.

  Similarly, **of** is NOT used after **100, 250, 3000 etc:**

  > If you kill 200 whales a year, they will soon disappear.

  Hundreds (of), thousands (of) etc are used only when you give a general idea of how many or how much: 'There were hundreds of stars in the sky.' 'They've spent thousands (of pounds) on improvements to the house.'

- Use **and** between **hundred** and the next number. (In American English, **and** is often omitted, especially in formal styles.)

  > *BrE* The club has about a hundred and thirty members.
  > *AmE* The club has about a hundred (and) thirty members.

I 1

✗ I and some of my classmates publish a monthly magazine.
✓ **Some of my classmates and I publish a monthly magazine.**

Someone **and I** (NOT **I and** someone): 'My husband and I belong to a diving club.'

2

✗ She is one year younger than I.
✓ **She is one year younger than I am.**
✓ **She is one year younger than me.**

In comparisons use **than me/him/her/us/them** (object pronouns) or **than I am/he is/she is/we are/they are**: 'You're stronger than him.' 'You're stronger than he is.'

idea

✗ I had the brilliant idea to invite Sonia to my party.
✓ **I had the brilliant idea of inviting Sonia to my party.**

the idea of doing sth: 'She doesn't like the idea of staying in the house on her own.'
Compare: 'It was a good idea to invite Sonia to your party.'

if 1

✗ If it will rain, I'll come and meet you in the car.
✓ **If it rains, I'll come and meet you in the car.**

See Language Note at WILL

2

See WOULD

3

See DEPEND 3

4

See SO 1

ill 1

✗ I am being trained to look after ill children.
✓ **I am being trained to look after sick children.**

Ill (= sick) is usually used after a verb: 'I told the doctor that I felt ill.' 'His father is seriously ill in hospital.'
Before a noun, use **sick**: 'Your father is a very sick man.'

2

✗ He wanted to be with his son who was badly ill.
✓ **He wanted to be with his son who was seriously ill.**

seriously ill (NOT **badly**): 'So far three people have died and five more are seriously ill.'

imaginary

✗ People tend to become less imaginary as they grow older.
✓ **People tend to become less imaginative as they grow older.**

imaginary = not existing in real life but only in someone's mind: 'This new novel takes the reader on an imaginary journey into space.' 'The

little boy kept firing an imaginary gun at me.'
imaginative = having or showing a powerful imagination: 'She is one of the most imaginative designers of her generation.' 'His paintings tend to be highly imaginative.'

imitate   ✗   I think I shall imitate my friend and join the club too.
✓   **I think I shall copy my friend and join the club too.**

imitate = do something in exactly the same way that someone else does it: 'Have you heard him trying to imitate an Englishman speaking French?' 'He walks as if he is trying to imitate Donald Duck.'
copy = do the same thing as someone else: 'As soon as I began cycling to work, people started copying me.' 'His little sister wants to copy him all the time.'

immedi-   ✗   'Let me know immediately she will arrive,' he shouted.
ately   **1**   ✓   **'Let me know immediately she arrives,' he shouted.**
See Language Note at WILL

2   ✗   At the airport he began immediately taking photographs.
✓   **At the airport he immediately began taking photographs.**
See Language Note at ALWAYS

immigrate   ✗   Some of those who can't find a job decide to immigrate.
✓   **Some of those who can't find a job decide to emigrate.**
✗   We're planning to immigrate to the United States next year.
✓   **We're planning to emigrate to the United States next year.**

The verb **immigrate** (= enter a foreign country and make your home there) is seldom used. Instead people tend to use **immigrant** and **immigration** (nouns): 'When jobs became scarce, the number of new immigrants suddenly decreased.' 'Immigration has decreased in recent years.'
emigrate = leave your own country and make your home in another one: 'His parents emigrated from Scotland to Canada in 1933.'

impact   ✗   I doubt whether it will cause an impact on the readers.
✓   **I doubt whether it will have an impact on the readers.**
See Language Note at DO

important 1   ✗   He said that money was not important for him.
✓   **He said that money was not important to him.**
If you care or think about something a lot, it is **important to** you (NOT **for**): 'The watch is very important to me because it belonged to my grandmother.' Compare: 'English is very important for my career.'

2   See CAUSE 4, PROBLEM 2

3   See THING 1, 2

impression 1   ✗   I decided to change my impression and had all my hair cut short.
✓   **I decided to change my image and had all my hair cut short.**
impression = an opinion or feeling that you have about someone or something, especially after just a short time: 'My impression is that she would make an excellent teacher.' 'He gives the impression of being someone you can trust.'

image = the general picture that you want people to have in their minds when they think of you or your company, organization etc: 'After all the bad publicity, the company needs to improve its image.'

2 ✗ My first impression about Californians was very positive.
   ✓ **My first impression of Californians was very positive.**
   impression of sb/sth: 'They went back to Japan with very different impressions of what England was like.'

3 ✗ He wanted to make a good impression to his girlfriend.
   ✓ **He wanted to make a good impression on his girlfriend.**
   make an impression on sb: 'His first priority was to make a favourable impression on the prison warden.'

impulse
   ✗ I hope your trip will provide impulse for the essay you will have to write when you get back.
   ✓ **I hope your trip will provide inspiration for the essay you will have to write when you get back.**
   impulse = a sudden desire to do something: 'I had a sudden impulse to walk out of the classroom and never return.' 'It's unwise to act on impulse.'
   inspiration = (a source of) creative energy: 'The inspiration for these early poems came from his relationship with Lucy Potter.'

in 1
   ✗ In 1st July we went to Italy by car.
   ✓ **On 1st July we went to Italy by car.**
   ✗ I made an appointment for the following Friday. In that day I got up early so as to have plenty of time.
   ✓ **I made an appointment for the following Friday. On that day I got up early so as to have plenty of time.**
   See Language Note at TIME

2
   ✗ I haven't seen any good films in this year.
   ✓ **I haven't seen any good films this year.**
   ✗ There was almost a nuclear disaster in last year.
   ✓ **There was almost a nuclear disaster last year.**
   ✗ We intend to visit the north of England in this summer.
   ✓ **We intend to visit the north of England this summer.**
   See Language Note at TIME

3
   ✗ We have 4 classes in a day.
   ✓ **We have 4 classes a day.**
   ✗ They usually work 39 hours in a week.
   ✓ **They usually work 39 hours a week.**
   Expressions of frequency, speed, duration etc do not contain **in**: 'The shop is open six days a week.' 'He visits his father three times a year.' 'Bananas cost fifty pence a pound.' 'I drove to the hospital at ninety miles an hour.'

4
   ✗ I noticed that nobody cried in the funeral.
   ✓ **I noticed that nobody cried at the funeral.**
   ✗ I'm sorry that I can't be there in the wedding.
   ✓ **I'm sorry that I can't be there at the wedding.**
   (be) **at** an event (Such as a wedding, party, meeting etc NOT **in**): 'I

didn't expect to see his ex-wife at the party.' 'Will Dr Sirinanda be at the conference.'

5 ✗ I'm a student in the University of Jordan.
✓ **I'm a student at the Univeristy of Jordan.**
✗ For the last year I have been studying in the British Council.
✓ **For the last year I have been studying at the British Council.**
(be/study/be a student/teach etc) at (a) college/university etc (NOT **in/of**): 'His wife teaches chemistry at Bristol University.' 'I'm a Hotel Management student at Henley College.'

incapable ✗ Most small children are incapable to sit still for more than five minutes.
✓ **Most small children are incapable of sitting still for more than five minutes.**
incapable of doing sth: 'James is incapable of staying awake after ten o'clock.'

include 1 ✗ One of the bottles including the virus had been stolen.
✓ **One of the bottles containing the virus had been stolen.**
✗ Classes should include no more than 20 students.
✓ **Classes should contain no more than 20 students.**
See Language Note on next page

2 ✗ Milk also includes vitamins.
✓ **Milk also contains vitamins.**
See Language Note on next page

3 ✗ The poem includes just two short verses.
✓ **The poem consists of just two short verses.**
✗ Education in Jordan includes three stages.
✓ **Education in Jordan consists of three stages.**
See Language Note on next page

4 ✗ I am including a photograph of myself.
✓ **I am enclosing a photograph of myself.**
See Language Note on next page

increase 1 ✗ I'd like to increase my English.
✓ **I'd like to improve my English.**
✗ We can increase the economic situation by working harder.
✓ **We can improve the economic situation by working harder.**
increase = become or make (something) greater in amount, number or degree: 'The government has increased taxes.' 'As their profits increase, the companies expand.' 'The number of words in the language is increasing all the time.'
improve = become or make (something) better: 'Efforts are being made to improve the quality of the medical services.'

2 ✗ The government is trying to increase the level of education.
✓ **The government is trying to raise the level of education.**
✗ In Hong Kong the standard of living has increased sharply.
✓ **In Hong Kong the standard of living has risen sharply.**

> When you are talking about the **level** or **standard** of something, use **raise/rise** (NOT **increase**): 'The standard of living continues to rise.'

CONTAIN • INCLUDE • ENCLOSE • CONSIST OF • COMPRISE • BE COMPOSED OF • BE MADE UP OF

contain	Use **contain** (1) when you say what a box, bottle, bag etc has inside it: 'The bag contained some old clothes.' (2) when you mention one or more of the things that something is made of or has in it: 'Water contains hydrogen and oxygen.' 'The film contained a number of violent scenes.'
include	If something **includes** another thing, it has it as one of its parts: 'The holiday package includes a two-day cruise along the Rhine.' 'The price includes a small charge for postage and packing.'
enclose	Use **enclose** when you tell someone what you are putting in the envelope or parcel that you are sending them: 'I'm enclosing a copy of the book review that you asked for.'
consist of **comprise** (formal) **be composed of** **be made up of**	When you mention all the parts that something has in it, use **consist of/comprise/be composed of/be made up of**: 'The book consists of six chapters and a brief introduction.' 'The earth's atmosphere is composed mainly of nitrogen, oxygen and carbon dioxide.' 'The house comprises two bedrooms, a bathroom, a kitchen, and a living room.' 'The US government is made up of two legislative assemblies.' Note that you will sometimes see comprise used with of. 'This investment scheme is comprised of two separate packages.' Most careful users consider this to be incorrect, preferring: 'This investment scheme comprises two separate packages.'

3　✗　The increase of crime is accelerating.
　✓　**The increase in crime is accelerating.**
　✗　There has been an increase of the number of cars.
　✓　**There has been an increase in the number of cars.**

> **increase in sth** (NOT **of**): 'There's been a sudden increase in political activity.' 'We can expect further increases in the cost of living.'

indeed 1　✗　As for his new novel, I think it's worth reading indeed.
　✓　**As for his new novel, I think it's certainly worth reading.**
　✗　He claims that many young people do not want jobs but this is indeed not the case.
　✓　**He claims that many young people do not want jobs but this is certainly not the case.**

> **Indeed** is used (1) to introduce a statement that strengthens a previous point: 'We don't need any more high street banks. Indeed, there are too many already.' (2) to show that you agree with a previous statement or opinion: 'Cancer research has indeed come a long way in recent years.' To strengthen a point or opinion that has not been mentioned before, use **certainly** or **definitely**: 'He doesn't treat his staff very well but he

certainly knows how to make money.' 'The first essay is excellent but the second one definitely doesn't deserve more than a 'C' grade.'

2   ✗ I'm afraid that I won't be able to come to your wedding. Indeed, I'm giving a lecture on that day.
   ✓ **I'm afraid that I won't be able to come to your wedding. As it happens, I'm giving a lecture on that day.**

To show that something that you are about to mention is connected by chance with something you have mentioned before, use **as it happens** or **it so happens that**: 'We've just seen a really beautiful house and it so happens that it's for sale.'

3   ✗ Secondary students are under great pressure indeed.
   ✓ **Secondary students are under very great pressure indeed.**
   ✗ We all had a good time indeed.
   ✓ **We all had a very good time indeed.**

very + adjective + noun + **indeed**: 'I thought it was a very clever answer indeed.'
very + adjective/adverb + **indeed**: 'The quality of the recording is very good indeed.' 'Some of the students did very well.'

4   ✗ America is a paradise for young people indeed.
   ✓ **America is indeed a paradise for young people.**
See Language Note at ALWAYS

independent   ✗ Nowadays young people want to be independent from their parents.
   ✓ **Nowadays young people want to be independent of their parents.**

independent of sb/sth (NOT **from**): 'Good students soon become independent of their teachers.'

indoor   ✗ As it was raining we decided to stay indoor.
   ✓ **As it was raining we decided to stay indoors.**

Indoor (WITHOUT **s**) is an adjective: 'an indoor tennis court', 'indoor athletics'.
Indoors (WITH **s**) is an adverb: 'I don't like spending the whole day indoors.'

indoors   ✗ Their new house even has an indoors swimming pool.
   ✓ **Their new house even has an indoor swimming pool.**
See note at INDOOR

industrious   ✗ The South has fewer industrious areas.
   ✓ **The South has fewer industrial areas.**

industrious = hard-working: 'Neil is indeed a quiet student, but you won't find anyone more industrious.'
industrial = having or connected with major industries: 'We visited some of the country's main industrial areas.' 'The economy has been hit by a series of industrial disputes.'

industry 1   ✗ The biggest industries in Jakobsberg are Philips and IBM.
   ✓ **The biggest companies in Jakobsberg are Philips and IBM.**
See Language Note on next page

COMPANY • FACTORY • INDUSTRY • MILL • PLANT • WORKS	
company	an organization that makes or sells goods or that sells services: 'My father works for an insurance company.' 'IBM is one of the biggest companies in the electronics industry.'
factory	a place where goods such as furniture, carpets, curtains, clothes, plates, toys, bicycles, sports equipment, drinks and packaged food are produced: 'The company's UK factory produces 500 golf trolleys a week.'
industry	(1) all the people, factories, companies etc involved in a major area of production: 'the steel industry', 'the clothing industry' (2) all industries considered together as a single thing: 'Industry has developed rapidly over the years at the expense of agriculture.'
mill	(1) a place where a particular type of material is made: 'a cotton mill', 'a textile mill', 'a steel mill', 'a paper mill' (2) a place where flour is made from grain: 'a flour mill'
plant	a factory or building where vehicles, engines, weapons, heavy machinery, drugs or industrial chemicals are produced, where chemical processes are carried out, or where power is generated: 'Vauxhall-Opel's UK car plants', 'Honda's new engine plant at Microconcord. Swindon', 'a sewage plant', 'a wood treatment plant', 'ICI's £100m plant, 'the Sellafield nuclear reprocessing plant in Cumbria'
works	an industrial building where materials such as cement, steel, and bricks are produced, or where industrial processes are carried out: 'The drop in car and van sales has led to redundancies in the country's steel works.'

2 ✗ Many industries have been closed because of the recession.
  ✓ **Many factories have been closed because of the recession.**
  ✗ There are car industries all over the place.
  ✓ **There are car factories/plants all over the place.**
  See Language Note above

3 ✗ They are demanding that all the nuclear industries are shut down.
  ✓ **They are demanding that all the nuclear plants are shut down.**
  See Language Note above

4 ✗ Another thing that education has changed is the industry.
  ✓ **Another thing that education has changed is industry.**
  ✗ The industry as a whole must become more environmentally friendly.
  ✓ **Industry as a whole must become more environmentally friendly.**

When **industry** means all industries seen together as one thing, it is an uncountable noun: 'She can't decide whether she wants a career in banking or in industry.'

in fact See Language Note at FACT

infancy ✗ Mr Fox had a very difficult infancy.
  ✓ **Mr Fox had a very difficult childhood.**

Infancy (= the period when a child is very young) is used mainly in formal and technical styles: 'In those days, large numbers of children died in infancy.'
To refer to the period when someone is a child, use **childhood**: 'The old photographs brought back memories of my childhood.'

infant ✗ I had to stay at home and look after my infants.
  ✓ **I had to stay at home and look after my children.**

Infant (= a baby or very young child) is used mainly in literary and technical styles: 'The infant, cradled in Mariam's arms, began to cry.' 'There are clear differences in temperament and speed of learning among infants at this early stage.'

inferior ✗ They still think that women are inferior than men.
  ✓ **They still think that women are inferior to men.**

inferior/superior to (NOT **than**): 'To suggest that women doctors are in some way inferior to their male counterparts is scandalous.' 'Why do they think they're so superior to the rest of us?'

influence 1 ✗ These drugs have no influence on the virus.
  ✓ **These drugs have no effect on the virus.**
  ✗ I asked him not to keep disturbing me, but it had no influence.
  ✓ **I asked him not to keep disturbing me, but it had no effect.**

If someone (or something) has an **influence**, they help to shape the way that someone or something develops: 'D.W. Griffith had an enormous influence on the motion picture industry.'
If something has an **effect**, it causes a change to take place in someone or something: 'The war had a disastrous effect on the economy.'

2 ✗ America has given a tremendous influence to Japanese society.
  ✓ **America has had a tremendous influence on Japanese society.**

have an influence on sb/sth (NOT **give ... to/in/for**): 'The book attempts to demonstrate the influence of the stars on people's lives.'

3 ✗ I don't think that longer prison sentences would influence on criminals.
  ✓ **I don't think that longer prison sentences would influence criminals.**

influence sb/sth (WITHOUT **on**): 'The revolution of 1789 influenced events far beyond France.'
Note the alternative: 'I don't think that longer prison sentences would deter criminals.'

informa-tion 1

✗ On Friday we'll be able to give you further information of the trip.
✓ **On Friday we'll be able to give you further information about the trip.**
✗ Can you give me any information for summer courses?
✓ **Can you give me any information about summer courses?**

information about/on sth (NOT **of/for**): 'These files contain detailed information about our overseas customers.'

2

✗ Would you please send me more informations about the course?
✓ **Would you please send me more information about the course?**
✗ Let me know if you need a further information.
✓ **Let me know if you need (any) further information.**

See Language Note at SCENERY

inhabit

✗ The bathroom was already inhabited.
✓ **The bathroom was already occupied.**

inhabit = (usually passive) live in a place or area, especially for a long time or permanently: 'The island is mainly inhabited by sheep.' 'The remoter mountain regions are still inhabited by indigenous tribes.'
occupy = use or live in a room, house or building for any length of time: 'Is that seat occupied?' 'The flat below was occupied by a young Sri Lankan couple.'

inhabitant 1

? The inhabitants certainly know how to make money from tourists.
✓ **The local inhabitants certainly know how to make money from tourists.**

The **inhabitants** of a particular town, country or area are the people who live there, especially considered in terms of quantity or history: 'Just ten years ago the town had only 12,000 inhabitants.' 'The first inhabitants of the island planted coffee beans.'
To refer to the people living in and around a village or town, who have shared interests and activities, use **local inhabitants/local residents/ local population** or (in informal styles) **locals**: 'The local residents are against the motorway proposal.'

2 ✗ The rapid growth of the world's inhabitants has produced serious social and economic problems.
✓ **The rapid growth of the world's population has produced serious social and economic problems.**

To refer to all the people in the world, or all the people living in a particular country, city, town etc, use **population**: 'Half the world's population doesn't have enough to eat.' 'To make it profitable, about a third of the population of France will have to visit Eurodisney each year.' 'The town has a population of 15,000.'

injure 1

✗ My car was seriously injured in the accident.
✓ **My car was badly damaged in the accident.**
✗ We must all stop injuring the environment.
✓ **We must all stop damaging the environment.**

> **Injure** is used only in connection with people and animals: 'Latest reports from the site of the crash indicate that three people are dead and twelve are seriously injured.'
> For objects, plants and machines, use **damage**: 'Some of the equipment had been badly damaged.'

2   ✗ He shot dead 22 innocent people and injured 23 others.
  ✓ **He shot dead 22 innocent people and wounded 23 others.**

> **wound** = injure a person or animal by using a weapon such as a gun or knife: 'He is accused of wounding a fellow prisoner.' 'The sergeant had been seriously wounded and was losing blood.'

3   ✗ Several people injured in the accident.
  ✓ **Several people were injured in the accident.**
  ✗ Fortunately the driver was wearing his seat belt and so he did not injure.
  ✓ **Fortunately the driver was wearing his seat belt and so he wasn't injured.**

> **Injure** is a transitive verb: 'Gibbs won't be playing because he's injured his knee.' In passive sentences, use **be injured**: 'You're lucky you weren't injured.'

4   ✗ I was afraid that she might injure.
  ✓ **I was afraid that she might injure herself.**

> See Language Note at MYSELF

5   ✗ He fell and was injured in the leg.
  ✓ **He fell and injured his leg.**

> **injure** + a part of the body (WITHOUT **in**): 'How did you manage to injure your shoulder?'
> Compare: 'He'd been wounded in the leg and couldn't walk.'

inquiry   ? After making several inquiries I finally discovered his address.
  ✓ **After making several enquiries, I finally discovered his address.**

> In a simple request for information, the usual word is **enquiry**: 'We've had a lot of enquiries in response to the advertisement.'
> When you mean 'a full investigation or a long serious study', the usual word is **inquiry**: 'a court of inquiry', 'There is to be an official inquiry into the cause of the crash.'

inside   ✗ Inside of the wallet there should be £20 and my Visa Card.
  ✓ **Inside the wallet there should be £20 and my Visa Card.**

> **inside sth** (WITHOUT **of**): 'Inside the box was a small silver spoon.'

insist   ✗ The porter insisted to help us with our baggage.
  ✓ **The porter insisted on helping us with our baggage.**
  ✓ **The porter insisted that he (should) help us with our baggage.**

> **insist on** (**doing**) **sth**: 'He insisted on paying for the meal himself.'
> **insist that sb** (**should**) **do sth**: 'He insisted that he (should) pay for the meal himself.'

in spite of   See SPITE

instead 1   ✗ Instead of to go to a disco, we went to the cinema.
 ✓ **Instead of going to a disco, we went to the cinema.**
 ✗ You should go out more instead to stay at home all the time.
 ✓ **You should go out more instead of staying at home all the time.**

instead of (doing) sth: 'Instead of waiting for a bus, we decided that it would be quicker to walk.'

2   ✗ We had planned to go to the museum but we went to the park instead of it.
 ✓ **We had planned to go to the museum but we went to the park instead.**

Instead means 'instead of it/that': 'Wendy said she was too tired to play badminton and so we went to the cinema instead.'

instructions   ✗ The machine is supplied with instructions how to use it.
 ✓ **The machine is supplied with instructions on how to use it.**
 ✗ I'm here to give you some instructions to cook Bin Dae Tuck.
 ✓ **I'm here to give you some instructions on how to cook Bin Dae Tuck.**

instructions on how to do sth: 'The crew has a full set of instructions on how to launch the satellite.'

intend   ✗ Students that are motivated intend to work harder.
 ✓ **Students that are motivated tend to work harder.**

intend = plan to do something: 'I intend to arrive early and make sure that I get a seat.'
tend = be likely or true in most cases: 'At that age, girls tend to be more mature than boys.'

intense   ✗ The government has embarked on an intense industrialization programme.
 ✓ **The government has embarked on an intensive industrialization programme.**

intense = strong or very great; extreme: 'intense heat', 'intense pleasure', 'intense pain', 'intense competition'
intensive = concentrated: 'an intensive English course', 'a period of intensive training'

intention   ✗ I don't have the slightest intention to accept the invitation.
 ✓ **I don't have the slightest intention of accepting the invitation.**
 ✗ We went to Stratford with the intention to see a play.
 ✓ **We went to Stratford with the intention of seeing a play.**

have no/not the slightest intention of doing sth: 'When the salesman realized that I had no intention of buying the car, he just walked off.'
with the intention of doing sth: 'I came to England with the intention of doing a PhD.'

interested 1   ✗ It was a very interested idea.
 ✓ **It was a very interesting idea.**
 See note at BORING

2 ✗ She is interested on learning French.
  ✓ **She is interested in learning French.**
  ✗ I am not really interested by the job.
  ✓ **I am not really interested in the job.**

> **interested in (doing) sth** (NOT **on/by/about**): 'I didn't know that you were interested in yoga.' 'The only thing she is interested in is having a good time.'

3 ✗ At school I wasn't interested to learn English.
  ✓ **At school I wasn't interested in learning English.**

> Use **be interested to hear/read/know** etc when you are talking about news or information: 'We were interested to learn that the research has been completed.' 'I'd be interested to know what you think of the idea.'
> Use **be interested in doing sth** when you are talking about someone who wants to do something: 'She's interested in setting up her own business.'

interesting ✗ I was interesting to hear she had got married.
  ✓ **I was interested to hear she had got married.**
  ✗ I am very interesting in community work.
  ✓ **I am very interested in community work.**

> See note at BORING

interior ✗ Solutions to the country's interior problems are still a long way away.
  ✓ **Solutions to the country's internal problems are still a long way away.**

> **interior** = on the inside of a building, room, vehicle etc: 'The interior doors are still sound but the exterior doors need replacing.'
> **the interior** = the part of a country that is a long way from the coast: 'The convoy set off at dawn for the interior.'
> **internal** = involving what happens within a particular country: 'Each country has the right to control its own internal affairs.'

interrupt ✗ The noise of the traffic interrupts the local residents.
  ✓ **The noise of the traffic disturbs the local residents.**

> **interrupt** = to stop someone while they are speaking or doing something, especially by saying something yourself: 'I'm sorry to interrupt but there's an urgent phone call for you.'
> **disturb** = make it difficult for someone to continue what they are doing: 'Will it disturb you if I listen to the radio?' 'I think we're disturbing Martin. Let's go and talk in your office.'

interruption ✗ Between the first two classes there is a ten minute interruption.
  ✓ **Between the first two classes there is a ten-minute break.**

> **interruption** = something that suddenly stops you from continuing what you are doing or saying: 'To avoid further interruption, we locked the office door.'
> **break** = a short period when students or workers are free to do what they want: 'At eleven o'clock there is a twenty-minute coffee break.' 'During their break the boys usually kick a ball around in the playground.'

intrude ✗ I hope I'm not intruding your privacy.
  ✓ **I hope I'm not intruding (on your privacy).**

✗ Reporters have no right to intrude into people's private lives.
✓ **Reporters have no right to intrude upon people's private lives.**

intrude (on/upon sb/sth): 'I'm not intruding, am I?' 'Governments should not intrude on the rights of the individual.'

invent 1

✗ It will not be long before scientists invent a cure for this terrible disease.
✓ **It will not be long before scientists discover a cure for this terrible disease.**

invent = create a machine, instrument, system or process which has never existed before: 'Who invented the telephone?' 'The cotton gin was invented by Eli Whitney in 1793.'
discover = find or find out something for the first time: 'Penicillin was discovered almost by accident.' 'I've just discovered a new way of cooking spaghetti.'

2

✗ I'm sure that your host families will invent lots of interesting things for you to do.
✓ **I'm sure that your host families will think of/up lots of interesting things for you to do.**

think of = produce a plan, idea or suggestion by thinking: 'Can you think of a good birthday present for David?' 'I can't think of any way of avoiding the problem.'
think up (also **dream up**) = produce a completely new plan, idea or suggestion by thinking hard about something: 'They've thought up a new advertising campaign.' 'Financial advisers will soon think up new ways for us to evade tax.'

3

✗ The word 'workaholic' was invented in America.
✓ **The word 'workaholic' was coined in America.**

coin a new word or expression: 'The term 'black hole' was coined in 1969 by the American scientist John Wheeler.'

invention

✗ Recent inventions in medicine have helped to reduce the rate of infant mortality.
✓ **Recent advances in medicine have helped to reduce the rate of infant mortality.**

When you are talking about the development of new ideas or techniques that have a good effect, use **advance/breakthrough/discovery**: 'This new treatment could be the breakthrough that cancer patients have been waiting for.'

invest

✗ Businessmen invest vast amounts on these industries.
✓ **Businessmen invest vast amounts in these industries.**
✗ We should invest more money to education.
✓ **We should invest more money in education.**

invest money/£1 million/time etc **in sth**: 'More money should be invested in local industries.' 'I've started investing in foreign currencies.'

investigate

✗ The Hong Kong government has already investigated into these problems.
✓ **The Hong Kong government has already investigated these problems.**

investigate sth (WITHOUT into): 'The cause of the accident is still being investigated.'
Compare: 'The army is conducting its own investigation into the explosion.' (noun + into)

invitation

✗ Thank you for the invitation for your wedding.
✓ **Thank you for the invitation to your wedding.**

invitation to a party, wedding, meeting etc: 'I've just had an invitation to a New Year's Eve party.'
Note the alternative: 'Thank you for the wedding invitation.'

invite

✗ We became friends and he invited me for his wedding.
✓ **We became friends and he invited me to his wedding.**
✗ I've been invited in a party on Friday.
✓ **I've been invited to a party on Friday.**

invite sb for a drink, meal, etc: 'She's invited us for a meal at the club.'
invite sb to dinner/lunch, a party, wedding, meeting etc: 'We don't have to invite them to dinner.' 'The President has been invited to an official reception at Buckingham Palace.'

involve

✗ My job involves to deal with customer complaints.
✓ **My job involves dealing with customer complaints.**

involve (doing) sth: 'A proper repair would involve stripping all the tiles off the roof.'

is

✗ Is very easy to get lost in a big city.
✓ **It's very easy to get lost in a big city.**
See IT 1

island 1

✗ I was on holiday with my parents on the island Capri.
✓ **I was on holiday with my parents on the island of Capri.**

the island/isle of + name: 'the holiday resort island of Langkawi', 'the Isle of Skye'

2

✗ Does anyone live in the island?
✓ **Does anyone live on the island?**
✗ I was born in a small village in Lantau Island.
✓ **I was born in a small village on Lantau Island.**

When island means 'a mass of land surrounded by water', or is part of a name, the usual preposition is on (NOT in): 'The prisoners were left on a small island, with neither food nor drinking water.' 'Mr Mandela was placed in a maximum security prison on Robben Island.'
When an island is considered in terms of its people, cities, schools, roads, traditions, economy etc, both in and on are used: 'There has been no serious outbreak of cholera in the island for over twenty years.' 'Elsewhere in the island most of these stone cottages have disappeared.'

it 1

✗ Is easy to buy exactly what you want in a big city.
✓ **It's easy to buy exactly what you want in a big city.**

When you comment on a situation, the subject of the sentence is usually it: 'It's impossible to read in the dark.' 'It was good to see you again.' 'It's hot today, isn't it?' 'It was a miracle that nobody was injured.'
Note that in this pattern it has no meaning. It simply fills the subject position.

2 See HAPPEN 1

3 See APPRECIATE 2, BEAR 2, FIND 2, LIKE 3

4 See NEED 1

it's
    ✗ The cat sat in front of the fire, cleaning it's whiskers.
    ✓ **The cat sat in front of the fire, cleaning its whiskers.**

> **it's** (WITH an apostrophe) = 'it is' or 'it has': 'It's still raining.' 'It's been raining again.'
> **its** (WITHOUT an apostrophe) = a possessive form like **my, his, their,** etc: 'The dog has hurt its nose again.'

its
    ✗ Its a nice place to have a holiday.
    ✓ **It's a nice place to have a holiday.**
    See IT'S

jargon

✗ I don't understand computer jargons.
✓ **I don't understand computer jargon.**
Jargon is an uncountable noun: 'The document was full of legal jargon.'

jealous

✗ Although I'm jealous about his achievements, he is my brother and I'm proud of him.
✓ **Although I'm jealous of his achievements, he is my brother and I'm proud of him.**
jealous of sb/sth: 'It's very common for older children to be jealous of a new baby.'

jewellery 1

✗ She had bought the ring at a jewellery.
✓ **She had bought the ring at a jeweller's.**
✗ I saw the same watch in a jewellery shop.
✓ **I saw the same watch in a jeweller's.**
jewellery = rings, bracelets, necklaces, watches, etc: 'The stolen jewellery has never been recovered.'
jeweller's = a shop which sells and repairs jewellery: 'I took the watch to my local jeweller's but they said it couldn't be repaired.'

2

✗ You should keep expensive jewelleries in a bank or safe.
✓ **You should keep expensive jewellery in a bank or safe.**
Jewellery is an uncountable noun: 'The thieves took nothing but cash and jewellery.'

job 1

✗ The photographer made quite a good job.
✓ **The photographer did quite a good job.**
✗ With the right tools, I could make the job in five minutes.
✓ **With the right tools, I could do the job in five minutes.**
do a job (NOT make): 'There are lots of jobs to do when we get home.'
(= pieces of work) 'There's no need to thank me. I was just doing my job.'
(= what I do to earn a living)
do a good/great/marvellous etc **job**: 'You can always rely on Charlie to do a good job.'
Note however the expression **make a good/bad job of sth**: 'She's made a good job of the decorating.' (= she has done it well)

2

✗ I'm willing to accept any job, even a half-time one.
✓ **I'm willing to accept any job, even a part-time one.**
See Language Note at OCCUPATION

3

? What is your job?
✓ **What do you do (for a living)?**
See Language Note at OCCUPATION

join 1   ✗ You should join in our tennis club.
✓ **You should join our tennis club.**

join a club, society etc (WITHOUT **in/up**): 'I'm thinking of joining the Labour Party.' 'He left his job and joined the army.'

2   ✗ I came to England a year ago to join with my husband.
✓ **I came to England a year ago to join my husband.**

join sb (WITHOUT **with**): 'You two go on ahead and I'll join you later.' 'Won't you join us for a drink?'

joke   ✗ He kept saying the same joke again and again.
✓ **He kept telling the same joke again and again.**

tell (sb) a joke (NOT **say**) = tell someone a short funny story to make them laugh: 'Come on, Peter! Tell us a joke!'
crack/make a joke = say something funny: 'He's always laughing and cracking jokes.'

journey 1   ✗ I've arranged a journey to Malta from April 15th to May 2nd.
✓ **I've arranged a trip to Malta from April 15th to May 2nd.**
✗ I booked a journey to Brighton for two weeks.
✓ **I booked a trip to Brighton for two weeks.**

See Language Note at TRIP

2   ✗ Then we'll rent a car and have a journey through Scotland.
✓ **Then we'll rent a car and go on a tour of Scotland.**

See Language Note at TRIP

3   ✗ It wasn't the first journey he had done to Paris.
✓ **It wasn't the first journey he had made to Paris.**

See Language Note at TRIP

judge 1   ✗ He was judged and sentenced to life imprisonment.
✓ **He was tried and sentenced to life imprisonment.**

be tried = be judged in a court of law: 'He is being tried for the murder of his wife and her lover.'

2   ✗ You shouldn't judge people for their appearance.
✓ **You shouldn't judge people by their appearance.**
✗ What standards should we judge them with?
✓ **What standards should we judge them by?**

judge sb by a particular measure: 'It's better to judge people by what they do, not just by what they say.'

jump   ✗ The price of vegetables jumped up overnight.
✓ **The price of vegetables jumped overnight.**

jump = (of an amount, price, level, etc) suddenly increase: 'House prices jumped almost 20% in the first quarter.'

junk   ✗ If you are caught dropping junk in the street, you are fined.
✓ **If you are caught dropping litter in the street, you are fined.**

junk = (informal) anything that you consider to be worthless or useless: 'The garden shed was full of old junk that hadn't been used for years.'

> **litter** = things such as empty packets, cans and bottles that are left in a public place: 'You can be fined up to £100 for dropping litter.'

just

✗ In the evening you should practise what you just have learned during the day.
✓ **In the evening you should practise what you have just learned during the day.**
See Language Note at ALWAYS

justice 1

✗ The legal system ensures the justice for everyone.
✓ **The legal system ensures justice for everyone.**
See note at THE 4

2

✗ The justice of a country uses the threat of punishment to control people.
✓ **A country's legal system uses the threat of punishment to control people.**

> **justice** = the principle of fair treatment upon which the laws of a country are based: 'the 1970 Administration of Justice Act', 'He has spent his whole life fighting for justice and freedom for all.' 'Relatives of the victims are now demanding justice.'
> **legal system** = the laws of a country and the ways in which these laws operate: 'When the colony becomes independent, it will maintain its present legal system.'

keep on ✗ He wants the new generation to keep on this tradition.
✓ **He wants the new generation to keep up this tradition.**

> **keep up** = continue a tradition, custom, habit, relationship etc (instead of letting it come to an end); continue to use a particular skill: 'We've managed to keep up our friendship despite all the problems and misunderstandings.' 'Try to keep up your English while you're back in Italy.'

keep up ✗ People of normal weight should keep up eating the food they are used to.
✓ **People of normal weight should keep (on) eating the food they are used to.**

> **keep (on) doing sth** (or **carry on doing sth**) = continue to do something (instead of stopping): 'Just keep (on) going till you come to a crossroads.' 'You should keep (on) taking the tablets until they're all gone.'
> Note the alternative: 'People of normal weight should just keep to their normal diet.'

key ✗ The key of our success is that we all worked very hard.
✓ **The key to our success is that we all worked very hard.**

> **key to** a problem or situation: 'The key to inflation is control of the money supply.'

kid ? Films of this type are not suitable for young kids.
✓ **Films of this type are not suitable for young children.**

> **kid** is used only in informal styles: 'I'll ring you back once the kids are in bed.'

kill See Language Note on next page

kind 1 ✗ I wonder if you would be so kind to send me further details and an application form.
✓ **I wonder if you would be so kind as to send me further details and an application form.**

> **be kind enough to do sth**: 'Would you be kind enough to forward the enclosed documents to Mr Tomkin's new address?'
> **be so kind as to do sth**: 'I wonder if you'd be so kind as to inform your colleagues of the new arrangements.'

2 ✗ All the people he met were very kind with him.
✓ **All the people he met were very kind to him.**

Choosing the right word:
GENERAL WORDS and EXACT WORDS

Some words have a general meaning, e.g. **big, beautiful, good, say, make, kill.** These words are useful, especially when you begin to learn English, because you can make use of them in a wide range of situations:

a big meal, a big kitchen, a big mistake, etc

For each general word, however, there is usually another word or phrase which comes closer to what you want to say, and which may also sound more natural in the context:

a substantial meal, a spacious kitchen, a serious mistake, etc

A major step towards fluency in English is getting to know plenty of exact words which can replace the more general words you have learned. Here are some words which can be used instead of the general word **kill**.

murder	To **murder** someone is to kill them deliberately and unlawfully: 'The key witness was murdered before he could testify.' A person who does this is a **murderer**.
massacre	**Massacre** is used when you talk about the deliberate killing of a large number of people, especially people who cannot defend themselves: 'Whole native populations were massacred when the European settlers arrived.'
slaughter	**Slaughter** is used when you talk about the deliberate killing of a large number of people, especially in a particularly cruel way: 'Men ran through the village burning houses and slaughtering anyone that got in their way.'
	To **slaughter** an animal is to kill it for its meat, skin, etc, or as part of a religious ceremony: 'The children couldn't understand why the cattle had to be slaughtered.'
execute	To **execute** someone (or **put** someone **to death**) is to kill someone as a punishment, according to the law: 'King Charles I was executed on 30th January 1639.'
assassinate	To **assassinate** someone is to deliberately kill a very famous or important person such as a political leader: 'President Lincoln was assassinated by John Wilkes Booth.' A person who does this is an **assassin**.
commit suicide	To **commit suicide** (or **take your own life**) is to deliberately kill yourself: 'Rather than be taken prisoner, they preferred to commit suicide.'
destroy	To **destroy** an animal (or **have** it **put down/to sleep**) is to kill it in a way that does not cause pain, especially because it is sick or injured: 'The cat had developed cancer and had to be destroyed.'

> **kind to** a person or animal (NOT **with**): 'She's always been kind to people less fortunate than herself.'

kind of 1
- ✗ There are many kind of job for people with qualifications.
- ✓ **There are many kinds of job for people with qualifications.**
- ✓ I enjoy all kind of sport.
- ✓ **I enjoy all kinds of sport.**

> **Kind, sort** and **type** are countable nouns. After **many, all, these** and other plural meanings, use **kinds/sorts/types** (WITH–**s**): 'These kinds of fruit do not grow in cold climates.'

2
- ✗ Imprisonment is not a good way of reducing this kind of crimes.
- ✓ **Imprisonment is not a good way of reducing this kind of crime.**
- ✓ **Imprisonment is not a good way of reducing these kinds of crime/s.**

> **kind/sort/type of** + singular form: 'this kind of envelope'
> **kinds/sorts/types of** + singular or plural form: 'these kinds of envelope/s'
> Note that after **kinds/sorts/types of** a plural form can sometimes sound awkward and careful users generally prefer a singular form.

kindly 1
- ✗ You are very kindly to spare me so much of your time.
- ✓ **You are very kind to spare me so much of your time.**
- ✗ She is always very kindly and helpful.
- ✓ **She is always very kind and helpful.**

> **Kindly** is nearly always used as an adverb: 'They've kindly offered to lend me their car while they're away.' 'Would you kindly sit down and stop being a nuisance.'

2
- ? I wonder if you would kindly correct my mistakes.
- ✓ **I wonder if you could possibly correct my mistakes.**
- ? Would you kindly open the door?
- ✓ **Would you mind opening the door, please?**

> **Kindly** is used to mean 'please' only in formal styles. When used inappropriately, it can sound sarcastic or even express anger: 'Would you kindly keep your hands to yourself.'

knock 1
- ✗ The woman got angry and knocked him.
- ✓ **The women got angry and hit him.**
- ✗ He thinks that someone knocked him on the head.
- ✓ **He thinks that someone hit him on the head.**

> When someone tries to hurt another person, they **hit** them: 'He still had a bruise from the time she had hit him.'

2
- ✗ When Sandra knocked the door, he was washing his face.
- ✓ **When Sandra knocked on the door, he was washing his face.**

> **knock on/at** a door, window etc: 'In future, don't come in without knocking on the door.'

know 1
- ✗ I ran downstairs to know what was happening.
- ✓ **I ran downstairs to find out what was happening.**

    ✗ Two police officers visited him to know where he had been on the night of the murder.

    ✓ **Two police officers visited him to find out where he had been on the night of the murder.**

    find out = get information about something that you want to know: 'We need to find out why these cars have stopped selling.'

2   ✗ The best way to know the city is to visit it on foot.

    ✓ **The best way to get to know the city is to visit it on foot.**

    ✗ When a woman goes out to work, she knows other people.

    ✓ **When a woman goes out to work, she gets to know other people.**

    know = be familiar with: 'I know Frankfurt very well.'
    get to know = become familiar with: 'Once you get to know her, I'm sure you'll like her.' 'We got to know each other very well during the week we spent together.'

3   ✗ I got to know the south of London very deeply.

    ✓ **I got to know the south of London very well.**

    (get to) know sb/sth very well (NOT **deeply**): 'I know Alex very well. We used to go to the same school.'

4   ✗ He knew well where he wanted to go.

    ✓ **He knew exactly/precisely where he wanted to go.**

    know sb/sth well = be fully familiar with: 'After living in Florence for two years, I know the city very well.' Compare: 'I'm completely against the idea, as you well know.'

knowledge 1 ✗ I don't have much knowledge about it.

    ✓ **I don't know much about it.**

    ✗ I only have a little knowledge about the United States.

    ✓ **I don't know very much about the United States.**

    ? The man had a good knowledge of car engines.

    ✓ **The man knew a lot about car engines.**

    When talking informally about how much someone knows about something, use the verb **know** (NOT **have ... knowledge**): 'I don't know anything at all about computers.' 'Talk to Pam. She knows a lot about horses.'
    Have ... knowledge is mainly used in formal styles when you give precise details of what someone knows: 'Tucker has an excellent knowledge of Sri Lankan tea plantations.'

2   ✗ I've learned a lot of knowledge during the course.

    ✓ **I've learned a lot during the course.**

    ✗ They get the knowledge of AIDS from the television.

    ✓ **They learn about AIDS from the television.**

    learn a lot/a great deal (NOT **learn/get ... knowledge**): 'I've learned a lot this year.' 'She's improving but she still has a lot to learn.'
    learn about sth: 'We've been learning about the American political system.'

3   ? I would like to get more knowledge of ancient history.

    ✓ **I would like to improve my knowledge of ancient history.**

improve/increase/further/brush up your knowledge (of sth): 'I'd like to improve my knowledge of Asian cultures.'

4 ✗ I am attending this course to improve my knowledges of English.
✓ **I am attending this course to improve my knowledge of English.**

Knowledge never has a plural ending: 'With all your knowledge, you should be a teacher.'

5 ✗ In this job you will need a good knowledge in English.
✓ **In this job you will need a good knowledge of English.**

knowledge of a subject (NOT **in/on**): 'She displayed an impressive knowledge of modern French literature.'

lack 1

✗ At school I used to lack in confidence.
✓ **At school I used to lack confidence.**
✗ She certainly doesn't lack of enthusiasm.
✓ **She certainly doesn't lack enthusiasm.**

> Do not confuse **lack sth** (verb + object, WITHOUT **in/of**) with **be lacking in sth** and **(a) lack of sth**: 'He lacks the confidence to start his own business.' 'At school he was found to be lacking in confidence.' 'She certainly doesn't show any lack of confidence.' 'I think I'm suffering from a lack of sleep.'

2

✗ The room was fine except for a total lack of radio and television.
✓ **The room was fine except that there was no radio or television.**
✗ Someone noticed the lack of salad dressing.
✓ **Someone noticed that there wasn't any salad dressing.**

> **Lack** is mainly used with abstract nouns: 'a lack of support/sympathy/freedom/sleep/energy'
> Avoid using **lack** with concrete nouns: 'We don't have any envelopes.' 'We're short of envelopes.' 'There aren't enough envelopes.'

lady

? At the front of the queue a man and a lady were arguing with the cashier.
✓ **At the front of the queue a man and a woman were arguing with the cashier.**

> **Lady** is used when you need to be polite, especially in formal styles: 'Ladies and gentlemen, may I have your attention please?' 'Please show these ladies the way to the cloakroom.'
> The usual word is **woman**: 'Isn't that the woman who teaches at the International School?'
> Note however that **old lady** is generally preferred to **old woman**, which sounds impolite: 'Can you help that old lady across the road?'

landscape

✗ Lots of kings chose to live here because of the beautiful landscape.
✓ **Lots of kings chose to live here because of the beautiful scenery.**
✗ The landscape surrounding the village is really beautiful.
✓ **The scenery surrounding the village is really beautiful.**

> **landscape** = (a view, painting or photograph of) a wide area of land, especially in the countryside: 'Having reached the top of the hill, we sat and admired the landscape that stretched far into the distance.' 'Constable is known for his beautiful Suffolk landscapes.'
> **scenery** = the natural features of the countryside (hills, valleys, fields etc) considered in terms of their beauty, especially those seen from a

particular place: 'The train journey takes you through some breathtaking scenery.' 'Cycling means that you can get fit and enjoy the scenery at the same time.'

lane
  ✗ It was so dark in the park that she kept wandering from the lane.
  ✓ **It was so dark in the park that she kept wandering from the path.**

lane = a narrow road or street: 'We rode our bikes along the little country lanes.'
path = a narrow strip of ground in a garden, park etc that is made for people to walk along: 'There used to be a path down to the stream, but it's all overgrown now.'

language
  ✗ I speak Arabic language all the time.
  ✓ **I speak Arabic all the time.**
  ✗ I spent the whole year learning English language.
  ✓ **I spent the whole year learning English.**
  ✗ They know Japanese language.
  ✓ **They know Japanese.**

speak/learn/know etc + name of a language (WITHOUT **language**): 'She speaks fluent English and a little German.' 'Do you know any Malay?' 'I'd like to learn Mandarin.'
Note that **the Arabic/English/Japanese language** may be used when you talk about a language in terms of its history, structure, users etc: 'The English language has evolved over many centuries.'

large
  ? The road wasn't large enough for two cars.
  ✓ **The road wasn't wide enough for two cars.**

When you are talking about the distance from one side to the other, use **wide** or **broad**: 'The river is much too wide to swim across.' 'How did you get such broad shoulders?'

last 1
  ✗ Did you hear what happened on last Friday?
  ✓ **Did you hear what happened last Friday?**
  ✗ He looks thinner than when I saw him in the last summer.
  ✓ **He looks thinner than when I saw him last summer.**
  ✗ The last Monday was a terrible day.
  ✓ **Last Monday was a terrible day.**

See Language Note at TIME

2
  ✗ In the last years many people have stopped smoking.
  ✓ **In recent years many people have stopped smoking.**

in recent weeks/months etc (NOT **last**): 'In recent months this stretch of the road has seen three serious accidents.'
Compare: 'Over the last few years many people have stopped smoking.'

3
  ✗ First we listened to the tape, then we answered some questions, and at last we wrote the story.
  ✓ **First we listened to the tape, then we answered some questions, and finally we wrote the story.**
  ✗ We went from one restaurant to another, but all of them were full. At last we decided to buy some pizzas and take them home.
  ✓ **We went from one restaurant to another, but all of them were full. In the end we decided to buy some pizzas and take them home.**

See Language Note at END

4   ✗ As a dress designer, I am very interested in the last fashions.
      ✓ **As a dress designer, I am very interested in the latest fashions.**

> **last** = (the one) before this one; (the one) at the end of a list, sequence or series: 'Our last meeting was in Rome.' 'I answered all the questions except the last one.'
> **latest** = designed/produced/published etc more recently than any other: 'Have you seen Toyota's latest models?' 'The BBC World Service always has the latest news.'

5   ✗ At last but not least, I must mention the climate.
      ✓ **Last but not least, I must mention the climate.**

> **last but not least** (WITHOUT **at**): 'Last but not least, I'd like to thank our sponsors for making this evening possible.'

lastly   ✗ Lastly I got bored with walking round the streets, and went back home.
      ✓ **In the end/Eventually I got bored with walking round the streets, and went back home.**

See Language Note at END

late   ✗ I often watch television until late night.
      ✓ **I often watch television until late at night.**
      ✗ Even late in the night, the roads are very busy.
      ✓ **Even late at night, the roads are very busy.**

> **late at night**: 'Hedgehogs like to roam around late at night, when most other animals are asleep.'

lately 1   ✗ Lately someone told me that the fire was caused by a cigarette.
      ✓ **Recently someone told me that the fire was caused by a cigarette.**

> Both **lately** and **recently** refer to a period of time that begins in the past and continues until now (the moment of speaking): 'Just lately/recently I have been wondering whether to look for a new job.'
> **Recently** is also used to refer to a point in time: 'Just recently she applied for a new job.'

2   ✗ One of the best films that I saw lately is 'Hook'.
      ✓ **One of the best films that I've seen lately is 'Hook'.**
      ✗ Lately I play a lot of Miles Davis tapes.
      ✓ **Lately I've been playing a lot of Miles Davis tapes.**
      ✗ We have a lot of rain lately.
      ✓ **We've had a lot of rain lately.**

> **Lately** is usually used with the present perfect tense: 'I haven't seen much of your sister lately. Has she gone away?'

latest   ✗ The latest election was won by the socialists.
      ✓ **The last election was won by the socialists.**
      ✗ In the latest decades of the twentieth century, the world has seen many changes.
      ✓ **In the last decades of the twentieth century, the world has seen many changes.**

See note at LAST 4

laughter ✗ His laughters filled the whole apartment.
✓ **His laughter filled the whole apartment.**

> **Laughter** is an uncountable noun: 'There was always a lot of laughter and joking when Henry came to dinner.'

lay ✗ The tourists were laying in the hot sun like corpses.
✓ **The tourists were lying in the hot sun like corpses.**
✗ We broke down the door and found him laying on the carpet.
✓ **We broke down the door and found him lying on the carpet.**

> **lay** (**laying, laid, laid**) = put something somewhere: 'She laid the money on the table in front of me.'
> **lie** (**lying, lay, lain**) = be in a horizontal position (on the ground/on a bed etc): 'He was lying on his back, staring up at the sky.' 'I could lie here all day!'

lay down ✗ I just wanted to lay down and have a rest.
✓ **I just wanted to lie down and have a rest.**

> **lay down** = put something down: 'Just lay the books down on the floor.'
> **lie down** = put your body into a horizontal position, especially on a bed: 'I think I'll go and lie down for half an hour.'

lead ✗ Ali asked us if we would lead him to the theatre one night.
✓ **Ali asked us if we would take him to the theatre one night.**
✗ After breakfast I led my daughter to school as usual.
✓ **After breakfast I took my daughter to school as usual.**

> See Language Note at TAKE

learn 1 ✗ In the museum I learned Balinese culture.
✓ **In the museum I learned about Balinese culture.**

> **learn** a foreign language: 'How long have you been learning Italian?'
> **learn about** a subject: 'Today we've been learning about the functions of the human brain.'

2 See KNOWLEDGE 2

leave 1 ✗ I leave from Bilbao on 12th June.
✓ **I leave Bilbao on 12th June.**
✗ I left from the shop without buying anything.
✓ **I left the shop without buying anything.**

> **leave** somewhere (usually WITHOUT **from**): 'If I leave the office at six, I'm home by ten to seven.'
> Use **leave from** only when you want to refer to the place where a journey, trip, excursion etc begins: 'The coach will be leaving from in front of the hotel at six o'clock sharp.'

2 ✗ Ken's aunt left to New York on 17th April.
✓ **Ken's aunt left for New York on 17th April.**

> **leave** (somewhere) **for** somewhere else (NOT **to**): 'She'll be leaving for London on the nine o'clock train.'

3 ✗ Every woman is entitled to a maternity leave.
✓ **Every woman is entitled to maternity leave.**

> **leave** (= a number of days, weeks or months when someone does not have to do their usual job) is usually an uncountable noun: 'Government

officers get six weeks' annual leave.' 'First she was on sick leave, then she took study leave, and now she's applied for maternity leave!'

lend 1 ✗ Could I lend your pen just for a minute?
✓ **Could I borrow your pen just for a minute?**
See note at BORROW

2 ✗ To lend a car, you have to have a driving licence.
✓ **To hire/rent a car, you have to have a driving licence.**
✗ We usually lend a villa so that we can cook for ourselves.
✓ **We usually rent a villa so that we can cook for ourselves.**
See note at HIRE

length 1 ? The length of the tunnel is about two miles.
✓ **The tunnel is about two miles long.**
When you mention how long something is, a phrase ending with **long** usually sounds more natural than **the length ... is**, especially in informal styles: 'The garden is almost seventy feet long.'

2 ? The length of the film is one and a half hours.
✓ **The film lasts one and half hours.**
last = take (a stated length of time) from start to finish: 'Each lesson lasts fifty minutes.' 'This afternoon's exciting match on centre court lasted exactly two hours and twelve minutes.'

lengthen ✗ The question is whether doctors should lengthen life when there is no hope of recovery.
✓ **The question is whether doctors should prolong life when there is no hope of recovery.**
lengthen = make something longer; become longer: 'We can use the old curtains, but they'll have to be lengthened.' 'As evening fell, the shadows lengthened.'
prolong = prevent a feeling, activity or life from ending: 'He asked her another question just to prolong the conversation.'

less 1 ✗ Teachers today are less stricter than they used to be.
✓ **Teachers today are less strict than they used to be.**
The comparative ending (**-er**) is NEVER used with **less** or **more**.

2 ✗ If there were less cars on the roads, there would be less accidents.
✓ **If there were fewer cars on the roads, there would be fewer accidents.**
Use **less** with an uncountable noun and **fewer** with the plural form of a countable noun: 'Less traffic would mean fewer accidents.'
Note that **less** is widely used in place of **fewer** in everyday conversation, but careful users regard this usage as non-standard.

lessen ✗ Fortunately, my workload has been lessened.
✓ **Fortunately, my workload has been reduced.**
✗ The best solution is to lessen the amount of traffic entering the town.
✓ **The best solution is to reduce the amount of traffic entering the town.**

Lessen is mainly used in connection with pain and feelings: 'I'll give you an injection to lessen the pain.' 'No amount of comforting could lessen Charles' disappointment.'
When you mean 'make something smaller in amount, number, price or size', use **reduce**: 'The workforce has been reduced by 50 percent.'

lesson 1

✗ I've been studying my lessons very hard.
✓ **I've been studying very hard.**
✗ After studying my lessons, I watched T.V.
✓ **After doing my homework/the exercises, I watched T.V.**

When you mean 'do work that has been set by a teacher', use **study, do your homework** or **do an exercise** (NOT **study a lesson**): 'I spent the whole evening studying.' 'Mrs Potts gave us three exercises to do for tomorrow.'

2

✗ After lunch we're doing a history lesson.
✓ **After lunch we're having a history lesson.**
✗ I follow lessons on Thursdays and Fridays.
✓ **I have lessons on Thursdays and Fridays.**
✗ I've started to do lessons in English and French.
✓ **I've started to have/take lessons in English and French.**

have a lesson (NOT **do/follow**): 'I didn't go into the classroom because the children were having a lesson.'
have/take lessons (= arrange for someone to teach you): 'If you want to improve your English, you should have/take lessons.'

let 1

✗ You can travel by train or let a car.
✓ **You can travel by train or rent/hire a car.**

let = allow someone to live in your house, flat etc in return for money: 'During the holiday season we let the cottage to tourists.'
rent/hire = See note at HIRE

2

✗ Do you think your parents will let you go to England?
✓ **Do you think your parents will let you go to England?**

let sb do sth (WITHOUT **to**): 'Why wouldn't Alice let you help her?'
Compare: 'Do you think your parents will allow you to go to England?'

level 1

✗ These courses are taught in postgraduate level.
✓ **These courses are taught at postgraduate level.**
✗ The volume of the radio should be kept in a low level.
✓ **The volume of the radio should be kept at a low level.**

at a particular **level** (NOT **in**) = having a particular degree of intensity, power, proficiency etc: 'Students at this level need individual tuition.' 'Talks are being held at the highest level.'
Compare: 'James likes school. He's now in Level 3.' (= in a class at Level 3)

2

✗ People in developed countries have a higher level of living.
✓ **People in developed countries have a higher standard of living.**

When you are talking about the quality of something, the usual word is **standard**: 'All his work is of a very high standard.' 'Our company accepts only the highest standards of workmanship.'

3 ✗ What will we do if the sea level continues to increase?
  ✓ **What will we do if the sea level continues to rise?**
  See note at INCREASE 2

lie ✗ I was sure the old woman was saying lies.
  ✓ **I was sure the old woman was telling lies.**
  tell a lie (NOT **say** or **speak**): 'I always know when he's telling lies.'

lied ✗ After a while he stopped running and lied down on the ground.
  ✓ **After a while he stopped running and lay down on the ground.**
  lie (lying, lied, lied) = say something which is not true in an attempt to deceive: 'I wonder why he lied about his age?'
  lie (lying, lay, lain) down = be in or get into a horizontal position: 'I lay down on the bed and fell sound asleep.'

life 1 ✗ The cost of life is very high in London.
  ✓ **The cost of living is very high in London.**
  ✗ During a recession, some people find it difficult to make a life.
  ✓ **During a recession, some people find it difficult to make a living.**
  Phrases connected with the idea of money end with **living** (NOT **life**): 'Salaries have not kept up with increases in the cost of living.' 'It's difficult to earn/make a living as an actress.' 'Acting is fun, but I wouldn't want to do it for a living.'

2 ✗ Television has taught me a lot about the American life.
  ✓ **Television has taught me a lot about the American way of life.**
  ? This busy type of life allows us no time to sit down and relax.
  ✓ **This busy lifestyle allows us no time to sit down and relax.**
  way of life = the way that a society, group or person chooses to live: 'I found the British way of life very strange at first.' 'The computer has transformed our whole way of life.'
  lifestyle = way of life, especially that of a particular person: 'As a photographer, she has a very hectic lifestyle.'

3 ✗ The life in the countryside is quiet and relaxed.
  ✓ **Life in the countryside is quiet and relaxed.**
  ✗ He didn't enjoy the life in the army at all.
  ✓ **He didn't enjoy life in the army at all.**
  When **life** means 'the way of life that is connected with a particular type of situation, group or occupation', it is usually used without **the**: 'I found city life too stressful.' 'Life in New York is full of excitement.' 'What do you think of married life?'

4 ✗ He was the most attractive man that I had met in my life.
  ✓ **He was the most attractive man that I had ever met.**
  When a superlative ('most attractive') is followed by a relative clause, use **that ... ever ...** (NOT **that ... in my/her etc life**): 'It was the best holiday we'd ever had.' 'This is the worst film I've ever seen.'

5 ✗ It was one of the happiest days in my life.
✓ **It was one of the happiest days of my life.**

superlative ('happiest') + noun + **of your life** (NOT **in**): 'She refers to her childhood as the most carefree time of her life.'
Compare: 'One of the most important things in life is good health.'

6 ✗ On Saturday nights there is usually life music at the club.
✓ **On Saturday nights there is usually live music at the club.**

live = heard or seen while it is actually being played or performed: 'Tonight's live concert comes from the Royal Opera House, Covent Garden.'

lighted ✗ It was dark inside so I lighted a match.
✓ **It was dark inside so I lit a match.**
✗ Suddenly a wonderful smile lighted up her face.
✓ **Suddenly a wonderful smile lit up her face.**
✗ The road was poorly lighted and it was difficult to see.
✓ **The road was poorly lit and it was difficult to see.**

In British English the usual past tense and past participle form of **light** is **lit**. **Lighted** is mainly used before a noun. Compare: 'He lit a cigarette.' 'The cigarette hadn't been lit.' 'He was holding a lighted cigarette.'

like 1 ✗ What he likes to know is how much it will cost.
✓ **What he would like to know is how much it will cost.**
✗ Do you like me to show you where to go?
✓ **Would you like me to show you where to go?**

When you mean 'want', use **would like**.
Compare: 'Do you like playing the piano?' (= Do you enjoy ... ?) 'Would you like to play the piano?' (= Do you want ... ?)

2 ✗ She would like that you ring her back after five o'clock.
✓ **She would like you to ring her back after five o'clock.**
✗ Would you like going for a walk with me?
✓ **Would you like to go for a walk with me?**

would like (**sb**) **to do sth**: 'Would you like me to help you with the packing?' 'I'd like you all to listen carefully.'

3 ✗ I don't like that my shoes get wet.
✓ **I don't like my shoes getting/to get wet.**
✓ **I don't like it when my shoes get wet.**
✗ I don't like when friends of mine get married.
✓ **I don't like it when friends of mine get married.**

like + **sb/sth** + **doing/to do sth** (NOT **that** clause): 'I don't like the children staying/to stay out late.'
like + **it** + **when/if** clause: 'I don't like it when the children stay out late.'

4 ? Everyone arrived late like they often do when you don't want them to.
✓ **Everyone arrived late as they often do when you don't want them to.**

Although the use of **like** as a conjunction is becoming fairly common and appears even in formal English, it has not yet been fully accepted by careful users.

5
- ✗ She spoke very loudly like I was deaf.
- ✓ **She spoke very loudly as if I was deaf.**

  The use of **like** to mean 'as if' is very informal and is usually regarded as non-standard.

limit
- ✗ One solution would be for the government to put a limit on when these programmes may be broadcast.
- ✓ **One solution would be for the government to place restrictions on when these programmes may be broadcast.**

  When you are talking about the control of something by laws, rules etc, use **restrict/restriction**: 'The government plans to restrict the sale of guns.' 'The 1986 law imposed new financial restrictions on private companies.'

linen
- ✗ We complained about the dirty bed linens.
- ✓ **We complained about the dirty bed linen.**

  Linen is an uncountable noun: 'The linen is changed once a week.'

list
- ✗ I looked to see if my name was in the list.
- ✓ **I looked to see if my name was on the list.**

  on a list (NOT **in**): 'If it's not on the list, we don't sell it.'

listen
- ✗ My mother never listens what I say.
- ✓ **My mother never listens to what I say.**
- ✗ He invited me to listen his new CD.
- ✓ **He invited me to listen to his new CD.**

  listen to sb/sth: 'You are listening to the BBC World Service.'

lit
- ✗ All I could see in the darkness was the end of his lit cigarette.
- ✓ **All I could see in the darkness was the end of his lighted cigarette.**

  See note at LIGHTED

litter 1
- ✗ In the cities the streets are full of litters.
- ✓ **In the cities the streets are full of litter.**

  Litter is an uncountable noun: 'Wherever you find crowds, you'll find litter.'

2
- ✗ Children should be taught that it is wrong to litter.
- ✓ **Children should be taught that it is wrong to drop litter.**
- ✗ If someone litters the street, someone else has to clear it up.
- ✓ **If someone drops litter in the street, someone else has to clear it up.**

  People **drop/leave litter** (= leave things such as empty packets, cans and bottles in a public place): 'There is a $100 fine for dropping litter.' Things **litter** a floor, street, area etc: 'Discarded clothing began to litter the dance floor.'

little 1
- ✗ He works in a little office building in Geneva.
- ✓ **He works in a small office building in Geneva.**
- ✗ His parents died when he was still a little child.
- ✓ **His parents died when he was still a small child.**

Little usually expresses an emotional attitude such as affection or dislike: 'We've rented a cosy little cottage in the countryside.' 'You shouldn't let that silly little man upset you.'
When you simply wish to describe the size of someone of something, use **small**: 'Their daughter is rather small for her age.' 'People are turning to smaller cars because they are cheaper to run.'

2

  ✗ The police asked for a little description of the car.
  ✓ **The police asked for a brief description of the car.**
  ✗ He told me that I needed a little operation.
  ✓ **He told me that I needed a minor operation.**
See Language Note at KILL

3

  ✗ Today there are too many people for too little jobs.
  ✓ **Today there are too many people for too few jobs.**
See note at FEW 1

a little 1

  ✗ It was my first interview and I was nervous a little.
  ✓ **It was my first interview and I was a little nervous.**

Put **a little** in front of the word it modifies (NOT after it): 'I felt a little sad.' 'The news was a little worrying.' Compare: 'The town had changed a little since my last visit.'

2

  ✗ It was a little difficult question.
  ✓ **It was a slightly difficult question.**

slightly + adjective + noun: 'a slightly solemn expression'

a little bit

  See BIT

live

  ✗ Whenever we go to the seaside, we live in a hotel.
  ✓ **Whenever we go to the seaside, we stay at a hotel.**
  ✗ At the hotel, we lived in room 101.
  ✓ **At the hotel, we stayed in room 101.**

stay at/in a hotel, youth hostel, etc (NOT **live in**): 'In London we usually stay at the Savoy.'

living 1

  ✗ The local farmers will never change their way of living.
  ✓ **The local farmers will never change their way of life.**
  ✗ We have different languages, traditions and living styles.
  ✓ **We have different languages, traditions and life styles.**
See note at LIFE 2

loan

  ✗ The military government loaned millions of dollars from the world bank.
  ✓ **The military government borrowed millions of dollars from the world bank.**

loan = (1) (noun) a sum of money that you borrow, usually from a bank: 'They are currently negotiating a $100 million loan.'
(2) (verb) lend a painting, work of art etc to an art gallery or museum: 'The pictures have been loaned to the National Gallery for the forthcoming exhibition.'
(3) (verb; especially in American English) let someone use something; lend: 'Why don't you ask John if he'll loan you his car?'
borrow = receive money or something that a bank or person agrees to

lend you: 'By the end of the war the Canadian government had borrowed over $5 million from its own citizens.'

long

✗ I am afraid it will take long to improve my English.
✓ **I am afraid it will take a long time to improve my English.**

Use **take long** in questions and negative sentences: 'How long does it take to get to London by train?' 'It doesn't take very long.'
Use **take a long time** in affirmative sentences: 'It might take a long time to sort out the problem.'

look 1

✗ Someone should inspect the kitchen twice a week to look whether everything is nice and clean.
✓ **Someone should inspect the kitchen twice a week to see whether everything is nice and clean.**
✗ Wait here and I'll look if I can find him for you.
✓ **Wait here and I'll see if I can find him for you.**

see = find out (by checking): 'I'll go and see whether they have any rooms available.' 'While you're in the kitchen, can you see if the eggs are cooked?'
Compare: 'I looked to see whether it was still raining.'

2

✗ Then I looked the person sitting next to her.
✓ **Then I looked at the person sitting next to her.**

look at sb/sth: 'I looked at the clock to see what time it was.' 'What are you looking at?'

3

✗ The report takes a close look on meat consumption.
✓ **The report takes a close look at meat consumption.**

have/take a look at sth: 'They're going to take a look at a new house this evening.'

4

See note at FEEL 2

look after

✗ Having received news of his death, the police stopped looking after him.
✓ **Having received news of his death, the police stopped looking for him.**

look after = take care of: 'Who will look after you if you are ill?'
look for = try to find: 'I wasted half the morning looking for my keys.'

look forward to 1

✗ I'm looking forward the day I can go home.
✓ **I'm looking forward to the day I can go home.**
✗ He said he was looking forward for his holidays.
✓ **He said he was looking forward to his holidays.**

look forward to sth (WITH **to**): 'We've only just come back from holiday but we're already looking forward to the next one.'

2

✗ I'm looking forward to hear from you.
✓ **I'm looking forward to hearing from you.**

look forward to doing sth: 'Simon is looking forward to having his own office again.'

look into ✗ Have you looked into your pocket?
  ✓ **Have you looked in your pocket?**
  ✗ I decided to look into the telephone directory.
  ✓ **I decided to look in the telephone directory.**

> **look in** a book, container or room to find something or someone (NOT **into**): 'I looked in the drawer but it wasn't there.' 'Go and look in the bedroom.'
> Compare: 'The police are looking into the matter.' (= are investigating)

look like 1 ✗ The two younger children looked like tired.
  ✓ **The two younger children looked tired.**
  ✗ The job was not as easy as it looked like.
  ✓ **The job was not as easy as it looked.**

> **look like** + noun phrase: 'She looks a bit like my sister.'
> **look** + adjective (WITHOUT **like**): 'The man looked very suspicious.' 'His wife looks much happier these day.'

  2 See HOW 1

lose 1 ✗ His illness has caused him to lose a lot of lessons.
  ✓ **His illness has caused him to miss a lot of lessons.**

> If you do not attend a class, meeting, activity, etc, you **miss** it: 'If you don't hurry up, you'll miss your appointment.' 'I'd hate to miss one of John's parties.'

  2 ✗ I don't care if they're lazy, as long as they don't lose my time.
  ✓ **I don't care if they're lazy, as long as they don't waste my time.**

> **waste your/sb's time** = (cause someone to) spend an amount of time without doing anything useful: 'I wish they'd stop asking me silly questions and wasting my time.'
> Compare: 'The puncture meant that we lost a lot of time.'

lost ✗ This morning I noticed that my purse was lost.
  ✓ **This morning I noticed that my purse was missing.**

> If something is not in the place where you left it and you cannot find it anywhere, it is **missing** (NOT **lost**): 'Police are still searching for the missing diamonds.' 'She was making her way towards immigration when she discovered that her passport was missing.'
> Compare: 'Oh no! I've lost my passport!'

lot/lots 1 ✗ She makes us do a lots of homework.
  ✓ **She makes us do a lot of homework.**
  ✓ **She makes us do lots of homework.**

> **a lot of** (WITH **a**): 'I bet she's got a lot of money.'
> **lots of** (WITHOUT **a**): 'I bet she's got lots of money.'

  2 ✗ Lot of people come here because it's near Morocco.
  ✓ **A lot of people come here because it's near Morocco.**
  ✗ Groceries here are lot cheaper than in Japan.
  ✓ **Groceries here are a lot cheaper than in Japan.**

> **a lot, a lot of** (WITH **a**): 'I've wasted a lot of time today.' 'He'll have to work a lot faster from now on.'

3   ✗ My husband and I met each other a lot of years ago.
      ✓ **My husband and I met each other many years ago.**
      ✗ The problem is that for a lot of years smoking was not considered to be anti-social.
      ✓ **The problem is that for many years smoking was not considered to be anti-social.**

> **many + weeks/months/years** (NOT **a lot of**): 'Many years have passed since we were at school together.'
> Compare: 'During the summer we spend a lot of time in the garden.'

4   ✗ There is a lot of countries in the same situation.
      ✓ **There are a lot of countries in the same situation.**

> See note at THERE 2

love   ✗ I'm sure that once you see Venice, you'll love it very much.
      ✓ **I'm sure that once you see Venice, you'll love it.**

> **love sb** (**very much**): 'I love him very much.'
> **love sth** (WITHOUT **very much**): 'I love tennis.'

luck 1   ✗ If you have luck, you'll be able to hear Carreras sing.
      ✓ **If you're lucky, you'll be able to hear Carreras sing.**
      ✓ **If you're in luck, you'll be able to hear Carreras sing.**
      ✗ That afternoon she had luck and found the keys at the bottom of a drawer.
      ✓ **That afternoon she was lucky and found the keys at the bottom of a drawer.**
      ✓ **That afternoon she had a stroke of luck and found the keys at the bottom of a drawer.**

> **be lucky, be in luck, (have) a stroke/bit of luck** (NOT **have luck**):
> 'We're lucky the coach didn't go without us.' 'You're in luck, there are still a few tickets left.' 'I'm so pleased she got the job. It's about time she had a bit of luck.'
> Note that when **luck** is used with **have**, it is always modified: 'I've had enough bad luck to last me a lifetime.' 'Some people have all the luck.' 'He hasn't had much luck recently.'

2   ✗ I'd just like to say goodbye and wish you a good luck.
      ✓ **I'd just like to say goodbye and wish you good luck.**
      ✗ What a rotten luck! There he was again, sitting right beside me.
      ✓ **What rotten luck! There he was again, sitting right beside me.**

> **Luck** is an uncountable noun: 'She's had a lot of bad luck recently.'
> 'Meeting the right partner is just a matter of luck.'

luggage 1   ✗ There was no room in the car for all our luggages.
      ✓ **There was no room in the car for all our luggage.**
      ✗ He had brought a heavy luggage with him.
      ✓ **He had brought some heavy luggage with him.**

> **Luggage** is an uncountable noun: 'Do you have any more luggage?'

2   ✗ I spent the morning packing my luggage.
      ✓ **I spent the morning packing (my bags/suitcases).**

> **pack** or **pack a bag/suitcase** (NOT **pack ... luggage**): 'I haven't finished packing yet.' 'That's not the way to pack a suitcase!'

lunch   See BREAKFAST

luxurious 1   ✗ You could stay at one of the big luxurious hotels, but the small hotels are far more reasonable.
✓ **You could stay at one of the big luxury hotels, but the small hotels are far more reasonable.**
✗ Consumers are offered more and more luxurious goods.
✓ **Consumers are offered more and more luxury goods.**

> To refer to a type or class of hotel, apartment, furniture, services etc, use **luxury** as a modifier: 'a luxury apartment in the heart of London', 'luxury bedroom suites imported direct from Italy', 'a luxury liner'.
> Use **luxurious** to describe something that is very comfortable and expensive: 'The car's soft cream leather interior was extremely luxurious.'

2   ✗ Many people today do not consider a car as a luxurious thing.
✓ **Many people today do not consider a car as a luxury.**

> **a luxury** = something that you do not need: 'We can hardly afford to buy food, yet alone waste money on luxuries.'

luxury 1   ✗ They don't have any money to spend on luxury things.
✓ **They don't have any money to spend on luxuries.**

> **luxuries** (plural of **luxury**), **luxury goods, luxury items** (but NOT **luxury things**): 'Tax on luxury goods is bound to be increased.'

2   ✗ Some successful criminals enjoy a luxury life.
✓ **Some successful criminals enjoy a life of luxury.**

> **A life of luxury** is a fixed phrase: 'His dream is to marry a princess and live a life of luxury.'

machine   ✗ Over eighty per cent of these cars are old, and so are their machines.
     ✓ **Over eighty per cent of these cars are old, and so are their engines.**

> **machine** = a piece of equipment which performs useful work, such as a sewing machine, washing machine or computer: 'To operate this machine, simply select the type of coffee you require and press the green button.' 'The latest machines can run both types of software.'
> **engine** = a device which provides the power for a motor vehicle, train, aircraft etc: 'It was difficult to make yourself heard above the roar of the engines.' 'Check the tyre pressures and top up the engine oil.'

mad 1   ✗ She began to think she was becoming mad.
     ✓ **She began to think she was going mad.**

> **go mad** (NOT **become**): 'Eventually, rejected by Hamlet, Ophelia goes mad and drowns herself.'

2   ✗ I've always been mad for tennis.
     ✓ **I've always been mad about tennis.**

> **be mad/crazy about sth** (NOT **for**) (informal) = like something very much: 'Why are so many people crazy about computer games?'

made   ✗ She claimed that the jumper was made from wool.
     ✓ **She claimed that the jumper was made of wool.**
     ✗ Many components are made by plastic.
     ✓ **Many components are made of plastic.**
     ✗ Margarine, which is made by natural ingredients, seems to be more acceptable.
     ✓ **Margarine, which is made from natural ingredients, seems to be more acceptable.**

> Use **made from** when the original materials have been completely changed and cannot be recognized: 'Bread is made from flour and water.'
> Use **made of** when the original materials have not been completely changed and you can still see them: 'Their dining table is made of solid oak.'
> Use **made by** when you mention the name of the company or person that has made something (NOT the names of materials): 'This new razor is made by Wilkinson Sword.'

mail   ✗ It takes seventeen trees to produce one ton of junk mails.
     ✓ **It takes seventeen trees to produce one ton of junk mail.**

> **Mail** (= letters and parcels) is an uncountable noun: 'Has there been any mail today?'

mainly 1 ✗ We were attracted by the clean air, the beautiful scenery, and mainly the peace and quiet.
✓ **We were attracted by the clean air, the beautiful scenery, and above all the peace and quiet.**
✗ What I like about her mainly is her sense of humour.
✓ **What I like about her above all is her sense of humour.**

> To show that one particular feature or item is more important than all the others, use **above all**: 'The person we're looking for has got to be smart, intelligent and above all trustworthy.' 'Above all, the government wants to avoid an increase in inflation.'

2 ✗ Mainly the film is about the madness of war.
✓ **The film is mainly about the madness of war.**
✗ Mainly these problems involve the definition of words.
✓ **These problems mainly involve the definition of words.**
> See Language Note at ALWAYS

majority 1 ? The majority of houses in Germany have fitted carpets.
✓ **Most houses in Germany have fitted carpets.**
> **The majority of** (= more than half) is usually used in formal styles: 'The majority of the government voted against the bill.'
> In other styles **most** (= nearly all) usually sounds more natural: 'Most people have never even heard of him.'

2 ✗ The majority of motorists is opposed to the scheme.
✓ **The majority of motorists are opposed to the scheme.**
> **the majority** + singular/plural verb: 'The majority is/are in favour of abolishing the death penalty.'
> **the majority of** + plural count noun + plural verb: 'The majority of voters are in favour of abolishing the death penalty.'

make 1 ✗ I didn't make anything in particular. I just stayed at home.
✓ **I didn't do anything in particular. I just stayed at home.**
✗ In Italy we have made a great deal to prevent pollution.
✓ **In Italy we have done a great deal to prevent pollution.**
✗ He looked as if he had made something wrong.
✓ **He looked as if he had done something wrong.**

> For actions, the usual verb is **do** (NOT **make**): 'Governments are not doing enough to reduce unemployment.' 'I'm so worried I don't know what to do.' See Language Note at DO

2 ✗ I made lots of fun in London.
✓ **I had lots of fun in London.**
✗ On Saturday we're making a party.
✓ **On Saturday we're having a party.**
> See Language Note at DO

3 ✗ The cold water made me shivering.
✓ **The cold water made me shiver.**
✗ What made you to decide to work in the theatre?
✓ **What made you decide to work in the theatre?**
> **make sb/sth do sth** (WITHOUT **to**): 'They made him take the examination again.'

Compare **be made to do sth**: 'He was made to take the examination again.'

make up ✗ The company rule is that all female employees must make up their faces.

    ✓ **The company rule is that all female employees must wear make-up.**

    ✗ She told me what to wear and showed me how to make up.

    ✓ **She told me what to wear and showed me how to put on my make-up.**

    wear/use make-up: 'Some women refuse to wear make-up.'
    put on your make-up: 'I've just got to put on my make-up and I'll be ready.'

man ✗ Every day the man is inventing new machines.

    ✓ **Every day man is inventing new machines.**

    When you mean 'the human race', use **man** (WITHOUT **the**): 'I can't believe that man has actually stepped foot on the moon.'

mankind 1 ✗ These bombs could lead to the destruction of the mankind.

    ✓ **These bombs could lead to the destruction of mankind.**

    mankind (= the human race) WITHOUT **the**: 'Travelling into space was a great advance for mankind.'

    2 ? The nature of mankind is very complicated.

    ✓ **Human nature is very complicated.**

    ? In art we discover the beauty of mankind's imagination.

    ✓ **In art we discover the beauty of the human imagination.**

    Mankind (or **the human race**) refers to all human beings considered as a group: 'The greatest danger to mankind is not science but ignorance.' 'These are the most devastating weapons mankind has ever devised.' 'What is mankind's long-term role in space?'
    When you mean 'belonging to or typical of people (as opposed to God, animals, machines etc)', the usual pattern is **human** + noun: 'Greed and envy are common human failings.'
    Note that phrases such as **human nature, human error, human interest** and **human weakness** are very common.

manner 1 ✗ Japanese manner is based on the idea that 'you are superior to me'.

    ✓ **Japanese manners are based on the idea that 'you are superior to me'.**

    See Language Note on next page

    2 ✗ American manner is all about freedom and equality.

    ✓ **American culture is all about freedom and equality.**

    See Language Note on next page

    3 ✗ Every society has its own laws and manners.

    ✓ **Every society has its own laws and traditions/customs.**

    See Language Note on next page

    4 ? One of the biggest differences I noticed was the American manner of being polite to strangers.

✓ **One of the biggest differences I noticed was the American custom of being polite to strangers.**
See Language Note below

5 ✗ We were taught how to speak in a good manner.
✓ **We were taught how to speak properly.**
If you do something in the right way, you do it **properly**: 'Failure to use the equipment properly may result in serious injury.' 'Since George passed away, Mavis has stopped eating properly.'

CULTURE • CUSTOM • HABIT • MANNER • MANNERS • TRADITION

culture	(1) the customs, ideas, art, etc, which are found in a particular society or group and which make it different from another society or group: 'Obeying your parents is a hallmark of Asian culture.' (2) the art, music, literature, etc, that is produced by a particular society: 'Professor Jackson is an expert on ancient Greek culture.' 'The Samba is an important part of Brazilian culture.'
custom	(1) something that the people in a particular society have done (in the same way) for a very long time, and which they consider to be normal or polite: 'One of their customs is to point with the thumb, not with index finger.' 'According to local custom, his body was carried to the top of a hill and cremated.' 'His knowledge of Malay and Indonesian customs proved invaluable when we got to Bali.' (2) something that a person usually does in a particular situation: 'His custom of making detailed preparatory drawings makes him unique amongst 18th century British painters.' 'On Wednesday evening, as was his custom, he went for a long walk.'
habit	something that a person does repeatedly, often without realizing it: 'She has a lot of little habits that I find really irritating.' 'In California I got into the habit of eating with just a fork.'
manner (singular)	the way someone behaves towards people: 'She impressed us all with her business-like manner.' 'His cheerful face and polite manner have won him a lot of friends.'
manners (plural)	the way someone behaves towards people, especially when compared with what is accepted as polite behaviour: 'The child has very good manners and always says thank you.'
tradition	a belief, custom or way of doing something that has been passed on from one generation to the next: 'The tradition was that when a man died, all his wealth and possessions would go to the eldest son.'

many 1 ✗ One of the policemen started asking me many questions.
  ✓ **One of the policemen started asking me a lot of questions.**
  ✗ We are given many tests.
  ✓ **We are given a lot of tests.**

> **Many** and **much** are used mainly in questions and negative sentences: 'Does he have many friends?' 'It appears that he doesn't have many friends.' In affirmative sentences, phrases such as **a lot of** and **plenty of** are used.
> Note however that **many** and **much** are used in affirmative sentences after **too, so,** and **as** ('You ask too many questions.') and sometimes in formal styles ('Many accidents arise as a result of negligence').

2 ✗ It's important to understand why there is so many violence in our world.
  ✓ **It's important to understand why there is so much violence in our world.**
  See note at MUCH 1

3 ✗ I had never seen so many and bright stars in the sky.
  ✓ **I had never seen so many bright stars in the sky.**
  ✗ There are not many and interesting Sunday newspapers.
  ✓ **There are not many interesting Sunday newspapers.**

> **many** + adjective + noun (WITHOUT **and**): 'He is convinced that many serious accidents could be prevented.'

mark 1 ✗ Her only distinguishing mark is her long blond hair.
  ✓ **Her only distinguishing feature is her long blond hair.**

> A **mark** on someone's face or body is a small area of skin that is a different colour from the rest: 'You've got two dark red marks on your nose where your glasses have been.'
> Things such as the colour of someone's eyes and hair, and the shape of their nose, chin and mouth are their **features**: 'As soon as he began to describe her features, I realized that he was talking about Mandy.'

2 ✗ Before buying a cassette recorder, I asked my friend if he could recommend a good mark.
  ✓ **Before buying a cassette recorder, I asked my friend if he could recommend a good make.**
  ✗ As for cigarettes, there are many different marks.
  ✓ **As for cigarettes, there are many different brands.**

> **mark** (also **Mk**) = a model, type or version (used mainly in trade names): 'a Mk II Jaguar'
> **make** = a particular type of car, washing machine, camera, etc: 'If you want a really good make, go for a Nikon or a Pentax.' 'Which make of television do you prefer, Sony or Panasonic?'
> **brand** = a particular type of soap, toothpaste, butter, cigarette, etc: 'I'm tired of being told which brand of washing powder I should use.'

market ✗ The magazine gives a list of all the computers in the market.
  ✓ **The magazine gives a list of all the computers on the market.**

> **on the market** (NOT **in**) = available in shops for people to buy; for sale: 'It's not the cheapest machine on the market, but it's certainly the best.'

marriage

✗ Why didn't you invite me to your marriage?
✓ **Why didn't you invite me to your wedding?**
✗ I have just received your marriage invitation.
✓ **I have just received your wedding invitation.**

> **marriage** = the ceremony of becoming husband and wife considered from a purely religious or legal point of view: 'Her parents are against the marriage.'
> **wedding** = the occasion when this ceremony takes place and the celebrations that follow it: 'I never see most of my relatives apart from at weddings.'

married

✗ She is married with a post office worker.
✓ **She is married to a post office worker.**

> **be/get married to sb** (NOT **with**): 'How long has she been married to him?'

marry

✗ He's going to ask her to marry with him.
✓ **He's going to ask her to marry him.**
✗ His daughter is expected to marry to a viscount.
✓ **His daughter is expected to marry a viscount.**
✗ After they get marry, they're going abroad.
✓ **After they get married, they're going abroad.**

> **marry sb** (WITHOUT **with/to**): 'Isn't he the man who married Elizabeth Taylor?'
> **get married (to sb)**: 'I can still remember the day I got married. United were playing at Wembley.'

master

✗ I have a master in Hotel Management.
✓ **I have a master's in Hotel Management.**
See DEGREE 1

match

✗ The green jacket doesn't match to the trousers.
✓ **The green jacket doesn't match the trousers.**
✗ We chose the sunflowers to match with the wallpaper.
✓ **We chose the sunflowers to match the wallpaper.**

> One thing **matches/doesn't match** another thing (WITHOUT **to/with**): 'You can't wear that blue tie. It doesn't match your shirt.'
> Compare: 'The green jacket doesn't go with the trousers.'

material

✗ In today's material society, most people think only about money.
✓ **In today's materialistic society, most people think only about money.**

> **material** = connected with the physical needs that people have (as opposed to spiritual or intellectual needs): 'In material terms they are very well off, but spiritually they are deprived.'
> **materialistic** = believing that money and the things that money can buy are more important than anything else: 'Modern society is becoming increasingly materialistic.'

mathematics

✗ Mathematics are my favourite subject.
✓ **Mathematics is my favourite subject.**

> **Mathematics** (the subject) is an uncountable noun: 'Mathematics is compulsory. Even if you don't like it, you still have to take it.'

matter 1 ✗ The matter is that we won't have enough room in the car to take your mother with us.
✓ **The problem is that we won't have enough room in the car to take your mother with us.**

Matter is used to mean 'problem' or 'trouble' only in questions and negative sentences: 'What's the matter?' 'Is anything the matter?' 'There's nothing the matter.'

2 ✗ It doesn't matter the nationality of the archaeologists.
✓ **The nationality of the archaeologists doesn't matter.**
✗ Doesn't matter the time.
✓ **The time doesn't matter.**

it doesn't matter + clause: 'It doesn't matter if you can't answer all the questions. Just do your best.'
subject + **doesn't matter**: 'The results don't matter. Just do your best.'

3 ✗ The flight attendant told us that there wasn't any matter; it was just a storm.
✓ **The flight attendant told us that nothing was the matter; it was just a storm.**

nothing/something is the matter or **there is nothing/something the matter**: 'I think there's something the matter with the central heating. It's cold in here.' 'Don't worry. Nothing's the matter. It's just a tiny cut.'

4 See FACT 3

5 See NO MATTER

matured ✗ He isn't matured enough to get married.
✓ **He isn't mature enough to get married.**
✗ Replacing such a politically matured leader will not be easy.
✓ **Replacing such a politically mature leader will not be easy.**

Use **matured/mature** when you are talking about wine, cheese etc: 'The whisky is kept here until it has matured/is mature.'
When you are talking about people, the usual word is **mature**: 'He's very mature for a boy of sixteen.'

may ✗ If I hadn't seen the car coming, I may have been killed.
✓ **If I hadn't seen the car coming, I might have been killed.**

To refer to something in the past that was possible but did not actually happen, use **might have** or **could have** (NOT **may have**): 'If you had worked harder, you might have passed the exam.'
Compare: 'I may have left it at home - I'm not sure.'

maybe 1 ✗ Maybe you'll find the film very boring.
✓ **You may find the film very boring.**
✗ Maybe you will have problems breathing.
✓ **You may have problems breathing.**

Instead of using **maybe ... will**, use **may** + infinitive: 'They may decide that our offer is too low, of course.'

2 ? Maybe this helps to explain why there are so many divorces.
✓ **Perhaps this helps to explain why there are so many divorces.**

Maybe is used mainly in informal styles: 'Maybe you should see a doctor.'
Perhaps is used in all styles: 'Perhaps he's gone home already.' 'Perhaps there are other factors that need to be considered.'

me 1

✗ I got me a drink and sat down on the sofa.
✓ **I got myself a drink and sat down on the sofa.**
✗ What can I tell you about me?
✓ **What can I tell you about myself?**
See Language Note at MYSELF

2

? I still remember the day me and my sister went to Buenos Aires by bus.
✓ **I still remember the day my sister and I went to Buenos Aires by bus.**

The pattern **me and ...** is sometimes heard in informal styles but is widely regarded as non-standard. The usual pattern is **... and I**: 'George and I have opened a joint account.'

meal 1

? You will be able to try some of the traditional meals.
✓ **You will be able to try some of the traditional dishes.**
See Language Note at PLATE

2

✗ We always take our meals in the canteen.
✓ **We always have our meals in the canteen.**

In British English the phrase is **have a meal** (NOT **take**): 'In the evening we had a three-course meal.'
In American English both **take a meal** and **have a meal** are used, although **take a meal** (more formal) is not very common.

mean

✗ Being a good flight attendant means to make your passengers feel relaxed.
✓ **Being a good flight attendant means making your passengers feel relaxed.**

mean to do sth = intend to do something: 'I've been meaning to write to you for ages.'
mean doing sth (or **mean + that** clause) = involve doing something: 'The new job will mean getting up an hour earlier in the morning.' 'The new job will mean that I have to get up ....'

means 1

✗ He was determined to get the money by all means.
✓ **He was determined to get the money by whatever means.**
✗ They intend to become famous by all means, even if they have to risk their lives.
✓ **They intend to become famous by whatever means, even if they have to risk their lives.**

By all means (= certainly) is used in formal spoken English to show that you are happy to accept someone's request or suggestion: 'Would you mind if I stayed a bit longer?' 'By all means.'
When you mean 'by using any method, even if it is unkind or illegal', use **by any means** or **by whatever means (are available/necessary)**: 'They are determined to get their hands on the property by whatever means are necessary.'

2   ✗ Learning English is a means to improve one's career prospects.
      ✓ **Learning English is a means of improving one's career prospects.**

> **means of (doing) sth** = a way or method: 'It's time we stopped using force as a means of settling disputes.' 'There must be an easier means of gaining their confidence.'
> **means to do sth** (or **means of doing sth**) = the thing that is required or necessary (to make something possible): 'These people have lost the means to support their families.' 'They would like to stop the war but lack the means to do so.'

3   ✗ By no means I want to suggest that people like being unemployed.
      ✓ **By no means do I want to suggest that people like being unemployed.**

> See Language Note at NOT

measure-ment   ✗ In my opinion, the authorities have to take even stricter measurements to save our archaeological treasures.
      ✓ **In my opinion, the authorities have to take even stricter measures to save our archaeological treasures.**

> **measurement** = the length, width etc of something: 'You can't buy new curtains without knowing the window measurements.'
> **measure** = an action intended to have a particular effect; a law or ruling: 'New measures are to be introduced in the fight against crime.'

media 1   ✗ Television is a very powerful media.
      ✓ **Television is a very powerful medium.**
      ✗ The medias, such as radio and television, tell us what is happening in the world.
      ✓ **The media, such as radio and television, tell us what is happening in the world.**

> When you are talking about television, radio and newspapers, use **medium** for singular reference: 'Children learn as much through the medium of television as they do by going to school.'
> Use **media** (WITHOUT **-s**) for plural and group reference: 'the mass media', 'the news media'.

2   ? In January 1990, the international news media was excited because it appeared that Mandela might be released.
      ✓ **In January 1990, the international news media were excited because it appeared that Mandela might be released.**

> **The media** usually takes a plural verb, especially in formal styles: 'The media have shown considerable interest in the trial.' A singular verb is sometimes heard in everyday conversation, but some careful users consider this to be incorrect.

medicine   ✗ After drinking the medicine, I felt sleepy.
      ✓ **After taking the medicine, I felt sleepy.**

> **take/have your medicine** (NOT **drink**): 'Have you taken/had your medicine today?'

medium 1   ✗ The medium score was about 6 out of 10.
      ✓ **The average score was about 6 out of 10.**

medium = neither large nor small, neither tall nor short, etc: 'The waiter was of medium height and walked with a slight limp.'
average = calculated by adding a set of quantities together and then dividing this total by the number of quantities in the set: 'The average age of students entering the college this year is 19.' 'Since 1991 house prices have been falling at an average annual rate of 8%.'

2   ✗ My ability in English is about medium.
       ✓ **My ability in English is about average.**

If someone's level of skill or ability is neither high nor low, it is **average**: 'Elizabeth shows above average intelligence for a child of three.'

meet 1   ✗ Could you meet with me outside the station?
            ✓ **Could you meet me outside the station?**
            ✗ The next time I met with her was in the supermarket.
            ✓ **The next time I met her was in the supermarket.**

meet with sb (mainly American English) = have a (previously arranged) meeting with someone: 'We met with their representatives to discuss the problem.'
meet sb (British and American English) = be in the same place as someone by chance or arrangement: 'Guess who I met on the way to the bank this morning?' 'I suggest we meet back here in an hour's time.'

2   ✗ Hello John. It's good to meet you.
       ✓ **Hello John. It's good to see you.**
       ✗ I can't wait to meet you again at Christmas.
       ✓ **I can't wait to see you again at Christmas.**

When you greet someone you know well, or talk about meeting them, use **see** (NOT **meet**): 'I hope you'll come and see us again soon.'

memorize   ✗ Following his death, a statue was erected to memorize him.
              ✓ **Following his death, a statue was erected in his memory.**

memorize = learn something so that you are able to repeat it exactly: 'Fortunately, I had memorized her telephone number and was able to ring her from the station.'
in memory of sb, to the memory of sb or **as a memorial (to sb)** = as a permanent reminder of someone after they have died: 'The charity was set up in memory of the late Lord Hinton.' 'It was built as a memorial to all those who died in the war.'

memory 1   ✗ Each visitor received a small gift as a memory.
              ✓ **Each visitor received a small gift as a souvenir.**
              ✗ I bought six postcards and a few small memories.
              ✓ **I bought six postcards and a few small souvenirs.**

memory = something that you remember and see as a picture in your mind, especially an experience that you had a long time ago: 'The old teddy bear brought back vivid memories of my childhood.'
souvenir = something that you buy or obtain in a particular place (especially while on holiday) and keep to remind you of it: 'The vase is a souvenir of my week in Venice.'

2   ✗ Casanova recorded his adventures in his memories.
       ✓ **Casanova recorded his adventures in his memoirs.**

To refer to someone's written account of (a period in) their life, use **memoirs** (pronounced /ˈmemwɑːz/): 'The former President's long awaited memoirs are to be published next month.'

3 ? You will remain in our memory and we all hope that you'll visit Greece again next summer.

✓ **We won't forget you and we all hope that you'll visit Greece again next summer.**

You promise that you will **not/never forget** someone or the time you spent with them: 'I'll never forget the magic week we spent together in Rome.' The phrase **remain in one's memory** is grammatical but sounds unnatural.

4 ✗ I have many happy memories about my childhood.

✓ **I have many happy memories of my childhood.**

memory of sth: 'He smiled to himself at the memory of his son's first day at school.' 'The order and discipline of the job brought back memories of his army days.'

menace ✗ Nowadays world peace is menaced.

✓ **Nowadays world peace is threatened.**

Menace is usually used as a noun or adjective: 'These street gangs are a social menace.' 'He was convicted of menacing behaviour.' **Menace** is not often used as a verb. It appears mainly in formal styles and means 'make or try to make someone feel their life or safety is in great danger': 'His mighty war machine continues to menace neighbouring countries.' When you are talking about something which is a danger to peace, survival, safety, health, happiness, etc, use **threaten**: 'These poisonous liquids threaten the drinking water supply of two million people.' 'AIDS could threaten the economic well-being of Asian countries.'

mend ? Old cars are easier to mend.

✓ **Old cars are easier to repair.**

mend (or **repair**) a roof, fence, watch, radio, camera, puncture etc: 'Once you've mended the kettle, we can have a cup of tea.'
repair a vehicle or something that is wrong with a vehicle: 'How will you get to work while your car is being repaired?'

mental ✗ Modern society provides us with material comforts but very few mental rewards.

✓ **Modern society provides us with material comforts but very few spiritual rewards.**

mental = affecting or taking place in the mind: 'People who have had mental illnesses are often unwilling to talk about them.'
spiritual = connected with the part of a person which has very deep thoughts and feelings: 'African music has a spiritual quality which is often lacking in Western music.'

mention ✗ The first place that foreigners think of when I mention about Indonesia is Bali.

✓ **The first place that foreigners think of when I mention Indonesia is Bali.**

mention sth (WITHOUT **about**): 'I don't suppose she mentioned her new address?' 'They mentioned how helpful you had been.'

menu 1 ✗ For the main menu we had fish, rice and vegetables.
   ✓ **For the main course we had fish, rice and vegetables.**
   See Language Note at PLATE

2 ✗ My favourite menu is cheese and mushroom omelette.
   ✓ **My favourite dish is cheese and mushroom omelette.**
   See Language Note at PLATE

method 1 ✗ We'll have to find new methods of amusing ourselves.
   ✓ **We'll have to find new ways of amusing ourselves.**
   Method (of/for doing sth) is used mainly in technical styles: 'Farming methods have undergone many changes in recent years.' 'The research project aims to develop new methods for trapping solar energy.'
   In non-technical styles, use **way (of doing/to do sth)**: 'There are several ways of answering the question.' 'The best way to contact him is by fax.'

2 ✗ Some companies are taking new methods for coping with environmental problems.
   ✓ **Some companies are adopting new methods for coping with environmental problems.**
   adopt a method: 'This new method of treating the disease has been widely adopted.'

midday ✗ We usually eat during the midday and again in the evening.
   ✓ **We usually eat at midday and again in the evening.**
   at midday (NOT **during**): 'At midday the sun is directly overhead.'
   Compare: 'During the middle of the day the sun is very hot.'

middle 1 ✗ The girl was of middle height and was wearing a blue suit.
   ✓ **The girl was of medium height and was wearing a blue suit.**
   When you are talking about someone's height, weight, etc, use **medium** (NOT **middle**): 'The man that police wish to question is of medium height and has a small black moustache.'

2 ✗ The wallet was middle brown and contained sixty dollars.
   ✓ **The wallet was medium brown and contained sixty dollars.**
   When you describe the colour of something, use **medium** (NOT **middle**): 'a medium grey suit' (= neither light grey nor dark grey but somewhere in between).

3 ✗ On the middle of September she is going on maternity leave.
   ✓ **In the middle of September she is going on maternity leave.**
   in the middle of (NOT **on**): 'The cat dropped the mouse right in the middle of the kitchen floor.' 'What do we do if the fire alarm starts ringing in the middle of an examination?'

Middle Age ✗ The history of the town dates back to the Middle Age.
   ✓ **The history of the town dates back to the Middle Ages.**
   middle age = the period in a person's life between youth and old age: 'People who live this type of life are lucky if they reach middle age.'
   Middle Ages = the period in European history from about 1100 to 1500 AD: 'Life in the Middle Ages was very simple.'

middle age ✗ Sitting next to me was a middle age man, probably about forty.
✓ **Sitting next to me was a middle-aged man, probably about forty.**
✗ The Rolling Stones are all middle-age now.
✓ **The Rolling Stones are all middle-aged now.**

The adjective is **middle-aged** (WITH **-d**): 'They would prefer a middle-aged woman to a young girl.'

Middle East ✗ Arabic is spoken all over Middle East.
✓ **Arabic is spoken all over the Middle East.**

the Middle East, the Far East (WITH **the**): 'Bahrain is in the Middle East.'

midnight ✗ Her plane is due to land in about midnight.
✓ **Her plane is due to land at about midnight.**
See Language Note at TIME

migrate ✗ A lot of new doctors migrate to America where they can earn more money.
✓ **A lot of new doctors emigrate to America where they can earn more money.**

migrate = (of birds, animals and people) travel from one place to spend a length of time in another, especially to find food, water, warmer weather, etc: 'How do birds know when to migrate and how do they find their way back home?'
emigrate = (of people) leave your own country and make your home in another one: 'There were no jobs back home so we decided to emigrate.'

million 1 ✗ Belgium has ten millions inhabitants.
✓ **Belgium has ten million inhabitants.**
✗ The paper has a circulation of approximately 3.9 millions.
✓ **The paper has a circulation of approximately 3.9 million.**
See Language Note at HUNDRED

2 ✗ We hung just over a million of little electric bulbs on the trees.
✓ **We hung just over a million little electric bulbs on the trees.**
✗ In the last ten years, more than two million of people have come to Milan to find work.
✓ **In the last ten years, more than two million people have come to Milan to find work.**
See Language Note at HUNDRED

3 ✗ Nearly half million people entered the country.
✓ **Nearly half a million people entered the country.**
See Language Note at HUNDRED

mind 1 ✗ I don't mind to wait a bit longer.
✓ **I don't mind waiting a bit longer.**

(not) mind doing sth: 'Would you mind posting this letter for me when you go into town?'

2 ✗ It was raining but we didn't mind it.
✓ **It was raining but we didn't mind.**

When the object of **mind** can be understood from the context, **mind** is not followed by a pronoun: 'Do you mind waiting a few minutes?' 'No, I don't mind.'

3

✗ The first thing that comes to my mind when I think about France is wine.
✓ **The first thing that comes to mind when I think about France is wine.**

come/spring to mind (WITHOUT **my, his, their,** etc): 'When I'm planning a camping holiday, the first thing that comes to mind is the weather.'

4

✗ Having in mind that the roads will be busy, I think that we should make an early start.
✓ **Bearing in mind that the roads will be busy, I think that we should make an early start.**

bear in mind (NOT **have**): 'Something else you need to bear in mind is the fact that not all countries have public transport.'

minute 1

✗ The train arrived at exactly twelve past three.
✓ **The train arrived at exactly twelve minutes past three.**

When telling the time, **minutes** must be used after all numbers except **five, ten, twenty,** and **twenty-five**.
Compare: 'It's twenty (minutes) past ten.' (**minutes** can be used)
'It's twenty-three minutes past ten.' (**minutes** must be used)

2

✗ The college is a twenty minutes bus ride from my flat.
✓ **The college is a twenty-minute bus ride from my flat.**
See Language Note at HUNDRED

mist

✗ Her flight was held up on account of the mist.
✓ **Her flight was held up on account of the fog.**

mist = tiny drops of water in the air that make it difficult to see things that are far away: 'As the day wore on, the early morning mist quickly disappeared.'
fog = very thick mist: 'Traffic on several stretches of the M1 was slowed to a walking pace this morning as the result of thick fog.'

mistake

✗ It doesn't matter if you do a slight mistake.
✓ **It doesn't matter if you make a slight mistake.**

make a mistake (NOT **do**): 'It's easy to make mistakes when you're tired.' See Language Note at DO

mister

✗ Dear Mister Southcroft ...
✓ **Dear Mr Southcroft ...**

Mister is always written **Mr**: 'Mr Jones called this morning about the central heating.' See also MR

moist

✗ Basement flats are often dark and moist.
✓ **Basement flats are often dark and damp.**

moist = slightly wet, especially in a pleasant way: 'The bread was still nice and moist.' 'These plants prefer a warm, moist atmosphere.'
damp = slightly wet, especially in a cold and unpleasant way: 'Our hotel room felt cold and damp.' 'On damp days, we have to dry the washing indoors.'

moment **1**   ✗   In that moment the door opened.
               ✓   **At that moment the door opened.**

> **in a moment** = very soon: 'I'll have to go in a moment.'
> **at that moment** = at that particular time: 'Just at that moment the telephone rang.'

        2   ✗   At the moment the girl opened her eyes.
            ✓   **At that moment the girl opened her eyes.**

> When you are telling a story or reporting what happened, use **at that moment**: 'At that moment the car skidded on the ice and went off the road.'
> Compare: 'At the moment I'm working in a restaurant.' (= now, at the present time)

        3   ✗   At the moment I saw him, I knew something was wrong.
            ✓   **The moment I saw him, I knew something was wrong.**

> **the moment** (WITHOUT **at**) = as soon as: 'He fell in love with Samantha the moment he set eyes on her.'

        4   ✗   I'd like to see him in my office the moment he will arrive.
            ✓   **I'd like to see him in my office the moment he arrives.**

> See Language Note at WILL

money   See GAIN 1

month   See Language Note at HUNDRED

monument   ✗   It is impossible to visit all the monuments of London in one day.
            ✓   **It is impossible to see all the sights of London in one day.**

> **monument** = (1) a structure, usually made of stone, that is built to remind people of an important event or famous person; memorial: 'The inscription at the foot of the monument read: *To all those who gave their lives so that others could live in freedom.*'
> (2) a building or structure that is preserved because of its historical importance: 'If you are interested in ancient monuments you will find the Pyramids fascinating.'
> **see the sights** = visit the interesting places in a city or country: 'I wanted to look round Moscow and see the sights.'

mood   ✗   The mood of the castle depends on the weather.
            ✓   **The atmosphere of the castle depends on the weather.**
            ?   The streets were very crowded and had a holiday mood.
            ✓   **The streets were very crowded and had a holiday atmosphere.**
            ✓   **The streets were full of people in a holiday mood.**

> **mood** = the way someone feels at a particular time, such as happy, angry, etc: 'I'd keep clear of George this morning - he's in one of his bad moods.'
> **atmosphere** = the general impression that a place gives you: 'Their house always has a warm, friendly atmosphere.'

more **1**   ✗   In Taiwan the food is more cheaper than in England.
            ✓   **In Taiwan the food is cheaper than in England.**

✗ These machines make farming much more easier.
✓ **These machines make farming much easier.**

> Do not use **more** with the **-er** form of an adjective or adverb: 'Leather bags are more expensive but they tend to last longer.'

2   See MUCH 2

3   See NO MORE

more or less ✗ Some women more or less are forced to work nowadays.
✓ **Some women are more or less forced to work nowadays.**

> **More or less** is usually placed immediately in front of the word or phrase that it modifies: 'The two words have more or less the same meaning.' 'My wife and I met each other more or less by accident.' 'That's more or less everything you need to know.'
> In everyday conversation **more or less** also comes at the end of a sentence: 'I guess that's everything you need to know, more or less.'

morning ✗ At morning I wake up at 6.30.
✓ **In the morning I wake up at 6.30.**
✗ The trains are very crowded in morning.
✓ **The trains are very crowded in the morning.**

> See Language Note at TIME

most 1 ✗ Where I come from, the most teachers have to teach at two schools in order to earn enough.
✓ **Where I come from, most teachers have to teach at two schools in order to earn enough.**

> When you mean 'nearly all', use **most** (NOT **the most**): 'Most universities provide a wide range of courses.'
> Use **the most** in comparisons: 'Which city has the most tourists?' 'Rome and Florence are indeed beautiful, but Venice is the most romantic.'

2 ✗ Both girls are clever but Edna is the most intelligent.
✓ **Both girls are clever but Edna is (the) more intelligent.**

> Use **(the) most** when comparing one person or thing with all others: 'This is the most ridiculous excuse I've ever heard.'
> When comparing just two people or things, use **(the) more**: 'Which is (the) more expensive - an ALR or an IBM?'
> Note that in everyday conversation some people use **(the) most** instead of **(the) more**, but careful users consider this to be incorrect.

mostly ✗ We see each other mostly every day.
✓ **We see each other almost every day.**
✗ Mostly every family has a television.
✓ **Nearly every family has a television.**

> Use **almost/nearly** with **all/every/everyone** etc (NOT **mostly**): 'Almost everyone in the office has had a cold recently.'
> Compare: 'The students here are mostly Swiss or German.' (= most of the students here ...)

motor ✗ It's an old car and the motor is very noisy.
✓ **It's an old car and the engine is very noisy.**

> **motor** = the part of a machine which turns electrical power into movement: 'My video camera isn't working. Either the battery is flat or there's something wrong with the motor.'
> **engine** = See note at MACHINE

move

   ✗ When they saw that I couldn't move myself, they called an ambulance.
   ✓ **When they saw that I couldn't move, they called an ambulance.**

> See Language Note at MYSELF

Mr 1

   ✗ Our English teacher is called Mr John.
   ✓ **Our English teacher is called Mr (John) Smith.**

> **Mr/Mrs/Miss/Ms** (+ first name) + surname: 'Mrs Waters', 'Mr Clive Upton'

2

   ✗ Dear Mr,
   ✓ **Dear Sir,**
   ✗ Dear Mr/Mrs,
   ✓ **Dear Sir/Madam,**

> When you are writing a formal letter and you know the surname of the addressee, begin **Dear Mr Smith, Dear Mrs Jones, Dear Ms Simpson** etc. When you do not know the person's surname, begin **Dear Sir, Dear Madam** or **Dear Sir/Madam**.

3

   ✗ Dear Mr Alan Jones,
   ✓ **Dear Mr Jones,**

> **Dear** is followed by **Mr/Mrs/Ms** + surname only (NOT first name + surname): 'Dear Mrs Jackson'

much 1

   ✗ We don't need to hire that much employees.
   ✓ **We don't need to hire that many employees.**
   ✗ There are as much disadvantages as advantages.
   ✓ **There are as many disadvantages as advantages.**
   ✗ There are too much people in Mexico.
   ✓ **There are too many people in Mexico.**

> **much** + uncountable noun: 'There isn't much traffic today.' 'There was too much furniture in the room.'
> **many** + plural (countable) noun: 'There aren't many cars today.' 'There were too many chairs in the room.'

2

   ✗ Nowadays, there are much more criminals than policemen.
   ✓ **Nowadays, there are far more criminals than policemen.**
   ✗ I make much too many mistakes.
   ✓ **I make far too many mistakes.**

> At the beginning of a phrase that ends with a plural (countable) noun, use **far** (NOT **much**). Compare: 'much more traffic', 'far more cars'

3

   ✗ As a doctor he earns much money.
   ✓ **As a doctor he earns a lot of money.**

> See note at MANY 1

4

   ✗ British culture is much different from ours.
   ✓ **British culture is very different from ours.**

✗ We were much afraid that we would miss the flight.
✓ **We were very afraid that we would miss the flight.**

> **Much** is used before an adjective (1) in questions and negative sentences: 'Is British culture much different from ours?' 'No, it isn't much different.' (2) before comparative forms: 'His last novel was much longer and much more interesting.' (3) before certain past participles acting as adjectives: 'Her drawings are much admired.'

5   See TOO MUCH 2

music 1

✗ Nowadays I prefer classical musics.
✓ **Nowadays I prefer classical music.**
✗ Are we allowed to play a pop music?
✓ **Are we allowed to play pop music?**

> **Music** is an uncountable noun: 'Her hobbies are gardening and music.'

2

✗ After leaving school, he joined a music band.
✓ **After leaving school, he joined a band.**

> **(jazz/rock) band** or **(pop/rock) group** (NOT **music band**): 'The band's new album has just been released.'

must 1

✗ People are not as careful as they must be and drop their litter in the streets.
✓ **People are not as careful as they should be and drop their litter in the streets.**

> Use **must** (or **have to**) when, for example, there is a law or rule and you are not free to choose or decide for yourself: 'Candidates must answer all the questions in Part A and two questions in Part B.'
> Use **should** (or **ought to**) when, for example, someone advises you to do something but you are free to choose or decide for yourself: 'At the end of the examination, you should check your answers.'

2

✗ The pupils mustn't go to the meeting if they don't want to.
✓ **The pupils needn't go to the meeting it they don't want to.**

> Use **must not/never** when you mean that it is essential that someone does not do something: 'The door to the X-ray room must never be opened when the red light is on.'
> When you mean that it is not necessary for someone to do something, use **needn't** or **don't need/have to**: 'You needn't pay now. You can wait until the furniture has been delivered.'

3

✗ You must be pleased to hear that I've already got the tickets.
✓ **You'll be pleased to hear that I've already got the tickets.**

> When you inform someone of something, use **will be** + **pleased/interested** + **to hear/know/learn** (NOT **must**): 'You will be pleased to know that your old friend Peter has been promoted to Associate Professor.'

4

✗ If you can't find her, she must hide somewhere.
✓ **If you can't find her, she must be hiding somewhere.**

> When you do not actually know where someone is or what they are doing, but certain facts allow you to guess, use **must be** or **must be doing**: 'If she isn't in her office, she must be in the canteen.' 'If she's in the canteen, she must be having her lunch.'

myself   See Language Note below

Using reflexive pronouns

The words listed below are called 'reflexive pronouns'.

SINGULAR	PLURAL
myself,	**ourselves** (NOT **ourself/s**)
yourself	**yourselves** (NOT **yourself/s**)
himself, herself	**themselves** (NOT **theirselves** or
itself, oneself	**themself/s**)

- These pronouns are always written as just ONE word, e.g. **myself, ourselves** (NOT **my self, our selves**):

> He managed to escape by disguising himself as a prison officer.

All the singular forms end with **-self**; all the plural forms end with **-selves**:
> You mustn't blame yourself, Helen. It wasn't your fault.
> I hope that you are both looking after yourselves.

- If the subject and the pronoun refer to the same person or thing, use **myself, himself, etc** (NOT **me, him**):
> We found ourselves in a difficult situation. (NOT 'we found us')
> She describes herself as a journalist. (NOT 'she describes her')
> I stood there looking at myself in the mirror. (NOT 'looking at me')

Note however that prepositions of place are usually followed by **me, him, etc** (NOT **myself, himself**): 'I could hear footsteps behind me.' 'Do you have any money on you?' 'He'd forgotten to bring his keys with him.'

- The verbs **enjoy, amuse, hurt, injure** and **familiarize** are often used with a reflexive pronoun:
> The children always enjoy themselves at the seaside.
> He'd fallen down the stairs and injured himself.

Feel and **relax** are not usually used with reflexive pronouns:
> He soon began to feel better. (NOT 'feel himself better.')
> After a hard day's work, I like to relax. (NOT 'relax myself.')

Note however the pattern **feel yourself doing sth**: 'I felt myself getting redder and redder.'

Specialize and **concentrate** are never used with reflexive pronouns.
> I want to specialize in tropical medicine. (NOT 'specialize myself')
> He can't concentrate with the radio on. (NOT 'concentrate himself')

- Do not use **wash yourself, dress yourself, etc** when you mention the simple things that people do as part of their daily routine:
> I always wash/have a wash before breakfast.
> I wish you would hurry up and get dressed.

If you use **wash yourself, dress yourself, etc** you draw attention to the special skill or ability that the action requires: 'Not many two-year-olds are able to wash and dress themselves.'

name 1
- ✗ This beautiful village is named 'Cadaques'.
- ✓ **This beautiful village is called 'Cadaques'.**
- ✗ I stayed in and watched a film named 'The Clockwork Orange'.
- ✓ **I stayed in and watched a film called 'The Clockwork Orange'.**
- ✗ What we used to name 'the Cold War' is now over.
- ✓ **What we used to call 'the Cold War' is now over.**

> When you mention the name by which someone or something is known, use **call/be called** (NOT **name/be named**): 'Most people call him Bob but he prefers to be called Robert.'
> Compare: 'They've named/called the baby Louise.' (= the name they have chosen for the baby is Louise)

2
- ✗ They named their children from their grandparents.
- ✓ **They named their children after their grandparents.**

> **name** a child **after sb**: 'We've decided to name her Sarah, after her grandmother.'
> In American English **name** a child **for sb** is also possible, although not very common.

narrow
- ✗ When immersed in water, the cloth narrows.
- ✓ **When immersed in water, the cloth shrinks.**

> **narrow** (of roads, rivers etc) = become less wide: 'Just beyond the bend, the river begins to narrow.'
> **shrink** (especially of cloth) = become smaller as a result of being wet or placed in water: 'I suggest you buy the larger size just in case it shrinks.'

nation
- ✗ It's hard to tell which nation he comes from.
- ✓ **It's hard to tell which country he comes from.**

> A person comes from, lives in, or feels part of a particular **country** (NOT **nation**): 'Some people in this country think that the leadership is too weak.' 'People living in former Soviet bloc countries are undergoing a difficult period of transition.'
> **Nation** is less common than **country** and is mainly used when a country is considered as a political or economic structure: 'Japan has become the richest nation in the world.' 'Representatives from the world's leading industrial nations will meet next month in Geneva.'
> Note the alternative: 'It's hard to tell his nationality.'

nationality
- ✗ My name is Iman Jalil and my nationality is Iraqi.
- ✓ **My name is Iman Jalil and I come from Iraq.**

> The usual way of referring to someone's nationality is to use **come from**: 'Most of the students in my class come from Oman or Bahrain.'
> **Nationality** is used mainly in formal styles: 'Visitors of Swedish

nationality do not require a visa.' 'Despite being born in Germany, these children do not have an automatic right to German nationality.'

native ✗ The airport extension is strongly opposed by the natives.
✓ **The airport extension is strongly opposed by the local residents.**

Nowadays the noun **native** is usually used in formal styles to refer to the place where someone was born: 'His real name was Harvey Pepper, a native of Montreal.' or to the country/region where a particular animal or plant has always grown: 'This useful herb is a native of southern Europe, but has adjusted well to colder climates.'
To refer to the people who live in and around a village, town or city, and have shared interests and activities, use **local residents**, **local population** or (in informal styles) **locals**: 'Local residents are against the motorway proposal.'

nature ✗ I have always found the nature fascinating.
✓ **I have always found nature fascinating.**

Ⓖ **Nature** (= the natural world of birds, trees, rivers etc) is never used with **the**: 'We must stop destroying nature before it is too late.'

near 1 ✗ He decided to visit a friend who lived very near from where he was at that moment.
✓ **He decided to visit a friend who lived very near (to) where he was at that moment.**

near or **near to** (NOT **near from**): 'The post office is near (to) the bank.' 'If we moved to Dallas, we would be nearer to my parents.'

2 ✗ I went near to the girl and told her my name.
✓ **I went up to the girl and told her my name.**
See note at TO 2

3 ✗ I sometimes meet friends in a near restaurant.
✓ **I sometimes meet friends in a nearby restaurant.**
✗ I ran to the telephone box which was near to call an ambulance.
✓ **I ran to the telephone box nearby to call an ambulance.**

To say that something is only a short distance from a place, use **nearby**: 'I stopped at one of the nearby cottages and asked the way.' 'It's very convenient having a supermarket nearby.'

nearby ✗ Their house is nearby the new airport.
✓ **Their house is near the new airport.**

Nearby is used as an adjective or adverb: 'We flew from a nearby airport.' 'There is an airport nearby.'
When you need a preposition, use **near**: 'The hotel is near the sea.'

nearly ✗ In the countryside there is nearly no pollution.
✓ **In the countryside there is hardly any pollution.**

Instead of saying **nearly no/nobody/never** etc, use **hardly any/anybody/ever** etc: 'Hardly any of my friends are married.' 'Hardly anybody objected to the idea.'

necessity ✗ It was then that I felt the necessity to improve my English.
✓ **It was then that I felt the need to improve my English.**

If something is a **necessity**, you must have it or do it, or it must happen: 'If you saw the terrible conditions in which these people are living, you would appreciate the necessity to step up foreign aid.' 'For anyone who runs a large business, a computer is an absolute necessity.'
Need has a similar meaning to **necessity** but it is also used in connection with something that you want to do/have/happen (although it is not essential): 'I began to feel the need for a change of life style.' 'Don't you ever feel the need to do something more creative?'

need 1

  ✗ It is no need to tell the police about the accident.
  ✓ **There is no need to tell the police about the accident.**

> **there is no need to do sth** (NOT **it is ...**): 'There's no need to start getting upset.'

2

  ✗ There is a great need of international understanding.
  ✓ **There is a great need for international understanding.**

> **a need for sth** (NOT **of**): 'The government is conscious of the need for more schools.' See NEED 3

3

  ✗ We have an urgent need of a new secretary.
  ✓ **We are in urgent need of a new secretary.**
  ✗ I'm in urgent need for a loan.
  ✓ **I'm in urgent need of a loan.**

> **be in need of sth** (= require): 'The car is in need of a good clean.' 'Are you in need of any assistance?'

4

  ✗ For a long time I have felt the need of improving my French.
  ✓ **For a long time I have felt the need to improve my French.**

> **a need to do sth** (NOT **of/for doing**): 'I don't understand their need to sell the house.'

5

  ✗ Tina needs leave her house at seven o'clock every morning.
  ✓ **Tina needs to leave her house at seven o'clock every morning.**

> In affirmative sentences, use **need to do sth** (WITH **to**): 'I need to get to the airport by seven at the latest.'
> Compare (1) the negative forms: 'She doesn't need to stay if she doesn't want to.' 'She needn't stay if she doesn't want.'
> (2) the question forms: 'Does she need to stay any longer?' 'Need she stay any longer?'

**need not/
needn't 1**

  ✗ During the day I need not work.
  ✓ **During the day I don't need/have to work.**
  ✗ They need not get a job if their parents are rich.
  ✓ **They don't need/have to get a job if their parents are rich.**

> Use **needn't/need not** (or **don't need/have to**) to refer to the situation 'now' (at the moment of speaking): 'You needn't rush. I'm not in a hurry.'
> To refer to general situations, you usually use **don't need to** or **don't have to**: 'You don't need/have to drive everywhere if there is a good bus service.'

2

  ✗ They need not to feel ashamed of themselves.
  ✓ **They needn't feel ashamed of themselves.**
  ✓ **They don't need to feel ashamed of themselves.**

✗ Catherine told her husband he needn't to worry.
✓ **Catherine told her husband he needn't worry.**
✓ **Catherine told her husband he didn't need to worry.**

needn't/need not do sth (WITHOUT **to**): 'You needn't wait if you're in a hurry.'
don't need to do sth (WITH **to**): 'You don't need to wait if you're in a hurry.'
Note that **need not** is used mainly in formal styles. In other styles, the usual form is **needn't**.

needless to say

✗ Needless to say that his films are very popular with children.
✓ **Needless to say, his films are very popular with children.**

Needless to say (an adverb meaning 'of course') is NOT followed by a **that** clause: 'Needless to say, I was delighted to see that I had passed.'

neglect

✗ Some teachers neglect how much a student can take in during one lesson.
✓ **Some teachers forget how much a student can take in during one lesson.**

neglect = (1) fail to look after someone or something properly: 'The garden has been badly neglected and will require a lot of attention.'
(2) (formal) fail to do something, especially something that you ought to do: 'The public are demanding to know why the government neglected to warn them of the oil shortage.'
forget = fail to realize something (and be guided by it): 'Children tend to forget that their parents like to have fun too.'

negligent

✗ There was a negligent amount of liquid in the test tube.
✓ **There was a negligible amount of liquid in the test tube.**

negligent = failing to take proper care, especially in your job; careless: 'The court decided that the pilot of the crashed aircraft had been negligent.'
negligible = (of an amount) so small that it has no effect and can be ignored: 'The cost of maintaining the machine is negligible.'

neither 1

✗ Inside the examination room we could neither smoke or talk.
✓ **Inside the examination room we could neither smoke nor talk.**
✗ His parents neither shouted at him or smacked him.
✓ **His parents neither shouted at him nor smacked him.**

neither ... nor ... (NOT **neither ... or ...**): 'The sales assistant was neither friendly nor helpful.'
Compare: 'You can either come with me or wait here.'

2

✗ Neither John's father nor mine couldn't understand the problem.
✓ **Neither John's father nor mine could understand the problem.**

After **neither** and **neither ... nor ...** the verb is affirmative (NOT negative): 'Neither applicant had the right qualifications.' 'Neither the teachers nor the students had been informed.'
See Language Note at NOT

3

✗ I have neither studied the language nor the culture.
✓ **I have studied neither the language nor the culture.**

Neither should be placed immediately before the first of the connected items and **nor** immediately before the second. Compare: 'I have neither studied nor experienced the culture.'

4 ✗ Neither teachers are coming.
  ✓ **Neither teacher is coming.**
  ✓ **Neither of the teachers is coming.**

After **neither** + singular noun, the verb is singular: 'Neither player wants a transfer.'
After **neither of** + plural noun, careful users prefer a singular verb: 'Neither of the players wants a transfer.' Some people use a plural verb, especially in informal styles: 'Neither of the players want a transfer.'

nervous 1 ✗ Thinking she might be hurt, I felt very nervous.
  ✓ **Thinking she might be hurt, I felt very anxious.**

nervous = worried and unable to relax, especially because you lack confidence: 'There's no need to be so nervous. It's only an interview.'
anxious = very worried about something which may happen or may have happened: 'I knew that there were no sharks around but all the same I couldn't help feeling anxious.'

2 ✗ What really made me nervous was the way he kept pulling my sleeve.
  ✓ **What really irritated me was the way he kept pulling my sleeve.**

nervous = worried and unable to relax: 'I hate the way the teacher watches me when I'm working - it makes me feel nervous.'
irritate = (of something unpleasant that happens repeatedly or continuously) make someone feel slightly angry; annoy: 'His attempts to sound important irritate people.'
Note the alternative: 'What I found really irritating was the way ... '

never 1 ✗ I asked him to never arrive late.
  ✓ **I asked him never to arrive late.**

Never and **not** usually go immediately in front of a **to** infinitive: 'He's promised never to do it again.'

2 ✗ You never can get really good beef in our local supermarket.
  ✓ **You can never get really good beef in our local supermarket.**
See Language Note at ALWAYS

3 ✗ My father did never have the opportunity to go to university.
  ✓ **My father never had the opportunity to go to university.**

Do is often used with **not** to make negative statements: 'I didn't answer the letter.' 'She doesn't invite strangers.' However, **do** is NOT used in this way with **never**: 'I never answered the letter.' 'She never invites strangers.'
The exception to this rule is when **do** is used for emphasis: 'You never did tell me why you decided to leave your last job.'

4 ✗ She said some of the rudest things I have never heard in all my life.
  ✓ **She said some of the rudest things I have ever heard in all my life.**

never = at no time: 'I've never met his wife.' 'I had never met his wife before yesterday.'

ever = at any time: 'Have you ever met his wife?'
Note that **ever** is often used after a superlative: 'His wife is the kindest person I've ever met.'

5 ✗ 'Nobody will never find me,' he thought.
✓ **'Nobody will ever find me,' he thought.**

After **nobody/nothing/rarely** and other words with a negative meaning, use **ever** (NOT **never**): 'After she won the national lottery, nothing was ever the same again.'
See also Language Note at NOT

6 ✗ Never I had seen such an ugly face.
✓ **Never had I seen such an ugly face.**

See Language Note at NOT

nevertheless ✗ I was born and grew up in Switzerland, nevertheless Italy is the country that I have grown to love and where I now live.
✓ **I was born and grew up in Switzerland. Nevertheless, Italy is the country that I have grown to love and where I now live.**
✓ **I was born and grew up in Switzerland but (nevertheless) Italy is the country that I have grown to love and where I now live.**

Unlike **but**, **nevertheless** is an adverb (NOT a conjunction): 'The survey was conducted on a very small scale. Nevertheless, the information gathered is likely to prove very useful.' 'As you may have heard, the existing workforce is soon to be reduced by 40 per cent. The management is nevertheless committed to maintaining the present level of production.' See also HOWEVER, THEREFORE 1

news ✗ The news are never very good nowadays.
✓ **The news is never very good nowadays.**
✗ I'm looking forward to hearing a good news from you.
✓ **I'm looking forward to hearing some good news from you.**

News is an uncountable noun: 'Why do Clive's letters never contain any news?' 'There's one piece of news that I'm sure will interest you.'

next ✗ I'm looking forward to seeing you on next Sunday.
✓ **I'm looking forward to seeing you next Sunday.**
✗ I have some spare time this week but the next week I'll have to start work.
✓ **I have some spare time this week but next week I'll have to start work.**

See Language Note at TIME

nice ✗ There is a nice and quiet room where I do my work.
✓ **There is a nice quiet room where I do my work.**
✓ **The room where I do my work is nice and quiet.**

Two-part adjectival phrases with **nice** such as 'nice and quiet and 'nice and clean' are always placed after the noun they modify: 'The house is always nice and tidy.' Do not use **and** after **nice** when it comes in front of a noun: 'Right now I could do with a nice cold drink.'

night 1 ✗ I don't like driving in the night.
✓ **I don't like driving at night.**

✗ It was about nine o'clock in the night when we heard a noise outside.
✓ **It was about nine o'clock at night when we heard a noise outside.**
See Language Note at TIME

2 ✗ 'Where were you in the night of June 3rd?' he asked.
✓ **'Where were you on the night of June 3rd?' he asked.**
See Language Note at TIME

no See NO ONE 1

no matter 1 ✗ No matter he tries hard, he never succeeds.
✓ **No matter how hard he tries, he never succeeds.**

no matter how/who/whether etc + subject + verb : 'No matter how much you help him, he never seems grateful.' 'No matter how late you set off, the roads are always busy.' 'No matter who you ask, they all say the same thing.'

2 ✗ After the sauna they run and jump in the river, no matter if it's freezing or not.
✓ **After the sauna they run and jump in the river, no matter whether it's freezing or not.**
✗ No matter they are rich or poor, they all come to us for advice.
✓ **No matter whether they are rich or poor, they all come to us for advice.**

no matter + **wh-**word (NOT **if**/nothing): 'I'm not interested in the job, no matter how much they offer me.' 'No matter what you ask her to do, she's always ready to help.'
Note that **no matter whether** tends to sound awkward and there are usually simpler alternatives: 'After the sauna they run and jump in the river, whether it's freezing or not.' 'Rich or poor, they all come to us for advice.'

3 ✗ No matter the recession, sales remained high.
✓ **In spite of the recession, sales remained high.**

No matter is always followed by a **wh-** clause: 'No matter what they did, they couldn't put the fire out.' 'No matter how cold it gets, we'll keep warm somehow.'
In front of a noun phrase, use **in spite of/despite**: 'In spite of the temperature outside, we managed to keep warm.'

no more ✗ My wife had left the hotel and I no more needed a double room.
✓ **My wife had left the hotel and I no longer needed a double room.**

When talking about time, use **no longer** (NOT **no more**): 'The offices are no longer occupied.'
Note the alternative: 'My wife had left the hotel and I didn't need a double room any more.'

no one 1 ✗ No one of us regrets volunteering.
✓ **None of us regrets volunteering.**
✓ **Not one of us regrets volunteering.**

When you mean 'not one', use **none** or (for emphasis) **not one**: 'None of the children could tell the time.' 'Not one of the trainees has a medical background.'

No one and nobody cannot be followed by **of** unless the phrase introduced by **of** is descriptive: 'No one of any importance was at the meeting.'

2   See NOBODY/NO ONE

no sooner
- ✗ No sooner we had arrived than it began to rain.
- ✓ **No sooner had we arrived than it began to rain.**
  See Language Note at NOT

nobody/ no one 1
- ✗ Nobody have complained about the noise.
- ✓ **Nobody has complained about the noise.**
- ✗ When I arrived, there were nobody at home.
- ✓ **When I arrived, there was nobody at home.**

  nobody/no one + singular verb: 'Is nobody going to help you?'

2
- ✗ He closed the door quietly so that nobody wouldn't hear him.
- ✓ **He closed the door quietly so that nobody would hear him.**
  See Language Note at NOT

3
- ✗ Nobody has done something yet.
- ✓ **Nobody has done anything yet.**
  See Language Note at NOT

noise 1
- ✗ I turned on the radio but there was no noise.
- ✓ **I turned on the radio but there was no sound.**
- ✗ He was woken up by the noise of broken glass.
- ✓ **He was woken up by the sound of broken glass.**

  noise = (1) loud unpleasant sounds heard as a single mass: 'The noise of the traffic gave me a headache.' 'People were making such a lot of noise that I couldn't hear what she was saying.' (2) a sound that is unpleasant and/or without meaning: 'The radio started making a funny noise.' 'What was that noise?'
  sound = something that is heard or received by the ear, especially something that you recognize or can give a meaning to: 'I've always loved the sound of a classical guitar.' 'I could hear the sound of someone crying in the next room.'

2
- ✗ I was woken up by a big noise outside the room.
- ✓ **I was woken up by a loud noise outside the room.**

  loud noise (NOT **big**): 'Habitual exposure to loud noises can damage the ear.'

3
- ✗ The restaurant was full and there was a loud noise.
- ✓ **The restaurant was full and there was a lot of noise.**
- ✗ You can talk as long as you don't make a loud noise.
- ✓ **You can talk as long as you don't make a lot of noise.**

  A loud noise (countable) describes what you hear when, for example, somebody slams a door or drops a plate. To refer to continuous noise made during an activity, use **noise** as an uncountable noun: 'They don't know the difference between music and noise.'

nominate
- ✗ Mr Tong was nominated manager of the company in 1984.
- ✓ **Mr Tong was appointed manager of the company in 1984.**

> **nominate** = suggest someone for election or selection (for a job or position): 'We need to nominate someone to take over from Harry as our new public relations officer.'
> **appoint** = give someone a job or position: 'Mr H. Wilks has been officially appointed as the society's new public relations officer.'

none 1   ✗ I checked the essay for mistakes but I couldn't find none.
         ✓ **I checked the essay for mistakes but I couldn't find any.**
         See Language Note at NOT

2   ✗ I told the police officer that in my opinion none of the two drivers was responsible.
     ✓ **I told the police officer that in my opinion neither of the two drivers was responsible.**

> When talking about two people or things, use **neither**. For three or more, use **none**.

noon   ✗ The cafeteria is always crowded in the noon.
        ✓ **The cafeteria is always crowded at noon.**
        See Language Note at TIME

North   ✗ I am now living in North England.
         ✓ **I am now living in the north of England.**

> **North** + noun, **South** + noun, etc, are mainly used in the names of countries and their internal divisions: 'North America', 'South Carolina'. To refer to approximate locations, use **the North/South**, **the north/south of** + noun, or **northern/southern** + noun, etc: 'They've bought a cottage in the south of France.' 'Northern England is supposed to be colder than the South.'

not 1   ✗ He told me to not spend too long in the sun.
         ✓ **He told me not to spend too long in the sun.**

> **Not** and **never** usually go immediately in front of a **to** infinitive: 'Try not to worry about anything.' 'It's hard not to feel sorry for him.'

2   See Language Note opposite

not only 1   ✗ He not only was a talented pianist but also a great composer.
             ✓ **He was not only a talented pianist but also a great composer.**

> The position of **not only** should be the same as the position of **but also** (i.e. immediately before an object, immediately before a main verb, etc). Compare: 'He injured not only his shoulder but also his elbow.' ('his shoulder' and 'his elbow' are both objects) 'He not only injured his back but also hurt his head.' ('injured' and 'hurt' are both verbs)

2   ✗ Not only I passed, but I got a distinction.
     ✓ **Not only did I pass, but I got a distinction.**
     See Language Note opposite

nothing   ✗ It was so dark that I couldn't see nothing.
           ✓ **It was so dark that I couldn't see anything.**
           See Language Note opposite

Using negative words

- Do not use two negative words in a clause. **No, nobody, nothing etc** cannot be used with **not, never, hardly, seldom, etc.**

> **Nobody could see me.** (NOT 'couldn't see')
> **Nobody ever asks me for my opinion.** (NOT 'never asks')
> **I checked the essay for mistakes but couldn't find any.** (NOT 'find none')

- After negative words, you usually use **any, anyone, anything, etc** (NOT **some, someone, something, etc**).

> **I hadn't seen anyone for over a week.**
> **Nobody is doing anything to help them.**

Follow the same rule if the context has a negative meaning.

> **He managed to get on the train without anyone seeing him.**
> **By six o'clock I am too tired to do anything else.**

- As a general rule, use **nobody/nothing etc** with an affirmative verb instead of **everybody/everything etc** with a negative verb.

> **Nobody is allowed to wear shoes in the mosque.** (NOT 'Everyone isn't')
> **None of the children are at school today.**

Compare: 'All the children aren't at school today.' This means that some of the children are at school today, but not all of them.

- When a sentence begins with **never, hardly, seldom, rarely, scarcely, nowhere, no sooner, not only, only when, by no means, under no circumstances etc**, the subject and auxiliary verb change places.

> **No sooner had we arrived than it began to rain.**
> **Under no circumstances should you wait any longer.**

- When there is no auxiliary verb, use **do**:

> **Only then did I realize that I was completely alone.**
> **Rarely do you meet such polite children nowadays.**

---

notice 1

   ✗ I wrote him a notice saying that the package had arrived.
   ✓ **I wrote him a note saying that the package had arrived.**

> **notice** = a short written statement giving information or directions, usually found in a public place: 'There was a notice on the wall saying "Private property. No parking."'
> **note** = a short informal letter or written message from one person to another: 'Just a quick note to say that Helen had a baby boy yesterday.'

2   ✗ It was so crowded that at first I didn't take any notice of him.
   ✓ **It was so crowded that at first I didn't see/notice him.**

> **take notice of** = pay attention to: 'Nobody ever takes any notice of what I say.'
> **notice** = become aware of; see: 'I didn't suspect anything until I noticed that my chequebook was missing.'

3   ✗ I could notice that he was not enjoying himself.
  ✓ **I noticed that he was not enjoying himself.**
  ✓ **I could see that he was not enjoying himself.**

> **Notice** is not used with **can/could**: 'They were so busy that they didn't notice how late it was getting.'

now 1   ✗ I'm sure you'll be happier from now.
  ✓ **I'm sure you'll be happier from now on.**
  ✗ From now I shall make all the decisions myself.
  ✓ **From now on I shall make all the decisions myself.**

> **from now on** (WITH **on**): 'From now on I'm going to work really hard and make sure I pass.'

2   See UNTIL NOW

nowadays 1 ✗ People live longer in nowadays.
  ✓ **People live longer nowadays.**

> **nowadays** (WITHOUT **in**): 'More women have executive jobs nowadays, especially in publishing.' 'Nowadays, computer skills are essential.'

2 ✗ This is a major problem for nowadays society.
  ✓ **This is a major problem for today's society.**

> **Nowadays** is an adverb (NOT an adjective): 'Video cameras are very popular nowadays.'

number 1   ✗ The number of heavy smokers are decreasing.
  ✓ **The number of heavy smokers is decreasing.**

> **the number of ...** + singular verb: 'The number of people claiming unemployment benefit has risen by 5 per cent in the last three months.'

2   ✗ A large number of cars was parked outside the school.
  ✓ **A large number of cars were parked outside the school.**

> **a number of ...** + plural verb: 'A number of viewers have complained about the excessive violence in the film.'

3   ✗ Harsher punishments will not reduce the number of crime.
  ✓ **Harsher punishments will not reduce the number of crimes.**
  ✓ **Harsher punishments will not reduce the amount of crime.**
  See note at AMOUNT 1

4   ✗ In England I met a big number of women in senior positions.
  ✓ **In England I met a large number of women in senior positions.**

> **a large/considerable number** (NOT **big**): 'A large number of fatal accidents are caused by drunken drivers.'

obey   ✗ He was a good boy and obeyed to his parents all the time.
✓ **He was a good boy and obeyed his parents all the time.**
obey sb/sth (WITHOUT **to**): 'Those who refused to obey orders were usually shot.'

object   ✗ My object is to improve my English as much as possible.
✓ **My objective is to improve my English as much as possible.**
object = the purpose of an action or event: 'The object of the game is to score as many points as possible.' 'Nobody knows the real object of their visit. They're keeping it a secret.'
objective = the thing that you are working towards and hope to achieve by the end of a course of action: 'The company's long-term objective is to increase sales overseas.' 'The course description began with a long list of aims and objectives.'

obligation   ✗ My obligations include doing the housework and picking up the children from school.
✓ **My duties include doing the housework and picking up the children from school.**
obligation = moral duty or responsibility: 'Having promised to cut taxes, the government now has an obligation to do so.' 'Anyone who rents a property is under an obligation to keep it clean and tidy.'
duty = what you have to do because it is a part of your job or because you think it is right: 'One of the principal's main duties is to improve the quality of teaching and learning in the school.'

oblige 1   ✗ You can't oblige children to study if they don't want to.
✓ **You can't force children to study if they don't want to.**
If someone makes you do something that you do not want to do, they **force/compel** you to do it (or **make** you do it): 'They forced him to hand over the money by threatening to kill him.'

2   ✗ In order to pay the hospital bill, it obliged me to sell my car.
✓ **In order to pay the hospital bill, I was obliged to sell my car.**
be/feel obliged to do sth (= have to/feel that you have to do something): 'Doctors are obliged to keep their patients' records secret.' 'Since the temperature outside was below freezing, I felt obliged to invite them in.'

obtain 1   ✗ It has taken women a long time to obtain equality.
✓ **It has taken women a long time to achieve equality.**
✗ With these new policies the government hopes to obtain economic stability.

✓ **With these new policies the government hopes to achieve economic stability.**

When you are talking about something that takes a long time and a great amount of work or effort, use **achieve** (NOT **obtain**): 'By the end of the course you really feel that you have achieved something.' 'The company intends to achieve all these goals within the next five years.' 'Her only purpose in life was to achieve stardom.'

2 ? Where did you obtain the ticket?
✓ **Where did you get the ticket?**
? He's been trying to obtain a part-time job.
✓ **He's been trying to get a part-time job.**

Obtain is mainly used in formal styles: 'Information about visas and passports can be obtained from your local library.'
The usual word for this meaning is **get**: 'How long does it take to get a visa?'

3 See DEGREE 4

occasion 1 ✗ The scholarship provided me with my first occasion to travel overseas.
✓ **The scholarship provided me with my first opportunity to travel overseas.**
✗ I never had occasion to take the Proficiency examination.
✓ **I never had a chance to take the Proficiency examination.**

occasion = the time when an event happens: 'I've been to Rome on several occasions.' (= several times)
opportunity = a time when it is possible to do something that you want to do: 'The meeting on Tuesday will be a good opportunity for you to make some new contacts.' 'She has considerable ability and should be given more opportunity to use it.'
chance = an informal word for 'opportunity': 'If I had the chance, I'd like to be an airline pilot.' 'I've been so busy this morning I haven't had a chance to sit down.' See also OPPORTUNITY

2 ✗ I remember that in the last occasion he had a very bad cold.
✓ **I remember that on the last occasion he had a very bad cold.**

on a particular **occasion** (NOT **in**): 'I am honoured that you have invited me to join you on this special occasion.'

occupation ✗ It used to be difficult for women to get good occupations.
✓ **It used to be difficult for women to get good jobs.**
✗ The important thing is to be happy in your occupation.
✓ **The important thing is to be happy in your job.**

See Language Note opposite

occur 1 ✗ The concert will occur at eight o'clock next Tuesday.
✓ **The concert will take place at eight o'clock next Tuesday.**

Occur is usually used in connection with unplanned events: 'Many of the serious accidents that occur are caused by human error.' 'Tornadoes occur when a warm weather front meets a body of very cold air.'
For planned events, use **take place**: 'The wedding will take place at St Andrew's church.'

JOB · DO · OCCUPATION · POST/POSITION · CAREER · TRADE · PROFESSION

job	Your **job** is what you do to earn your living: 'You'll never get a job if you don't have any qualifications.' 'She'd like to change her job but can't find anything better.' Your **job** is also the particular type of work that you do: 'John's new job sounds really interesting.' 'I know she works for the BBC but I'm not sure what job she does.' A **job** may be **full-time** or **part-time** (NOT **half-time** or **half-day**): 'All she could get was a part-time job at a petrol station.'
do (for a living)	When you want to know about the type of work that someone does, the usual questions are **What do you do? What does she do for a living? etc** 'What does your father do?' - 'He's a police inspector.'
occupation	**Occupation** and **job** have similar meanings. However, **occupation** is far less common than **job** and is used mainly in formal and official styles: 'Please give brief details of your employment history and present occupation.' 'People in manual occupations seem to suffer less from stress.'
post/position	The particular job that you have in a company or organization is your **post** or **position**: 'She's been appointed to the post of deputy principal.' 'He's applied for the position of sales manager.' **Post** and **position** are used mainly in formal styles and often refer to jobs which have a lot of responsibility.
career	Your **career** is your working life, or the series of jobs that you have during your working life: 'The scandal brought his career in politics to a sudden end.' 'Later on in his career, he became first secretary at the British Embassy in Washington.' Your **career** is also the particular kind of work for which you are trained and that you intend to do for a long time: 'I wanted to find out more about careers in publishing.'
trade	A **trade** is a type of work in which you do or make things with your hands: 'Most of the men had worked in skilled trades such as carpentry or printing.' 'My grandfather was a bricklayer by trade.'
profession	A **profession** is a type of work such as medicine, teaching, or law which requires a high level of training or education: 'Until recently, medicine has been a male-dominated profession.' 'She entered the teaching profession in 1987.'

2   ✗ You'd better tell them exactly what occurred.
      ✓ **You'd better tell them exactly what happened.**

> **Occur** is used mainly in formal styles: 'These violent incidents frequently occur without any warning.'
> The usual word is **happen**: 'The accident happened just outside my house.'

o'clock 1   ✗ It was twenty past four o'clock when the train arrived.
      ✓ **It was twenty past four when the train arrived.**

✗ They finished their dinner at about 7.30 o'clock.
✓ **They finished their dinner at about 7.30.**

Do not use **o'clock** for times that include minutes or parts of an hour. Compare: 'It's four o'clock.' 'It's ten past four.'

2

✗ By seven o'clock p.m. the child had been found.
✓ **By seven p.m. the child had been found.**
✓ **By seven o'clock (in the evening) the child had been found.**

Use EITHER **o'clock** OR **a.m./p.m.** (NOT both).

3

✗ I start work at 9.00 o'clock.
✓ **I start work at 9 o'clock.**

Do not use **o'clock** after **6.00, 7.00** etc. Compare: '8 a.m.', '8.00', '8.00 a.m.', '8 o'clock'.

of 1

✗ The demonstration was attended by several hundreds of people.
✓ **The demonstration was attended by several hundred people.**
✗ Over a thousand of people have died from the disease.
✓ **Over a thousand people have died from the disease.**

See Language Note at HUNDRED

2

✗ Arlon is one of the oldest towns of Belgium.
✓ **Arlon is one of the oldest towns in Belgium.**
✗ We stayed in one of the most beautiful villages of Kent.
✓ **We stayed in one of the most beautiful villages in Kent.**

To refer to the country/region/area etc where something is or takes place, use **in** (NOT **of**): 'the longest river in Brazil', 'the second largest city in Spain', 'one of the most picturesque spots in the whole of Tuscany'

3

✗ I arrived in London on 25th of November.
✓ **I arrived in London on 25th November.**

You say 'the 25th of November' or 'November the 25th' but you write '25th November' or 'November 25th' (WITHOUT **the** or **of**).

4

✗ The old man didn't give me a minute of peace.
✓ **The old man didn't give me a minute's peace.**

When you say how long something lasts, you usually use **-'s/-s'** (NOT **of**): 'a week's holiday', 'three months' maternity leave'
Note however the pattern with **of** + **v-ing**: 'After two months of doing nothing, I decided it was time to get on with my life.'

5

✗ The bicycle of Paul was too big for me.
✓ **Paul's bicycle was too big for me.**
✗ This coat isn't mine. It's of a friend.
✓ **This coat isn't mine. It's a friend's.**

To say that something belongs to or is connected with someone, use **-'s/-s'** (NOT **of**). Compare: 'Pam's husband', 'Julia's house', 'her father's car', 'a beginners' course in French conversation'

6

✗ He is a good friend of them.
✓ **He is a good friend of theirs.**

✗ A friend of you phoned and wants you to call her.
✓ **A friend of yours phoned and wants you to call her.**

When the meaning is possessive, use **of** + **mine/yours/his/ hers/ours/theirs**. Compare:
'That's a photograph of him.' (= showing him)
'That's a photograph of his.' (= belonging to or taken by him)

7 ✗ The scenery reminded her of a painting of Renoir.
✓ **The scenery reminded her of a painting by Renoir.**

To introduce the person who wrote/painted/composed something, use **by**: 'I'm reading a novel by Thomas Hardy.'
Compare: 'a painting of Renoir' (= a picture that someone painted of Renoir) 'a painting by Renoir' (= a picture that Renoir painted)

8 See OFF 2

of course See COURSE 3

off 1 ✗ Don't forget to off the lights before you go out.
✓ **Don't forget to turn off the lights before you go out.**

turn off/on (or **switch off/on**) a light, television, electric kettle etc: 'Let's turn on the radio and listen to the news.'

2 ✗ The glass fell off of the table.
✓ **The glass fell off the table.**

off + **sb/sth** (WITHOUT **of**): 'I wish he'd wipe that silly smile off his face.'

offence ✗ Public caning would deter other students from doing the offence.
✓ **Public caning would deter other students from committing the offence.**

commit an offence (NOT **do**): 'He is accused of committing various minor offences.'

offer 1 ✗ Her parents have offered me to go on holiday with them.
✓ **Her parents have invited me to go on holiday with them.**

offer to do sth = express willingness to do something: 'She's offered to help me.'
invite sb to (do) sth = ask someone if they would like to come to a party, wedding etc, or join you in a social activity: 'Have you invited Mark and Valerie to the party?'

2 ✗ The old man then offered something to eat to the little boy.
✓ **The old man then offered the little boy something to eat.**

The usual pattern is **offer sb sth** (**offer** + indirect object + direct object): 'He offered me a job.' 'They've offered Maria a place on the intermediate course.'
Use **offer** something **to** someone only when the direct object is a pronoun or is much shorter than the indirect object: 'She offered it to George but he didn't want it.' 'I offered the apple to the first child that could answer my question.'

officer 1 ✗ Most of my friends got jobs as shop assistants or officers.
✓ **Most of my friends got jobs as shop assistants or office workers.**

officer = a person with a position of rank or authority, especially someone in the armed forces, police force or government service: 'a club for army officers and their families', 'local government officers', 'a customs officer'
office worker = a person who works in an office: 'Between five and six the trains are packed with office workers.'

2 ✗ A British Airways officer told us that there was a delay.
✓ **A British Airways official told us that there was a delay.**
official = a person with a position of authority in an organization: 'WHO officials are monitoring the spread of the disease.'

official ✗ She is good at organizing people without seeming arrogant or official.
✓ **She is good at organizing people without seeming arrogant or officious.**
official = done by or connected with a person or group in authority; formal: 'an official letter', 'an official inquiry', 'official approval'
officious (expressing dislike or disapproval) = too eager to give orders or make people keep to rules which are unimportant: 'An officious little man at the check-in insisted that my luggage was half a kilo overweight.'

often ✗ Often people stop smoking when they are ill.
✓ **People often stop smoking when they are ill.**
✗ He often has said that he would like to be young again.
✓ **He has often said that he would like to be young again.**
✗ The trains often are late.
✓ **The trains are often late.**
See Language Note at ALWAYS

oily ? The chips were so oily that I couldn't eat them.
✓ **The chips were so greasy that I couldn't eat them.**
The usual word for describing food that is unpleasant because it is cooked and presented with too much fat or oil is greasy: 'I ate the tomato and left all the greasy chips.'

old 1 ✗ He is married to a twenty years old American girl.
✓ **He is married to a twenty-year-old American girl.**
✗ Eight-years-old Sarah had a few surprises up her sleeve.
✓ **Eight-year-old Sarah had a few surprises up her sleeve.**
Use years old after the verb be: 'Sarah is eight years old.'
In front of a noun, use a compound adjective (WITH two hyphens and a singular noun): 'a three-week-old baby', 'a ten-year-old daughter'
Nouns of measurement ('year', 'week', 'gram', 'mile' etc) are always singular when used in compound adjectives: 'a ten-second silence', 'a six-minute wait', 'a five-mile race'.

2 ✗ He fell in love with a young girl of nineteen years old.
✓ **He fell in love with a young girl of nineteen.**
noun + of + number: 'a child of five', 'a man of sixty'
Compare: 'The girl was nineteen years old.'

3 ✗ The old should not be brushed aside by society.
✓ **The elderly should not be brushed aside by society.**

To refer to old people in general, use **the elderly**: 'The building has been converted into a retirement home for the elderly.'

on 1

✗ On last Monday we went to the Railway Museum.
✓ **Last Monday we went to the Railway Museum.**
✗ On every Saturday morning we go shopping.
✓ **Every Saturday morning we go shopping.**
See Language Note at TIME

2

✗ I was surprised to see your picture on the newspaper.
✓ **I was surprised to see your picture in the newspaper.**

You see a report, advertisement, photograph, etc **in** a newspaper or magazine (NOT **on**): 'I came across the article in this month's edition of Woman's World.'

once 1

✗ You may remember we had once a long talk in the hotel bar.
✓ **You may remember we once had a long talk in the hotel bar.**
See Language Note at ALWAYS

2

✗ Once it will stop raining, we can go out.
✓ **Once it stops raining, we can go out.**
✓ **Once it has stopped raining, we can go out.**
See Language Note at WILL

one 1

✗ Fluency in English is one of the best qualifications you can have.
✓ **Fluency in English is one of the best qualifications you can have.**

Do not use **the** in front of **one of**: 'We stayed at one of the cheaper hotels.' 'She is one of the strongest political leaders in the world today.'

2

✗ The sea is one of our main source of food.
✓ **The sea is one of our main sources of food.**

The noun/pronoun following **one of** is always plural: 'one of my friends', 'one of her teachers', 'one of the biggest islands in the world'.

3

✗ One of the eggs were bad.
✓ **One of the eggs was bad.**
? She is one of those children who refuses to share things.
✓ **She is one of those children who refuse to share things.**

After a phrase beginning with **one of**, the verb is singular: 'One of the main disadvantages is the cost of the battery.'
However when **one of** is followed by a relative clause, the verb in the relative clause is usually plural: 'He's one of those people who are always complaining.'
In informal styles, some people use a singular verb, but careful users regard this as incorrect.

4

✗ After we had been to Helen's house, we went to Paul's one.
✓ **After we had been to Helen's house, we went to Paul's.**

Avoid **one/ones** immediately after an **-'s/-s** form, especially in formal styles: 'No, it's not mine - it's my wife's.'
Compare: 'John's new one is the same as yours.' (= **-'s/-s** form + adjective + noun)

5   ✗   If you can carry those books, I'll bring these ones.
        ✓   **If you can carry those books, I'll bring these.**
        ✗   This book will be of interest to all those ones involved in the tourist industry.
        ✓   **This book will be of interest to all those involved in the tourist industry.**

> Avoid **ones** immediately after **these/those**, especially in formal styles: 'Within this group, there are those who are willing to take risks and those who are more cautious.'
> Compare: 'These plastic ones are cheaper.' (= **these/those** + adjective + noun)

6   ✗   All the shoes and handbags they sell are handmade ones.
        ✓   **All the shoes and handbags they sell are handmade.**

> Avoid **one/ones** after an adjective which can be used on its own, especially in formal styles: 'The new proposals are impractical.'
> Compare: 'We could do with a new one/some new ones.'

7   ✗   British children have more opportunities than Tunisian ones.
        ✓   **British children have more opportunities than Tunisian children.**
        ✗   Young people learn more quickly than older ones.
        ✓   **Young people learn more quickly than older people.**

> **Ones** is usually used to refer to things: 'Rechargeable batteries are more expensive than ordinary ones.' 'The red ones are fine, but I prefer the white ones.' **Ones** may also be used to refer to particular people: 'The older children laughed but the younger ones were scared.'
> In general statements about groups of people, **ones** is usually avoided: 'French students have to work harder than British students.'

8   ✗   One mustn't waste ones time when there is so much to do.
        ✓   **One mustn't waste one's time when there is so much to do.**
        ✗   Getting married for economic reasons is not a good start to ones married life.
        ✓   **Getting married for economic reasons is not a good start to one's married life.**

> The possessive form is **one's** (WITH **'s**): 'It is difficult to estimate one's chances of success.' See also IT'S

9   ✗   One cannot succeed unless he works hard.
        ✓   **One cannot succeed unless one works hard.**

> In British English (unlike American English) it is not possible to change from **one** to **he/his/her** etc.
> Note, however, that most speakers find the repetition of **one** awkward and try to avoid it: 'One cannot succeed without working hard.' 'Success calls for a lot of hard work.' See also Language Note at HE

10   See EVERYONE 1

one another   ✗   The children get on well one another.
        ✓   **The children get on well with one another.**
        ✗   They had good opinions one another.
        ✓   **They had good opinions of one another.**

You use prepositions in front of **one another** (pronoun) in the same way as you use prepositions in front of **him, her, us,** etc. Compare: 'I often write to her.' 'We often write to one another.' See also EACH OTHER

only 1

✗ The level of pollution can only be reduced by the introduction of new laws.
✓ **The level of pollution can be reduced only by the introduction of new laws.**

To avoid confusion in written English, **only** is usually placed as near as possible to the word or phrase that it modifies. Compare: 'Alison only posted the letter to Mr Jones.' (= she didn't write it) 'Alison posted only the letter to Mr Jones.' (= she didn't post the other letters)
In spoken English the position of **only** is less important because the speaker uses stress to make the meaning clear.

2

✗ If you only would stay longer, your English would improve.
✓ **If only you would stay longer, your English would improve.**
✓ **If you would only stay longer, your English would improve.**

When **if only** is used to express a wish, the two words usually stay together: 'If only I could stop smoking.' Sometimes, **only** is placed in front of the main verb 'If I could only stop smoking.'

3

✗ Only when it started to rain he noticed that he had left his raincoat somewhere.
✓ **Only when it started to rain did he notice that he had left his raincoat somewhere.**

See Language Note at NOT

4

See NOT ONLY

open 1

✗ I got out of bed and opened the radio to listen to the news.
✓ **I got out of bed and turned/switched on the radio to listen to the news.**

turn on/off (or **switch on/off**) a light/radio/television (NOT **open/close**): 'The children are not allowed to turn on the television without permission.'

2

✗ If anyone tried to open a new topic, she would immediately interrupt.
✓ **If anyone tried to introduce a new topic, she would immediately interrupt.**

introduce a (new) topic/subject/argument (NOT **open**): 'You can't introduce new material in the last section of a report.'

opened

✗ I couldn't buy a newspaper because the shop wasn't opened.
✓ **I couldn't buy a newspaper because the shop wasn't open.**

Use **opened** to describe an action and **open** to describe a state. Compare: 'The shop was opened at 8 a.m. and stayed open until 6 p.m.'

operate

✗ Have you heard what happened to the last patient he operated?
✓ **Have you heard what happened to the last patient he operated on?**

	✗	My niece was recently operated for appendicitis.
	✓	**My niece was recently operated on for appendicitis.**

operate on sb: 'He is too weak at the moment to be operated on.'

operation
✗ My mother is taking an operation tomorrow.
✓ **My mother is having an operation tomorrow.**
✗ Mr Barrett is going to get an operation on his back.
✓ **Mr Barrett is going to have an operation on his back.**
See Language Note at DO

opinion 1
✗ According to Henry's opinion, less money should be spent on weapons.
✓ **In Henry's opinion, less money should be spent on weapons.**
✓ **According to Henry, less money should be spent on weapons.**

according to sb: 'According to Peter, deforestation is a very serious problem.'
in sb's opinion (NOT **according to ... opinion**): 'In Peter's opinion, deforestation is a very serious problem.'

2
✗ They are not afraid of saying their opinions.
✓ **They are not afraid of expressing their opinions.**

express/give your opinion (NOT **say**): 'The newspapers express a wide range of political opinions.'

opportunity
✗ There is an opportunity that David's father will come tonight.
✓ **There is a chance that David's father will come tonight.**

When you talk about the likelihood of something happening, use **chance** (NOT **opportunity**): 'I think she has a good chance of passing.' 'There's very little chance that anyone has survived the crash.'
Compare: 'Tomorrow's test will be an opportunity/a chance for you to find out how much you know.' (= a particular time when something is possible)

oppose
✗ I oppose to violence.
✓ **I am opposed to violence.**

oppose sth (WITHOUT **to**) = think that something is wrong and try to stop it from happening or being accepted: 'Many leading scientists vigorously opposed Darwin's ideas.'
be opposed to sth = feel strongly that something is wrong: 'Many people are opposed to the use of fur by the clothing industry.'

opposite 1
✗ People have opposite opinions about this matter.
✓ **People have different opinions about this matter.**
✗ The Americans I met were opposite to what I had imagined.
✓ **The Americans I met were very different from what I had imagined.**
✗ My own country and the USA are totally opposite of each other.
✓ **My own country and the USA are totally different (from each other).**

Use **opposite** and **the opposite of** only when you mean that two things are as different as it is possible to be: 'I thought that the medicine would make him sleepy, but it had the opposite effect.' 'The opposite of *long* is

short.' 'The two men went off in opposite directions.' (= one went to the left and one to the right)
To describe people's opinions, life styles, ways of thinking etc, the usual word is **different**: 'These two schools of thought are completely different.'

2   ✗   On the wall opposite to the door, there was a large painting.
  ✓   **On the wall opposite the door, there was a large painting.**
  ✗   The phone booths are opposite of the tube station.
  ✓   **The phone booths are opposite the tube station.**

One thing is **opposite** another thing (WITHOUT **to/of**): 'The nearest bus stop is opposite the bank.'

3   ✗   The opposite woman was knitting a cardigan.
  ✓   **The woman opposite was knitting a cardigan.**

When **opposite** means 'facing the speaker or the person/place being talked about', it comes immediately after the noun: 'The house opposite is also for sale.'

or 1   ✗   At night we used to go out with our friends or stayed at home listening to music.
  ✓   **At night we used to go out with our friends or stay at home listening to music.**

When you use **or** to join two verbs, both verbs should have the same form. Compare: 'We used to go to the cinema or watch the television.' 'We went to the cinema or watched the television.'

2   ✗   I think the microphone or the recording mechanism are broken.
  ✓   **I think the microphone or the recording mechanism is broken.**

When each of the nouns joined by **or** is singular, the verb is usually singular: 'It is important to understand what one's son or daughter expects out of life.'

3   See NEITHER 1

oral   ✗   Her oral English is very fluent and clear.
  ✓   **Her spoken English is very fluent and clear.**

The use of **oral** to mean 'spoken' is restricted to certain technical phrases used in education: 'oral skills', 'an oral examination'.

order 1   ✗   I was so excited that I forgot to order them to check that the camera was working properly.
  ✓   **I was so excited that I forgot to ask them to check that the camera was working properly.**

You cannot **order** someone to do something unless you have the power to do so. Compare: 'The teacher ordered the child to sit down.' 'She asked her teacher if he could check her homework.'

2   ✗   I've ordered two seats for tomorrow night's performance.
  ✓   **I've booked two seats for tomorrow night's performance.**
  See note at BOOK

3 ? Turning on the radio, I noticed immediately that it was out of order.

✓ **Turning on the radio, I noticed immediately that it was not working properly.**

The phrase **out of order** is used mainly on notices stating that things such as public telephones, ticket machines, photocopiers etc are not working.

original 1 ✗ Archaeological treasures should be kept in the original country.

✓ **Archaeological treasures should be kept in the country of origin.**

country of origin = the country where something was made or discovered: 'They refuse to release these antiquities until the country of origin is properly established.'

2 ✗ Many craftsmen have given up their original skills to work in factories.

✓ **Many craftsmen have given up their traditional skills to work in factories.**

✗ She was wearing an original Japanese 'yukata'.

✓ **She was wearing a traditional Japanese 'yukata'.**

original = (1) completely new: 'Nobody expected that the bikini, with its daringly original design, would catch on as it did.'
(2) the one that exists first (usually followed later by other ones): 'The original edition contained only 170 pages.' 'The tennis court to the side of the house was the idea of the original owner.'
traditional = done or used by a group or society for a very long time: 'The dancers were wearing traditional African dress.' 'Kumar gave the traditional Hindu greeting.'

originate 1 ✗ One of our teachers originates from Scotland.

✓ **One of our teachers comes from Scotland.**

Originate is used in connection with things, ideas, customs etc (NOT people): 'No one really knows how the solar system originated.'
If you are born in and/or grow up in a particular place, town, country etc, you **come from** that place: 'Where does Agneta come from - Sweden or Norway?'

2 ✗ 'Alcohol', 'alcove' and 'sofa' originate in Arabic.

✓ **'Alcohol', 'alcove' and 'sofa' come from Arabic.**

Words that enter a language from other languages **come from** (or **are derived from**) those languages: 'The name 'terrier' comes from the Latin word 'terra' meaning 'the earth'.'

other 1 ✗ 'Go and play with some others children,' she said.

✓ **'Go and play with some other children,' she said.**

When used before a noun, **other** never has an **s**: 'Do you have any other shoes besides the brown ones?'
Compare: 'Besides the brown shoes, do you have any others?'

2 ✗ It tells us all about nouns, verbs, adjectives and others.

✓ **It tells us all about such things as nouns, verbs and adjectives.**

Do not use **and others** at the end of a list of examples. In some styles it is possible to use **etc** for this purpose, but in formal styles it is safer to use **such as** (or **such ... as**): 'Candidates' performance in the test was influenced by factors such as age, sex, attitude and first language.'

otherwise ✗ Remember to get there early otherwise you may not get a seat.
    ✓ **Remember to get there early. Otherwise you may not get a seat.**
    ✓ **Remember to get there early or you may not get a seat.**

Unlike **or, otherwise** is an adverb (NOT a conjunction): 'I'm glad that you told me about the show being cancelled. Otherwise I'd have travelled all the way to Glasgow for nothing.'

out ✗ When we came out the restaurant, it was half past eleven.
    ✓ **When we came out of the restaurant, it was half past eleven.**
    ✗ She suddenly stood up and ran out from the room.
    ✓ **She suddenly stood up and ran out of the room.**

verb of movement + **out**: 'I'm afraid Mr Baker has just gone out.'
verb of movement + **out of** + somewhere (NOT **out** or **out from**): 'I've just seen Mr Baker going out of the building.'
In informal styles, **out** is sometimes used instead of **out of**: 'I saw someone jump out the window.' However, careful users consider this to be incorrect.

out of date ✗ Doctors read these journals so as not to become out of date.
    ✓ **Doctors read these journals so as to keep up to date.**

Out of date (before a noun **out-of-date**) is used in connection with information, ideas, knowledge, technology etc (NOT people): 'A significant proportion of what children are studying at school will be out of date within the space of a few years.'
If you always have the latest information about something, you **keep up to date** (**with** developments) or **keep abreast** (**of** developments): 'Lecturers are expected to keep abreast of developments in their subject areas.'

outdoor ✗ She makes the dog stay outdoor during the summer.
    ✓ **She makes the dog stay outdoors during the summer.**

Outdoor (WITHOUT **s**) is an adjective: 'He enjoys the outdoor life.'
Outdoors (WITH **s**) is an adverb: 'He likes to work outdoors.'

outdoors ✗ There are lots of outdoors activities in and around Coimbra.
    ✓ **There are lots of outdoor activities in and around Coimbra.**

See note at OUTDOOR

outside 1 ✗ The new airport makes it easy to go outside the country.
    ✓ **The new airport makes it easy to get out of the country.**
    ✗ I'll be going outside London for a few days.
    ✓ **I'll be going out of London for a few days.**

When you mean 'away from', use **(get/go) out of** (NOT **outside**): 'It does you good to get out of the city now and again.' 'Without a false passport, he would never have been able to get out of the country.'

2

✗ She was listening outside of the door.
✓ **She was listening outside the door.**

In British English, **outside** is not used with **of**: 'You aren't allowed to park outside the bank.'
In American English, both **outside** and **outside of** are used.

3

See HOME 4, 5

overall 1

✗ His idea of a good time included the sun, the sea, jokes, laughter, and overall friendship.
✓ **His idea of a good time included the sun, the sea, jokes, laughter, and above all friendship.**

overall = (adv) (1) including everything: 'How much will the holiday cost, overall?' (2) generally: 'Overall, the weather in this area is good.'
overall = (adj) including everything: 'We're concerned about the overall effect of these films on younger viewers.'
above all = most importantly: 'Get plenty of sleep, eats lots of good food, and above all try to relax.' 'The sort of person we are looking for must be well qualified, suitably experienced, easy to get on with, and above all able to work independently.'

2

✗ In spite of the film's many faults, in the overall it's worth seeing.
✓ **In spite of the film's many faults, on the whole it's worth seeing.**
✗ England is okay on the overall, although some places are very dirty.
✓ **England is okay on the whole, although some places are very dirty.**

on the whole = in general: 'On the whole, the people I've been dealing with have been very cooperative.'
Compare: 'Her overall command of English is excellent.' 'On the whole her command of English is excellent.'

3

✗ The important thing is your score in overall.
✓ **The important thing is your overall score.**

Overall may be used as an adjective or adverb (NOT as a noun after **in/on**): 'The examination counts for 60 per cent of your overall grade.' 'You would have done better overall if you hadn't spent so long on the essay question.'

overdue

✗ I suddenly realized that my driving licence was overdue.
✓ **I suddenly realized that my driving licence had expired.**

Be/become overdue is used of payments, library books, video films that you have rented etc: 'Even if the books are only one day overdue, you still have to pay a fine.'
Expire is used of a licence, contract, membership card, etc: 'I wanted to pay by Visa but my card had expired.'

overnight

✗ I recently stayed an overnight at your hotel.
✓ **I recently stayed overnight at your hotel.**
✗ I am writing to complain about my overnight at your hotel.
✓ **I am writing to complain about the night I spent at your hotel.**

Overnight is used as an adverb and adjective (NOT as a noun):
'I missed the connecting flight and had to stay at the airport overnight.' 'If we travel overnight, we'll be there in time for breakfast.' 'The overnight coach arrives in London at six in the morning.'

owing to

✗ They come here looking for work owing to the wages are higher.
✓ **They come here looking for work because the wages are higher.**

Owing to is a preposition (NOT a conjunction): 'Owing to various political and economic factors, the land reclamation project has been discontinued.'

own 1

✗ I had the whole beach for my own.
✓ **I had the whole beach to myself.**

Own (= belonging to you, or only to be used by you) is used either in front of a noun, or in the phrase **of your own**: 'I wish I had my own car.' 'I wish I had a car of my own.'
have sb/sth (all) to yourself = be the only person or people in a place, using something, talking to someone, etc: 'After the children had gone, we had the house all to ourselves.'

2

✗ He's decided to resign and work for his own.
✓ **He's decided to resign and work for himself.**
✗ They want everything for their own.
✓ **They want everything for themselves.**

do/want sth for yourself (NOT **for your own**): 'He's kept all the money for himself.'
Compare: 'He prefers to work on his own.' (= without anyone's help; alone).

3

✗ I didn't have a room for my own but had to share one.
✓ **I didn't have a room of my own but had to share one.**

of your own (NOT **for**): 'Timothy has now decided that he wants a bicycle of his own.'

4

✗ I now have enough money to buy an own car.
✓ **I now have enough money to buy my own car.**

Own always follows **my/her/their/Jill's** etc (NOT **an**) 'their own children', 'her own flat', 'Tina's own radio'.

P*p*

pace

✗ I want to learn English in my own pace.
✓ **I want to learn English at my own pace.**

You do something **at your own pace** (NOT **in/by etc**): 'With computer assisted language learning, students can work at their own pace.'

package 1

✗ I bought six eggs and a package of tea.
✓ **I bought six eggs and a packet of tea.**
✗ He smokes about one package a day.
✓ **He smokes about one packet a day.**
See Language Note below

2 ✗ There are so many unnecessary packages nowadays.
✓ **There is so much unnecessary packaging nowadays.**
See Language Note below

3

✗ I enclose a stamped addressed envelope and a cheque for £5 for postage and package.
✓ **I enclose a stamped addressed envelope and a cheque for £5 for postage and packing.**
See Language Note below

PACKET • PACKAGE • PACKAGING • PACKING • PACK	
package	a small parcel, usually sent by post: 'Sending both packages by airmail could work out very expensive.'
packet	a box, bag, container etc with a number of things or an amount of something inside, especially one that is sold in shops: 'a packet of cigarettes/biscuits/envelopes/balloons'. Another word for **packet** is **pack**, especially in American English: 'a pack of cigarettes'.
packaging	material that is put round things that are sold in shops, especially to encourage people to buy them: 'I wonder how much it would cost without all the fancy packaging.'
packing	material that is put round things to protect them, especially from getting damaged in the post: 'Please remember to add an extra £2.00 per order for postage and packing.' 'I think you should keep all the packing in case you ever want to ship the organ back to the UK one day.'

painful

   ✗ The operation was successful but I still feel very painful.
   ✓ **The operation was successful but I still feel a lot of pain.**

> **painful** = causing pain: 'The finger I trapped in the door is still very painful.' 'The child wriggled free and gave me a painful kick on the ankle.'

pair 1

   ✗ The old pair next door have been married for 65 years.
   ✓ **The old couple next door have been married for 65 years.**

> **Pair** usually refers to things (e.g. 'a pair of scissors/socks') or to two people who are seen (doing something) together: 'It's about time the pair of you did some work.' 'The German pair need just two more points for the match.' **Pair** also refers to two animals that stay together and produce young: 'a pair of swifts with a family to feed'.
> The usual word for a husband and wife (or two people in a similar relationship) is **couple**: 'Married couples should benefit from the new tax legislation.'

2

   ✗ Have you always worn a pair of glasses?
   ✓ **Have you always worn glasses?**

> **Pair of** is usually used for individual reference (NOT general reference): 'I've bought two pairs of shoes for the children.'
> Compare: 'They sell shoes and handbags .' (NOT 'pairs of shoes')

paper

   ✗ Each of us was given a clean paper to write on.
   ✓ **Each of us was given a clean sheet of paper to write on.**

> When it refers to the material that you write on, **paper** is an uncountable noun: 'The printer has run out of paper.' 'On the back of the piece of paper she had written her address.'

pardon 1

   ✗ I asked the teacher if I could be pardoned for a few minutes.
   ✓ **I asked the teacher if I could be excused for a few minutes.**

> **pardon** = (formal) forgive: 'I'm sure they will pardon the occasional mistake.'
> **excuse** = give someone permission to stay away from school, work etc, or leave a classroom, meeting etc: 'Can I be excused from swimming today please? I've got a cold.'

2

   ✗ I beg your pardon, but I was very busy and couldn't spare the time.
   ✓ **I'm sorry, but I was very busy and couldn't spare the time.**
   ✗ I'd like to beg your pardon because I was late.
   ✓ **I'm sorry I was late.**
   ✓ **Please forgive me for being late.**

> **I beg your pardon** is used (1) to apologize to a stranger because you have bumped into them by accident, sat in their seat by mistake, etc: 'I beg your pardon. I didn't know the table was reserved.'
> (2) to politely ask someone to repeat what they have said: 'Does this bus go to Marble Arch?' 'I beg your pardon?' 'This bus, does it go to Marble Arch?'
> (3) when someone has said something that makes you feel surprised, shocked, angry etc: 'Who's that man with the long nose?' 'I beg your pardon! That happens to be my husband.'
> Note that in formal situations you can use **excuse/forgive me** instead of **I'm sorry**: 'Please excuse me for taking so long to answer your letter.'

parking 1 ✗ The car was parking outside the flat all night.
          ✓ **The car was parked outside the flat all night.**

> Use **park** when you are talking about what a driver does: 'You're not allowed to park (your car) in the city centre.' 'Where've you parked (your car)?'
> To talk about a vehicle that has been left somewhere and is not moving, use **parked**: 'That Ford van has been parked there for over a week.' 'The street is always full of parked cars.'

      2 ✗ It took me an hour to find a parking.
          ✓ **It took me an hour to find a parking space.**
          ✗ What the town needs is an underground parking.
          ✓ **What the town needs is underground parking.**
          ✓ **What the town needs is an underground car park.**

> **a parking space/place** = a place in a street, car park etc where a vehicle can be left: 'My first attempt to back into the parking space was a disaster.'
> **a car park** (AmE **parking lot**) = a large open area or building where cars can be left: 'The supermarket has its own car park.'
> **parking** (uncountable noun) = space(s) where vehicles can be left: 'Parking is available at Whitefriars Street.' 'There's ample parking in front of the hotel.'

part 1 ✗ A part of the difficulty was caused by her poor English.
          ✓ **Part of the difficulty was caused by her poor English.**

> It is unusual to use **a** before **part of** unless **part of** has an adjective in front of it. Compare: 'Lack of money was part of the problem.' 'Lack of money was a large part of the problem.'

      2 ✗ The country is vast and occupies the most part of the continent.
          ✓ **The country is vast and occupies most of the continent.**
          ✗ For the most part of his life he was devoted to his work.
          ✓ **For most of his life he was devoted to his work.**

> **most of** (NOT **most part of**): 'She spent most of the morning in bed.'
> Note however the fixed phrase **for the most part** (= almost completely; mainly): 'The machines have for the most part been replaced.'

      3 ✗ He refuses to part from his old camera.
          ✓ **He refuses to part with his old camera.**

> **part from** a person: 'The two sisters were parted from each other when they were sent to different schools.'
> **part with** a thing: 'Getting them to part with the money won't be easy.'

      4 ✗ The annual celebration takes part in Valencia on 19th March.
          ✓ **The annual celebration takes place in Valencia on 19th March.**
          ✗ The election will take part within the next two years.
          ✓ **The election will take place within the next two years.**

> When you **take part in** an activity, you do it together with other people: 'Altogether there are seventy-three competitors taking part in the race.' 'She's been invited to take part in a TV quiz programme.'
> **take place** = (of a planned event) happen: 'The next meeting of the Nature Society will take place on Tuesday 3rd March.'

5 x Did you take part in Yolanda's party on Saturday?
  ✓ **Did you go to Yolanda's party on Saturday?**
    go to a party/wedding etc (NOT **take part in**): 'We can't go to the party if we haven't been invited.'

6 x I think you ought to take part in a club.
  ✓ **I think you ought to join a club.**
    join a club/society etc (NOT **take part in**): 'Guy is thinking about joining the drama society.'

participate ✗ Teams from all Asian countries will participate the event.
  ✓ **Teams from all Asian countries will participate in the event.**
    participate in sth = (formal) take part in: 'Our students are encouraged to participate in extra-curricular activities.'

partly ✗ Putting fluoride in the water may solve the problem partly.
  ✓ **Putting fluoride in the water may solve the problem to some extent.**
  ✓ **Putting fluoride in the water may partly solve the problem.**
    At the end of a clause use **to some extent/to a certain extent** or **to some degree/to a (certain) degree** (NOT **partly**). Compare: 'I partly agree with him.' 'I agree with him to some extent.'

party 1 ✗ On Christmas Day we always make a big party.
  ✓ **On Christmas Day we always have a big party.**
  ✗ Next Saturday we're celebrating a small party at John's house.
  ✓ **Next Saturday we're having a small party at John's house.**
  ✗ The party was being made at a friend's house.
  ✓ **The party was being held at a friend's house.**
    have/hold/throw a party (NOT **make/celebrate**): 'Let's have a party and invite all our friends.'
    celebrate Christmas, the New Year, someone's birthday, retirement, promotion etc: 'Next month we're having a party to celebrate our sixth wedding anniversary.'
    A party **is held** somewhere (NOT **made/celebrated**): 'Where is the garden party being held?' See Language Note at DO

2 See TAKE PART 5

pass 1 ✗ We like to pass our holidays near the sea.
  ✓ **We like to spend our holidays near the sea.**
  ✗ We passed the night in a cheap hotel.
  ✓ **We spent the night in a cheap hotel.**
  ✗ I passed Christmas in London.
  ✓ **I spent Christmas in London.**
    You **spend** your holidays/a period of time somewhere (NOT **pass**): 'We spent a lazy afternoon down by the river.'
    When **pass** is used in connection with time, it is usually intransitive: 'Two weeks passed and there was still no reply.'

2 ✗ It has passed almost a year since we first met each other.
  ✓ **It's almost a year since we first met each other.**
  ✓ **We first met each other almost a year ago.**
  ? Almost a year has passed since we first met each other.

In sentences about the passage of time, the subject of **pass** is always a time phrase: 'Another five minutes passed and the taxi still didn't appear.' Note however that this pattern is used mainly in narrative styles.

3   See EXAM/EXAMINATION 2

pass up   ✗ The essays have to be passed up by next Monday.
✓ **The essays have to be handed in by next Monday.**

When you give a piece of written work to a teacher, lecturer, etc, you **hand** it **in**: 'All assignments have to be handed in by Monday 3rd October.'

past 1   ✗ I was 8 years old when my father past away.
✓ **I was 8 years old when my father passed away.**
✗ Several taxis past me without stopping.
✓ **Several taxis passed me without stopping.**

The past tense and past participle of the verb pass is passed (NOT past): 'She's passed all her exams.' 'I passed him in the corridor but he didn't say anything.' 'These remedies have been passed down from one generation to the next.'
Past is (1) an adjective: 'For the past week he's been ill in bed.'
(2) a preposition: 'She walked past me very quickly.'
(3) an adverb: 'She walked past very quickly.'
(4) a noun: 'He never speaks about his past.'
Past is NOT used as a verb.

2   ✗ It was a little past five when the game finished.
✓ **It was just after five when the game finished.**

Use **past** when you mention exact times: 'eight minutes past three', 'a quarter past two', 'twenty-five past seven'. Otherwise use **just after, shortly after, etc**: 'Her flight arrived shortly after midnight.'

pattern   ✗ Their daily pattern doesn't include enough exercise.
✓ **Their daily routine doesn't include enough exercise.**

To refer to the things that you do every day, usually in the same order, use **routine**: 'The trip to Oslo was quite exhausting, but at least it provided an escape from the same old routine.'

pay 1   ✗ 'Who paid the tickets?' I asked.
✓ **'Who paid for the tickets?' I asked.**

pay (an amount of money) **for sth**: 'Let me pay for the meal this time.' 'I can't afford to pay $200 for a suit.' 'How much did she pay for the car?'

2   ✗ Very few office workers get a good pay.
✓ **Very few office workers get good pay.**

Pay is an uncountable noun: 'They've given him a week's leave without pay.'

pay back   ✗ The manager offered to pay me back the cost of the camera.
✓ **The manager offered to refund the cost of the camera.**
✓ **The manager offered me a refund of the cost of the camera.**

pay back money that was borrowed: 'He's promised to pay me back when he gets his next salary.'
refund money that was paid for something: 'If it doesn't work, bring it

back and we'll refund your money.' 'She assured me that my $500 deposit would be refunded.'
a refund (of sth): 'You'll receive a refund of up to £50 if the concert is cancelled.' 'Season ticket holders are entitled to a full refund.'

payment 1 ✗ Dr Schneider charges a high payment but he is very good.
  ✓ **Dr Schneider charges a high fee but he is very good.**

  payment = an amount of money that is paid for something: 'I had to get rid of the car because I couldn't keep up the payments.'
  fee = an amount of money paid to a doctor, lawyer, or other professional person: 'The fee for one hour's private tuition is $60.'

2 ✗ For the first month the payment by the hour is 650 yen.
  ✓ **For the first month the hourly rate is 650 yen.**

  hourly/daily/weekly rate = the amount that someone charges or is paid for each hour/day/week that they work: 'He charges an hourly rate of $600 plus expenses.'

3 See CHEAP 1

peculiar ✗ She said she liked the jumper because the colour was very peculiar.
  ✓ **She said she liked the jumper because the colour was very unusual.**

  peculiar = strange, especially in a surprising or unpleasant way: 'I'm not sure about this cheese. The taste is a bit peculiar.' 'Just because I don't like computers, everyone thinks I'm a bit peculiar.'
  unusual = uncommon or rare: 'Where did you buy this cheese? The taste is very unusual.' 'At one time it was unusual for women to enter politics.'

people 1 ✗ After a hard day, all people need to relax.
  ✓ **After a hard day, everyone needs to relax.**
  ✗ In Avanos every people smile at you.
  ✓ **In Avanos everyone smiles at you.**

  everybody/everyone (NOT **all/every people**): 'Everyone needs someone to love.' See also PERSON 1

2 ✗ Peoples come from all over the world to visit the city.
  ✓ **People come from all over the world to visit the city.**

  a people (countable) = a race: 'His dream is that the peoples of the world will one day unite.'
  people (plural noun) = men, women and children: 'He finds it difficult to get along with people.'

3 ✗ There was few people at the funeral.
  ✓ **There were few people at the funeral.**
  ✗ I think people who does these things should be punished.
  ✓ **I think people who do these things should be punished.**

  People is a plural noun and takes a plural verb: 'People have been very kind to me.'

percentage ✗ Only a small percentage of the windmills still works.
✓ **Only a small percentage of the windmills still work.**

If the noun after **percentage of** is plural, the verb is plural: 'A high percentage of these school leavers have no qualifications.'

perfect ✗ I am pleased to say that the tape recorder now works perfect.
✓ **I am pleased to say that the tape recorder now works perfectly.**

Perfect is an adjective: 'My grandmother enjoys perfect health.'
Perfectly is an adverb: 'The baby is perfectly healthy.'

perform ✗ In his last film he performed a middle-aged school teacher.
✓ **In his last film he played a middle-aged school teacher.**

play a particular part or role in a film, play etc (NOT **perform**): 'What's the name of that good-looking American actor who played Butch Cassidy?'
Compare: 'She has never performed in front of a live audience before.' 'Tonight's concert will be performed by the Boston Symphony Orchestra.'

perhaps ? Perhaps I will even decide to get married after all.
✓ **I may even decide to get married after all.**
? Perhaps it will be a good chance for you to have a rest.
✓ **It may be a good chance for you to have a rest.**

May/might usually sounds more natural than **perhaps ... will**: 'My mother may need to have an operation.' 'You might feel that the course is too difficult.'

period ✗ These traditions took a long period of time to evolve.
✓ **These traditions took a long time to evolve.**
✗ She needs somewhere to live for a period of time.
✓ **She needs somewhere to live for a while.**

a (long/short) time/while (WITHOUT **period**): 'You can stay here for a while, if you like.' 'Learning a foreign language can take a very long time.'

permis- ✗ To get a job in Switzerland, foreigners need a special
sion 1 permission.
✓ **To get a job in Switzerland, foreigners need special permission.**

Permission is an uncountable noun: 'If you want to put up a tent, you'll have to get the farmer's permission.' 'Nobody is allowed to leave early without permission.'

2 ✗ Eventually he gave me the permission to stay at home.
✓ **Eventually he gave me (his) permission to stay at home.**

(their/his mother's/the headmaster's) permission but NOT **the permission**: 'I'm sure that they'll let you use the library but it's better to have official permission.'

permit ✗ Overpopulation doesn't permit these countries to develop.
✓ **Overpopulation stops/prevents these countries from developing.**

Permit is used in situations where there is a rule, law or authority that controls what people can do: 'The law permits foreign investors to own up to 25% of British companies.' 'As children we were never permitted to leave the table until everyone had finished.'

person 1   ✗   Very soon every person will have a portable computer.
    ✓   **Very soon everyone will have a portable computer.**
    ✗   Any person can vote in the election.
    ✓   **Anyone can vote in the election.**

> **everyone/anyone etc** (NOT **every/any person**): 'Not everyone has leadership potential.' See also PEOPLE 1

2   ✗   Her husband talked so much that all the other persons in the room had to keep quiet.
    ✓   **Her husband talked so much that all the other people in the room had to keep quiet.**

> The plural of **person** is usually **people**: 'Thousands of people had gathered outside the palace to catch a glimpse of the new princess.' **Persons** is used mainly in public notices and other formal contexts: 'Seating capacity - 12 persons.'

personal   ✗   The meals can be improved if the canteen personal agree to cooperate.
    ✓   **The meals can be improved if the canteen personnel agree to cooperate.**

> See note at PERSONNEL

personality   ✗   He is a man of strong personality who will fight for what is right.
    ✓   **He is a man of strong character who will fight for what is right.**

> When talking about a person's moral quality, use **character** (NOT **personality**). Compare: 'For a career in sales, you need a forceful personality.' 'People of character and integrity never turn their backs on the truth.'

personnel   ✗   Her books deal mainly with personnel relationships, especially marital problems.
    ✓   **Her books deal mainly with personal relationships, especially marital problems.**

> **personal** /ˈpɜːsənəl/ (adjective) = concerning or belonging to one person in particular; individual or private: 'The novel is based on the author's own personal experience.' 'Our bank manager assured us that she would give the matter her personal attention.'
> **personnel** /pɜːsəˈnel/ (noun) = all the people employed in a company, office etc: 'In the event of a fire, all personnel must report to the reception area.' 'The personnel officer wants you to call and arrange an interview.'

phenomena   ✗   This phenomena is called 'culture shock'.
    ✓   **This phenomenon is called 'culture shock'.**

> **Phenomena** is the plural of **phenomenon**: 'The breakdown of family life is a relatively recent phenomenon.' 'Mathematics explains a wide variety of natural phenomena.'

phone 1   ✗   She phoned to the hospital to ask about her husband.
    ✓   **She phoned the hospital to ask about her husband.**
    ✗   Just phone to 555-879 and I'll come and get you.
    ✓   **Just phone 555-879 and I'll come and get you.**

> **phone/telephone/ring/call** a person/place/number (WITHOUT **to**): 'You must promise to phone me as soon as you get there.'
> Note that speakers of American English do not use **ring** for this meaning.

2

  ✗ I talked to him for a long time by phone last night.
  ✓ **I talked to him for a long time on/over the phone last night.**

> In British English the phrase is **(talk/speak to sb) on/over the phone** (NOT **by phone**): 'He didn't want to discuss it over the phone.'
> Note that in American English both **by phone** and **on/over the phone** are used, although **by phone** is not common.

piano

  See PLAY

picnic 1

  ✗ We decided to make a picnic in the field opposite the house.
  ✓ **We decided to have a picnic in the field opposite the house.**
  See Language Note at DO

2

  ✗ On our day off, we went picnic.
  ✓ **On our day off, we went on a picnic.**

> **go on/for a picnic** (NOT **go picnic/go to/on picnic**: 'The last time I went on a picnic I was chased by a bull.' 'Lucy loves going on picnics.'

piece

  ✗ The pencils were free and so I took two pieces.
  ✓ **The pencils were free and so I took two.**

> **Piece** is NOT used with countable nouns. Compare: 'a piece of cheese', 'a piece of furniture', 'a piece of luck'.

pillow

  ✗ The pillows had been removed from the sofa and scattered on the floor.
  ✓ **The cushions had been removed from the sofa and scattered on the floor.**

> **pillow** = a bag-like object filled with soft material that you rest your head on when you are in bed: 'No sooner had his head touched the pillow than he was sound asleep.'
> **cushion** = a bag-like object filled with soft material that you put on a chair, sofa etc to make it more comfortable: 'Would you like a cushion for your back?'

pitiful

  ✗ We both felt pitiful when we saw how lonely she was.
  ✓ **We both felt pity for her when we saw how lonely she was.**
  See PITY 1

pity 1

  ✗ When I saw these pity children, my eyes filled with tears.
  ✓ **When I saw these pitiful children, my eyes filled with tears.**

> **pity** (noun) = a feeling that you have when you feel sad and sorry for someone because of their situation: 'They don't want out pity. They need our help.'
> **pitiful** (adjective) = causing people to feel sad and sorry: 'The horses were in a pitiful condition, thin and covered with sores.'

2

  ✗ She expected me to feel pity on her and help her.
  ✓ **She expected me to take pity on her and help her.**
  ✓ **She expected me to feel pity for her and help her.**

> **take pity on**: 'Eventually a kind motorist took pity on us and offered us a lift.'
> **feel pity for**: 'Being a widow, she expects you to feel pity for her.'

place 1 ✗ I hope there's enough place in the wardrobe for all your clothes.
      ✓ **I hope there's enough room in the wardrobe for all your clothes.**

> **place** = an area or a particular part of an area: 'The best place to sit is right in front of the stage.'
> **room** (or **space**) = an empty part of something that can be used or filled: 'There's room in the back seat for all three of you.'

2 ✗ I left the coat in my room but it may not be in that place any longer.
    ✓ **I left the coat in my room but it may not be there any longer.**

> **there** = in/to that place: 'It's a long way to New Zealand but I'd love to go there.'

3 ✗ When I lived at home, my father did not let me go to any place on my own.
    ✓ **When I lived at home, my father did not let me go anywhere on my own.**

> **anywhere** = in/to any place: 'Have you seen my comb anywhere?'

4 ✗ He was looking for a place where to spend the night.
    ✓ **He was looking for somewhere to spend the night.**
    ✗ There was no place where to park.
    ✓ **There was nowhere to park.**

> **somewhere/nowhere/anywhere + to-v**: 'She needs somewhere to stay.'
> Compare: 'He was looking for a place where he could spend the night.'

planet ✗ I was born in a little planet in outer space.
    ✓ **I was born on a little planet in outer space.**

> **on a planet** (NOT **in**): 'Is there life on other planets?'

plate ✗ You'll be able to try some of the local plates.
    ✓ **You'll be able to try some of the local dishes.**
    See Language Note on next page

play ✗ I've been playing piano since I was eight.
    ✓ **I've been playing the piano since I was eight.**

> In British English the phrase is **play the piano/guitar/violin etc** (WITH **the**): 'She's learning to play the flute.'
> In American English **the** is sometime omitted.

pleasant ✗ We would be very pleasant if you could attend.
    ✓ **We would be very pleased if you could attend.**

> **pleasant** = (of a person) polite and friendly: 'I've always found Bob very pleasant to work with.'
> **pleased** = happy, satisfied: 'I was very pleased to hear that you're feeling better.' 'She's pleased that the exams are over.'

please ✗ Please, if you cannot come, let me know as soon as possible.
    ✓ **Please let me know as soon as possible if you cannot come.**

> **Please** does not usually come immediately before a subordinate clause ('if you cannot come').
> Note the usual positions: 'Please let me know as soon as you can.' 'Will you please let me know as soon as you can?' 'Will you let me know as soon as you can, please?'

MEAL • MENU • COURSE • DISH • THE DISHES • PLATE

meal	A **meal** is the food that you eat at about the same time each day: 'After the meal we went to a discotheque.' 'We usually have our main meal in the evening.'
menu	A **menu** is a list of all the things that you can order in a restaurant: 'I tried to read the menu but it was all in French.' 'Is there any fish on the menu?'
course	A meal may be served in separate stages. Each stage is called a **course:** 'The main course was disappointing, but the dessert was excellent.' 'I'm not hungry enough to eat a three-course meal.'
dish	A **dish** is (1) food prepared in a particular way and served as a meal or part of a meal: 'My favourite Italian dish is lasagne.' 'For the main course there were six different meat dishes to choose from.' (2) a (usually shallow) container that food is placed in and then cooked or served: 'I hope this dish is ovenproof!'
the dishes	**The dishe**s is a collective term for all the plates, bowls, cups, etc, that are used during a meal: 'Whose turn is it to wash the dishes tonight?'
plate	A **plate** is (1) a (usually round) flat object that food is placed on, especially just before it is eaten: 'All the clean plates are still in the dishwasher.' 'I'd never seen anyone put so much food on their plate.' (2) (also **plateful**) the amount of food on a plate: 'How can you eat two large plates of spaghetti and still feel hungry?'

pleasure 1 ✗ As mayor of this town, it gives me a great pleasure to welcome you.
  ✓ **As mayor of this town, it gives me great pleasure to welcome you.**

> **it gives sb great pleasure to do sth** (WITHOUT **a**): 'It gives me great pleasure to introduce today's guest speaker.'
> Compare: 'It is a great pleasure for me to introduce ...'

2 ✗ A lot of people work for their pleasure, not because of financial obligations.
  ✓ **A lot of people work for pleasure, not because of financial obligations.**

> **do sth for pleasure** (WITHOUT **his/our/their** etc): 'She used to be in the national team but now she swims just for pleasure.'

3 ✗ It's the first time that I've had the pleasure to meet her.
  ✓ **It's the first time that I've had the pleasure of meeting her.**

> **be pleased to do sth** BUT **have the pleasure of doing sth**: 'In Java I had the pleasure of attending a traditional wedding ceremony.'

p.m.   See o'clock 3

point 1   ✗ There's no point to complain about the service.
    ✓ **There's no point (in) complaining about the service.**

    there is no/little point (in) doing sth (NOT **to do**): 'There's no point in going on Sunday - all the shops will be shut.'

2   ✗ I had to spend forty-eight hours listening to him with a gun pointed to my head.
    ✓ **I had to spend forty-eight hours listening to him with a gun pointed at my head.**

    point at = hold a weapon, camera etc so that it is in line with someone or something: 'Never point a gun at anyone.' 'With a knife pointed at my chest, I was in no position to argue.'
    Compare: ' "I'd like one of those," he said, pointing to/at a Mercedes.'

point of view 1   ✗ From my point of view, the war is likely to continue.
    ✓ **In my opinion, the war is likely to continue.**

    Use **from ... point of view** to introduce the particular position from which a situation is seen and judged: 'From the government's point of view, a June election would make very good sense.' 'From a financial point of view, the proposal has many advantages.'
    To introduce your opinion about something, use **in my opinion** : 'In my opinion, the public isn't ready for another election.'

2   ✗ On a cultural point of view, it is always interesting to live in a foreign country.
    ✓ **From a cultural point of view, it is always interesting to live in a foreign country.**

    from a particular **point of view** (NOT **on/in/at/to etc**): 'From an environmental point of view, the battery-driven car is very attractive.'

police 1   ✗ The police was not able to find anything.
    ✓ **The police were not able to find anything.**

    Police is always used with a plural verb: 'The police have a very difficult job to do.'

2   ✗ He was charged with shooting a police.
    ✓ **He was charged with shooting a police officer.**

    the police = the police force in general: 'If you get any more of these phone calls, you should contact the police.'
    policeman, policewoman, police officer = a member of the police force: 'There are two police officers outside waiting to see you.'

pollution   ✗ The world's most serious ecological problem is the pollution.
    ✓ **The world's most serious ecological problem is pollution.**
    See the 4

poor   ✗ He gave all his money to the poors.
    ✓ **He gave all his money to the poor.**

    the poor (WITHOUT **-s**) = all people that are poor: 'In a recession it is always the poor that suffer the most.'

position

✗ I should like to explain our government's position about nuclear weapons.

✓ **I should like to explain our government's position on nuclear weapons.**

position on sth (NOT **about**): 'The President has made his position on taxation perfectly clear.'

possib- ility 1

✗ We are considering the possibility to do the job ourselves.

✓ **We are considering the possibility of doing the job ourselves.**

possibility of (doing) sth: 'Is there any possibility of (getting) a refund?' Compare: 'Is it possible to get a refund?'

2

✗ My visit to Tokyo was a good possibility for me to learn some Japanese.

✓ **My visit to Tokyo was a good opportunity to learn some Japanese.**

✗ A person who wants to go out to work should be given the possibility to do so.

✓ **A person who wants to go out to work should be given the opportunity to do so.**

Use **possibility** when you are talking about something that may happen: 'There is also a possibility that the peacekeeping forces could themselves come under attack.'
To refer to a situation in which it is possible for someone to do something, use **opportunity**: 'The exchange scheme provides young people with the opportunity to visit a foreign country.'

possible 1

✗ If you find my book, could you possible return it to me?

✓ **If you find my book, could you possibly return it to me?**

Possible is an adjective: 'It's quite possible that someone picked up your bag by mistake.' 'There are several possible answers.'
Possibly is an adverb: 'I wonder if you could possibly send me some more information.' 'How could you possibly suspect your own brother of doing such a thing?'

2

✗ It could be possible that I left the wallet back at the hotel.

✓ **It's possible that I left the wallet back at the hotel.**

✗ I was wondering whether it could be possible to arrange another meeting.

✓ **I was wondering whether it might be possible to arrange another meeting.**

Do not use **can/could** before **possible**. When you are talking about a past event, use **it is possible**: 'It's quite possible that the letter was sent to the wrong address.' When you are talking about a future event, use **it may/ might be possible**: 'She thinks that it may be possible to get the watch repaired.'

3

✗ Is it possible that I come and see you tomorrow?

✓ **Is it possible for me to come and see you tomorrow?**

✗ She asked me if it was possible that you ring her back after 5 p.m.

✓ **She asked me if it was possible for you to ring her back after 5 p.m.**

In enquiries and polite requests, use **possible (for sb) to do sth** (NOT **possible that**): 'Would it be possible for me to open a bank account?' Compare: 'It's quite possible that they've got stuck in a traffic jam.'

power

✗ The illness has left her with no power.
✓ **The illness has left her with no energy.**

A person's **power** refers to their social, economic or political influence: 'The royal family has very little power these days.' 'The major investors have the power to make or break a company.'
When talking about someone's physical condition, use **energy** or **strength** (NOT **power**): 'I don't have the time or energy to go out in the evenings.' 'Her doctor has told her to take things easy until she gets her strength back.'

practice

✗ I think it's a great idea and should be put in practice.
✓ **I think it's a great idea and should be put into practice.**

put sth into practice (NOT **in**): 'The aim of the project is to give students the opportunity to put what they have learned into practice.'

prefer 1

✗ I'd prefer to staying at a different hotel this time.
✓ **I'd prefer to stay at a different hotel this time.**

prefer to do sth (NOT **to doing**): 'They'd prefer to wait and see what happens.'

2

✗ I'd prefer renting a small flat rather than live with a host family.
✓ **I'd prefer to rent a small flat rather than live with a host family.**

When you are talking about a future or imaginary event, use **(would) prefer + to do sth** (NOT **doing**): 'I think I'd prefer to wait a bit longer, just in case the others show up.'
Compare: 'I've always preferred eating at home to eating in restaurants.'

3

✗ Why do you prefer the theatre than the cinema?
✓ **Why do you prefer the theatre to the cinema?**
✗ I prefer drawing than painting.
✓ **I prefer drawing to painting.**

prefer (doing) sth to (doing) sth else (NOT **than**): 'He normally prefers classical music to rock.' 'Most women prefer breastfeeding to bottle feeding.'
Compare: 'I'd rather live in the North than in the South.' 'Most women would rather go out to work than stay at home all day.'

preferable 1

✗ Going swimming is more preferable to playing football.
✓ **Going swimming is preferable to playing football.**

Do not use **more** with an adjective which contains the sense 'more' as part of its meaning. **Preferable** means 'better or more suitable': 'As far as I'm concerned, anything would be preferable to spending another night here.'

2

✗ For most teenagers, living in the countryside is preferable than living in a city.
✓ **For most teenagers, living in the countryside is preferable to living in a city.**

One thing is **preferable to** another thing (NOT **than**): 'An old computer is preferable to no computer at all.'

preference ✗ Our preferences in music are very similar.
　　　　　　　✓ **Our tastes in music are very similar.**
　　　　　　　✗ I know Carlos very well and I know his preferences.
　　　　　　　✓ **I know Carlos very well and so I know his tastes/what he likes.**

> **Preference** usually refers to what someone prefers on a particular occasion: 'We could eat Chinese, Indian or Italian. Do you have any preference?' 'My own preference is for a hotel with its own swimming pool.'
>
> When you are talking about the particular style or styles that someone (always) likes or buys, use **taste**: 'While in Italy she developed a taste for Renaissance art.' 'When it comes to clothes, he has very expensive taste.'

prepare ✗ I was preparing myself to go to bed when the phone rang.
　　　　　　? **I was preparing to go to bed when the phone rang.**
　　　　　　✓ **I was getting ready to go to bed when the phone rang.**

> If you **prepare yourself** (**for sth**), you get yourself into a suitable mental or physical state for something that you expect to happen: 'Relatives of the victims were told to prepare themselves for a long wait.' 'The villagers are preparing themselves for further flooding.'
> When you **get ready** or **prepare** to do something, you make yourself ready to do it: 'The company is preparing to expand its European network.' 'I had my breakfast and got ready to go to school.'
> Note that **get ready** is very common in spoken English and is often used in connection with the simple things that people do as part of their daily routine.

present 1 ✗ They decided to present a tiny kitten to their son.
　　　　　　　✓ **They decided to give their son a tiny kitten.**

> **present** (verb) = give something (to someone) during an official ceremony or meeting: 'The company's vice-president will now present the prize for the Best Salesperson of the Year.' 'Before leaving London, Mr Bush was presented with a petition from the Campaign for Nuclear Disarmament.'

2 ✗ Before leaving the examination room we had to present our answer papers.
　　✓ **Before leaving the examination room we had to hand in our answer papers.**
> See note at PASS UP

3 ✗ In the present she is involved in a project at the Housing Research Institute.
　　✓ **At present she is involved in a project at the Housing Research Institute.**
> **at present** or **at the present time** (NOT **in the present**): 'I'm afraid that we're out of stock at present.'
> Compare: 'In future, don't keep the customers waiting.'

4 ? At present I'm trying to improve my English.
　　✓ **At the moment I'm trying to improve my English.**
> **At present** is used mainly in formal styles: 'At present there is insufficient evidence for the police to press charges.'
> In other styles use **at the moment, just now** or **right now**: 'Alan is in bed with flu at the moment.' 'Mrs Blake is too busy to see anyone just now.'

presently   ?   Presently, nearly every machine used in the home is made of plastic.
✓   **At present, nearly every machine used in the home is made of plastic.**

Presently is used to mean 'soon' in both British and American English: 'The car will arrive presently to take Her Majesty back to the palace.' In American English **presently** is also used to mean 'now, at present, currently': 'The President is presently undergoing minor surgery.' The American usage is gradually becoming accepted outside the USA, but careful users of British English consider it to be non-standard.

pressure **1** ✗   All these 'tests put an unnecessary pressure on students.
✓   **All these tests put unnecessary pressure on students.**

Pressure is an uncountable noun: 'To stem the flow of blood, firm pressure should be applied.' 'They will never agree to the proposal unless there is pressure from above.'

2 ✗   This growing demand for housing gives pressure to the farmland and recreational areas.
✓   **This growing demand for housing puts pressure on the farmland and recreational areas.**

put pressure on sb/sth (NOT **give**): 'His parents are putting pressure on him to leave school and get a job.'

pretend **1** ✗   The government pretends to nationalize all the major industries.
✓   **The government intends to nationalize all the major industries.**

pretend = behave in a way that aims to give someone a false impression: 'He got into the conference centre by pretending to be a security guard. 'She hurried past, pretending not to see me.'
intend = be planning to do something: 'As soon as the baby can be left with someone, she intends to go back to work.'

2 ✗   He pretends that he wasn't informed about the meeting.
✓   **He claims that he wasn't informed about the meeting.**

claim = state that something is true, especially when there is no proof or evidence that it is true: 'She claims to have been a close friend of John Lennon.'

prevent **1** ✗   Stricter punishments would prevent people from doing these things.
✓   **Stricter punishments would deter people from doing these things.**

prevent = stop someone from doing something: 'They locked all the doors to prevent him escaping.'
deter = discourage someone from doing something: 'Tougher laws are needed to deter people from drinking and driving.'

2 ✗   Stricter punishments may help to prevent society from serious crime.
✓   **Stricter punishments may help to protect society from serious crime.**

prevent = stop something from happening: 'Bad weather prevented the plane from taking off.' 'Good tyres help to prevent accidents.'

protect = keep someone or something safe: 'The camera comes with a free leather carrying case to protect it.' 'It is the responsibility of the police and the courts to protect us from these killers and maniacs.'

3 ✗ His parents tried to prevent him to join the army.
✓ **His parents tried to prevent him from joining the army.**

prevent sb (from) doing sth: 'Girls should not be prevented from taking part in these sports.'

prevention ✗ I decided to take a big stick with me, just as a prevention.
✓ **I decided to take a big stick with me, just as a precaution.**

prevention = the act of stopping something from happening: 'The police are also concerned with the prevention of crime.'
precaution = an action taken in an attempt to avoid possible danger, damage, injury, etc: 'Some drivers have had alarms fitted as an extra precaution.'

price 1 ✗ The price of keeping a person in prison for a year is enormous.
✓ **The cost of keeping a person in prison for a year is enormous.**

See Language Note opposite

2 See CHEAP 1

print ✗ The magazine is printed every month.
✓ **The magazine is published every month.**

print = produce copies of a book, newspaper, etc. by using machines: 'Due to increased demand, another six thousand copies are to be printed.'
publish = produce and distribute (a book, magazine, newspaper, etc) for sale to the public: The first edition was published in 1989.' 'Amateur Photographer is published every Tuesday.'

prison ✗ Sending people to the prison is not the way to reduce crime.
✓ **Sending people to prison is not the way to reduce crime.**

See note at SCHOOL 1

probably ✗ They probably will understand and try to help you.
✓ **They will probably understand and try to help you.**

See Language Note at ALWAYS

problem 1 ✗ I experienced problems to find the right accommodation.
✓ **I experienced problems in finding the right accommodation.**

have/experience a problem/problems (in) doing sth (NOT **to do**): 'You shouldn't have any problems in getting a visa.'

2 ✗ Unemployment is a very important problem.
✓ **Unemployment is a very serious problem.**

a serious problem (NOT **important**): 'Teenage vandalism is a serious problem in this area.'

3 ✗ When population growth is not controlled, serious problems can happen.

✓ **When population growth is not controlled, serious problems can arise.**
problem + **arise/occur** (NOT **happen**): 'How did the problem first arise?'

PRICE • COST • COSTS • CHARGE • FEE • RATE • RENTAL • FARE • RENT

price	The **price** of something is the amount of money that you must pay in order to buy it: 'I'm interested in the car, but the price is too high.' 'Food prices are relatively low at present.'
cost	The **cost** of something is the amount of money you must pay to buy, do, make or use it: 'The cost of having the car repaired was £340.' **the cost of living** (fixed phrase) = the general amount that the people living in a particular area or country have to pay for necessary goods and services: 'In urban areas the cost of living tends to be higher.'
costs	Your **costs** are the total amount of money you spend over a period of time in order to make or produce something, or continue an activity: 'Our costs have doubled over the last five years as a result of the increase in oil prices.'
charge	A **charge** is the amount of money that you must pay for a service or to be allowed to use something: 'The waiter explained that the bill included a 10% service charge.' 'There is also a small charge for delivery and installation.' If you do not have to pay for something, it is provided **free of charge**: 'The company has offered to install the software free of charge.'
fee	A **fee** is **1** a charge that you must pay to be allowed to do something: 'Most art galleries charge an entrance fee.' 'Every new student has to pay a registration fee.' **2** (usually **fees**) a charge that you must pay for professional services such as those provided by doctors, lawyers, consultants, tutors, schools etc: 'My parents couldn't afford the school fees.' 'Last year alone, the company paid over $12 million in legal fees.'
rate	A **rate** is the amount of money that you have to pay for a service or for hiring something, especially one that is calculated on an hourly, weekly or monthly basis: 'His hourly rate is £60.' 'For a five-star hotel, the rates are very reasonable.'
rental	The **rental** is the amount of money that you have to pay to a hire company to use something for a fixed period of time: 'The car rental is $45 a day and you need a clean driving licence.' 'The rental on the TV doesn't include repairs.' See also CHEAP 1
fare	a **fare** is the cost of a journey on a bus, train etc: 'How much is the train fare from Toronto to Montreal?' 'She spends $20 per week on bus fares.'
rent	**Rent** is the money you pay every week or month to live in or use a place that doesn't belong to you: 'The rent is £500 inclusive of bills.'

proceed

✗ The main film was proceeded by a short cartoon.
✓ **The main film was preceded by a short cartoon.**

> **proceed** = (begin and) continue: 'After a five-minute delay, the lecture proceeded.' 'According to latest reports, negotiations are proceeding smoothly.'
> **precede** = come, go, or happen (immediately) before someone or something: 'Churchill was a much stronger leader than the man who preceded him.' 'The snowfall was preceded by a sudden drop in temperature.'

process

✗ The production of plastic paper clips has seven processes.
✓ **The production of plastic paper clips has seven stages.**

> **process** = a series of actions or operations that are performed in order to make or do something: 'The process begins with the gathering of the coffee beans.'
> **stage** = one of the actions or operations in a process: 'During the next stage in the process the beans are dried.'

professor

✗ He has applied for a job as a professor in a language school.
✓ **He has applied for a job as a teacher in a language school.**

> In Britain a **professor** is the most senior teacher in a university: 'My professor was the famous historian A.J.P. Taylor.'
> In the United States a **professor** is any university teacher who has a second degree.

profit

✗ The company has gained enormous profits in recent years.
✓ **The company has made enormous profits in recent years.**

> **make a profit** (NOT **gain**): 'Derek would never sell you anything without making a good profit.' 'The company made a profit of $53 million last year.'

progress

✗ We have made a great progress in the field of medicine.
✓ **We have made great progress in the field of medicine.**

> See Language Note at SCENERY

prohibit

✗ Even the teachers were prohibited to walk on the lawn.
✓ **Even the teachers were prohibited from walking on the lawn.**

> **prohibit sb from doing sth**: 'The government intends to prohibit shopkeepers from selling cigarettes to children.'

promotion

✗ In some professions it is still difficult for women to get promotions.
✓ **In some professions it is still difficult for women to get promotion.**

> In phrases such as **get promotion, apply for promotion** and **chance/s of promotion,** the noun **promotion** is usually uncountable: 'Women should have the same chance of promotion as their male counterparts.' Compare: 'With so many staff leaving, we can expect a few more promotions.'

proof

✗ These bones are a proof that the animals really existed.
✓ **These bones are proof that the animals really existed.**

✗ Today we have scientific proofs that tobacco is harmful.
✓ **Today we have scientific proof that tobacco is harmful.**

Proof (= evidence) is usually an uncountable noun: 'Investigators now have proof of his involvement in the arms deal.'

propaganda ✗ The television company receives most of its money from propaganda.
✓ **The television company receives most of its money from advertising.**

Propaganda is used in a political context: 'Roadside hoardings displayed anti-Western propaganda.' 'In times of war the public are bombarded with propaganda.'
Advertising is used in a commercial context: 'Car manufacturers spend billions of dollars a year on advertising.'

property ✗ The police eventually found most of the stolen properties.
✓ **The police eventually found most of the stolen property.**

Property (= things that belong to someone) is an uncountable noun: 'Personal property should not be left unattended.'

proportion ✗ The country's small food supply is not proportion about the size of the population.
✓ **The country's food supply is small in proportion to the size of the population.**

Something is small/large etc **in proportion to/with** something else: 'Her feet are very small in proportion to the rest of her body.'

proposal ✗ The proposal of building a new motorway received little support.
✓ **The proposal to build a new motorway received little support.**

proposal to do sth: 'The proposal to close the hospital was rejected.'

propose **1** ✗ I propose you to talk to John about it.
✓ **I suggest that you talk to John about it.**

propose = formally suggest an idea, plan or course of action, especially to an official person or group that has the power to decide: 'May I propose that we postpone further discussion of this matter until our next meeting.'

2 ✗ A friend of mine has proposed me a job in his restaurant.
✓ **A friend of mine has offered me a job in his restaurant.**
✗ He proposed to put them up for a few days.
✓ **He offered to put them up for a few days.**

offer = (1) tell someone that they can have something if they want it: 'He offered me a cup of tea.' 'She was offered a job on a local newspaper.' (2) tell someone that you are willing to do something: 'He offered to drive me back to my hotel.'

3 ✗ I would like to propose to double the number of computers in each office.
✓ **I would like to propose that the number of computers in each office is/be doubled.**
✓ **I would like to propose doubling the number of computers in each office.**

✗ I propose the library opening hours to be increased.
✓ **I propose that the library opening hours are/be increased.**
propose to do sth = intend: 'We would like to know what action you propose to take.'
propose that sb does/(should) do sth (or **propose doing sth**) = formally suggest: 'He has proposed that each existing member accept responsibility for recruiting two new members.' 'In the end it was proposed that the students concerned should be given a verbal warning.'

prospect   ✗ There is little prospect for the situation to improve.
✓ **There is little prospect of the situation improving.**
prospect of doing sth/sth happening: 'With all the political unrest, there is little prospect of attracting foreign investment.'

protest   ✗ She told the shop assistant that she wanted to protest about the cardigan she had bought.
✓ **She told the shop assistant that she wanted to complain about the cardigan she had bought.**
protest = say or do something to show that you strongly disagree with something: 'The crowds were protesting against the government's purchase of nuclear weapons.'
complain = say that you are annoyed or unhappy about something: 'He's always complaining about the weather.' 'If you think you've been overcharged, you should complain to the manager.'

provide 1   ✗ My job provides me the opportunity to meet new people every day.
✓ **My job provides me with the opportunity to meet new people every day.**
provide sb with sth: 'Money from the aid programme will be used to provide the farmers with better tools.'

2   ✗ The government does not provide enough food to the population.
✓ **The government does not provide enough food for the population.**
✗ I was very pleased with the room you provided to me.
✓ **I was very pleased with the room you provided for me.**
provide sth for sb/sth: 'The hotel also provides facilities for business meetings and conferences.'

3   ✗ In my view, a father should provide his family.
✓ **In my view, a father should provide for his family.**
provide for sb = support someone by paying for all their food, clothes etc: 'How can you provide for your children when you don't have a job?'

publicity   ✗ I think governments should ban the publicity of tobacco.
✓ **I think governments should ban the advertising of tobacco.**
If something is given **publicity**, there is an attempt to inform the public about it: 'Scandals involving prominent politicians always receive widespread publicity.'
Advertising is the activity of trying to persuade people to buy something: 'The big software companies spend millions each year on advertising.'

punishment   ✗ The police are in favour of stricter punishments.
 ✓ **The police are in favour of harsher punishments.**

 severe/harsh punishment (NOT **strict/strong**): 'A prison sentence seems a very severe punishment for tax evasion.'

pure   ✗ We opened the window to get some pure air.
 ✓ **We opened the window to get some fresh air.**
 ✗ I always keep a few bottles of pure water on the boat.
 ✓ **I always keep a few bottles of fresh/drinking water on the boat.**

 Use **pure** when you mean 'completely clean': 'The water in the lake is so pure that you can drink it.'
 The usual word for describing air and water is **fresh**: 'Her doctor has prescribed a good holiday and lots of fresh air.'

purpose   ✗ The purpose why I have come here is to improve my English.
 ✓ **The reason why I have come here is to improve my English.**
 ✗ The purpose of staying in the United States is to complete my PhD.
 ✓ **My reason for staying in the United States is to complete my PhD.**

 purpose = what you hope to achieve by doing something; aim: 'The main purpose of the trip is to see Helen's parents.' 'Their purpose in coming here is to promote Australian universities.'
 reason = the thing that causes someone to do something: 'The reason why she left him was probably to do with his drinking problem.' 'Did they give you a reason for rejecting your application?'

put off   ✗ Once indoors, he immediately put off his wet clothes and dried himself.
 ✓ **Once indoors, he immediately took off his wet clothes and dried himself.**

 See Language Note at WEAR

qualification ✗ I am taking another course to improve my qualification.
✓ **I am taking another course to improve my qualifications.**

qualifications (plural) = all the examination passes, skills and experience that you need for a particular job: 'I'd like to apply for the job but I don't have the right qualifications.'
qualification = a degree, diploma, certificate etc: 'Do you have a postgraduate qualification?' Speakers of American English use **degree, diploma, certificate etc** for this meaning.

quality ✗ Switzerland produces goods with a very high quality.
✓ **Switzerland produces goods of a very high quality.**

of (a) high/low/poor quality (NOT **with**): 'Japanese electrical products tend to be of much higher quality.'

quarrel ? Sometimes we quarrel about which programme to watch.
✓ **Sometimes we argue about which programme to watch.**

When people **quarrel** they argue angrily, especially for a long time about something that is unimportant: 'If you two boys don't stop quarrelling, you can go straight to bed.'
People can **argue** without feeling angry or looking silly: 'Most evenings we would sit in the kitchen arguing about politics.'

quarter ✗ He served his country for over quarter of a century.
✓ **He served his country for over a quarter of a century.**

a quarter (of sth): 'He's had almost a quarter of the cake all to himself.'

quicker ✗ We are able to exchange information quicker than in the past.
✓ **We are able to exchange information more quickly than in the past.**

Quicker is sometimes used as an adverb, but only in informal styles.
More quickly is always acceptable: 'He spoke more quickly than usual.'

quickly ? I went quickly to the nearest phone booth.
✓ **I ran to the nearest phone booth.**

Go quickly usually sounds unnatural. The same meaning can be expressed by verbs such as **hurry, rush, run, dash, sprint, etc**: 'As soon as we saw the rain clouds, we hurried back home.'

quiet See NICE

quite 1 ✗ This year the work at university is quite harder than last year.
✓ **This year the work at university is rather harder than last year.**

Before comparative forms use **rather, slightly, somewhat** or (especially in informal styles) **a bit, a little** (NOT **quite**): 'My new office is rather smaller than my old one.' 'He's slightly older than me.'
Note however the common exception: 'Yes, I'm feeling quite better, thank you.' (= completely recovered)

2 ✗ In the circumstances, it was a quite rude answer.
   ✓ **In the circumstances, it was quite a rude answer.**

When **quite** means 'rather/fairly', it comes in front of **a/an**: 'The survey covered quite a wide range of newspapers.' 'On the whole, it was quite a good essay.'
Compare: 'a rather/fairly/pretty rude answer'

3 ✗ There are quite many foreign students in London.
   ✓ **There are quite a lot of foreign students in London.**

quite a lot (of) NOT **quite many/much**: 'Quite a lot of time has already been wasted.' I've made quite a lot of new friends.'

radio

✗ I always listen to the news in the radio.
✓ **I always listen to the news on the radio.**
✗ On radio there was a current affairs programme.
✓ **On the radio there was a current affairs programme.**

On the radio, on (the) television (NOT **in**): 'It's strange to hear your own voice on the radio.' 'What's on television tonight?'

rain 1

✗ It was heavy rain yesterday.
✓ **It rained heavily yesterday.**
✓ **There was some heavy rain yesterday.**

When you begin with **it**, use **rain** as a verb: 'It's raining again!' 'This month it's rained nearly every day.'
When you begin with **there**, use **rain** as a noun: 'There's been a lot of rain this month.'

2

✗ Two minutes later it started pouring rain.
✓ **Two minutes later it started pouring with rain.**
✗ The next day the sky poured heavily.
✓ **The next day it poured with rain.**

it + pour with rain: 'Whenever I forget my umbrella, it pours with rain.' 'We can't go out – it's pouring with rain.'

rainfall

✗ There was no rainfall for over three months.
✓ **There was no rain for over three months.**
✓ **It didn't rain for over three months.**

rainfall = the amount of rain that usually falls in an area during a certain period: 'The whole region has a very low rainfall at this time of the year.'
Note that **rainfall** is mainly used in technical styles.

rainy

? The afternoon was very rainy.
✓ **The afternoon was very wet.**
? It's rainy again today.
✓ **It's wet again today.**
✓ **It's raining again today.**

When **rainy** is used it generally comes in front of words like **day, afternoon, Sunday** and **season** (NOT after a verb): 'The baby was born on a rainy Sunday in June.' 'When does the rainy season begin?'
The more usual word is wet: 'Apart from a couple of wet afternoons, the weather was fine.' 'If it's wet tomorrow, we'll go on Monday instead.'

raise 1

✗ When I was a child, I used to raise my own flowers in a corner of the garden.
✓ **When I was a child, I used to grow my own flowers in a corner of the garden.**

raise plants, vegetables, animals etc, especially on a farm to sell as food: 'He grew up in Nebraska where his parents raised chickens.'
grow plants, flowers, vegetables, etc, in a garden for pleasure: 'This year I thought I'd try growing a few tomatoes.'

2   ✗   They offered to raise up my salary.
         ✓   **They offered to raise my salary.**

raise sth (WITHOUT **up**): 'If you want to ask a question, just raise your hand.' 'The age of retirement should be lowered, not raised.'

3   ✗   The cost of living has raised by 20 per cent this year.
         ✓   **The cost of living has risen by 20 per cent this year.**
         ✗   Sales raised rapidly.
         ✓   **Sales rose rapidly.**
         ✗   The rain had caused the water level to raise.
         ✓   **The rain had caused the water level to rise.**

Raise (raising, raised, raised) is a transitive verb: 'They wouldn't dare to raise taxes just before an election.'
Rise (rising, rose, risen) is intransitive: 'The divorce rate has risen steadily over the last forty years.' 'Prices rose again last month.'

4   ✗   There has been an enormous raise in house prices.
         ✓   **There has been an enormous rise in house prices.**

a raise = (American English) an increase in wages or salary: 'The State Government simply can't afford to give all teachers a raise.'
a rise = an increase in quantity, cost, price, salary etc: 'For those on low incomes, another rise in the cost of living could be devastating.'

rank   ✗   After dealing with customer enquiries for a year I was promoted to a higher rank and given my own office.
            ✓   **After dealing with customer enquiries for a year I was promoted to a more senior position and given my own office.**

Rank usually refers to someone's position in the army, navy, police force etc, where there are fixed levels of authority such as sergeant or captain 'She joined the police force in 1990 and quickly rose to the rank of sergeant.'

rapid/   ✗   These new trains are very rapid.
rapidly   ✓   **These new trains are very fast.**
              ✗   I rapidly took the gun out of my pocket.
              ✓   **I quickly took the gun out of my pocket.**

When used in connection with movement, **rapid** and **rapidly** usually refer to something that happens at a very fast rate: 'She could hear rapid footsteps approaching.' 'The patient often develops a fever and breathing becomes rapid.'
Note that these words are mainly used to describe the speed with which something changes, develops, spreads etc: 'Investors have profited from the country's rapid economic growth.' 'Unemployment has been increasing rapidly over the past 8 years.'

rare 1   ✗   Water is very rare in some parts of the country.
               ✓   **Water is very scarce in some parts of the country.**

If certain things are **rare** there are only a few of them in existence: 'Rare coins are usually worth a lot of money.' A **rare** event is one that hardly ever happens: 'I was lucky enough to witness one of her rare public performances.'

To describe something that is usually common but for some reason is difficult to obtain at a particular time or in a particular place, use **scarce**: 'After the war, food and clothing were scarce.'

2   ✗   I think that my name is rare.
    ✓   **I think that my name is unusual.**
    ✗   In San Francisco I saw some rare architecture.
    ✓   **In San Francisco I saw some unusual architecture.**

If something is different from what is usual, it is **unusual**: 'The bread had an unusual flavour.' 'Kit. That's an unusual name.'

3   ✗   It is not rare that women have a job nowadays.
    ✓   **It is not unusual for women to have a job nowadays.**

not unusual (for sb) to do sth (NOT **not rare**): 'It's not unusual to see business people cycling to work these days.'

rarely   See Language Note at NOT

rather 1   ?   The bed was rather comfortable.
    ✓   **The bed was quite comfortable.**
    ?   The weather is rather good today.
    ✓   **The weather is quite good today.**

When **rather** means 'to a small extent', it is usually used with words that express negative qualities: 'The bed was rather uncomfortable.' 'The lesson was rather boring.' 'He's always been rather lazy.'
When **rather** is used with words that express positive qualities, it makes the quality stronger: 'These cakes are rather nice! Try one!'

2   ✗   They rather violent films to romantic ones.
    ✓   **They prefer violent films to romantic ones.**
    ✓   **They'd rather see violent films than romantic ones.**
    ✗   I rather take him to somewhere less crowded.
    ✓   **I'd rather take him to somewhere less crowded.**
    ✓   **I prefer to take him to somewhere less crowded.**

When you mean 'prefer', use **prefer/would rather/would prefer** (NOT **rather** on its own): 'She says she'd rather speak to you herself about it.'

3   ✗   I'd rather prefer just to lie on the beach.
    ✓   **I'd rather just lie on the beach.**
    ✓   **I'd prefer just to lie on the beach.**

Do not use **rather** and **prefer** together: 'If the weather's fine, we'd rather play tennis.'

4   ✗   I told her I would rather to go by train than to fly.
    ✓   **I told her I would rather go by train than fly.**
    ✗   I would rather going abroad for my holidays.
    ✓   **I would rather go abroad for my holidays.**

would rather do sth (NOT **to do** or **doing**): 'They'd rather wait and see what happens.'

reach

   ✗ When the blue car reached to the corner, it stopped.
   ✓ **When the blue car reached the corner, it stopped.**

   reach sth (WITHOUT **to/at**): 'Eventually the two sides reached an agreement.' 'We reached London just after 3 o'clock.'

**react/
reaction**

   ✗ It's time the government reacted on the crisis.
   ✓ **It's time the government reacted to the crisis.**
   ✗ Their reaction on the article was predictable.
   ✓ **Their reaction to the article was predictable.**

   react/reaction to sth (NOT **on/at**): 'People reacted to the speech in different ways.' 'Reactions to the news of the merger were less positive than expected.'

realize **1**

   ✗ The criminal mind is not always easy to realize.
   ✓ **The criminal mind is not always easy to understand.**
   ✗ I didn't realize the meaning of 'junk mail'.
   ✓ **I didn't understand the meaning of 'junk mail'.**
   See Language Note below

  2

   ✗ The school year is divided into three terms, as you realize.
   ✓ **The school year is divided into three terms, as you know.**
   ✗ Nobody realized whether he was coming.
   ✓ **Nobody knew whether he was coming.**
   See Language Note below

  3

   ✗ Our own mistakes are sometimes difficult to realize.
   ✓ **Our own mistakes are sometimes difficult to recognize.**
   ✗ I'm sure you will realize the song when you hear it.
   ✓ **I'm sure you will recognize the song when you hear it.**
   See Language Note below

KNOW • REALIZE • RECOGNIZE • UNDERSTAND

know	be aware of a fact or particular piece of information: 'Do you know their new telephone number?' 'I know she's fond of you. She told me so herself.'
realize	suddenly become aware of a fact or the true meaning of something, especially because you have thought about it or received new information about it: 'I suddenly realized that the thumping I could hear was the sound of my own heart.' 'It was only when I saw the expression on the doctor's face that I realized the seriousness of her illness.'
recognize	know what something is because you have seen/heard/ smelled it before; know who someone is because you have seen them before: 'I'm sorry I didn't recognize you - you've had your hair cut!'
understand	know what something means, what causes something, how something operates, how someone feels, etc: 'I've never really understood physics.' 'Such behaviour is very difficult to understand.'

4 ✗ The headmaster realized his threat and sent the children home.
 ✓ **The headmaster carried out his threat and sent the children home.**
 ✗ Many people in developing countries do not realize family planning.
 ✓ **Many people in developing countries do not practise family planning.**

> When **realize** means 'make something actually happen or become real', it is usually used with words such as **ambition, intention, expectation, hope, dream, fear**: 'I feel confident that the high expectations I have of my new job will be realized.'

really 1 ✗ That's really a good idea.
 ✓ **That's a really good idea.**
 ✓ **That really is a good idea.**
 ✗ It was only a short trip but we had really a good time.
 ✓ **It was only a short trip but we had a really good time.**
 ✓ **It was only a short trip but we really had a good time.**

> The position of **really** (= very) is a matter of emphasis. Very often it comes immediately before the adjective or adverb it modifies: 'some really good news', 'a really old car'. Otherwise, it is usually placed immediately in front of the main verb: 'You really fooled me.' 'We're really enjoying ourselves.'

2 ✗ To his great amazement, little Nicola really won the race.
 ✓ **To his great amazement, little Nicola actually won the race.**

> **Really** and **actually** are sometimes interchangeable: 'She sold the piano for a lot more than it was actually/really worth.'
> When you mean 'strange as it may seem', use **actually** (NOT **really**): 'Instead of running away as he normally does, he actually offered to stay and help.'

reason 1 ✗ What was the reason for the traffic jam?
 ✓ **What was the cause of the traffic jam?**
 See note at CAUSE 1

2 ✗ My reason of coming here is to improve my English.
 ✓ **My reason for coming here is to improve my English.**
 ✗ There are several good reasons to have children.
 ✓ **There are several good reasons for having children.**

> **reason for (doing) sth**: 'He wanted to know the reason for your absence.' 'What reasons do you have for thinking that?'

3 ✗ The main reason because I am here is to study for my Master's degree.
 ✓ **The main reason why I am here is to study for my Master's degree.**
 ✓ **My main reason for being here is to study for my Master's degree.**
 ✗ The weather here is always warm and this is the reason because there are so many public swimming pools.
 ✓ **The weather here is always warm and this is (the reason) why there are so many public swimming pools.**

> **reason why** (NOT **because/how**): 'Most of you are aware of (the reason) why I've called this meeting.'
> **reason for doing sth**: 'Most of you are aware of my reason for calling this meeting.'

4 ✗ My reason for not buying the car was because it was too expensive.
  ✓ **My reason for not buying the car was that it was too expensive.**

> **the/sb's reason ... is that** (NOT **is because**): 'Her reason for going all the way to the Bahamas is that she wants some winter sunshine.'

5 ✗ I don't agree with them by many reasons.
  ✓ **I don't agree with them for many reasons.**
  ✗ The closing date for applications was last Saturday and by this reason we cannot offer you a place on the course.
  ✓ **The closing date for applications was last Saturday and for this reason we cannot offer you a place on the course.**

> **for ... reason/s** (NOT **by**): 'For these reasons next year's rice harvests are likely to be very disappointing.'

6 See CAUSE 5

reason-able 1 ✗ I was far too upset and emotional to make a reasonable decision.
  ✓ **I was far too upset and emotional to make a rational decision.**

> **reasonable** = fair, sensible or acceptable: 'Dividing up the work equally seems like a very reasonable decision.' 'They'll accept any reasonable offer.'
> **rational** = produced by means of careful, logical thinking: 'There must be some rational explanation - things can't just disappear!'

2 ✗ She usually gets reasonable good marks.
  ✓ **She usually gets reasonably good marks.**

> When you mean 'fairly/quite', use **reasonably** (adverb): 'The team played reasonably well on Saturday, but something was missing in the attack.'

recall ✗ May I recall you what happened that day?
  ✓ **May I remind you of what happened that day?**

> **recall** (fairly formal) = remember: 'I really can't recall what his wife looks like.'
> **remind** = cause (someone) to remember: 'The painting reminded me of my last holiday in Bali.' 'Remind me to buy a new toothbrush while we're out.'

recent 1 ✗ Over the recent 30 years there has been a great deal of industrial development.
  ✓ **Over the last 30 years there has been a great deal of industrial development.**

> When you mention a number, use **last** (NOT **recent**). Compare: 'In recent months house prices have fallen.' 'Over the last 12 months house prices have fallen.'

2 ✗ Tennis has become popular in Germany in the recent years.
 ✓ **Tennis has become popular in Germany in recent years.**
 ✗ Recent years the crime rate has increased.
 ✓ **In recent years the crime rate has increased.**

> **in recent weeks/months/years**: 'Flight cancellations have increased in recent weeks.'

recognize ✗ On the plane home, I suddenly recognized that I had left my coat at the hotel.
 ✓ **On the plane home, I suddenly realized that I had left my coat at the hotel.**

> See Language Note at REALIZE

recommend ✗ I recommend you a walk along the Seine.
 ✓ **I recommend a walk along the Seine.**
 ✗ I wouldn't recommend to let your children watch it.
 ✓ **I wouldn't recommend that you let your children watch it.**
 ✓ **I wouldn't recommend letting your children watch it.**

> **recommend sth**: 'Can you recommend a good hotel?'
> **recommend that**: 'My accountant recommends that I should open an offshore account.' 'We recommend you choose your wedding ring about three months in advance.' 'They recommend that 100 be regarded as a minimum number.'
> **recommend doing sth**: 'I'd never recommend sending a young child to boarding school.'
> British English also uses **recommend sb to do sth**: 'I wouldn't recommend you to let your children watch it.'

reference ✗ In reference to your letter of 6th September, I am pleased to confirm that the books have now arrived.
 ✓ **With reference to your letter of 6th September, I am pleased to confirm that the books have now arrived.**

> **with reference to sth** (NOT **in**): 'With reference to your recent article in *Amateur Gardening*, there are one or two questions that I would like to ask.'
> See also REGARD 1, REGARDING

refrain ✗ We all refrained telling her what we really thought.
 ✓ **We all refrained from telling her what we really thought.**

> **refrain from (doing) sth** (fairly formal): 'I suggest that you refrain from making similar statements until you are sure of your facts.'

refuse 1 ✗ He refused their lifestyle and decided to seek a simpler alternative.
 ✓ **He rejected their lifestyle and decided to seek a simpler alternative.**
 ✗ I refuse the idea that men and women are psychologically different.
 ✓ **I reject the idea that men and women are psychologically different.**

> **refuse** = say no (when someone wants you to do or accept something): 'Some of the staff refuse to attend lunchtime meetings.' 'We can't possibly refuse the invitation.' 'Simon had to refuse the job offer because it would have meant moving house again.'

reject = say that you do not support (an idea, belief, suggestion, plan, proposal, etc): 'Vegetarians reject the theory that you must eat meat to get all the nutrients you need.' 'The belief that a woman's place is in the home has been widely rejected.'

2 ✗ He felt refused by the man he admired most.
  ✓ **He felt rejected by the man he admired most.**

If someone makes you feel that you are no longer loved, needed etc, they **reject** you (and you feel **rejected**): 'It's terrible to feel rejected by someone you care for.'

regard 1 ✗ With regards to accommodation, there are several excellent hotels.
  ✓ **With regard to accommodation, there are several excellent hotels.**
  ✗ As regard our working environment, the machines make too much noise.
  ✓ **As regards our working environment, the machines make too much noise.**

with regard to (WITHOUT **s**): 'With regard to the minutes of our last meeting, may I first draw your attention to Item 3.'
as regards (WITH **s**): 'As regards transport, I would suggest that we hire a mini-bus for the days in question.'
See also REFERENCE, REGARDING

2 ✗ He shows no regard to other people.
  ✓ **He shows no regard for other people.**

regard for sb/sth (= respect for): 'He always does a good job and I have a high regard for him.'

regarding ✗ Regarding to your letter of 22 November, I have referred your query to our accounts department.
  ✓ **Regarding your letter of 22 November, I have referred your query to our accounts department.**

regarding (WITHOUT **to**): 'If you have any questions regarding any of our services, please feel free to contact me.'
See also REFERENCE, REGARD 1

regardless ✗ We have to train every day, regardless the weather.
  ✓ **We have to train every day, regardless of the weather.**

regardless of sth: 'The school accepts all students, regardless of educational level and background.'

regret ✗ In any case I didn't regret to stay at home.
  ✓ **In any case I didn't regret staying at home.**
  ✗ I now regret not to have worked harder at school.
  ✓ **I now regret not having worked harder at school.**

Regret is followed by a to-infinitive in formal letters to introduce a piece of bad news: 'I regret to inform you that your application for a scholarship has been unsuccessful.'
When you are talking about the past, use **regret doing sth** or **regret that**: 'I have often regretted leaving the police force.' 'I wonder if they ever regret not having gone to live abroad?' 'Now that it was too late, he regretted that he hadn't worked harder at school.'

related **1**   ✗   Many of these illnesses are related with smoking.

           ✓   **Many of these illnesses are related to smoking.**

               One thing is **related to** another thing (NOT **with**): 'Poverty is often directly related to unemployment.'

2   ✗   The size of a family is deeply related to parental income.

           ✓   **The size of a family is closely related to parental income.**

               closely related (NOT **deeply**): 'His thesis is that drugs, boredom and juvenile crime are closely related.'

relation **1**   ✗   I thought that offering to help him might improve our relation.

           ✓   **I thought that offering to help him might improve our relationship.**

           ✗   The relation between teachers and students is very friendly.

           ✓   **The relationship between teachers and students is very friendly.**

               See Language Note below

2   ✗   The new government is trying to improve its relation with America.

           ✓   **The new government is trying to improve relations with America.**

               See Language Note below

RELATION • RELATIONSHIP • RELATIONS

relation	(1) the way in which one person or thing is connected with another: 'We've been studying the relation between gender and income.' 'This latest murder bears no relation to the earlier killings.' (2) someone who belongs to your family; relative: 'She took me back home to meet all her friends and relations.'
relationship	the way that two people, groups or countries feel about each other and behave towards each other: 'What kind of relationship did you have with your father?' 'Successful companies know the importance of establishing good relationships with their customers.' 'This decision will not affect the relationship between France and its European partners.'
relations (plural noun)	the way that two groups, countries or regions publicly or officially feel about and behave towards each other: 'Relations between the two countries have steadily deteriorated in recent years.' 'The police are making great efforts to improve relations with the public.'

relax   ✗   I usually relax myself by taking a hot bath.

           ✓   **I usually relax by taking a hot bath.**

               See Language Note at MYSELF

rely

    ✗ I think it all relies on whether you like being on your own.
    ✓ **I think it all depends on whether you like being on your own.**
    ✗ A country's strength relies on unity.
    ✓ **A country's strength depends on unity.**

> When you mean that one thing is decided or shaped by another thing, use **depend on** (NOT **rely on**): 'The cost of the trip depends on how long you go for and where you stay.'
> Compare: 'Since his wife died, he has had nobody that he could really depend/ rely on.'

remark

    ✗ As soon as I came in I remarked your note on the table.
    ✓ **As soon as I came in I noticed your note on the table.**

> **remark** = say what you think or have noticed about someone or something: ' "There's a strange smell in here," she remarked.' 'Sarah remarked that the fire was going out, but nobody seemed to care.' 'I couldn't help remarking on his new hair style.'
> **notice** = become aware of someone or something: 'If we keep very quiet, they may not notice us.' 'Have you noticed that she has stopped wearing her wedding ring?'

remember

    ✗ 'He went to the doctor's yesterday.' - 'Yes, I can remember. He looked very ill.'
    ✓ **'He went to the doctor's yesterday.' - 'Yes, I remember. He looked very ill.'**
    ✗ Can you remember me? I used to sit at the back of your class.
    ✓ **Do you remember me? I used to sit at the back of your class.**

> When **remember** means 'bring the memory of a person or thing into your mind (i.e. **recall**) then **can/could** is usually optional: 'I (can) still remember the sad look on her face.' Use **can/could** to suggest effort: 'I just can't remember how the film ended.' 'I wish I could remember their address."
> When **remember** means 'have or keep the memory of a person or thing in your mind', it is usually used WITHOUT **can/could**: 'I hope you still remember me.' 'I'll always remember the night we first met.'

remind **1**

    ✗ I remind the happy days we spent together at college.
    ✓ **I remember the happy days we spent together at college.**

> **remind** = cause (someone) to remember something: 'The smell of fresh coffee always reminds me of Salvo's.'
> Compare: 'Whenever I look at the photograph, I am reminded of the happy days we spent together at college.'

    2 ✗ The flowers reminded him his garden.
    ✓ **The flowers reminded him of his garden.**

> **remind sb of sth** = cause someone to think about something: 'She reminds me of a girl I knew when I was at school.' 'As the horse came closer, I was suddenly reminded of my first riding lesson and a little pony called Duke.'

rent

    ✗ If you like riding, there are horses you can rent.
    ✓ **If you like riding, there are horses you can hire.**
    ✗ How much will it cost to rent some skis?
    ✓ **How much will it cost to hire some skis?**

> See note at HIRE 1

repeat	✗	I asked her to repeat again what she had said.
	✓	**I asked her to repeat what she had said.**

repeat sth (WITHOUT **again**): 'Would you mind repeating the question?'
' "I just can't believe it," he repeated.'
If you **repeat** something **again**, you repeat it a second time.

replace	✗	He offered to replace the old battery by a new one.
	✓	**He offered to replace the old battery with a new one.**

replace sb/sth with sb/sth (NOT **by**): 'The firm has been dismissing experienced staff and replacing them with school leavers.'

reply 1	✗	It's about time they replied my letter.
	✓	**It's about time they replied to my letter.**

reply to a letter/invitation/advertisement etc: 'Since Margaret hasn't replied to the invitation, we're assuming she isn't coming.'
Compare: 'It's about time they answered my letter.'

2	✗	He replied to me that he had grown up in a family of footballers.
	✓	**He replied that he had grown up in a family of footballers.**
	✗	'There's going to be a storm,' the captain replied me.
	✓	**'There's going to be a storm,' the captain replied.**

When **reply** is used as a reporting verb, the 'listener' is not mentioned:
' "I'm sure you're right," George replied.' 'She replied that she was too busy.'

request	✗	We had to request for more help.
	✓	**We had to request more help.**

request sth (WITHOUT **for**): 'The pilot requested permission to land, but this was refused.'
Compare: 'Our request for more help was turned down.' (noun + **for**)

research 1	✗	I'm doing a research into the causes of child abuse.
	✓	**I'm doing research into the causes of child abuse.**
	✗	The government invests a lot of money in scientific researches.
	✓	**The government invests a lot of money in scientific research.**

Research is usually an uncountable noun: 'A team of American scientists is carrying out research into the effects of acid rain.'
Researches (plural) is also used, especially in formal styles of British English and usually refers to a series of related studies by a particular person or team: 'His researches go back to the 1950s.' 'Their more recent researches point to a decline in the mortality rate.' The more usual word for this meaning, especially in American English, is **studies**.

2	✗	The project involves research of major lung diseases.
	✓	**The project involves research into major lung diseases.**

research into/on sth: 'We need more research into public attitudes to nuclear power.' 'To date, there has been very little research done on the subject.'
research on sb: 'It's a review of recent research on East Anglian fishermen.' 'She wishes to pursue her research on Edward VI.'

3	✗	Where is he making his research?
	✓	**Where is he doing his research?**

do/carry out/conduct/be engaged in research: 'We have received a small grant to conduct research into housing design for older women.' See Language Note at DO

reserve   ✗ We've reserved the school hall for the evening.
             ✓ **We've booked the school hall for the evening.**
             ✗ I've finally managed to reserve a two-room house on the beach.
             ✓ **I've finally managed to book a two-room house on the beach.**

reserve (or **book**) = arrange for a seat on a train, a seat in a theatre, a table in a restaurant etc, to be kept for you to use at a certain time: 'I'd like to reserve two seats in the front row for tomorrow night's performance.'
book = (British English) arrange for a hotel room, holiday accommodation etc, to be kept for you to use at a certain time: 'We've booked a holiday cottage in the Lake District for the first two weeks in June.' Note that in American English the usual word for this meaning is **reserve**.

resist **1**   ✗ She couldn't resist his rudeness any longer and walked out of the room.
             ✓ **She couldn't stand his rudeness any longer and walked out of the room.**

resist = fight against; oppose: 'We shall resist any changes that threaten our personal freedom.'
can't stand/bear (= be unable to tolerate): 'I'd like to live in Africa but I don't think I could bear the heat.'

2   ✗ The old couple resisted to all the pressure that was put on them to move.
       ✓ **The old couple resisted all the pressure that was put on them to move.**
       ✗ Without weapons there was no way of resisting against the attack.
       ✓ **Without weapons there was no way of resisting the attack.**

resist sb/sth (WITHOUT **to/against**): 'By resisting the Mafia's attempts to control the region, Dolci was putting his own life in danger.'
Compare: 'Much of the resistance to social and political change comes from people who oppose the government.' (noun + **to**)

resource   ✗ Tourism is the main resource of money for these people.
              ✓ **Tourism is the main source of money for these people.**
              ✗ Teachers are often regarded as a resource of knowledge.
              ✓ **Teachers are often regarded as a source of knowledge.**

resource = (1) something that can be used to make a particular task or activity easier: 'All the teaching resources - books, cassettes and so on - are kept in a special room.' (2) something that a country has and uses to create wealth, such as oil or natural gas: 'Brunei is rich in natural resources.'
source = the place where something comes from or the thing from which we can get it: 'We collect the information from various sources.' 'Beans and lentils are a very good source of protein.'

respect   ✗ They should respect to each other's opinions.
             ✓ **They should respect each other's opinions.**

respect sb/sth (WITHOUT **to**): 'He's not the most popular teacher, but all the students respect him.' 'She always told us exactly what she thought, and we respected her for that.'

respectful

✗ Some former prisoners are now respectful citizens.
✓ **Some former prisoners are now respectable citizens.**
✗ If you wish to make a good impression, you'll have to look a bit more respectful.
✓ **If you wish to make a good impression, you'll have to look a bit more respectable.**

respectful = having or showing respect for someone, especially someone older than you or senior to you: 'The principal has warned him that unless he shows a more respectful attitude towards his teachers, he will have to leave.'
respectable = displaying socially acceptable standards in appearance or behaviour: 'Surprisingly, many of these young offenders come from respectable families.' 'Nobody is going to give you a job unless you make yourself look a bit more respectable.'

respond/ response

✗ I don't care what they say, as long as I get a respond.
✓ **I don't care what they say, as long as I get a response.**
✗ We're still waiting for them to response.
✓ **We're still waiting for them to respond.**

Respond is a verb: 'I'm surprised they responded so quickly.'
Response is a noun: 'I'm surprised we got such a quick response.' 'In response to your last comment, I'm afraid I don't agree.'

responsible

✗ Drugs are responsible of a large number of deaths.
✓ **Drugs are responsible for a large number of deaths.**
✗ I'm also responsible to decide on the best way to manufacture a product.
✓ **I'm also responsible for deciding on the best way to manufacture a product.**

responsible for (doing) sth: 'Who's responsible for roof repairs - you or the landlord?' 'The person responsible for leaking the story to the press has been forced to resign.'

result

✗ Nowadays we hear a lot about pollution and its results on our health.
✓ **Nowadays we hear a lot about pollution and its effects on our health.**

result = the situation or action that develops from a previous situation or action: 'The result of the crisis was that in 1649 the king was beheaded.' 'The anti-smoking campaign has produced excellent results.'
effect (on sb/sth) = a change in condition that is caused by something: 'The drug had no effect on him.' (= there was no change in his condition) 'Wine always has an effect on me - it makes me want to sing.'

retire

✗ After just two months he retired and went to work for a smaller company.
✓ **After just two months he resigned and went to work for a smaller company.**

retire = leave your job at the end of your working life, usually because you have reached a particular age: 'In the UK, men usually retire at the

age of 65 and women at 60.' 'If you retire early, you won't get your full pension.'
resign = leave your job because you do not like it, because you have found a better one, etc: 'If she doesn't get a salary increase, she's going to resign.'

return

✗ She returned back after half an hour.
✓ **She returned after half an hour.**
✗ When is he going to return back the money he owes you?
✓ **When is he going to return the money he owes you?**

Return contains the meaning 'back': 'He had to return to India to look after his mother.' 'He's left a note asking you to return the book he lent you.'

revenge 1

✗ One day these innocent victims must be revenged.
✓ **One day these innocent victims must be avenged.**
✗ The damage done to his honour would have to be revenged.
✓ **The damage done to his honour would have to be avenged.**

Revenge is usually used as a noun: 'Once they know who planted the bomb, they are likely to seek revenge.' 'She did it in revenge for all the lies he had told her.'
The verb is **avenge**: 'They swore to avenge this humiliating defeat.' 'He considers it his duty to avenge his brother's death.'

2

✗ I'm your twin brother and I'm here to revenge.
✓ **I'm your twin brother and I'm here to get my revenge.**
✗ He swore to revenge on the doctor.
✓ **He swore to take revenge on the doctor.**

get/take (your) revenge (on sb): 'He decided that the easiest way to get his revenge was to disinherit her.' 'She has vowed to take revenge on each and every one of them.'

reward

✗ Two of the German films were given rewards.
✓ **Two of the German films were given awards.**
See AWARD

richness

✗ They go to Hollywood in search of richness and fame.
✓ **They go to Hollywood in search of wealth and fame.**

If someone has a large amount of money, property etc, they are very **wealthy** or have considerable **wealth** (NOT **richness**): 'The country's wealth is in the hands of a small minority.'

right

✗ Every child has a right of free education.
✓ **Every child has a right to free education.**
✗ Until recently, women did not have the right of voting.
✓ **Until recently, women did not have the right to vote.**

right to (do) sth (NOT **of**): 'The law gives you the right to remain silent.' 'Each partner has a right to a company car.'

ring

✗ I rang to the college to explain my absence.
✓ **I rang the college to explain my absence.**
See PHONE 1

rise

✗ Many firms try to survive by rising productivity.
✓ **Many firms try to survive by raising productivity.**
See RAISE 3

risk
   ✗ Not one of us would risk to go out on our own.
   ✓ **Not one of us would risk going out on our own.**

   risk doing sth (NOT **to do**): 'I couldn't risk taking a photograph - there were too many soldiers around.'

rob
   ✗ The wicked old man robbed all my money.
   ✓ **The wicked old man stole all my money.**
   ✗ They robbed $6000 from the office safe.
   ✓ **They stole $6000 from the office safe.**
   ✗ While he was asleep, she robbed him his watch.
   ✓ **While he was asleep, she stole his watch.**

   steal sth: 'Someone has stolen her car.' 'My watch has been stolen.' 'The girl has obviously stolen his heart.'
   rob sb (of sth): 'The two youths had tried to rob him, but he managed to fight them off.' 'The old couple were robbed of their life's savings.'

roof
   ✗ In the bedroom, the roof looked very damp.
   ✓ **In the bedroom, the ceiling looked very damp.**
   ✗ The bedroom roof was one huge mirror.
   ✓ **The bedroom ceiling was one huge mirror.**

   roof = the covering on top of a building that protects it from the weather: 'If the rain is coming in, there must be a hole in the roof.' 'All the rooves were covered in snow.'
   ceiling = the part of a room that is above your head: 'When he stands on tip-toe, he can almost touch the ceiling.'

row
   ✗ There was already a long row of passengers waiting to be checked in.
   ✓ **There was already a long queue of passengers waiting to be checked in.**

   row = a line of people or things: 'Along one side of the river there was a row of cottages.' 'When our coach arrived at the hotel, the staff were standing in a row waiting to greet us.' 'At school I always used to sit in the front row.'
   queue = (British English) a line of people standing one behind the other, waiting for a bus, to buy a ticket, etc: 'I never go to the bank at lunchtime because of the long queues.'

row

queue

rude
   ✗ The shop assistant was very rude with me.
   ✓ **The shop assistant was very rude to me.**
   rude to sb (NOT **with**): 'Why is he so rude to people?'

run
   ✗ The car was running too fast for me to see the number plate.
   ✓ **The car was moving too fast for me to see the number plate.**
   Vehicles **travel**, **move** or **go** at a certain speed in a certain direction (NOT **run**): 'We're travelling at just under 70 miles an hour.' 'How fast was the train going when the accident occurred?'

's/s'   **1**

✗ The shopkeeper said the fault was the manufacturers responsibility.
✓ **The shopkeeper said the fault was the manufacturer's responsibility.**

When talking about something which is possessed by or connected with someone, use **'s/s'**: 'Tim's new car', 'one of Sandra's friends', 'her parents' bedroom', 'our children's education'.

       2

✗ The children were playing marbles on the kitchen's floor.
✓ **The children were playing marbles on the floor of the kitchen.**
✓ **The children were playing marbles on the kitchen floor.**
✗ Some of the tree's leaves had fallen on top of the car.
✓ **Some of the leaves (of the tree) had fallen on top of the car.**

The possessive **'s/s'** is used mainly with nouns that refer to people and animals. Compare: 'All her father's tools were missing.' (NOT 'tools of her father') 'The handles of the tools were all made of wood' (NOT tools' handles')
Note also that some nouns can be used like adjectives (WITHOUT **'s/s'**): 'the *kitchen* floor', 'a *garden* shed', 'a *pencil* sharpener'.

       3

✗ These vitamin pills are always available at the chemist.
✓ **These vitamin pills are always available at the chemist's.**

The word for the shop ends in **'s**: 'You can buy them at the greengrocer's in the high street.' 'I'll stop off at the butcher's on the way home.'

sack

✗ When I took the two oranges out of the sack, I discovered that one of them was bad.
✓ **When I took the two oranges out of the bag, I discovered that one of them was bad.**

sack = a very large strong bag: 'He's hurt his back trying to lift a sack of potatoes.'
bag = a container made of cloth, paper, leather etc: 'Somewhere in this shopping bag there's a bag of sweets.'

safety

✗ In Japan even the big cities are very safety.
✓ **In Japan even the big cities are very safe.**
✗ She doesn't feel safety when she is on her own.
✓ **She doesn't feel safe when she is on her own.**
✗ Promise that you will drive safety.
✓ **Promise that you will drive safely.**

Safety is a noun (NOT an adjective/adverb): 'The boy has been missing for six days, and there are fears for his safety.' 'The firefighters rescued the children and carried them to safety.'

sake
   ✗ I came here for my children sake.
   ✓ **I came here for my children's sake.**

> **for ... -'s/-s' sake**: 'For Wendy's sake, we've postponed the wedding until the first week in April. She'll be back from Italy by then.'

salary
   ✗ The salary is 800 yen an hour.
   ✓ **The pay/wage is 800 yen an hour.**
   ✗ The basic salary is £60 per week.
   ✓ **The basic pay/wage is £60 per week.**

> A **salary** is the amount of money that someone earns for a year's work, usually paid once a month directly into their bank account: 'I'll pay you back at the end of the month when I get my salary.' 'She's on a salary of £23,000 a year.'
> If someone is paid once a week, they receive **wages**. In the past, **wages** were always paid in cash: 'He opened the envelope and counted his wages.' When you are thinking about rates or levels of payment (rather than actual coins and bank notes), use **wage**: 'She earns a pretty good wage.' 'They're demanding a 20 per cent wage increase.' 'They've raised the minimum wage from $4.25 an hour to $5.50.'
> **Pay** is a general word for the (amount of) money people get for the work they do: 'He's lost a month's pay.' 'They've been given a pay rise of £20 a week.'
> Note that in informal styles these words are often used with the same meaning.

sale 1
   ✗ This company prefers to employ girls to sale their products.
   ✓ **This company prefers to employ girls to sell their products.**

> **Sale** /seɪl/ is a noun: 'This new law makes the sale of pirated video tapes a criminal offence.' 'Are you sure the house is for sale?'
> The verb is **sell** /sel/: 'They were selling all the shoes half-price.'

    2
   ✗ I bought both pairs of shoes on a sale.
   ✓ **I bought both pairs of shoes in a sale.**

> You buy something **in a sale** (NOT **on**): 'I got the shoes half-price in a sale.'
> Compare: 'Shiseido moisturizing cream is on sale in most department stores, priced £4.99.'

salute
   ✗ A group of officials were at the airport to salute the visitors.
   ✓ **A group of officials were at the airport to welcome the visitors.**

> **salute** (of members of the armed forces) make a formal sign of respect, especially by raising the right arm: 'Always salute a superior officer.'
> **welcome** = meet someone when they arrive and show that you are pleased that they have come: 'The visitors were welcomed at reception and shown where to go.'

same 1
   ✗ Paris has the same level of pollution with Los Angeles.
   ✓ **Paris has the same level of pollution as Los Angeles.**
   ✗ The belt is made of the same material like the coat.
   ✓ **The belt is made of the same material as the coat.**
   ✗ There were thousands of girls in the same situation than me.
   ✓ **There were thousands of girls in the same situation as me.**

the **same ... as** (NOT **with/like/than**): 'She goes to the same school as my sister.' 'Women have the same abilities as men.'

2 ✗ The breakfast was same as usual.
  ✓ **The breakfast was the same as usual.**
  ✗ The milk cartons are same as in Japan.
  ✓ **The milk cartons are the same as in Japan.**
  the **same as** (WITH **the**): 'Her car is the same as mine.'

3 ✗ I'd like to visit Vietnam and Malaysia one day, as same as you.
  ✓ **I'd like to visit Vietnam and Malaysia one day, the same as you.**
  ✓ **I'd like to visit Vietnam and Malaysia one day, (just) like you.**
  ✗ She had a face as same as a beauty queen's.
  ✓ **She had a face (just) like a beauty queen's.**
  the **same as** or **(just) like** (NOT **as same as**): 'New York was not the same as I'd imagined. It was worse.'

satis-factory ✗ For many people, a part-time job can be very satisfactory.
  ✓ **For many people, a part-time job can be very satisfying.**
  satisfactory = good enough to be acceptable: 'Students are asked to leave the college if their work is not satisfactory.'
  satisfying = giving pleasure or contentment: 'There's something very satisfying about baking your own bread.'

satisfied 1 ✗ The salary they offered was more than satisfied.
  ✓ **The salary they offered was more than satisfactory.**
  ✗ Her examination results were not satisfied.
  ✓ **Her examination results were not satisfactory.**
  satisfied = (of a person) feeling pleased or content: 'Despite the team's convincing 3-0 victory, the manager wasn't satisfied.'

2 ✗ I was completely satisfied of the quality of her work.
  ✓ **I was completely satisfied with the quality of her work.**
  ✗ He seemed quite satisfied from my progress.
  ✓ **He seemed quite satisfied with my progress.**
  satisfied with sb/sth (NOT **of/from**): 'I wasn't at all satisfied with the quality of the workmanship.'

satisfying ✗ The service in the hotel was not at all satisfying.
  ✓ **The service in the hotel was not at all satisfactory.**
  See note at SATISFACTORY

save ✗ The police telephoned his parents to tell them that he was save.
  ✓ **The police telephoned his parents to tell them that he was safe.**
  Save /seɪv/ is a verb: 'This new drug is likely to save hundreds of lives.' 'Thanks to the local fire brigade, all three children were saved.'
  The adjective is **safe** /seɪf/: 'Since the break-in, I never feel safe in the house.' 'You should keep your passport somewhere safe.'

say 1 ✗ The policeman said me to go with him to the police station.
  ✓ **The policeman told me to go with him to the police station.**

   ✗ She said to me to ask you to phone her.
   ✓ **She told me to ask you to phone her.**

> **tell sb to do sth** (NOT **say**): 'I told them to wait for you outside.'

2   ✗ When he arrived, they said him that his friend had died.
   ✓ **When he arrived, they told him that his friend had died.**
   ✓ **When he arrived, they said that his friend had died.**

> **say that**: 'She said that she might be late.'
> **tell sb that**: 'She told me that she might be late.'

3   ✗ He was tired of people saying him what to do.
   ✓ **He was tired of people telling him what to do.**

> **say sth**: 'I forgot to say goodbye.'
> **tell sb sth**: 'Eventually he told me the truth.'

4   ✗ In our next class we're going to say about pollution.
   ✓ **In our next class we're going to talk about pollution.**
   ✗ The magazine also says about English football.
   ✓ **The magazine also talks about English football.**

> **talk about** a particular topic (NOT **say about**): 'He refuses to talk about politics.' 'She's always talking about her father's health.'

5   See JOKE, LIE

scarce   ✗ If you are interested in scarce birds, you should visit the bird garden.
   ✓ **If you are interested in rare birds, you should visit the bird garden.**
   ✗ Chocolate was very rare during the war.
   ✓ **Chocolate was very scarce during the war.**

> See note at RARE 1

scarcely   ✗ He sends them money but scarcely goes to see them.
   ✓ **He sends them money but rarely goes to see them.**

> When you are talking about frequency, use **rarely** (= almost never): 'Since she moved to Glasgow, we rarely see each other.'

scene 1   ✗ From the window, there was a beautiful scene of the lake.
   ✓ **From the window, there was a beautiful view of the lake.**

> **scene** = what you see when you are in a particular place, especially something that is unusual, shocking etc: 'Some of the scenes inside the concentration camp were too horrific to describe.' 'The President arrived by helicopter to witness a scene of total chaos.'
> **view** = the whole area that you can see from somewhere, especially when you can see a long way into the distance: 'Remember to book a room with a view of the sea.'

2   ✗ The driver stopped now and again so that we could enjoy the scene.
   ✓ **The driver stopped now and again so that we could enjoy the scenery.**

> **scenery** = the natural features of the countryside, especially when seen from a particular place: 'The Lake District is famous for its magnificent scenery.'

scenery   ✗ What a beautiful scenery!
   ✓ **What beautiful scenery!**
   ✗ You'll be very impressed by the beautiful sceneries.
   ✓ **You'll be very impressed by the beautiful scenery.**

> **Scenery** is an uncountable noun: 'Some of the scenery is quite spectacular.'
> See Language Note below.

Using uncountable nouns

• Uncountable nouns do NOT have a plural form:
Where can we put all the furniture? (NOT 'furnitures')

• Uncountable nouns are NOT used with **a/an** or words which have a singular or plural meaning (e.g. **another, these, many, two**):
She needs some information. (NOT 'an information')
Who'd like some more bread? (NOT 'another bread')

• To refer to a specific amount, use **piece of, bit of, slice of, cup of, etc**:
Sometimes it may be possible to use a countable noun instead. Compare:
They gave her two pieces of useful information.
For breakfast I had three pieces of toast and two cups of tea.

• After an uncountable noun, the verb is singular:
The traffic seems to get worse every day. (NOT 'seem')
New equipment is urgently needed. (NOT 'are')

• Remember that nouns can have both countable and uncountable meanings. Compare:
Are the lenses made of <u>glass</u> or plastic? (uncountable)
Would you like a <u>glass</u> or a cup? (countable)

The government spends a great deal on <u>education</u>. (uncountable)
want their daughter to have a good <u>education</u>. (countable)

See also THE 4

---

school 1   ✗ Her daughter wants to leave the school and get married.
   ✓ **Her daughter wants to leave school and get married.**
   ✗ He still isn't old enough to go to a school.
   ✓ **He still isn't old enough to go to school.**

> Use **the/a/my etc** only when you are talking about a particular school:
> 'She goes to a very good school.' 'Our two boys go to the same school.'
> When you refer to school as a type of place or activity, use **leave school, start school, go to school, etc** (WITHOUT the/a/my etc):
> 'Most children go to primary school at the age of five.'
> The same rule applies to **kindergarten, college, university, church, prison, jail** and (in British English but not American English) **hospital**.
> Compare: 'They deserve to be put in prison.' 'The new prison has a special security wing for dangerous criminals.'
> See also CINEMA

2 ✗ Most Norwegians speak English quite well because everybody has to learn it in school.
✓ **Most Norwegians speak English quite well because everybody has to learn it at school.**

> In British English the phrase is **at school** (NOT **in**): 'What did you do at school today?'
> Note that in American English both **in school** and **at school** are used.

3 See VISIT 3

scientific ✗ I'm studying for a scientific degree.
✓ **I'm studying for a science degree.**
✗ He's good at scientific subjects.
✓ **He's good at science subjects.**
✗ The Scientific Centre is next to the History Museum.
✓ **The Science Centre is next to the History Museum.**

> **Scientific** is mainly used to describe something that is done or produced by scientists: 'We still don't have a scientific explanation for these mysterious events.' 'Many scientific research projects are funded by the private sector.'
> When you mean 'used for, devoted to, based on or specializing in science', use **science** + noun: 'a new science laboratory', 'a science lesson', 'science fiction'.

scissors ✗ First you cut along the dotted line with a scissors
✓ **First you cut along the dotted line with some scissors.**

> **Scissors** is a plural noun: 'Do we have any sharp scissors?' 'I could do with a new pair of scissors.'

sea ✗ Every day Kino went out to the sea to look for the pearl.
✓ **Every day Kino went out to sea to look for the pearl.**

> go/head/swim/drift etc **out to sea** (WITHOUT **the**): 'Just ten minutes after getting on board, we were heading out to sea.'

search 1 ✗ Rescue teams are still searching survivors.
✓ **Rescue teams are still searching for survivors.**
✗ I searched my passport everywhere but couldn't find it.
✓ **I searched for my passport everywhere but couldn't find it.**

> **search** = (1) examine someone's clothing or pockets to discover whether they are carrying a gun, drugs, stolen goods etc: 'They searched him twice but didn't find anything.' (2) examine an area/house/cupboard etc carefully to try to find someone or something: 'I've searched the whole house from top to bottom.'
> **search for** = try to find someone or something, especially by looking everywhere very carefully: 'We spent the whole morning searching for the ring.' 'At this time of the year, thousands of school leavers are searching for jobs.'

2 ✗ I decided to search for another hotel further down the road.
✓ **I decided to look for another hotel further down the road.**

> Use **search for** (and **seek**) only when someone or something is very difficult to find: 'Investigators are still searching for clues as to the cause of the crash.'

Otherwise, use **look for**: 'I'll stay here with the bags while you go and look for a taxi.' 'If you're looking for some new shoes, you should try Clinkard's.'

seat

✗ Let's go and seat out in the garden.
✓ **Let's go and sit out in the garden.**

seat /siːt/ is a noun: 'You should book your seat two weeks in advance.'
sit /sɪt/ is a verb: 'My legs were aching but there was nowhere to sit.'

seaweed

✗ The first diver reappeared covered in seaweeds.
✓ **The first diver reappeared covered in seaweed.**

seaweed is an uncountable noun: 'Can you really eat seaweed?'

see 1

✗ He sat there all morning seeing the planes taking off.
✓ **He sat there all morning watching the planes taking off.**
✗ The teacher told us to see what he was doing.
✓ **The teacher told us to watch what he was doing.**

see = notice something with your eyes, especially without concentrating or paying attention: 'Did you see anyone go out?' 'Turn the light on if you can't see.'
watch = look at someone or something and pay careful attention, especially for a long time: 'She watched the man with interest as he made his way through the crowd.' 'After dinner we usually sit down and watch the news.'

2

✗ I'm sending you the magazine so you can see by yourself how beautiful the country is.
✓ **I'm sending you the magazine so you can see for yourself how beautiful the country is.**

see sth for yourself (NOT **by**) = check that something is really true, correct, as described etc by seeing it with your own eyes: 'If you think I'm exaggerating, come and see for yourself.'

seek 1

? I'm seeking someone to play squash with.
✓ **I'm looking for someone to play squash with.**

Seek is used mainly in formal styles: 'The aim of the hostel is to give help to those seeking friendship or simply shelter for the night.'
See also note at SEARCH 2

2

✗ He sat nearer the tree, seeking for protection.
✓ **He sat nearer the tree, seeking protection.**

seek sb/sth (WITHOUT **for**): 'Economics graduate, aged 25, seeks interesting part-time work in the West London area.'

seem 1

? Even the teacher seemed to be unable to answer the question.
✓ **Even the teacher seemed unable to answer the question.**
? She seemed to be sorry for causing so much trouble.
✓ **She seemed sorry for causing so much trouble.**

When **seem** is followed by an adjective, **to be** is usually avoided: 'After the guests had gone home, the room seemed empty.' 'It seems strange that she didn't say goodbye.'
Compare: 'There seems to be a problem with the carburettor.'

2
? 'Steel Magnolias' seemed to be a comedy at first.
✓ **'Steel Magnolias' seemed like a comedy at first.**
? This kind of diet seems to be a punishment.
✓ **This kind of diet seems like a punishment.**

> When you are making a comparison, use **seem like**: 'Suddenly she seemed like a complete stranger.' 'The last few days had seemed like a dream.'

seldom
See Language Note at NOT

selling 1
✗ They make all their money from the selling of vegetables.
✓ **They make all their money from the sale of vegetables.**

> To refer to the act of selling something, use **the sale of**: 'The money that comes from the sale of these drugs is used to buy weapons.'

2
✗ The first proposal would reduce the selling figures of the local shops.
✓ **The first proposal would reduce the sales figures of the local shops.**

> **sales** = the number of things that are sold by a company: 'They've recruited a top advertising agency to help boost sales.' 'Last month's sales figures are very pleasing.'

send 1
✗ Could you send me to the airport on Saturday?
✓ **Could you take me to the airport on Saturday?**
✗ The ministry's policy is for ambulances to send patients to designated hospitals within their zones.
✓ **The ministry's policy is for ambulances to take patients to designated hospitals within their zones.**
See Language Note at TAKE

2
✗ I will send to you a cheque for the full amount.
✓ **I will send you a cheque for the full amount.**

> **send sb sth** (WITHOUT **to**): 'Don't forget to send me a postcard.'

sensibility
✗ I felt terribly annoyed by his lack of sensibility.
✓ **I felt terribly annoyed by his lack of sensitivity.**

> To refer to the ability to understand other people's feelings and problems, use **sensitivity**: 'To teach young children, you need lots of sensitivity and imagination.'

sensible
✗ Children are very sensible; they all need love and attention.
✓ **Children are very sensitive; they all need love and attention.**

> Use **sensible** to describe someone who makes good decisions based on reason, and never behaves in a stupid or dangerous way: 'I'm glad to see that she was sensible enough to bring some warm clothes.' 'Be sensible - you can't wear high heels to a garden party.'
> Use **sensitive** to describe someone who is easily upset or offended: 'He's very sensitive about his weight, so try not to mention it.' 'Don't be so sensitive - he was only joking.'

separate
? Americans can be separated into a number of ethnic groups.
✓ **Americans can be divided into a number of ethnic groups.**

? England was separated into 650 constituencies.

✓ **England was divided into 650 constituencies.**

> **separate** = place or keep (people or things) apart from one another: 'Break an egg into a bowl and separate the white from the yolk.'
> **divide** = cause something to consist of (or be seen as) a number of parts, groups, sections etc: 'The manufacturing process is divided into three stages.'

several

✗ The phrase 'the role of women' appeared just several years ago.

✓ **The phrase 'the role of women' appeared just a few years ago.**

✗ Try to forget your work for several hours and relax.

✓ **Try to forget your work for a few hours and relax.**

> **Several** means 'some but not many': 'Chicken will keep for several days in a refrigerator.'
> When you are talking about a very small number, use **a few**: 'He was here just a few minutes ago so he can't be far away.'

severe 1

? My parents weren't at all severe with me. In fact, I was allowed to do what I liked.

✓ **My parents weren't at all strict with me. In fact, I was allowed to do what I liked.**

> **severe** = not kind or friendly; showing no humour or sympathy: 'Mr Cameron's angry voice and severe expression used to frighten the children.'
> **strict** = demanding that rules or laws are always obeyed: 'Teachers have to be strict or the children take advantage of them.' 'The company is very strict about employees getting to work on time.'

2

✗ There are severe rules as to what you can wear to school.

✓ **There are strict rules as to what you can wear to school.**

> When **severe** refers to punishment, criticism, damage etc, it means 'harsh': 'Driving while drunk could endanger other people's lives, so penalties are severe.' 'This non-intervention policy has attracted severe criticism.'
> To describe a rule or law that must always be obeyed, use **strict**: 'The deer and other animals in the park are protected by strict laws.'

shade

✗ I thought I saw someone's shade go past the window.

✓ **I thought I saw someone's shadow go past the window.**

See note at SHADOW

shadow

✗ I sat down in the shadow of a huge eucalyptus tree.

✓ **I sat down in the shade of a huge eucalyptus tree.**

> **shade** = sheltered from the sun: 'It's too hot here. Let's go and find some shade.' 'The branches provided plenty of shade.'
> **shadow** = a dark shape that you see on a wall or surface when a light shines behind someone or something: 'The setting sun cast long shadows down the beach.'

shall 1

✗ The next meeting shall take place in Vienna.

✓ **The next meeting will take place in Vienna.**

> For future reference, use **will** with the second and third person: 'I'm confident you will not be disappointed.' 'If we don't hurry, the match will

have started.' Use **will/shall** with the first person (**I/we**): 'This time next week I will/shall be in Florence.' 'I'm sure we will/shall be seeing each other again.'

2   See Language Note at WILL

shame
- ✗ When I speak English I sometimes feel shame.
- ✓ **When I speak English I sometimes feel embarrassed.**
- ✗ The Chinese feel shame when they see people kissing in public.
- ✓ **The Chinese feel embarrassed when they see people kissing in public.**

See ASHAMED

she, s/he   See Language Note at HE

sheep
- ✗ A lot of cows and sheeps died because of the polluted water.
- ✓ **A lot of cows and sheep died because of the polluted water.**

The plural form of **sheep** is the same as the singular form: 'one sheep', 'two sheep'.

shoot 1
- ✗ The day after his 35th birthday, he shot 22 innocent people to death.
- ✓ **The day after his 35th birthday, he shot dead 22 innocent people.**
- ✗ The prisoners were either hanged or shot to death.
- ✓ **The prisoners were either hanged or shot.**

beat/hack/stab sb to death BUT **shoot sb dead** or **shoot and kill sb** (NOT **shoot sb to death**): 'Hector Petersen was shot dead by South African police in June 1976.'
Note that **shoot** by itself can mean 'shoot and kill': 'After shooting his victims, he buried the bodies in a nearby field.'

2
- ✗ Someone in the crowd ran up and shot a gun to the president.
- ✓ **Someone in the crowd ran up and fired a gun at the president.**

fire a gun (at sb), NOT **shoot a gun**: 'As part of the celebration they drove through the streets firing guns in the air.'
Note the alternative: 'Someone in the crowd ran up and fired at the president.'

shopping
- ✗ In the afternoon we went for shopping.
- ✓ **In the afternoon we went shopping.**
- ✗ I go to shopping twice a week.
- ✓ **I go shopping twice a week.**

go shopping (WITHOUT **to/for**): 'Some people fly to London just to go shopping.'
Compare: 'We'd thought we'd go to the shops this afternoon.'

shortly
- ✗ She spoke very shortly about how they had lived during the war.
- ✓ **She spoke very briefly about how they had lived during the war.**

shortly = (1) impatiently; not politely: 'He answered rather shortly that he was NOT the slightest bit interested.' (2) very soon: 'The accident happened shortly after they moved into their new house.'

briefly = for a short time: 'We talked briefly about the financial side of the agreement and then moved on to other matters.'

should **1**   ✗   I have friends who should love to stay at home, but they have to go to work.
   ✓   **I have friends who would love to stay at home, but they have to go to work.**

When talking about an imaginary situation, use **should/would** in the main clause after a first person subject: 'I should/would accept the job if I were you.'
After a second or third person subject, use **would** in the main clause (NOT **should**): 'He would accept the job if the salary were better.'

2   See BETTER 2

shout   ✗   She made me so annoyed I felt like shouting to her.
   ✓   **She made me so annoyed I felt like shouting at her.**

When you speak to someone in a loud voice because you are angry, you **shout at** them: 'I can't stand it when the children start fighting and shouting at each other.'

side **1**   ✗   On the other side, I can understand why she feels disappointed.
   ✓   **On the other hand, I can understand why she feels disappointed.**

on the one hand ... on the other hand (NOT **side**): 'On the other hand, the airline has an excellent safety record.'

2   ✗   It shows us what is happening in the other side of the world.
   ✓   **It shows us what is happening on the other side of the world.**

on the other side of sth (NOT **in**): 'The bank is on the other side of the road.' 'What's on the other side?'

*sightsee   ✗   You will be able to sightsee the volcanoes.
   ✓   **You will be able to see/visit the volcanoes.**
   ✗   I enjoy sightseeing new places when I'm abroad.
   ✓   **I enjoy seeing/visiting new places when I'm abroad.**

The verb **sightsee** does not exist.

sight-seeing **1**   ✗   After lunch we went for sightseeing.
   ✓   **After lunch we went sightseeing.**
   ✗   They wanted me to take them for sightseeing.
   ✓   **They wanted me to take them sightseeing.**

go sightseeing, take sb sightseeing, etc (WITHOUT **for**): 'Today we're just relaxing by the pool and tomorrow we're going sightseeing.'

2   ✗   We're going to do a sightseeing tomorrow.
   ✓   **We're going (to do some) sightseeing tomorrow.**

Sightseeing is an uncountable noun: 'Some people aren't interested in sightseeing.'

3   ✗   We visited all the famous sightseeing places.
   ✓   **We saw all the famous sights.**

✗ Nagasaki is famous for its sightseeing spots.
✓ **Nagasaki is famous for its tourist attractions.**

To refer to places that tourists like to visit, use **sights** (plural) or **tourist attraction/spot** (NOT **sightseeing place/spot**): 'I've always wanted to see the sights of London.'

signature   ✗ The signature of the new protocol took place in Rio de Janeiro.
✓ **The signing of the new protocol took place in Rio de Janeiro.**

signature = your name, written in the way that you usually write it on a cheque, business letter etc: 'These letters need your signature, Mr Ross.' 'You can tell by the signature if the painting is genuine.'
To refer to the event at which two or more people sign a legal or formal agreement, use **signing**: 'The signing of the peace agreement is scheduled to take place in Zurich at the end of the month.'

silent   ? After a hard day's work, I like to be silent.
✓ **After a hard day's work, I like to be quiet.**

silent = without any sound at all: 'Apart from the regular ticking of the clock, the room was completely silent.'
quiet = without unwanted noise or activity; peaceful: 'After a few quiet days in the countryside, we felt ready to face London again.'

since   1   ✗ I am studying law since 1992.
✓ **I have been studying law since 1992.**
✗ Since that journey, I never sailed again.
✓ **Since that journey, I have never sailed again.**

When you talk about an action or situation which began in the past and continues into the present, use a present perfect tense: 'I've been waiting here since 9 o'clock.'
In informal American English, the past tense is also used for this purpose.
See also FOR 4

2   ✗ I have been living in London since four weeks now.
✓ **I have been living in London for four weeks now.**
✗ I've been working in a bank since two years ago.
✓ **I've been working in a bank for (the last) two years.**

since + beginning of period: 'since 3 p.m.'
for + length of period: 'for two and a half hours'
Compare: 'I have been living in London for almost two years, since October 1994.'

3   ✗ Since the last few years, unemployment has been increasing.
✓ **Over/during the last few years, unemployment has been increasing.**

since + beginning of period: 'I've been living in Paris since July.'
over/during + the period of time within which something happens or develops: 'Over the last eighteen months there have been three tax increases.'

4   ✗ I stayed at your hotel for three nights, since 23rd November to 26th November.
✓ **I stayed at your hotel for three nights, from 23rd November to 26th November.**

from ... to ... : 'from Monday to Wednesday', 'from 7 a.m. to 3 p.m.', 'from 1947 to 1966'

5 ✗ Bring Eva with you. It's ages since I haven't seen her.
✓ **Bring Eva with you. It's ages since I (last) saw her.**
✗ It's a long time since I haven't seen you last.
✓ **It's a long time since I saw you last.**

it's ages/a long time /two weeks (etc) since + past tense (NOT present perfect; WITHOUT **not**): 'It's almost a year since I arrived.' 'It must be ages since we last had a meal together.'

6 See SO 1

sincerely See YOURS 1

sink ✗ I knew that if I fell into the sea, I would sink.
✓ **I knew that if I fell into the sea, I would drown.**

Sink is used in connection with ships, boats and objects which go down and disappear beneath the surface of water: 'The ship had been holed in the collision and was beginning to sink.'
Drown is used in connection with someone who dies because water stops them from breathing: 'One of the boys had fallen into the river and drowned.'

sit See ARMCHAIR

size **1** ✗ I'm afraid that the pullover you sent me has the wrong size.
✓ **I'm afraid that the pullover you sent me is the wrong size.**

be a certain **size** (NOT **have**): 'If the boots are size 43, they should fit me.'

2 ✗ As far as I remember, you both have the same size.
✓ **As far as I remember, you both take the same size.**
✓ **As far as I remember, you are both the same size.**

be/take a certain **size** (NOT **have**): 'What size are you?' 'Before the baby was born, I used to take a size 12.'

skilful ✗ 'You're lucky to have such skilful children,' she said.
✓ **'You're lucky to have such talented children,' she said.**

skilful = having or showing skill (gained from instruction and practice): 'Although he lacked Tyson's knock-out punch, he was the more skilful of the two boxers.'
talented = having or showing a natural ability to do something well: 'This talented young musician gave his first public performance at the age of five.'

sleep **1** ✗ I slept at ten o'clock last night.
✓ **I went to bed at ten o'clock last night.**

sleep = be asleep: 'Nurse Burnley works all night and sleeps all day.'
go to bed = get into bed at the end of the day: 'After dinner I had a hot bath and then went to bed.'

2 ✗ I started sleeping and didn't wake up till the next morning.
✓ **I fell asleep and didn't wake up till the next morning.**

✗ After showing the conductor my ticket, I started sleeping again.
✓ **After showing the conductor my ticket, I went back to sleep.**

go to sleep or **fall asleep** = enter a state of unconsciousness, especially so that your mind and body can rest: 'As soon as I started to read her a story, she went to sleep.'
go back to sleep or **fall asleep again** = go to sleep again: 'The alarm clock rang at 7.45 but I just turned over and went back to sleep.'

smell 1

✗ You can feel the smell of the fish a mile away.
✓ **You can smell the fish a mile away.**
✗ I could feel the smell of his cigar all over the house.
✓ **I could smell his cigar all over the house.**

smell sth (NOT **feel the smell of**): 'I can smell something burning.'
Compare: 'The whole house smelled of his cigar.'

2

See note at FEEL 2

smile

✗ She smiled to me as if she knew me.
✓ **She smiled at me as if she knew me.**

smile at sb (NOT **to**): 'For many parents the biggest thrill is when their baby first smiles at them.'

smoke

✗ People eventually get ill from inhaling the smokes.
✓ **People eventually get ill from inhaling the smoke.**

Smoke is an uncountable noun: 'The room was full of smoke.'

snack

✗ She usually has lunch at a snack in Barceloneta Square.
✓ **She usually has lunch at a snack bar in Barceloneta Square.**

snack = a light meal or something that you eat between meals: 'Instead of going out to lunch, I usually have a quick snack in my office.'
snack bar = a café or similar place where you can buy a light meal: 'The snack bar gets very busy at lunchtime.'

so 1

✗ Since it's his birthday on Monday, so he's having a party.
✓ **Since it's his birthday on Monday, he's having a party.**
✓ **It's his birthday on Monday, so he's having a party.**
✗ If you're a naughty boy, so the big crocodile will come and eat you.
✓ **If you're a naughty boy, the big crocodile will come and eat you.**

If the first clause begins with **if, since, as** or **because,** do NOT begin the second clause with **so** (or **that's why**). See also BUT

2

✗ During the summer all the hotels are so busy.
✓ **During the summer all the hotels are very busy.**

Use **so** + adjective (1) to mean 'to such a high degree or great extent': 'I was so tired that I fell asleep on the train.' 'I didn't expect the hotels to be so busy.'
(2) to express strong personal emotion: 'It was very kind of you to help me. I'm so grateful.'
Otherwise, use **very/extremely** + adjective: 'She was very tired and found it difficult to stay awake.'

3   ✗ My English is so poor so my wife has to translate everything.
         ✓ **My English is so poor that my wife has to translate everything.**

> **so** + adjective/adverb + **that** clause: 'She was so clever that all the universities wanted her.' 'The pianist played so badly that the audience walked out.'
> Compare: 'My English is very poor so my wife has to translate everything.'

4   ✗ We were not prepared for so cold weather.
         ✓ **We were not prepared for such cold weather.**
         ✗ I was annoyed with myself for being so fool.
         ✓ **I was annoyed with myself for being such a fool.**

> A phrase that ends with a noun ('weather', 'fool') usually begins with **such** (NOT **so**): 'We hadn't expected such a warm welcome.' 'You're lucky to have such delightful children.'
> Compare: 'Why is it always so cold in here?' 'The food was so bad that nobody could eat it.'

5   See THAT 4

so that ✗ He hadn't taken any warm clothes with him so that he felt cold.
             ✓ **He hadn't taken any warm clothes with him so he felt cold.**

> **So that** is used to express the purpose of an action: 'We took our umbrellas so that we wouldn't get wet.'
> **So** is used to express the result of an action: 'I'd forgotten to take my umbrella so I got wet.'

so-called ✗ Most of these drugs come from the so-called Golden Triangle.
               ✓ **Most of these drugs come from what is called the Golden Triangle.**
               ✗ During the so-called denitrification process, bacteria convert fixed nitrogen into molecular nitrogen.
               ✓ **During what is known as the denitrification process, bacteria convert fixed nitrogen into molecular nitrogen.**

> Use **so-called** when you want to suggest that the name that has been given to something is incorrect or not suitable: 'I went to see the playwright's so-called masterpiece and was very disappointed by it.'
> To introduce the name by which something is generally known, use **be known as, be referred to as** or **be called**: 'The distance that light travels in a year is called a light year.' 'Zaire was formerly known as the Congo.'

social **1** ✗ The next election was won by the Social Party.
                   ✓ **The next election was won by the Socialist Party.**

> **social** = connected with (life in a) society: 'Government attempts to tackle two of today's most serious social problems - crime and unemployment - have had no effect.'
> **socialist** = connected with socialism (the political system that favours equality of opportunity and public as opposed to private ownership): 'Why is it that so many of these so-called socialists send their children to fee-paying schools?'

         2 ✗ Our new neighbours are not very social.
                ✓ **Our new neighbours are not very sociable.**

A person who enjoys meeting and being with other people is **sociable**: 'You'll like John - he's very sociable and easy to get on with.'

society   ✗   I was asked to give a talk about women and their role in the society.
    ✓   **I was asked to give a talk about women and their role in society.**

> When it means 'the general system which helps people to live together in an organized way', **society** is uncountable and is used without **the**: 'People who drink and drive are a danger to society.'
> Compare: 'Britain is a multi-racial society.'

solution   ✗   Let us hope that there will be a peaceful solution of these problems.
    ✓   **Let us hope that there will be a peaceful solution to these problems.**

> **solution to** a problem or difficult situation (NOT **of**): 'Divorce is not necessarily the best solution to an unhappy marriage, especially when there are children involved.'

some   **1**   ✗   The refugees don't have some rights at all.
    ✓   **The refugees don't have any rights at all.**

> See Language Note at NOT

    2   ?   Do you have some questions?
    ✓   **Do you have any questions?**

> Use **some, something etc** in offers, requests, and questions that expect or hope for a 'yes' answer: 'Who'd like something to eat?' 'Could you give me some help, please?' 'Aren't there some letters to be posted?'
> In other questions, use **any, anything etc**: 'Did you get any letters today?' 'Have you seen any good films recently?'

    3   ✗   I'm not sure if she has some brothers or sisters.
    ✓   **I'm not sure if she has any brothers or sisters.**

> When talking about something unknown or uncertain (e.g. after **if/whether**), use **any, anyone etc**: 'I doubt whether anyone will object.' 'I'm not sure if I've got any envelopes that size.'

    4   ✗   On Tuesday we're going to London for some days.
    ✓   **On Tuesday we're going to London for a few days.**

> To refer to a very small number or amount, use **a few** (+ plural count noun) or **a little** (+ uncountable noun). Compare:
> Tina: 'I need some washing powder.'
> Alex: 'How much?'
> Tina: 'Oh, just a little.'

somebody/   ✗   She hadn't seen somebody for over a week.
someone 1   ✓   **She hadn't seen anybody for over a week.**
    ✗   Somehow he had to get on the train without someone seeing him.
    ✓   **Somehow he had to get on the train without anyone seeing him.**

> See Language Note at NOT

2 ✗ I ran over to the car to see if someone was injured.
✓ **I ran over to the car to see if anyone was injured.**
See note at SOME 3

something 1 ✗ At first we couldn't see something suspicious.
✓ **At first we couldn't see anything suspicious.**
✗ By six o'clock I am too tired to do something else.
✓ **By six o'clock I am too tired to do anything else.**
See Language Note at NOT

2 ✗ Does your country export something?
✓ **Does your country export anything?**
See note at SOME 2

3 ✗ If the drawer is stuck, you'll have to use a knife or something like that.
✓ **If the drawer is stuck, you'll have to use a knife or something.**
✗ They never complain because they are afraid or something like that.
✓ **They never complain because they are afraid or something.**
✗ We could go shopping or something else.
✓ **We could go shopping or something.**
In informal styles use **... or something** (NOT **... or something else/like that**): 'Why don't you buy her a book or something?' 'We could stay here and play cards or something.'

some- ✗ The poor bus service makes it difficult to get somewhere.
where 1 ✓ **The poor bus service makes it difficult to get anywhere.**
See Language Note at NOT

2 ✗ Let's go to somewhere different for a change.
✓ **Let's go somewhere different for a change.**
The prepositions **in, at,** and **to** are usually omitted in front of **somewhere/anywhere.** 'He wants you to give him a lift somewhere.' Compare: 'He wants you to give him a lift to the station.'

soon 1 ✗ As it soon will be Christmas I'm anxious to get the television repaired as quickly as possible.
✓ **As it will soon be Christmas, I'm anxious to get the television repaired as quickly as possible.**
See Language Note at ALWAYS

2 ✗ I'll phone you as soon as I'll arrive.
✓ **I'll phone you as soon as I arrive.**
See Language Note at WILL

sorry ✗ I'm sorry for my terrible handwriting.
✓ **I'm sorry about my terrible handwriting.**
✗ Unfortunately I can't come to your wedding because my exams begin on that day. I'm sorry for that.
✓ **Unfortunately I can't come to your wedding because my exams begin on that day. I'm sorry about that.**

be **sorry about** + noun/pronoun: 'I'm terribly sorry about your camera - I didn't mean to drop it.' 'I'm so sorry about all the mistakes.'
be **sorry about/for** + doing sth: 'I'm sorry about/for taking so long to answer your letter.'

sort of 1　✗　These sort of activities help students to become independent.
✓　**These sorts of activities help students to become independent.**
See note at KIND OF 1

2　✗　I hate people who ask that sort of questions.
✓　**I hate people who ask that sort of question.**
✓　**I hate people who ask those sorts of question/s.**
See note at KIND OF 2

sound 1　✗　The engine was old and was making a lot of sound.
✓　**The engine was old and was making a lot of noise.**
See note at NOISE 1

2　✗　Her voice sounded more seriously than before.
✓　**Her voice sounded more serious than before.**
See note at FEEL 4

South　　See NORTH

space　✗　There are hundreds of millions of stars in the space.
✓　**There are hundreds of millions of stars in space.**
When you mean 'everything beyond the Earth's atmosphere', use **space** (WITHOUT **the**): 'He was the first German astronaut to travel in space.'

speak 1　✗　We hadn't seen each other for a year and so we spent the whole night speaking.
✓　**We hadn't seen each other for a year and so we spent the whole night talking.**
?　We spoke about where we would go for our next holiday.
✓　**We talked about where we would go for our next holiday.**
When just one person does all or most of the talking, either **speak** or **talk** may be used: 'He spoke/talked about his years in the army.'
When two or more people have a conversation, the usual word is **talk** (NOT **speak**): 'We must have been talking for hours.' 'If someone brings me a problem, we just sit down and talk about it.'

2　✗　Neither of my parents speaks in English.
✓　**Neither of my parents speaks English.**
speak in (English) = use (English) on a particular occasion: 'My grandparents won't understand a thing if the priest speaks in French.'
speak (English) = know (English) and use it habitually: 'Do you speak German?' 'We'll have to find someone who speaks English.'

3　✗　We were shown how to speak with customers and handle complaints.
✓　**We were shown how to speak to customers and handle complaints.**

In British English the usual phrase is **speak to** someone: 'If you need any more information, you should speak to Mrs Hall.'
Note that in American English both **speak to** and **speak with** are used.

specialize ✗ I intend to specialize myself in French literature.
✓ **I intend to specialize in French literature.**
See Language Note at MYSELF

specially 1 ✗ Ordering a meal can be very difficult, specially when there is no menu.
✓ **Ordering a meal can be very difficult, especially when there is no menu.**
✗ They should not drop bombs on innocent people, specially children.
✓ **They should not drop bombs on innocent people, especially children.**
✗ I also enjoy water sports and I am specially interested in sailing.
✓ **I also enjoy water sports and I am especially interested in sailing.**

Use **specially** when you mean that something is done or made for a particular purpose: 'We've come all the way from Frankfurt specially to see you.' 'The stamps were specially designed to commemorate the fiftieth anniversary of the United Nations.'
For all other meanings, use **especially**: 'Paris is always full of tourists, especially during the summer months.' 'Middle-aged men, especially those who are overweight, are susceptible to heart-attacks.'

2 ✗ To live in Britain you need a lot of money. Specially London is very expensive.
✓ **To live in Britain you need a lot of money. London especially is very expensive.**

To draw attention to the situation in which your statement is particularly true, use **especially**. See note at ESPECIALLY 2

spectator ✗ The spectators laughed at every joke.
✓ **The audience laughed at every joke.**

spectator = a person who goes to watch a sporting event such as a football match: 'The new stadium can hold up to 60,000 spectators.' 'The police should stop spectators from running onto the pitch.'
audience = see note at AUDIENCE

speech 1 ✗ I was invited to make a speech on the radio.
✓ **I was invited to give a talk on the radio.**

A **speech** is usually made by a politician or by an important person at a meeting, social occasion, or dinner: 'The Prime Minister's speech included a fierce attack on the unions.'
A **talk** is usually informative and is often given by a lecturer: 'The title of Dr Chase's talk is "Solar Energy and the Nuclear Debate".'

2 ✗ I was asked to do a speech welcoming the new students.
✓ **I was asked to give a speech welcoming the new students.**

give/make a speech (NOT **do**): 'After the meal the bride's father stood up and made a short speech.'

speed 1   ✗   I jumped in and swam towards the child at my fastest speed.
         ✓   **I jumped in and swam towards the child as fast as I could.**
         ✗   The world's population has increased at a very rapid speed.
         ✓   **The world's population has increased very rapidly.**

> Phases with **speed** are usually used in connection with vehicles and machines: 'At the time of the crash, the train was travelling at full speed.' 'These cars are capable of very high speeds.'

      2   ✗   These new trains can travel in very high speeds.
         ✓   **These new trains can travel at very high speeds.**
         ✗   The car in front of ours continued with the same speed.
         ✓   **The car in front of ours continued at the same speed.**

> **at** a particular **speed** (NOT **with/in**) 'If we continue at this speed, we'll be there in an hour.' 'According to the police report, the car had been travelling at a speed of 110 miles per hour.'

      3   ?   He always drives at a very fast speed.
         ✓   **He always drives at top speed.**

> **at great/high/top/full/breakneck speed**: 'He jumped into the car and drove off at great speed.'

spend 1   ✗   They don't have any money to spend for luxuries.
         ✓   **They don't have any money to spend on luxuries.**
         ✗   He spends everything he earns for his children.
         ✓   **He spends everything he earns on his children.**

> **spend your time/money/$12/£5 etc + on sb/sth** (NOT **for**): 'I spend about half my salary on food.' 'You should spend more time on your homework.'

      2   ✗   Parents should spend more time to look after their children.
         ✓   **Parents should spend more time looking after their children.**
         ✗   I never spend more than an hour a day for studying.
         ✓   **I never spend more than an hour a day studying.**
         ✗   She spends most of her free time on reading.
         ✓   **She spends most of her free time reading.**

> **spend your time/five minutes/two days etc + doing sth**: 'She spends all her time working on her thesis.'

      3   See TIME 8, 9

spite 1   ✗   I believe that every criminal, in spite of the circumstances, should be severely punished.
         ✓   **I believe that every criminal, regardless of the circumstances, should be severely punished.**

> Use **in spite of** to introduce a fact that is in sharp contrast with another fact: 'In spite of all their money, they still aren't happy.'
> Use **regardless of** to emphasize that a particular fact does not change a course of action, even though it may be a difficulty: 'We're determined to have a holiday this year, regardless of how much it costs.'

      2   ✗   In spite of staying at home, I decided to continue my studies in the United States.
         ✓   **Instead of staying at home, I decided to continue my studies in the United States.**

> When the situation involves a choice between two actions or things, use **instead of** (NOT **in spite of**): 'Instead of building more roads, we should be investing in the railway.'

3   ✗ They refused to play in the rain in spite of the crowd protested.
     ✓ **They refused to play in the rain in spite of the crowd's protests.**
     See note at DESPITE 1

sport 1   ✗ Sports help us to keep fit.
     ✓ **Sport helps us to keep fit.**

> a **sport** (countable) = a particular type of sport: 'Cricket is a very popular sport in Yorkshire.'
> **sport** (uncountable) = sport in general: 'She writes articles on sport and travel.' 'I'm not very good at sport.'

2   ✗ I need some new sport shoes.
     ✓ **I need some new sports shoes.**
     ✗ She bought a bright red sport car.
     ✓ **She bought a bright red sports car.**

> Use **sports** in front of a noun (NOT **sport**): 'a sports centre', 'a sports club', 'sports equipment', 'sports injuries'.

3   ✗ He makes all types of sport.
     ✓ **He does all types of sport.**

> I **do sport** (NOT **make**): 'Do you do any sport at school?'

spread   ✗ Rumours spread out very quickly.
     ✓ **Rumours spread very quickly.**
     ✗ The computer mania is still spreading out.
     ✓ **The computer mania is still spreading.**

> When you mean 'grow, develop or become increasingly common' use **spread** (WITHOUT **out**): 'They couldn't stop the fire from spreading.' 'Dissatisfaction with the present government seems to be spreading.' Compare: 'The search party spread out across the field.' 'Her clothes were all spread out on the bed, ready to be packed.'

squeeze   ✗ The train was so full that I was frightened of getting squeezed.
     ✓ **The train was so full that I was frightened of getting squashed.**

> **squeeze** = (1) press something firmly, especially by closing your hand round it: 'She squeezed my arm and told me not to worry.'
> (2) get liquid, cream, paste etc from something by pressing it firmly: 'Squeeze the lemons and then pour the juice into a jug.'
> (3) force someone or something into a small space: 'Somehow we managed to squeeze everyone into the car.'
> **squash** (or **crush**) = press something, usually with great force, so that it becomes flat or broken: 'Mind you don't squash the tomatoes.'

staff   ✗ The assembly and packing department has 50 staffs.
     ✓ **The assembly and packing department has 50 staff.**
     ✓ **The assembly and packing department has a staff of 50.**

The noun **staff** refers to a whole group of people, (NOT a single person): '(The) staff at the Central Hospital have rejected the new pay offer.' 'Several senior members of staff have opted for early retirement.'

statistic

✗ This view is supported by statistic published in 1985.
✓ **This view is supported by statistics published in 1985.**

statistic (singular) refers to one piece of data: 'This terrible crime will soon become nothing more than a statistic in police records.' **statistics** (plural) refers to a set of data: 'Statistics show that the population has almost doubled in the last twenty years.'

stay

✗ He's invited us to stay a few days with him.
✓ **He's invited us to spend a few days with him.**

spend a period of time somewhere (NOT **stay**): 'We spent the afternoon at John's house.' 'Where are you going to spend Christmas?' Note the alternative: 'He's invited us to stay with him for a few days.'

steal **1**

✗ The bank in our town has been stolen twice this year.
✓ **The bank in our town has been robbed twice this year.**

rob a bank, post office etc (NOT **steal**): 'Apart from the two cashiers, nobody realized that the bank was being robbed.'

2

✗ If you look wealthy, you are likely to be stolen.
✓ **If you look wealthy, you are likely to be robbed.**

See note at ROB

3

✗ After ten years he discovered that his partner had been stealing him.
✓ **After ten years he discovered that his partner had been stealing from him.**

steal from sb (WITH **from**): 'She was found guilty of stealing from her previous employer.'

still **1**

✗ I enjoy this type of music still now.
✓ **I still enjoy this type of music.**
✗ The accident happened over ten years ago but still now I get upset when I think about it.
✓ **The accident happened over ten years ago but I still get upset when I think about it.**

still (NOT **still now**): 'My sister still believes in Santa Claus but I don't.'

2

✗ It is my first time abroad and so I feel still excited and confused.
✓ **It is my first time abroad and so I still feel excited and confused.**
✗ My country still is not very rich, but at least everyone has enough food to eat.
✓ **My country is still not very rich, but at least everyone has enough food to eat.**

See Language Note at ALWAYS

stimulant

✗ Political stability acts as a stimulant for foreign investment.
✓ **Political stability acts as a stimulus for foreign investment.**

A **stimulant** is a drug, medicine etc, which makes the mind or body more

active: 'The caffeine in coffee acts as a stimulant.'
When you are not talking about a drug or medicine, use **stimulus** (= something which causes activity, growth, or greater effort): 'The new textbook provided a good stimulus for both teachers and students.'

stimulus   See note at STIMULANT

stop 1 ✗ This policy is supposed to stop people to buy foreign cars.
✓ **This policy is supposed to stop people from buying foreign cars.**

stop sb/sth (from) doing sth (NOT **to do**), = prevent someone (from) doing something or something from happening: 'Her parents tried to stop her from going abroad.'

2 ✗ The child couldn't stop from talking.
✓ **The child couldn't stop talking.**

stop doing sth (WITHOUT **from**) = cease an activity: 'It's actually stopped raining at last.'
Compare: 'The rain stopped us from going out.'

3 ✗ I stopped to play the piano at the age of eight.
✓ **I stopped playing the piano at the age of eight.**
✗ He loved toys and couldn't stop to look at them.
✓ **He loved toys and couldn't stop looking at them.**

stop doing sth = cease or discontinue an activity: 'I stopped reading and turned out the light.'
stop to do sth = halt or pause (in order to do something): 'Although I was in a hurry, I stopped to talk to him.'

storey   ✗ They live on the second storey.
✓ **They live on the second floor.**

Storey is usually used to describe the structure of a building: 'These office blocks are usually three or four storeys high.' 'a multi-storey car park', 'a detached two-storey house'.
When you are talking about where someone lives/works/goes etc, use **floor**: 'My flat is on the seventh floor.' 'We took the lift up to the third floor.'

strange 1 ✗ The children were told not to talk to strange people.
✓ **The children were told not to talk to strangers.**

A **strange** person is someone who behaves in a way that other people find disturbing or difficult to understand: 'I find Barbara a bit strange. She won't look at you even when you speak to her.'
A **stranger** is someone you have never met before: 'We've told our children not to accept sweets from strangers.'

2 ? When I arrived in England, I felt strange.
✓ **When I arrived in England, everything seemed strange.**

When you are talking about how you feel when you first arrive in a new country, city or situation, it is more usual to say that the country seems strange rather than 'I feel strange': 'Things are bound to seem a bit strange for the first few days.'

3 ✗ LA seemed very strange for me at first.
✓ **LA seemed very strange to me at first.**

Something unfamiliar is **strange to** you (NOT **for**): 'These customs can seem very strange to non-Westerners.'

stranger ✗ There are a lot of strangers visiting England.
✓ **There are a lot of foreigners visiting England.**

stranger = a person you have never met before: 'Although he was a total stranger, he started asking me for money!'
foreigner = a person from another country: 'Foreigners need a visa to enter the country.'

strict See PUNISHMENT

strike ✗ The whole workforce is threatening to go on a strike.
✓ **The whole workforce is threatening to go on strike.**

go/be on strike (WITHOUT **a**): 'Transport workers have gone on strike for better pay and shorter hours.' 'The miners are still on strike.'
Note however: 'Some of the prisoners have gone on (a) hunger strike.'

strong See note at PUNISHMENT

strongly ✗ When the plane took off, she held my hand strongly.
✓ **When the plane took off, she held my hand tightly.**

Strongly is used with verbs such as **suggest, advise, recommend, agree/disagree, believe, feel etc** (NOT with verbs that refer to actions): 'I would strongly advise you to think again.'

student ✗ I'm a student of Goldsmith's College.
✓ **I'm a student at Goldsmith's College.**
See IN 5

study 1 ✗ Next July I'm going to the USA to continue my study.
✓ **Next July I'm going to the USA to continue my studies.**

To refer to the work that a student does at a college or university, use **studies**: 'After the war he resumed his studies at the University of Turin.'
Compare: 'They are conducting a study of sex education in local secondary schools.'

2 ✗ She's studying history in Oxford University.
✓ **She's studying history at Oxford University.**
See IN 5

stuff ✗ He'd left all his tennis stuffs at home.
✓ **He'd left all his tennis stuff at home.**

Stuff is an uncountable noun: 'He asked if he could bring his stuff over to my place.'

style ? I'd like to live abroad and have a different style of life.
✓ **I'd like to live abroad and have a different lifestyle.**
? I find this living style very attractive.
✓ **I find this lifestyle very attractive.**
See note at LIFE 2

**subcon-
scious**
  ✗ The driver of the car was taken to hospital subconscious.
  ✓ **The driver of the car was taken to hospital unconscious.**

> **subconscious** = (of a thought or desire) existing or occurring in the mind without the person being aware of it: 'His dream about crossing the ocean single-handed probably arose from a subconscious desire for fame.'
> **unconscious** = (of a person) in a sleep-like state, especially because you are ill or have been hit on the head: 'The cleaner found him lying unconscious on the bathroom floor.'

subject
  ✗ The subject of my thesis is about women in the popular press.
  ✓ **The subject of my thesis is women in the popular press.**

> **Subject** is not followed by **about**. Note the alternative: 'My thesis is about women in the popular press.'

succeed
  ✗ Not many of us succeed to achieve our ambitions.
  ✓ **Not many of us succeed in achieving our ambitions.**

> **succeed in doing sth** (NOT **to do sth**): 'Having finally succeeded in mounting the horse, I was determined to stay on it.'

such
  ✗ She was always a such intelligent woman.
  ✓ **She was always such an intelligent woman.**

> **Such** always comes at the beginning of a noun phrase: 'It's such a good film that I'd like to see it again.'

suddenly
  ✗ Late one evening, as I was getting into the bath, suddenly I heard a strange noise.
  ✓ **Late one evening, as I was getting into the bath, I suddenly heard a strange noise.**

> See Language Note at ALWAYS

suffer 1
  ✗ The woman was so unpleasant that none of us could suffer her.
  ✓ **The woman was so unpleasant that none of us could tolerate her.**

> See note at SUPPORT

2
  ✗ The other passenger suffered from serious leg injuries.
  ✓ **The other passenger suffered serious leg injuries.**
  ✗ Most of the carriers suffer hemophilia.
  ✓ **Most of the carriers suffer from hemophilia.**

> **suffer** an injury, pain, loss, defeat etc (WITHOUT **from**): 'She can walk again, but she still suffers a lot of pain.' 'The party suffered yet another humiliating defeat in the recent by-election.'
> **suffer from** a disease, poverty, starvation etc: 'A lot of the children we saw were suffering from malnutrition.' 'Aunt Linda suffers from arthritis.'

suggest 1
  ✗ I suggest you to take more exercise.
  ✓ **I suggest (that) you take more exercise.**

> **suggest (that) sb (should) do sth**: 'I suggest you try the chemist's in the high street.' 'The chairman suggested that the two sides should meet again the following day.'

2 ✗ She suggested to go to the zoo.
✓ **She suggested going to the zoo.**

suggest doing sth (NOT **to do**): 'He suggested meeting us for a drink after the concert.'

suit 1 ✗ Short hair suits to her.
✓ **Short hair suits her.**

If something looks good on someone, it **suits** them (WITHOUT **to**): 'Do you think this colour suits me?' 'That blouse doesn't suit you.'

2 ✗ Red wine doesn't suit fish.
✓ **Red wine doesn't go with fish.**

When you are talking about the effect of having two different things together, use **go with** (NOT **suit**): 'I like the wallpaper, but it doesn't go with the carpet.' 'This jacket will go really well with your grey trousers.'

suitable 1 ✗ I didn't feel suitable to a career in medicine.
✓ **I didn't feel suited to a career in medicine.**

suitable (for) = right or appropriate for a particular purpose: 'The film isn't really suitable for children.' 'We'd like to give her the job but her qualifications aren't suitable.'
suited to = having the qualifications, experience, personality etc that make you suitable for a particular job or situation: 'Her interest in poetry makes her better suited to a literature course.'

2 ✗ The food they gave us wasn't suitable to be eaten.
✓ **The food they gave us wasn't fit to eat.**

be fit to eat/drink/live in etc = (of the condition or quality of something) good enough for the stated purpose: 'The house hadn't been cleaned for months and wasn't fit to live in.'

*sunbath ✗ In the afternoon we had a sunbath on the beach.
✓ **In the afternoon we sunbathed on the beach.**

The noun **sunbath** does not exist. Use the verb **sunbathe** /'sʌnbeɪð/or **do some sunbathing/go sunbathing**: 'I found him back at the hotel, sunbathing by the pool.' 'The sky had clouded over so we couldn't do any sunbathing.'

superior ✗ The second hotel was far superior than the first one.
✓ **The second hotel was far superior to the first one.**
See note at INFERIOR

supply ✗ We shall supply you everything you need.
✓ **We shall supply you with everything you need.**

supply sb with something: 'The workers are supplied with masks and special protective clothing.'

support ✗ He couldn't support the way his father used to shout at him.
✓ **He couldn't tolerate the way his father used to shout at him.**
✗ Are you prepared to support the noise of the traffic?
✓ **Are you prepared to put up with the noise of the traffic?**

tolerate, put up with, stand sb/sth (NOT **support/suffer**) = be willing to accept someone or something, even though the person or situation is unpleasant: 'I'm surprised that she tolerates his behaviour.' 'It's not a bad job, as long as you can stand the long hours.'

suppose 1 ✗ All their products are suppose to be guaranteed for six months.

✓ **All their products are supposed to be guaranteed for six months.**

be supposed to be/do sth (WITH **-d**): 'How many pages are we supposed to write?' 'You're supposed to be there in five minutes.'

2 ✗ It's a very unusual coat and so I suppose you will not have any trouble finding it.

✓ **It's a very unusual coat and so I don't suppose you will have any trouble finding it.**

See note at THINK 6

surely 1 ✗ It was an absolutely terrible flight. The next time I go to Rio, I will surely go by train.

✓ **It was an absolutely terrible flight. The next time I go to Rio, I will definitely go by train.**

Surely is used to express a strong belief in the truth or likelihood of what you are saying, and often to encourage the listener to express agreement: 'Surely they should have arrived by now!' 'A twenty-dollar parking fine! Surely someone's made a mistake!' 'You don't need to wear a coat in this weather, surely?'
Definitely expresses a sense of complete certainty about something: 'She said she'd definitely be back by dinner time.' 'This is definitely the best film she's ever made.'

2 ✗ On the first day we'll just stay at the hotel and rest because the journey will be surely tiring.

✓ **On the first day we'll just stay at the hotel and rest because the journey is bound to be tiring.**

If you feel sure that something is going to happen, you say that it **is bound/sure to** happen: 'At the interview they're bound to ask you about your last job.' 'Once drivers get impatient, accidents are sure to happen.'

3 ✗ He said he felt worried because of all the recent air disasters. Surely I became worried too.

✓ **He said he felt worried because of all the recent air disasters. Naturally I became worried too.**

When you mean 'as anyone would expect', use **naturally** or **of course**: 'She's just lost her job and so naturally she's feeling a bit depressed.' 'Henry is still in France but he'll be back in time for the wedding of course.'

surprised 1 ? When we heard about the accident, we were all surprised and didn't know what to say.

✓ **When we heard about the accident, we were all shocked and didn't know what to say.**

When someone is surprised and upset because something unpleasant has happened, they are **shocked**: 'When reports came in that the child's body had been found, everyone was deeply shocked.'

2 ✗ Paola was very surprised for the low prices.
  ✓ **Paola was very surprised at the low prices.**
  ✗ I was pleasantly surprised about the variety of food in England.
  ✓ **I was pleasantly surprised by the variety of food in England.**

surprised at/by sth (NOT **about/for/of etc**): 'I was surprised at the difference in their ages - he was old enough to be her father.' 'I knew she would do well and wasn't at all surprised by her results.'

suspect ✗ Army intelligence suspected him as a secret agent.
  ✓ **Army intelligence suspected him of being a secret agent.**

suspect sb of (doing/being) sth (NOT **as**): 'The police suspect her of receiving stolen goods.' 'Their father is suspected of being connected with the local mafia.'

suspicious ✗ Before I actually started to use one, I was suspicious about the value of computers.
  ✓ **Before I actually started to use one, I was sceptical about the value of computers.**

suspicious = thinking that someone may be guilty of doing something wrong: 'I started to get suspicious when he refused to tell me where he had been.'
sceptical /'skeptikəl/ = tending not to believe what people say about something: 'Many doctors remain highly sceptical about the value of alternative medicine.'

sympathetic ✗ He's a selfish, greedy little man and not at all sympathetic.
  ✓ **He's a selfish, greedy little man and not at all likeable.**

sympathetic = feeling or showing sympathy: 'He expected people to be sympathetic because he was an orphan.'
likeable = easy to like: 'If Philip weren't so arrogant, he'd be quite likeable.'

take 1   ✗ When you come to dinner on Sunday, take your fiancée with you so I can meet her.
   ✓ **When you come to dinner on Sunday, bring your fiancée with you so I can meet her.**
   ✗ He asked if he could come to your party and take a friend with him.
   ✓ **He asked if he could come to your party and bring a friend with him.**
   See Language Note on next page

2   See BREAKFAST 3, MEAL 2

take care   See CARE

take notice of   See NOTICE 2

take part in   See PART 4, 5, 6

talk 1   ✗ I couldn't talk English in those days.
   ✓ **I couldn't speak English in those days.**
   speak English/French/Thai etc (NOT **talk**): 'Do you speak Italian?' 'I didn't know you could speak Greek.'

2   ✗ I'd like to talk you about a dream I had last night.
   ✓ **I'd like to tell you about a dream I had last night.**
   When there is something that you want someone to know, you **tell** them about it: 'She told me about her holiday plans.'
   When you have a conversation, you **talk** (to someone) about something: 'We talked about where we could go at the weekend.'

3   ✗ There's something I'd like to talk you about.
   ✓ **There's something I'd like to talk to you about.**
   talk to sb (**about sth**): 'The manager would like to talk to you when you have a moment.'

4   ✗ I didn't want to talk with him because I was in a hurry.
   ✓ **I didn't want to talk to him because I was in a hurry.**
   In British English the usual phrase is **talk to** someone: 'Who were you talking to just now?'
   Note that in American English both **talk to** and **talk with** are used.

tall   ✗ I prefer rooms with tall ceilings.
   ✓ **I prefer rooms with high ceilings.**
   See note at HIGH

BRING • TAKE • LEAD • SEND • FETCH • CARRY • COLLECT • PICK UP

bring	**Bring** means 'come with sb/sth' (NOT 'go'): 'Could you bring me a glass of water, please?' 'I'll see you tomorrow at the club, and remember to bring your tennis racket!'
take	**Take** means 'go with sb/sth' (NOT 'come'): 'You take the shopping indoors and I'll put the car away.' 'When I go on holiday, I like to take a good book with me.'
	You usually **take** someone home, to school or to a cinema/restaurant/ airport etc (NOT **bring/lead/send/carry**): 'Lucy took us to Stratford to see a play.' 'If you need a lift to the station, ask Peter to take you.'
lead	If you **lead** someone to a place, you guide them there by walking in front of them, holding them by the arm, etc: 'Some blind people like to be led across the road.' 'The children led me through the wood to their secret hiding place.'
send	If you **send** a person somewhere, you tell them to go there. You do not go with them: 'My company sends one of us to Singapore every six months.'
fetch	If you **fetch** something, you go to the place where it is and come back with it: 'We waited at reception while the porter fetched our luggage.'
carry	If you go somewhere with something in your hands, in your arms, on your back etc, you **carry** it: 'She carried her chair into the garden and sat in the sun.' 'In some countries women carry their babies on their backs.'
collect/fetch	If you **collect** or **fetch** someone (**from** somewhere), you go there and bring them back with you: 'I have to collect the children from school at 4 o'clock.'
pick up	If you **pick up** someone (**at** a place), you go to the place where they are waiting, usually in a car or other vehicle, and then take them somewhere: 'I'll pick you up at your house just after seven. That gives us half an hour to get to the stadium.'

taste 1   ✗ During your visit you'll be able to taste some of the local Catalan specialities.
   ✓ **During your visit you'll be able to try some of the local Catalan specialities.**

When you **taste** something, you put a little into your mouth to see what it is like: 'The chef stirred the soup, tasted it, and then added a little salt. When you have something to eat or drink for the first time, you **try** it. 'I think I'll try the onion soup. What's it like?'

2   ✗ I buy all my family's clothes because my husband has such a
poor taste.
✓ **I buy all my family's clothes because my husband has such
poor taste.**

have good/poor/little/no taste (in sth), (WITHOUT a/an): 'She certainly
has remarkably good taste in clothes.'

3   ✗ We all thought that the joke was of a very bad taste.
✓ **We all thought that the joke was in very bad taste.**

be in good/poor/bad taste: 'These advertisements are in very bad taste
and in my opinion should be banned.'

4   See NOTE AT FEEL 2

tasteful   ✗ The food was excellent and very tasteful.
✓ **The food was excellent and very tasty.**

tasteful = chosen or produced by someone who is able to judge which
kinds of art, music, furniture, etc, are attractive: 'The design of the room
was very tasteful - pale colours, matching fabrics, and soft corner
lighting.'
tasty = (of food) having a pleasant taste : 'These sausages are really
tasty - where did you buy them?'

taxi   ✗ To save time, we decided to go with a taxi.
✓ **To save time, we decided to go by taxi.**
✓ **To save time, we decided to go in a taxi.**

You go somewhere by taxi or in a taxi (NOT with): 'If you go by taxi,
you're likely to get stuck in a traffic jam.'

tears   ✗ All of a sudden the child burst in tears.
✓ **All of a sudden the child burst into tears.**
✗ When the policeman had gone, she broke in tears.
✓ **When the policeman had gone, she burst into tears.**

burst into tears or break down (in tears): 'Laura burst into tears and
ran out of the room.' 'She still can't talk about the war without breaking
down in tears.'

technique 1 ✗ The main cause of unemployment is modern technique.
✓ **The main cause of unemployment is modern technology.**

technique = a way of doing something, especially one that requires
special training: 'Thanks to these new surgical techniques, patients
spend far shorter periods in hospital.' 'The purpose of these seminars is
to keep our staff up to date with the latest teaching and testing
techniques.'
technology = (the study of) the use of scientific theories and methods
for practical purposes: 'Can you imagine what the world would be like
without science and technology?' 'Space research has produced major
advances in computer technology.'

2 ✗ The job requires proper technique training.
✓ **The job requires proper technical training.**
✗ He used a lot of technique language that I didn't understand.
✓ **He used a lot of technical language that I didn't understand.**

technical = (1) involving or requiring detailed knowledge, especially of an industrial or scientific subject: 'The flight was cancelled because of a serious technical problem.'
(2) requiring special knowledge to be understood: 'Engineering students need a lot of technical English.'

technology 1 ✗ The modern technology has changed our whole way of life.
✓ **Modern technology has changed our whole way of life.**
See note at THE 4

2 ✗ A fine example of modern technologies can be seen in the Indonesian fishing industry.
✓ **A fine example of modern technology can be seen in the Indonesian fishing industry.**

When **technology** has a general meaning it is uncountable: 'The country's economic fate depends on access to foreign technology.' Use **technology** as a countable noun only when you refer to a particular area of activity: 'The system uses advanced computer and satellite technologies.'

3 ✗ High technology requires massive investment.
✓ **Advanced technology requires massive investment.**

advanced technology (NOT **high**): 'The United States government has agreed to provide both capital and advanced technology.'

telephone See PHONE

television 1 ✗ The whole world watched the cup final on televisions.
✓ **The whole world watched the cup final on television.**

Television (also **TV**) is usually uncountable: 'The children watch a lot of television.' 'The article explains how television affects family life.' As a countable noun it means 'a television set': 'Some parents buy two televisions - one for the children to watch and one for themselves.'

2 ✗ Cigarettes are no longer advertised in television.
✓ **Cigarettes are no longer advertised on television.**
See note at RADIO

tell 1 ✗ The article tells about the history of Rome.
✓ **The article is about the history of Rome.**
? The story tells of a princess and a frog.
✓ **The story is about a princess and a frog.**

You usually say that a book, story, article etc **is about** a particular subject: 'The novel is about the experiences of a young German soldier during the First World War.'
Tell of is used only in literary styles: 'The poem tells of the deeds of a young Greek soldier during the Trojan War.' **Tell about** does not exist.

2 ✗ He told that he hadn't eaten anything for over a week.
✓ **He told them that he hadn't eaten anything for over a week.**
✓ **He said that he hadn't eaten anything for over a week.**

tell sb sth (WITH indirect object): 'Jim told me that you've been offered a new job.'
say sth (WITHOUT indirect object): 'Jim said that you've been offered a new job.'

3   ✗ John said that he was trying to get to London. 'That's where I'm going,' told the man.
✓ **John said that he was trying to get to London. 'That's where I'm going,' said the man.**

Say is used with both direct and indirect speech: '"I'm not going,"' he said.' 'He said he wasn't going.'
Tell is used only with indirect speech: 'He told me he wasn't going.'

4   ✗ Kiri was always telling about herself and her problems.
✓ **Kiri was always talking about herself and her problems.**

talk about sth (NOT **tell about**): 'Once she felt more relaxed, she began to talk about her real reasons for coming to see me.'
Compare **tell sb about sth**: 'Did you tell him about the party on Saturday?' 'Don't forget to tell the doctor about your headaches.'

tendency   ✗ I have a tendency to agree with the statement.
✓ **I tend to agree with the statement.**

To introduce an opinion, use **tend to** (NOT **tendency**): 'She tends to think that small firms should receive greater government support.'
Compare: 'Ann tends/has a tendency to get up late.' (= Ann often gets up late)

terrible   ✗ The traffic jams are very terrible.
✓ **The traffic jams are (absolutely) terrible.**

See note at VERY 2

terrorism   ✗ One of the world's greatest problems is the terrorism.
✓ **One of the world's greatest problems is terrorism.**

See note at THE 4

test   ✗ On my first day at the school, I had to make a test.
✓ **On my first day at the school, I had to take a test.**

take/do a test (NOT **make**): 'Before they start their courses, all the new students take a placement test.'
See Language Note at DO

text   ✗ She said she was writing a text about France for her local newspaper.
✓ **She said she was writing an article about France for her local newspaper.**

text = (1) the words in a book, magazine, etc (as opposed to the illustrations); any written material: 'Alongside each drawing there were several lines of text.' 'A single disk can hold up to 1000 pages of text.'
(2) a book or piece of writing on an academic subject: 'The first two texts on the reading list are general introductions.'
(3) the written version of a play, speech etc: 'Only 'The Times' printed the full text of the President's speech.'
article = a piece of writing in a newspaper or magazine: 'I've just been reading an interesting article on alternative medicine.'

-th   ✗ It was their 23th wedding anniversary.
✓ **It was their 23rd wedding anniversary.**

Use **-th** when the word for the number ends with '-th': '6th May' (= sixth), '18th May' (= eighteenth). Do not use **-th** with (numbers ending) **1, 2, 3**.
Compare: '1st May' (first), '2nd May' (second), '3rd May' (third)

thank 1 ✗ I thank you very much for your last letter.
    ✓ **Thank you very much for your last letter.**
    ✗ First I thank you for answering my letter so quickly.
    ✓ **First I'd like to thank you for answering my letter so quickly.**

> Use **thanks** (informal), **thank you** or (especially in formal styles) **I would/should like to thank you** (NOT **I thank you**): 'On behalf of the team, I'd like to thank you for your invaluable advice and support.'

2 ✗ Thank you for agree to listen.
    ✓ **Thank you for agreeing to listen.**
    ✗ Thank you that you give me a chance to explain the situation.
    ✓ **Thank you for giving me a chance to explain the situation.**

> **thank sb for doing sth**: 'Thank you for being so understanding.'

3 ? Thank you in advance for your help.
    ✓ (Usually better to omit)

> You can use **thank you in advance** if the person you are writing to has already said that they will do something for you: 'It was kind of you to offer to send me a copy. Thank you in advance.' You can also use this phrase if you are in a position of authority and know that the person you are writing to will do what you have asked.
> Otherwise, **thank you in advance** should not be used since it can cause offence.

4 ✗ Thank to the microwave, we always have a hot breakfast.
    ✓ **Thanks to the microwave, we always have a hot breakfast.**

> **thanks to sb/sth** (WITH-**s**): 'Thanks to parents' generosity, the school will soon have its own swimming-pool.'

thankful ✗ I'm very thankful to you for giving me this opportunity.
    ✓ **I'm very grateful to you for giving me this opportunity.**

> **thankful** = happy and relieved that something (good) has happened: 'We should all be thankful that nobody was hurt.'
> **grateful** = full of thanks: 'Dr Cameron has received dozens of letters from grateful patients.' 'We'd be grateful if you could let us have your views on this matter.'

thanks ✗ First of all, thanks for your most interesting question.
    ✓ **First of all, thank you for your most interesting question.**

> **Thanks** is informal: 'Hello, John. Thanks for coming. I was hoping you could make it.' **Thank you** is more formal. See note at THANK 1

that 1 ✗ It is two months now that I left Germany.
    ✓ **It is two months now since I left Germany.**

> **a week/two months etc** + **since** something happened (NOT **that**): 'It's almost two years since I started my PhD.'

2 ✗ The weather has been very good, except for two days that it rained.
    ✓ **The weather has been very good, except for two days when it rained.**

> When the meaning is 'at/on/in/during which' (referring to time), use **when** (NOT **that**): 'These are the times when Dr Roberts will be able to see you.'
> Compare: 'I shall always remember the two days that I spent in Paris.'

3

  ✗ I was shocked by the sight that I could hardly speak.
  ✓ **I was so shocked by the sight that I could hardly speak.**

> **so** + adjective/adverb + **that** clause: 'I'm so tired that I can't keep awake.' 'He spoke so quickly that nobody could understand him.'

4

  ✗ He closed the door quietly that nobody would hear him.
  ✓ **He closed the door quietly so that nobody would hear him.**

> Use **so that** to express purpose (NOT **that**): 'The burglars turned off all the lights so that they wouldn't be seen.'

5

  ✗ Children are not as easy to please nowadays that they were in the past.
  ✓ **Children are not as easy to please nowadays as they were in the past.**

> When making a comparison, use **as/so ... as** (NOT **as/so ... that**): 'It's as hard to get into university today as it was ten years ago.'

6

  ✗ It worried me that the letter had not arrived, especially that it had never happened before.
  ✓ **It worried me that the letter had not arrived, especially since/as it had never happened before.**

> When giving a reason for something, use **since** or **as** (NOT **that**): 'Instead of cooking, why don't we get a take-away, especially as it's so late.'

7

  ✗ Sitting next to me was an old lady, that seemed to be sound asleep.
  ✓ **Sitting next to me was an old lady, who seemed to be sound asleep.**

> **That** is used to introduce an identifying relative clause (one which identifies, defines, or restricts the preceding noun): 'The woman that is sitting behind us is Tom's music teacher.' 'The man that I marry will have lots of money.'
> **That** is not used to introduce a non-identifying relative clause (one which simply adds more information about the noun).

8

  ✗ If you haven't sent it yet, I'd be pleased if you would do that as soon as possible.
  ✓ **If you haven't sent it yet, I'd be pleased if you would do so as soon as possible.**

> To make a precise reference to a previously mentioned action, use **do so** (NOT **do that**): 'I asked him politely to take his feet off the seat but he refused to do so.'

the 1

  ✗ She is arriving on March the 25th.
  ✓ **She is arriving on March 25th.**

> When you say the date, use 'March the twenty-fifth' or 'the twenty-fifth of March'.
> When you write the date, use 'March 25th' or '25th March' (WITHOUT **the** and **of**).

2

  ✗ Very few people can speak the English well in Japan.
  ✓ **Very few people can speak English well in Japan.**

> speak/learn/know etc + name of a language (WITHOUT **the**): 'She speaks fluent German.' 'Do you know any Malay?' 'I'd like to learn Mandarin.'
> Note that **the + English/Japanese etc + language** may be used when you talk about a language in terms of its history, structure, users etc: 'The English language has evolved over many centuries.'

3

✗ I have just seen a new magazine about the computers.
✓ **I have just seen a new magazine about computers.**

> Do not use **the** with the plural form of a countable noun when it is used in a general sense. Compare: 'She likes cats.' (= cats in general) 'The cats we saw in Venice looked very hungry.' (= a particular group of cats)

4

✗ A lot of people are afraid of the death.
✓ **A lot of people are afraid of death.**
✗ Nowadays the pollution is a very serious problem.
✓ **Nowadays pollution is a very serious problem.**
✗ My main hobby is the photography.
✓ **My main hobby is photography.**

> Do not use **the** with an uncountable noun when it is used in a general sense: 'She hates dishonesty.' 'Power doesn't interest him.'
> **The** is used when the sense is restricted: 'She hates the dishonesty of the man.' 'The power enjoyed by politicians doesn't interest him.'

5

✗ Diseases such as the AIDS and the cancer cause a lot of suffering.
✓ **Diseases such as AIDS and cancer cause a lot of suffering.**

> Do not use **the** before the name of a disease: 'He caught pneumonia and had to spend three weeks in bed.'

6

✗ Our plane arrived at the Gatwick Airport.
✓ **Our plane arrived at Gatwick Airport.**

> Do not use **the** before the names of airports and railway stations: 'Charles de Gaulle (Airport)', 'Narita (Airport)', 'Charing Cross (Station)'

7

✗ The language school is in the Malibu Street.
✓ **The language school is in Malibu Street.**

> **The** is not usually used in the names of streets and roads: 'Oxford Street', 'Fifth Avenue', 'Fir Tree Avenue', 'Blue Pool Road'.
> Note that when someone mentions 'the Oxford road' or 'the London road', they mean the road that leads to Oxford/London.

8

✗ Climbing the Mount Fuji in winter can be very dangerous.
✓ **Climbing Mount Fuji in winter can be very dangerous.**

> Do not use **the** with the name of a mountain: 'Mount Everest', 'Mount Fuji', 'Mount Olympus'. Note, however, that **the** is used with the names of groups of mountains: 'the Alps', 'the Andes', 'the Himalayas'.

9

✗ They were both found guilty and sent to the prison.
✓ **They were both found guilty and sent to prison.**
See note at SCHOOL 1

10

✗ Yellow River has caused many terrible floods.
✓ **The Yellow River has caused many terrible floods.**

Always use **the** with the names of canals, rivers, seas and oceans:: 'the Suez Canal', 'the Ganges', 'the (River) Thames', 'the Atlantic (Ocean)', 'the Mediterranean (Sea)'

11

✗ It is more than ten years since I visited West Indies.
✓ **It is more than ten years since I visited the West Indies.**

Most plural names begin with **the**: 'the Bahamas', 'the Himalayas', 'the United States', 'the Philippines'.

12

✗ This is my second visit to UK.
✓ **This is my second visit to the UK.**

Use **the** with any country whose name includes 'state', 'union', 'republic', 'kingdom' etc: 'the UK', 'the United Kingdom', 'the USA', 'the United States', 'the People's Republic of China'.

13

✗ Only very wealthy tourists can afford to stay at Imperial Hotel.
✓ **Only very wealthy tourists can afford to stay at the Imperial Hotel.**

The names of hotels and restaurants usually begin with **the**: 'the Hilton', 'the Mandarin', 'the Sheraton'.
Note that names which have a possessive form are exceptions: 'Claridge's', 'Salvo's', 'Tiffany's'

14

✗ This system was brought to Hong Kong by British.
✓ **This system was brought to Hong Kong by the British.**

To refer to the people of a country, use **the** + adjective: 'the British', 'the French', 'the Portuguese', 'the Swiss'.

15

✗ The hotel is not suitable for disabled.
✓ **The hotel is not suitable for the disabled.**

the poor, the sick, the deaf, the disabled, etc = all people who are poor/sick/deaf/disabled: 'The rich get richer and the poor get poorer.' 'She devoted her life to looking after the sick.'

16

See NATURE ✓

then 1

✗ We took a bus to the city centre then caught a train to London.
✓ **We took a bus to the city centre and then caught a train to London.**

Then is an adverb (NOT a conjunction). It cannot be used to link clauses.

2

✗ After my father retires, then I shall help him financially.
✓ **After my father retires, I shall help him financially.**

Then (= at that time) is used after a time clause only when it introduces a result or consequence. Compare: 'When you've seen the trees, then you'll know why I came to live here.' (= as a result of seeing the trees)

there 1

✗ If you aren't busy is something I'd like to ask you about.
✓ **If you aren't busy, there's something I'd like to ask you about.**

When you say that something exists or takes place, the sentence must have a subject. When there is no other subject, use **there**: 'There's a hair in your soup.' 'Suddenly there was a loud bang.' 'There are two police

officers waiting to see you.'
Note that in this pattern **there** has no meaning. It simply fills the subject position.

2   ✗ There was four people in the car.
            ✓ **There were four people in the car.**
            ✗ In Barcelona there is plenty of things for visitors to do.
            ✓ **In Barcelona there are plenty of things for visitors to do.**
            ✗ There was a lot of girls watching the game.
            ✓ **There were a lot of girls watching the game.**

Use **there is/was** when the following noun is singular/uncountable: 'There was a letter on the mat.' 'There was smoke all over the house.' Use **there are/were** when the following noun is plural: 'There were babies crying in every room.' 'There are many times when I would prefer to be alone.'
Note that **a lot of, plenty of, etc** do not affect the number of the verb. Compare: 'There *was* a lot of *traffic* on the road.' 'There *were* a lot of *cars* on the road.'

3   ✗ My sister often goes to the indoor pool but I don't like going to there.
            ✓ **My sister often goes to the indoor pool but I don't like going there.**

See note at HERE 2

4   See GOOD 4

5   See WHERE 1

therefore 1 ✗ She has lived in New York for many years therefore she regards New York as her home.
            ✓ **She has lived in New York for many years and (therefore) regards New York as her home.**

Therefore is an adverb (NOT a conjunction). It cannot be used to link clauses. See also HOWEVER, NEVERTHELESS

2   ? The child looked lost and therefore I asked him if I could help.
            ✓ **The child looked lost and so I asked him if I could help.**

Therefore is used mainly in formal styles: 'Crops have been badly affected by the drought and therefore food will be in short supply.'
In non-formal styles use **so**: 'It was quite late so I didn't stay long.'

these 1 ✗ The present government doesn't care enough about the poorer sections of our society. Businessmen are encouraged to exploit workers and make huge profits. In spite of all these, I believe in the principles of free enterprise.
            ✓ **The present government doesn't care enough about the poorer sections of our society. Businessmen are encouraged to exploit workers and make huge profits. In spite of all this, I believe in the principles of free enterprise.**

To refer back to the points that you have just made, use **(all) this** (NOT **(all) these**): 'In spite of all this, we managed to enjoy ourselves.' 'I find all this very confusing.'

2	See ONE 5

thing 1   ?   Being punctual is a very important thing.
         ✓   **Being punctual is very important.**

> Avoid using **thing** after an adjective when the adjective can be used on its own: 'To obtain a bank loan when you don't have a job can be very difficult.'
> Note however the commonly used phrase **a/the good thing**: 'Most people agree that democracy is a good thing.' 'The good thing about this school is that the teachers are all so enthusiastic.'

2   ✗   I have a very important thing to ask you.
      ✓   **I have something very important to ask you.**
      ✗   If you need any special thing, please let me know.
      ✓   **If you need anything special, please let me know.**

> **something** + adjective, **anything** + adjective, **somewhere** + adjective, **nothing** + adjective, etc: 'Did you notice anything unusual?' 'Let's go somewhere different tonight.'

3   ?   My brother knows many things about England.
      ✓   **My brother knows a lot about England.**
      ?   Asian countries have learned many things from western countries.
      ✓   **Asian countries have learned a great deal from western countries.**

> The use of **many things** often sounds unnatural. Instead, use **a lot, a great deal, etc**: 'She said that she had a lot to do.' 'In just one or two sessions you can learn a great deal.'
> Note also the phrase **all about**: 'The best person to ask is David - he knows all about tropical plants.' (= he knows everything about ...)

4   See BAD 2

think 1   ✗   I was thinking if you would like to have lunch before visiting the museum.
         ✓   **I was wondering if you would like to have lunch before visiting the museum.**

> To introduce a polite request or invitation, use **I was wondering if/whether**: 'I was wondering if you'd like to play tennis on Saturday.' 'Sally was wondering whether you could give her some advice.'

2   ✗   We should spend more time thinking why people do such terrible things.
      ✓   **We should spend more time thinking about why people do such terrible things.**
      ✗   While she was away, he often thought on her.
      ✓   **While she was away, he often thought about her.**

> **think about sb/sth** (= give a lot of thought to): 'She's worried about her father and can't stop thinking about him.' 'Have you ever thought about what you'd like to do for a living?' 'You look serious - what're you thinking about?'

3   ✗   He's thinking to make another trip to Italy next month.
      ✓   **He's thinking about making another trip to Italy next month.**

✗ We're thinking on going to the beach after lunch.
✓ **We're thinking of going to the beach after lunch.**

> When you are talking about possible future actions, use **think about/of doing sth**: 'They're thinking of starting their own health food business.' 'We're thinking about going to Disneyworld again next year.'

4

✗ He advised me to think deeply about it before making a decision.
✓ **He advised me to think seriously about it before making a decision.**

> **think seriously/carefully** (NOT **deeply**) (**about sth**), especially before making a decision: 'The job has a lot of attractions and in my opinion you should think seriously about it.'

5

✗ Some foreigners are thinking the Japanese are rich.
✓ **Some foreigners think the Japanese are rich.**

See Language Note at CONTAIN

6

✗ I think she didn't understand what you said.
✓ **I don't think she understood what you said.**

> **Do not think (that)** is more usual than **think (that) ... not**. This applies to **believe, imagine, suppose, feel** etc: 'I don't imagine they'll be coming after all.' 'I don't suppose you could give me a lift?'

this

✗ Will you be at home on this Sunday afternoon?
✓ **Will you be at home this Sunday afternoon?**
✓ **Will you be at home on Sunday afternoon?**
✗ My exams are on this month.
✓ **My exams are this month.**

See Language Note at TIME

those

See ONE 5

though

See note at BUT

thought 1

? People's attitudes and thoughts don't change overnight.
✓ **People's attitudes and opinions don't change overnight.**

> **thought** = something that you (suddenly) think of, remember or realize: 'Has the thought ever occurred to you that he might be guilty?' 'Does anyone have any thoughts about where we should eat?'
> **opinion/view** = what you feel about something, especially after thinking about it for a long time: 'Journalists are supposed to report the facts, not personal opinions.' 'If you want my opinion - I think he's guilty.'

2

✗ They are prepared to kill in order to defend their thoughts.
✓ **They are prepared to kill in order to defend their beliefs.**

> **belief** = a strong feeling that something is true or untrue, good or bad etc: 'In the old days people were persecuted for their religious beliefs.' 'The poet's belief in life after death is not evident in these early poems.'

thousand

See Language Note at HUNDRED

threat

✗ They used to threat each other with atomic bombs.
✓ **They used to threaten each other with atomic bombs.**

> **Threat** is a noun: 'The letter was full of threats and accusations.' 'The President said he would stand firm and not give in to threats from terrorists.'
> The verb is **threaten**: 'Whenever they have an argument, she threatens to leave him.' 'He is threatening the magazine with legal action unless they publish a full apology.'

throw 1

✗ He picked up a small stone and threw it to Sally's window.
✓ **He picked up a small stone and threw it at Sally's window.**

> You **throw** an object **at** the person or thing you want to hit (NOT **to**): 'One day Dr Roseberry lost his temper and threw a book at me.'

2

✗ Some smokers just throw their cigarette ends.
✓ **Some smokers just throw their cigarette ends on the ground.**

> **throw sth + away/down/on the ground etc**: 'You could save the paper for recycling instead of just throwing it away.'

thunder

✗ I heard a terribly loud noise, like a thunder.
✓ **I heard a terribly loud noise, like thunder.**
✗ We waited for the thunders and lightning to stop.
✓ **We waited for the thunder and lightning to stop.**

> **Thunder** is an uncountable noun: 'When Mr Cameron got angry, his voice was as loud as thunder.'

thus

✗ My house is near Greenwich Park and thus we'll be able to visit the famous Observatory.
✓ **My house is near Greenwich Park and so we'll be able to visit the famous Observatory.**

> **Thus** is used only in formal styles: 'All vaccines carry some risk of side effects. Thus emergency equipment and appropriate drugs should be available at all immunization sessions.'
> In non-formal styles use **so**: 'The smell of paint can give you a headache and so it's a good idea to keep the windows open.'

till

✗ I managed to drive the car till the nearest hospital.
✓ **I managed to drive the car as far as the nearest hospital.**

> See note at UNTIL 1

time 1

✗ The journey takes long time.
✓ **The journey takes a long time.**
✗ Long time ago there was a queen named Isabel.
✓ **A long time ago there was a queen named Isabel.**

> **a long time** (WITH **a**): 'The film lasted a long time.'

2

✗ In the present time the situation is getting worse.
✓ **At the present time the situation is getting worse.**
✗ We both left the building in the same time.
✓ **We both left the building at the same time.**
✗ Most families get together in Christmas time.
✓ **Most families get together at Christmas time.**
✗ He was born in the right time and in the right place.
✓ **He was born at the right time and in the right place.**

> See Language Note on page 333

3

   ✗ Last time Singapore used to be a fishing village.
   ✓ **Many years ago Singapore used to be a fishing village.**
   ✗ Last time you promised to join me on a trip to Beijing.
   ✓ **The last time we met you promised to join me on a trip to Beijing.**

> **The last time** (always with **the**) refers to a particular occasion: 'The last time we saw each other she said that she was going to get married.' 'This is the last time I'm coming here!'
> To refer to a period in the (distant) past, use **previously, formerly, many years ago, in the old days, etc**: 'The new road changed people's lives enormously - previously the only way of reaching the village was on foot.' 'Zimbabwe was formerly known as Rhodesia.' 'In the old days the only way to get to India was by ship.'

4

   ✗ The fire brigade arrived just on time, before the fire could spread.
   ✓ **The fire brigade arrived just in time, before the fire could spread.**
   ✗ They had to rush to get to work in time.
   ✓ **They had to rush to get to work on time.**

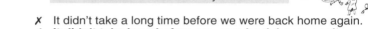

> **in time** = not late; early enough: 'Make sure you arrive in time to see the beginning of the film.'
> **on time** = (arriving) at the right time; punctual(ly): 'The train arrived at 17.28 - exactly on time.'

5

   ✗ It didn't take a long time before we were back home again.
   ✓ **It didn't take long before we were back home again.**

> **not take/be long** (WITHOUT **time**): 'The dinner won't be long - about another five minutes.'

6

   ✗ Medical science is developing every time.
   ✓ **Medical science is developing all the time.**
   ✗ I think about you every time.
   ✓ **I think about you all the time.**

> When you mean 'continuously', use **all the time** (NOT **every time**): 'They seem to be arguing all the time.'
> Compare: 'Every time I go skiing, I come home feeling years younger.'

7

   See SPEND 1, 2

8

   ✗ We went to the cinema to spend the time until the train arrived.
   ✓ **We went to the cinema to pass the time until the train arrived.**

> When you have nothing important to do and you spend time doing something in order to avoid being bored, you **pass the time**: 'At the airport we bought a pack of playing cards to help pass the time.'

9

   ✗ We spent a very good time in New York.
   ✓ **We had a very good time in New York.**

> **have** a good/marvellous **time** (NOT **spend**): 'In those days all I cared about was having a good time.'

times 1

   ✗ Many times there is nothing worth watching on TV.
   ✓ **Very often there is nothing worth watching on TV.**

Using prepositions in time phrases

in

main parts of the day	**in the morning/afternoon/evening**: 'In the morning we went for a walk along the Seine.' Compare: **at night**: 'I don't like driving at night.'
months, years, seasons, centuries	She'll be coming back home in March.' 'In 1989 he decided to join the army.' 'They're getting married in the autumn.' 'In the twentieth century there have been two World Wars.'
at the end of a stated period	''I'll be back in a couple of minutes.' 'In two weeks' time she's going on leave.'

on

specific days/dates/mornings/afternoons, etc	'on Tuesday', 'on 3rd April', 'on Monday night', 'on New Year's Day', 'on the day of my arrival'

at

clock times	'The shops open at 9 o'clock.' 'Her flight is due in at 6.35.'
main points of time in the day	**at midnight/noon/dawn/lunchtime, etc**: 'We usually open our presents at midnight.' 'He turned up in my office at noon, expecting a free lunch.'
weekend (British English)	**at the weekend**: 'What are you doing at the weekend?' **at weekends:** 'I never do any work at weekends.' BUT (American English) **on the weekend**
the holiday period around **Christmas, Easter, Hannukkah, Ramadan, etc**	**at Christmas, at Easter, at Hannukkah, at Ramadan**: 'We like to stay at home at Christmas.' 'At Ramadan the roads tend to be very quiet.' BUT **on Christmas Day, on Easter Sunday**
phrases with **time**	'I'm afraid that at the present time we're out of stock.' 'You've come at a bad time.' BUT note the idioms: **in time, on time, about time**
Note: **In, on, at, etc** are NOT used before time phrases beginning with **this, every** and **last/next** (= the one that has just gone/is about to come) '	We can't afford a holiday this year.' 'Where did you go last weekend?' 'My exams finish next Tuesday afternoon.' Note also that **the** is NOT used in these phrases. Compare: 'The meeting is to be held on the last Friday in April.' In this sentence **last** does not mean 'the one that has just gone'.
In, on, at, etc are NOT used before phrases ending with **ago**	'He left the office five minutes ago.' 'I first met her in Glasgow about two years ago.'

Do not use **many times** unless you are thinking about the total number of times that something happens: 'I've tried phoning her many times during the past week, but nobody answers.' 'He'd told me the same story many times before.'
When you are thinking about the general frequency with which something happens, use **often**: 'When people are tired, they often make mistakes.'

2   ?　He couldn't see where he was going and fell down many times.
　　✓　**He couldn't see where he was going and kept falling down.**
　　✗　People tell me many times that America is a dangerous country.
　　✓　**People are always telling me that America is a dangerous country.**

If you do something repeatedly, you **keep doing** it or you **are always doing** it: 'Why does she keep writing to you?' 'At school I was always getting into trouble.'

timetable   ✗　The manager's timetable next week is very busy.
　　✓　**The manager's schedule next week is very busy.**

timetable = a list or plan showing the times when lessons take place or the times when buses, trains etc arrive and leave: 'According to my timetable, history is on Mondays and Thursdays.'
schedule = a detailed plan of all the things that have to be done during a certain period: 'It's important that we all try and keep to the schedule.' 'The project is running 6 months behind schedule.'

tiresome   ✗　The flight from Hong Kong to London was very tiresome.
　　✓　**The flight from Hong Kong to London was very tiring.**
　　✗　After two tiresome days, we both needed some sleep.
　　✓　**After two tiring days, we both needed some sleep.**

tiresome = annoying or irritating: 'I find these so-called jokes extremely tiresome.
'tiring = causing tiredness; exhausting: 'Looking at a computer screen all day can be very tiring.'

title   ✗　The newspaper titles were all about the earthquake.
　　✓　**The newspaper headlines were all about the earthquake.**

title = the name of a book, play, painting, piece of music etc: 'I can remember the title of the book but not the author.'
headline = the heading above a report in a newspaper, especially at the top of the front page: 'Have you seen today's headlines? There's been another car bomb in London.'

titled   ✗　He was reading a short story by Saki titled 'The Open Window'.
　　✓　**He was reading a short story by Saki called 'The Open Window'.**
　　✗　She sent me an article from *Life Magazine* titled 'A Soldier's Anguish'.
　　✓　**She sent me an article from *Life Magazine* entitled 'A Soldier's Anguish'.**

To introduce the name of a book, story, film, article, song, painting etc, use **be called** or, especially in formal styles, **(be) entitled**: 'Her latest novel is called *Educating Peter*.'
Compare: 'The title of her latest novel is *Educating Peter*.'

to 1
    ✗ At that moment he noticed a man running to him.
    ✓ **At that moment he noticed a man running towards him.**

> When you are talking about direction, use **towards** (NOT **to**): 'If you walk along the river bank towards Skipton, you come to a bridge.' 'Keep going towards Manchester until you see the sign for the airport.'

2
    ✗ He came into the shop and went to the woman behind the counter.
    ✓ **He came into the shop and went up to the woman behind the counter.**
    ✗ She stood up, walked to John, and asked him what he was doing.
    ✓ **She stood up, walked over to John, and asked him what he was doing.**

> When you go towards someone and stop in front of them, you go **up to, over to** or **across to** them (NOT **to** or **near to**): 'One of the Japanese students walked slowly up to me and, with a huge smile, handed me a rose.'

3
    See DOWNSTAIRS, HERE 2, HOME 1

4
    See NOT 1

toast
    ✗ I usually have a cup of coffee and a toast for breakfast.
    ✓ **I usually have a cup of coffee and some toast for breakfast.**
    ✗ You make some toasts and I'll set the table.
    ✓ **You make some toast and I'll set the table.**

> **Toast** is an uncountable noun: 'There's some toast for you in the kitchen.' 'How many pieces/slices of toast would you like?'

toilet
    ✗ One of the children wanted to go to toilet.
    ✓ **One of the children wanted to go to the toilet.**

> **go to the toilet** (WITH **the**): 'He won't be long. He's just gone to the toilet.'

too 1
    ✗ I was too happy when I received your letter today.
    ✓ **I was very happy when I received your letter today.**
    ✗ Bearing in mind that it is too far from here, we should make an early start.
    ✓ **Bearing in mind that it is a long way from here, we should make an early start.**

> **too** = more than is good, reasonable or acceptable: 'He was driving too fast and couldn't stop in time.' 'The meat was too tough to eat.'
> Compare: 'I was very tired but not too tired to go out.'

2
    ✗ For some reason they didn't receive the fax and your letter hasn't arrived too.
    ✓ **For some reason they didn't receive the fax and your letter hasn't arrived either.**

> In a negative clause use **either** (NOT **too/also/as well**): 'The cheese cake was disappointing and the coffee wasn't very special either.'
> Compare: 'The food was excellent and the service was good too.'

3
    ✗ In my opinion, this is a too traditional approach.
    ✓ **In my opinion, this is too traditional an approach.**

too + adjective + **a/an** + noun: 'I'd accept the offer if I were you - it's too good an opportunity to miss.'

too many   ✗ It's an interesting magazine with too many good ideas.
　　　　　　　✓ **It's an interesting magazine with a lot of good ideas.**

too many = more than is acceptable or required: 'I don't like television - there are too many advertisements.' 'You can't have too many friends.'

too much 1 ✗ There are simply too much people in the world.
　　　　　　　✓ **There are simply too many people in the world.**
　　　　　　　✗ I noticed that he had had a couple of drinks too much.
　　　　　　　✓ **I noticed that he had had a couple of drinks too many.**
　　　　　　　See MUCH 1

2 ✗ 'If you are too much selfish, nobody will like you,' she said.
　　　✓ **'If you are too selfish, nobody will like you,' she said.**
　　　✗ The English course was too much difficult for me.
　　　✓ **The English course was too difficult for me.**

too much + noun: 'I hope I haven't caused you too much trouble.'
too + adjective/adverb (WITHOUT **much**): 'The dress was too expensive. '
'If you speak too quickly, he doesn't understand.'
Compare: 'The English course was much/far too difficult for me.'

top   ✗ You will find my address on top of the letter.
　　　　✓ **You will find my address at the top of the letter.**

at the top/bottom of a page or sheet of paper (NOT **on**): 'Please write your name clearly at the top of each page.'
Compare: 'I eventually found the keys on top of the television.'

touch 1   ✗ People living in the city were not touched by the famine.
　　　　　✓ **People living in the city were not affected by the famine.**

When you mean 'have an effect on', use **affect** (NOT **touch**): 'How will these new taxes affect people on low incomes?' 'Farms in the south of the country have been seriously affected by the drought.'

2 ✗ It's good to go out to work because you get in touch with other people.
　　　✓ **It's good to go out to work because you come into contact with other people.**

get in touch with = communicate with (someone) by letter or telephone: 'Don't wait until Christmas before you get in touch.' 'Mrs Taylor wants you to get in touch with her.'
come into contact with = meet: 'In my profession I come into contact with a lot of teachers.'

touristic   ✗ It is one of the most popular touristic resorts in Spain.
　　　　　　✓ **It is one of the most popular tourist resorts in Spain.**

Touristic and **touristy** are used, especially in informal styles, to describe a place that is unpleasantly full of things for tourists to see and do: 'He refuses to go there any more - it's become too touristy.'
When you simply mean 'visited or preferred by tourists', use **tourist** + noun: 'London is full of tourist attractions.' 'During the tourist season the hotels are packed.'

training   ✗   I made my training with the Swiss Bank in London.
          ✓   **I did my training with the Swiss Bank in London.**
             See Language Note at DO

translate   ✗   The novel has been translated to English and French.
          ✓   **The novel has been translated into English and French.**
             translate sth (from one language) **into** another language (NOT **to**):
             'Each letter has to be translated from Swedish into German.'

transport   ✗   Some countries don't have a public transport.
          ✓   **Some countries don't have (any) public transport.**
             Transport is an uncountable noun: 'How will you get there without transport?' 'People should be encouraged to use public transport.'

**transport-
ation**   ✗   Apart from housing, transportation is also a problem.
          ✓   **Apart from housing, transport is also a problem.**
             In British English **transportation** usually refers to the process or business of moving things, especially goods, from one place to another: 'Information regarding the transportation and storage of nuclear waste is difficult to obtain.'
             The word for the system that carries passengers (or goods) from one place to another is **transport**: 'I spent most of my money on hotels, food and transport.' 'Trains are still my favourite form of transport.'
             Note that in American English **transportation** is used for this meaning.

travel 1   ✗   The travel takes about half an hour.
          ✓   **The journey takes about half an hour.**
          ✗   For long travels we use the train.
          ✓   **For long journeys we use the train.**
             See Language Note on next page

2   ✗   He was exhausted from all the travels.
          ✓   **He was exhausted from all the travelling.**
             See Language Note on next page

treasure   ✗   There is always controversy when a treasure is discovered.
          ✓   **There is always controversy when treasure is discovered.**
             Treasure (= a collection of valuable objects) is an uncountable noun: 'It's an adventure story about a search for buried treasure.'

tremble   ✗   It was so cold that I couldn't stop trembling.
          ✓   **It was so cold that I couldn't stop shivering.**

             You **tremble** when you are afraid, nervous, upset or excited: 'As she opened the envelope, her hands started trembling and she started to cry.' 'She trembled with excitement just at the thought of seeing him again.'
             When you are cold, you **shiver**: 'I stood at the bus stop shivering and wishing that I'd worn my coat.'

trouble 1

  ✗ I'm sorry to cause you so many troubles.
  ✓ **I'm sorry to cause you so much trouble.**
  ✗ I'm having some troubles with my supervisor.
  ✓ **I'm having some trouble with my supervisor.**

> **Trouble** (= difficulties or problems) is an uncountable noun: 'I hope you didn't have any trouble getting here.' 'His back has been giving him a lot of trouble recently.'
> Note the alternative: 'I'm sorry to cause you so many problems.'

JOURNEY • TRIP • TRAVEL • TRAVELS • VOYAGE • TOUR

journey	When you travel to a place that is far away or to a place that you visit regularly, you **go on/make** a **journey** (NOT **do/have**): 'You can't go on a journey to Alaska without making careful preparations.' 'The journey to work takes about half an hour by train.' 'If the roads are flooded, we'll have to make the journey by boat.'
trip	When you go to a place and come back again, especially for a short visit, you go on/make/take a **trip**: 'How was your trip to San Francisco?' 'She's away on a business trip and won't be back until Monday.'
travel	**Travel** (uncountable) is the general activity of moving about the world or from place to place: 'She enjoys foreign travel immensely.' 'New computer technology has made air travel considerably safer.' A word with a similar meaning is **travelling**. This **-ing** form is often used after verbs and prepositions: 'I hate travelling on my own.' 'The job involves a certain amount of travelling.' (NOT 'of travel') In compound nouns, **travel** is used: 'foreign travel', 'air travel' (NOT 'air travelling').
travels	Someone's **travels** (plural) are the journeys they make (and the experiences they have) during a long visit to one or more foreign countries: 'I accompanied the South African team throughout their travels in Australia and New Zealand.' 'We filmed a lot of wild animals on our travels.'
voyage	A **voyage** is a long journey in a boat or ship: 'Heavy seas and strong winds made the voyage from Europe very unpleasant.'
tour	A tour is a journey that you make for pleasure during which you visit a number or different places within a country, region etc: 'For our next holiday we're going on a ten-day tour of the Lake District.' Politicians and entertainers sometimes go on a tour as part of their work, making a planned series of visits in order to meet people or perform: 'The Prime Minister will be returning on Monday from a three-week tour of Southeast Asia.' A tour is also a short trip around a city, factory, museum etc: 'After lunch we were taken on a guided tour of York Minster.'

2 ✗ Sometimes my little brother is a real trouble.
    ✓ **Sometimes my little brother is a real nuisance.**

> A person or thing that annoys you or gives you problems is a **nuisance**: 'The post office closes early today, which is a bit of a nuisance.' 'Alan! Stop being a nuisance and find something to do!'

true
    ✗ I hope all your dreams become true.
    ✓ **I hope all your dreams come true.**

> **come true** (NOT **become**): 'His dream came true on the day apartheid was abolished.' 'If scientists' predictions come true, the Earth's temperature will rise by five degrees in the next fifty years.'

trust
    ✗ After he was caught stealing, nobody trusted in him.
    ✓ **After he was caught stealing, nobody trusted him.**

> **trust in** = (formal or literary) have faith in: 'All will be well as long as you trust in God.'
> **trust** (WITHOUT **in**)= believe that someone is honest (and will not hurt or deceive you): 'He's just a bit too friendly and I'm afraid I don't trust him.' 'I'm the only person he'll trust to look after his money.'

truth
    ✗ We all thought he was saying the truth.
    ✓ **We all thought he was telling the truth.**

> **tell the truth** (NOT **say**): 'I'm still not convinced that he's telling the truth.'

turn back
    ✗ Having woken up, he sat up in his seat and turned back to see who was making all the noise.
    ✓ **Having woken up, he sat up in his seat and turned round to see who was making all the noise.**

> **turn back** = stop and begin to return to the place you started from: 'If the bridge has been destroyed, we'll have to turn back.'
> **turn round** (AmE **turn around**) = move so that you are looking in the opposite direction: 'If you turn round, I'll fasten your dress for you.'

turn round
    ✗ The alarm clock rang at 7.45 but I just turned round and went back to sleep.
    ✓ **The alarm clock rang at 7.45 but I just turned over and went back to sleep.**

> When you are lying down and you move so that you are looking in the opposite direction, you **turn over**: 'Every time I turn over, the bed squeaks.'

turn up
    ✗ George turned up to be the father of one of my old schoolfriends.
    ✓ **George turned out to be the father of one of my old school-friends.**
    ✗ Our presence turned up to be unnecessary.
    ✓ **Our presence turned out to be unnecessary.**

> **Turn up** means 'arrive, appear, or be found': 'He turned up at the party dressed in pink pyjamas!' 'I can't find my keys, but I expect they'll turn up somewhere.'
> When you are talking about the final result of something, use **turn out**: 'After a bad start, the party turned out to be a great success.'

TV

   ✗ After dinner we watched a film in TV.
   ✓ **After dinner we watched a film on TV.**
    See note at RADIO

type 1

   ✗ The manager of the shop told me that he was not responsible for these type of fault.
   ✓ **The manager of the shop told me that he was not responsible for these types of fault.**
    See note at KIND OF 1

2

   ✗ This type of shoes don't damage the grass.
   ✓ **This type of shoe doesn't damage the grass.**
   ✓ **These types of shoe/s don't damage the grass.**
    See note at KIND OF 2

typical 1

   ✗ Angelo took us to a typical restaurant.
   ✓ **Angelo took us to a typical Italian restaurant.**
    After **typical** you usually mention the exact group to which someone or something belongs: 'McGarron looked like a typical American car salesman.' 'The old fireplace and the few pieces of typical Basque furniture give the room a homely atmosphere.'

2

   ✗ After dinner it is typical to sing carols.
   ✓ **After dinner we usually sing carols.**
   ✓ **After dinner it is customary to sing carols.**
    When you are talking about what usually happens at a particular time of the year, use **usually** or (especially in formal styles) **customary**: 'It's customary to kiss the bride.'

Uu

UK

✗ This is my first visit to UK.
✓ **This is my first visit to the UK.**
See note at THE 12

under

✗ Prices are not allowed to fall under this level.
✓ **Prices are not allowed to fall below this level.**
See note at BELOW 1

understand 1

✗ People find it difficult to understand about the Japanese.
✓ **People find it difficult to understand the Japanese.**
understand sb/sth (WITHOUT **about**): 'After twenty years of marriage, we still don't understand each other.'

2

✗ You have to know our culture in order to understand us deeply.
✓ **You have to know our culture in order to understand us properly.**
✓ **You have to know our culture in order to really understand us.**
✗ Reading helps us to understand the world more deeply.
✓ **Reading helps us to understand the world better.**
understand sb/sth properly/better; fully/really understand sb/sth (NOT **deeply**): 'Make sure that you understand the instructions properly before you begin.' 'Nobody fully understands how the drug actually works.'
Note the alternative: 'Reading helps us to develop our understanding of the world.'

3

✗ At first I wasn't understanding anything.
✓ **At first I didn't understand anything.**
See Language Note at CONTAIN

unemployment

✗ The unemployment is a serious problem in my country.
✓ **Unemployment is a serious problem in my country.**
See THE 4

uniform

✗ Every year we make new uniforms for the carnival.
✓ **Every year we make new costumes for the carnival.**
uniform = a set of clothes worn by soldiers, police officers, nurses etc when on duty, and children in some schools: 'Some children hate having to wear their school uniform.'
costume = a set of clothes worn by actors or public performers: 'She used to work for a theatre company, designing and making costumes.' 'The tourist guides at the castle all wear medieval costumes.'

unique	?	It's one of the most unique pieces of architecture in Spain.
	✓	**It's one of the most unusual pieces of architecture in Spain.**

Unique usually describes something that is the only one of its kind: 'Lennon will be remembered for his songs and for his unique sense of humour.'
In informal styles **unique** is sometimes used with **more/most/rather etc.** to mean 'unusual': 'This rather unique little restaurant is very popular with the locals.' This use of **unique** is considered by careful users to be incorrect.

United Kingdom	✗	I spent two months travelling around United Kingdom.
	✓	**I spent two months travelling around the United Kingdom.**

See note at THE 12

United Nations	✗	The purpose of United Nations is to protect human rights.
	✓	**The purpose of the United Nations is to protect human rights.**

See note at THE 12

United States	✗	I met people from Canada and United States.
	✓	**I met people from Canada and the United States.**

See note at THE 12

university 1	✗	I am studying sociology at the London University.
	✓	**I am studying sociology at London University.**
	✓	**I am studying sociology at the University of London.**

London/Leeds University (WITHOUT **the**)
the University of London/Leeds (WITH **the**)
In formal written styles the usual form is 'the University of London'.

2	✗	After leaving school, we all went to the university.
	✓	**After leaving school, we all went to university.**

Users of American English would say: 'After graduating from high school, we all went to college.'
See note at SCHOOL 1

3	✗	My sister is studying music in university.
	✓	**My sister is studying music at university.**
	✗	I want to study Public Administration in the University of Southern California.
	✓	**I want to study Public Administration at the University of Southern California.**

See IN 5

unknown	?	I don't like driving on unknown roads.
	✓	**I don't like driving on unfamiliar roads.**
	?	The names on the list were unknown to me.
	✓	**The names on the list were unfamiliar to me.**

unknown usually describes something that people in general do not know or know very little about: 'Whether or not there is life on any of these planets remains unknown.' 'There are still some unknown species of animals in the South American rainforests.'
Something that you yourself have not seen, heard or experienced before

is **unfamiliar (to** you): 'The voice on the phone sounded unfamiliar.' 'It took Steven some time to get used to his unfamiliar surroundings.'

unless 1

✗ Bring something to eat unless you get hungry.
✓ **Bring something to eat in case you get hungry.**

When you are talking about something that is done as a precaution, use **in case** (NOT **unless**): 'You should take a book with you in case you have to wait.'

2

✗ We can go in my car unless if you prefer to walk.
✓ **We can go in my car unless you prefer to walk.**

Unless (= if ... not) is NOT used with **if**: 'That's all for today unless anyone has any questions.' 'Don't say anything unless you have to.'

3

✗ He won't go to sleep unless you will tell him a story.
✓ **He won't go to sleep unless you tell him story.**
See Language Note at WILL 4

unsatis-factory

✗ To tell you the truth, it's the most unsatisfactory job I've ever had.
✓ **To tell you the truth, it's the most unsatisfying job I've ever had.**
See note at SATISFACTORY

until 1

✗ The new tunnel means that we can drive until London.
✓ **The new tunnel means that we can drive (all the way) to London.**
✗ The magazine covers everything from politics until what's happening in Hollywood.
✓ **The magazine covers everything from politics to what's happening in Hollywood.**

Until and **till** are usually used in connection with time: 'The shops are open until six o'clock on weekdays.'
When you are talking about distance, area, or scope, use **to** or **as far as**: 'Do you know which bus goes to Marble Arch?' 'I got a lift as far as Sheffield and then I took a train.' 'You can get anything from a sandwich to a three-course meal.'

2

✗ The school caters for children until the age of eleven.
✓ **The school caters for children up to the age of eleven.**

up to a particular age (NOT **until**): 'The competition is open to all children up to the age of eleven.'

3

✗ I will have finished this book until tomorrow.
✓ **I will have finished this book by tomorrow.**
✗ Could you let us know your decision until the end of October.
✓ **Could you let us know your decision by the end of October.**

Until is used for an action or state continuing up to a certain time: 'The shops are open until five thirty.' 'I'll wait here until you get back.'
By is used for an action which happens before or no later than a certain time: 'I have to submit my dissertation by the end of next year.'

4 ✗ I'll wait here until you will return.
  ✓ **I'll wait here until you return.**
  See Language Note at WILL

until now 1 ✗ Until now we have received over sixty applications.
  ✓ **So far we have received over sixty applications.**
  ✗ I've only been here for two months until now.
  ✓ **I've only been here for two months so far.**

When you are talking about a situation that is (probably) going to continue into the future, use **so far** or (in formal styles) **to date**: 'So far this week it's hardly stopped raining.' 'To date there have been ten attempts on the President's life.'

2 ✗ Her husband is alive until now.
  ✓ **Her husband is still alive.**
  ? Until now their customs and beliefs remain unchanged.
  ✓ **To this day their customs and beliefs remain unchanged.**

When you want to say that something is the same now as it was in the past, use **still**: 'I've read the first chapter three times and I still don't understand it.' 'Despite her doctor's advice, she still eats anything she likes.'
To give emphasis to this meaning, especially at the beginning of a sentence, use **to this day ... (still)**: 'To this day I still don't understand why they got divorced.'

3 ✗ The letter hasn't arrived until now.
  ✓ **The letter hasn't arrived yet.**

When you mean that up to the moment of speaking something has not happened, use **yet**: 'Her plane hasn't landed yet.'

4 ✗ It's the best hotel that I've stayed at until now.
  ✓ **It's the best hotel that I've ever stayed at.**

When you mean 'at any time (in the past) up to the moment of speaking', use **ever**: 'This is the worst earthquake that the country has ever experienced.'

unusual ✗ It is not unusual that two families share the same house.
  ✓ **It is not unusual for two families to share the same house.**
  See USUAL 1

upstairs See DOWNSTAIRS

up-to-date ✗ Italian women like to keep up with up-to-date fashions.
  ✓ **Italian women like to keep up with the latest fashions.**
  ✗ Television also gives us the up-to-date news and information.
  ✓ **Television also gives us the latest news and information.**

up-to-date (also **up to date**) = (1) (of machinery, equipment, methods, books etc) modern, especially because based on the most recent knowledge, information, inventions etc: 'Our computer system is reasonably up-to-date but it's not flexible enough.' 'This map is no good. I need one that's up-to-date.'
(2) (of people) having the most recent information about something: 'The aim of the survey is to find out how many doctors keep up to date with developments in medical research.'
latest = See note at LAST 4

USA   ✗ I was travelling on a flight from USA to Paris.
              ✓ **I was travelling on a flight from the USA to Paris.**
              See note at THE 12

use 1   ✗ The meals we use to eat are very simple.
              ✓ **The meals we (usually) eat are very simple.**
              ✗ When I'm not busy, I use to play the guitar.
              ✓ **When I'm not busy, I (usually) play the guitar.**

> When you are talking about a present habit, use the present simple tense (NOT **use to do**): 'I (usually) have two cups of coffee at breakfast.'

2   ✗ In my previous job I use to travel a lot.
              ✓ **In my previous job I used to travel a lot.**

> When you are talking about a past habit, use **used to do sth** (with silent **d**): 'Before I had the accident I used to cycle to work.'

3   ✗ It took me a long time to get use to the local accent.
              ✓ **It took me a long time to get used to the local accent.**

> **be/get used to (doing) sth** (with silent **d**) = be in or get into the habit of doing/hearing/seeing etc something, so that it no longer seems strange or difficult: 'Being a city girl, she wasn't used to sitting on a horse.' 'I didn't like the taste of the water at first, but I'm getting used to it.'

4   ✗ On a beautiful day like today it's no use staying at home.
              ✓ **On a beautiful day like today there's no point in staying at home.**
              ✗ It's no use having lessons if you don't want to learn.
              ✓ **There's no point in having lessons if you don't want to learn.**

> Use **it's no use/good doing sth** when you mean that a particular action will not help to deal with a need or difficulty: 'For spellings, it's no use looking in a grammar book. What you need is a dictionary.'
> When you mean that something has no useful purpose, use **there's no point in doing sth**: 'There's no point in having a dictionary if you never use it.'

5   ✗ There's no use in waiting any longer.
              ✓ **There's no point in waiting any longer.**

> **it's no use ...** (NOT **there**): 'It's no use complaining.'
> **there's no point ...** (NOT **it**) 'There's no point in getting upset.'

used   ✗ We soon got used to live in the countryside.
              ✓ **We soon got used to living in the countryside.**
              See note at USE 3

useless 1 ✗ In garage sales people get rid of their useless things.
              ✓ **In garage sales people get rid of the things they don't use.**

> If something is **useless** it is not useful: 'These scissors are useless - they don't even cut paper.' 'The report contains a lot of useless information.'

2   ✗ I don't like history because I think it's useless for me.
              ✓ **I don't like history because I think it's of no use to me.**

✗ Why do we have to learn useless words?
✓ **Why do we have to learn words that are of no use?**

> If something does not help you to do what you want to do, it is **(of) no use (to you)**: 'I use my computer for writing and so a typewriter is of no use to me.' 'This map's no use - it doesn't show the minor roads.'

3
✗ Staying in a big hotel would involve useless expense.
✓ **Staying in a big hotel would involve unnecessary expense.**
? Without all this useless packaging, food would be cheaper.
✓ **Without all this unnecessary packaging, food would be cheaper.**

> If something is not necessary, it is **unnecessary** (NOT **useless**): 'People who refuse to stop smoking are taking an unnecessary risk.' 'Sports that cause animals unnecessary suffering should be banned.'

usual 1
✗ In Finland it's usual that women go out to work.
✓ **In Finland it's usual for women to go out to work.**

> **it's usual/unusual (for sb) to do sth** (NOT **that**): 'Is it usual for him to be so late?' 'It's very unusual to see these flowers at this time of the year.'

2
✗ I thought it was just a usual parcel but then it began to move across the table.
✓ **I thought it was just an ordinary parcel but then it began to move across the table.**

> **usual** = that is usually used, seen, done etc: 'She was sitting in her usual chair by the fire.' 'We arranged to meet at the usual time.' 'He was speaking in his usual calm tone.'
> **ordinary** = without any special features or qualities: 'It was just an ordinary house in an ordinary street.' 'From the moment I met her, I knew she was no ordinary kind of girl.'

usually
✗ As usually, he arrived five minutes late.
✓ **As usual, he arrived five minutes late.**
✗ The food wasn't the same as usually.
✓ **The food wasn't the same as usual.**

> **as usual** (NOT **as usually**): 'John's late as usual.' 'As usual, everyone was out in the garden when I arrived.'
> **the same as usual** (NOT ... **as usually**): 'Apart from his hair, he looked the same as usual.'

utterly
✗ I utterly hope you won't be angry with me.
✓ **I sincerely hope you won't be angry with me.**
✗ I have to make sure that our customers are utterly satisfied.
✓ **I have to make sure that our customers are completely satisfied.**

> **Utterly** is usually used with words that have a negative meaning or express strong disapproval such as (adjectives) **ridiculous, absurd, irrelevant, useless, wrong, impossible,** (adjectival participles) **confused, amazed, dejected, ruined,** (verbs) **reject, detest, destroy**: 'This new tin opener is utterly useless.' 'The whole idea is utterly absurd.' 'I'm utterly amazed.' 'The entire building was utterly destroyed.'

vain
? The police did their best to rescue the hostages but in vain.
✗ **The police did their best to rescue the hostages but without success.**
? She tried to get him to listen but in vain.
✓ **She tried in vain to get him to listen.**
✓ **She tried to get him to listen but it was all in vain.**
✓ **She tried to get him to listen but to no avail.**

> **In vain** usually comes after verbs such as **try, search, hunt, look, wait, fight etc** or after the verb **be**: 'Her voice was beginning to rise and she tried in vain to control it.' 'A team of surgeons battled in vain to save him.' 'I was never in any doubt that my efforts would be in vain.' In other situations, use **without success or to no avail**: 'They did everything they could to protect her, but (all) to no avail.

valuable 1
✗ The magazine is printed on very valuable paper.
✓ **The magazine is printed on very expensive paper.**
✗ They always buy valuable brands such as Polo, Louis Vuitton, and Yves St Laurent.
✓ **They always buy expensive brands such as Polo, Louis Vuitton, and Yves St Laurent.**

> **valuable** = worth a lot of money: 'Your stamp collection must be quite valuable by now.' 'If the painting is genuine, it could be extremely valuable.'
> **expensive** = costing a lot of money, especially when compared with other things of the same type: 'He only buys silk ties, even though they're more expensive.' 'Why are these bananas so expensive?'

2
✗ They will steal all your money and valuable things.
✓ **They will steal all your money and valuables.**

> When you mean valuable things such as jewellery, cameras, etc, use **valuables** (always plural): 'The management advises guests to deposit their valuables in the hotel safe.'

3
✗ The small hotels are usually very valuable for money but the big ones are expensive.
✓ **The small hotels are usually good value but the big ones are expensive.**

> If something is worth what you pay for it, it is **good value (for money)** or **(good) value for money**: 'At just under $90 the Sony is very good value.' 'Having paid £200 for the suit, I expect to get better value for money.'

value 1
✗ The large size is very value.
✓ **The large size is very good value.**
> See note at VALUABLE 3

2

✗ In any case, the car gives you an exceptional value for money.
✓ **In any case, the car gives you exceptional value for money.**

be good/excellent/exceptional value (for money) (WITHOUT **a/an**): '£600 might seem expensive for a two-week holiday, but when you look at all the extras it's quite good value.'

vegetable

✗ I buy a lot of fresh fruit and vegetable.
✓ **I buy a lot of fresh fruit and vegetables.**

Unlike **fruit**, **vegetable** is a countable noun: 'Alan has never been keen on vegetables.'

very 1

✗ He looked very funny that I couldn't help laughing.
✓ **He looked so funny that I couldn't help laughing.**

so + adjective/adverb + **that** clause: 'The music was so loud that I started to get a headache.'

2

✗ Meno Park in Central Tokyo is very huge.
✓ **Meno Park in Central Tokyo is (absolutely) huge.**
✗ The traffic jams are very terrible.
✓ **The traffic jams are (absolutely) terrible.**
✗ I'm very convinced that he is telling the truth.
✓ **I'm (absolutely) convinced that he is telling the truth.**

Do not use **very** or **extremely** with adjectives which already have a strong meaning, e.g. **boiling** (= very hot), **convinced** (= very sure), **exhausted** (= very tired), **huge** (= very big), **terrible** (= very bad). If you want to increase the strength of these words, use **absolutely** or (depending on the particular adjective) **completely, totally, utterly** or **quite**: 'By the time I got home I was completely exhausted.' With adjectives which do not have a strong meaning, use **very** or **extremely** (NOT **absolutely, completely** etc): 'By the time I got back home I was very tired.'

3

✗ Their services are very appreciated by the hospital management.
✓ **Their services are greatly appreciated by the hospital management.**

Very may be used with past participles that are like adjectives and refer to a state: 'very bored/worried/interested/pleased'.
Past participles with a strongly passive meaning are usually modified by **greatly** or **(very) much**: 'His work is much admired.' 'This courageous woman, who helped so many of us, will be greatly missed.'

4

✗ Although he was very in love with Marianne, he wanted to marry a rich heiress.
✓ **Although he was very much in love with Marianne, he wanted to marry a rich heiress.**

Very is not used before a phrase beginning with a preposition (e.g. 'in love with', 'in need of', 'at odds with'). However, in such cases it is often possible to use **very much**: 'These proposals are very much in keeping with the President's own ideas.'
Note the alternative: 'Although he was deeply in love ...'

very much 1

✗ I enjoyed very much my stay in the USA.
✓ **I enjoyed my stay in the USA very much.**
✗ I would like very much to visit some of the places that I have

been reading about.
✓ **I would very much like to visit some of the places that I have been reading about.**

Do not put **very much** between a verb (e.g 'enjoyed') and its object (e.g. 'my stay in the USA'). When the object is short, **very much** goes at the end of the sentence or in front of the verb. When the object is long, **very much** usually goes in front of the verb: 'I very much hope that you and your family have a safe journey.'

2 ✗ It costs very much.
✓ **It costs a lot (of money).**
✗ New doors cost very much because wood is so expensive.
✓ **New doors cost a lot (of money) because wood is so expensive.**

With some verbs (e.g. **cost, pay, charge, eat**) it is possible to use **very much** in questions and negative sentences: 'Did it cost very much?' 'It didn't cost very much.'
However, in affirmative sentences **very much** is usually replaced by **a lot**: 'It will cost quite a lot to have the job done properly.'

3 See LOVE

view 1 ✗ The view of all the blood on the ground made her feel ill.
✓ **The sight of all the blood on the ground made her feel ill.**

View refers to the whole area that you can see from somewhere, especially when you can see a long way into the distance: 'His studio has a spectacular view over Sydney Harbour Bridge.' 'I've booked a room with a view of the sea.'
When you are talking about the act of seeing something, use **the sight of**: 'The sight of so many people dying from disease and hunger is something I will never forget.'

2 ✗ Come over here and watch the view.
✓ **Come over here and look at the view.**
✗ We just sat there and saw the view.
✓ **We just sat there and admired the view.**
✗ From the top of the tower you see a wonderful view of the city.
✓ **From the top of the tower you get a wonderful view of the city.**

look at/admire/enjoy the view (NOT **see/watch**): 'We asked the coach driver to stop so that we could look at the view.'
have/get a (good) view from a particular place (NOT **see**): 'If you stand where I am, you get a much better view.'

3 See POINT OF VIEW

violence ✗ Some of these films are full of the violence.
✓ **Some of these films are full of violence.**
See note at THE 4

vision ✗ We'd like to know your personal vision of the situation.
✓ **We'd like to know your personal view of the situation.**

vision = a picture in the mind of what the future will be like: 'This romantic vision of a world without war is far removed from reality.'

view = the way you think about something that exists now: 'This report sets out the views of our members very clearly.' 'At that time there was a widely-held view that fascism was not a threat to Europe.'

visit 1

✗ Afterwards we visited a restaurant for dinner.
✓ **Afterwards we went to a restaurant for dinner.**

You **visit** places that are of special interest, especially when you are a tourist or official guest: 'By the end of the day I was fed up with visiting museums and all the travelling around.' 'Later in the day Her Majesty will be visiting the Great Ormond Street Children's Hospital.'
You **go to** a restaurant, market, library, someone's house etc: 'If it rains, we could always go to the cinema.' 'I've got to go to the dentist's.'

2

? Thank you for visiting me.
✓ **Thank you for coming to see me.**
? He's gone back to Iran to pay a visit to his family.
✓ **He's gone back to Iran to see his family.**

When you are talking about visiting someone for pleasure or business, **go/come to see sb** (or **go/come and see sb**) usually sounds more natural than **visit sb** or **pay sb a visit**: 'She's gone to see her brother.' 'Let's go and see Peter and take him some grapes.'

3

✗ I've been visiting a language school in Cambridge.
✓ **I've been going to a language school in Cambridge.**

go to or (more formal) **attend** a school, college, class etc (= go there regularly as a student): 'Her son goes to a small private school near Chingford.' 'I've started going to evening classes.'
Compare: 'Government inspectors visit the school twice a year.'

4

✗ If I ever visit to Canada, I'll go when it's warm.
✓ **If I ever visit Canada, I'll go when it's warm.**

You **visit** a place (WITHOUT **to**): 'He has visited all the countries in Europe.'
Compare: 'The President's July visit to El Salvador has been postponed.' (noun + **to**)

vocabulary

✗ The article contained a lot of American English vocabularies.
✓ **The article contained a lot of American English words.**

vocabulary = all the words in a language or all the words (in a language) that someone knows: 'English has a vast vocabulary.' 'By the end of the course students should have an active vocabulary of around 2000 words.'

voice 1

✗ 'You're late!' he said with an angry voice.
✓ **'You're late!' he said in an angry voice.**

in a loud/deep/sad etc **voice** (NOT **with**): 'She spoke in such a soft voice that we couldn't hear anything.'
Compare: 'She speaks with a strong accent.'

2

✗ Students should feel able to voice out their opinions.
✓ **Students should feel able to voice their opinions.**

voice your feelings and opinions (WITHOUT **out**): 'I'm not just voicing my own opinions - we all feel the same.' 'Whenever one of us voices the slightest disapproval, the chairman takes offence.'

voluntary

    ✗ The hospital could not operate without voluntaries.
    ✓ **The hospital could not operate without voluntary helpers.**
    ✗ In my opinion, these young voluntaries should be congratulated.
    ✓ **In my opinion, these young volunteers should be congratulated.**

> **Voluntary** is an adjective (NOT a noun). It describes someone who agrees to work without being paid, or work that is not paid: 'On Saturdays she does voluntary work at an old people's home.'
> The noun is **volunteer** = someone who decides to do something when they are not forced to do it: 'I need three volunteers to help me move the piano.'

vote 1

    ✗ Next year a new president will be voted.
    ✓ **Next year a new president will be elected.**
    ✗ On the day of the vote, they couldn't be bothered to go and vote.
    ✓ **On the day of the election, they couldn't be bothered to go and vote.**

> **vote** = show which person or which course of action you prefer, especially by marking a piece of paper or raising your hand: 'Who will you be voting for at the next election?' 'Fifty-three per cent of Danes voted in favour of the Maastricht treaty.'
> **elect** = choose a leader or representative by voting: 'Roman Catholic cardinals are meeting at the Vatican to elect a new Pope.' 'Williams was elected with a clear majority.'
> **election** = an occasion when people vote: 'Who's going to win the next election?'

2

    ✗ People are not allowed to vote more than one candidate.
    ✓ **People are not allowed to vote for more than one candidate.**

> **vote for sb**: 'I'm not prepared to vote for someone who keeps changing his mind.'

3

    ✗ Every night they voted what they would do the next day.
    ✓ **Every night they voted on what they would do the next day.**

> **vote on** a particular question or issue: 'The Council voted on a motion to close the hospital.'

voyage

    ✗ She didn't say much about her voyage to Germany.
    ✓ **She didn't say much about her trip to Germany.**
    ✗ On the first day we'll rest because the voyage will be tiring.
    ✓ **On the first day we'll rest because the journey will be tiring.**

See Language Note at TRIP

wage

    ✗ He has an annual wage of $40,000.
    ✓ **He has an annual salary of $40,000.**
    See note at SALARY

wages

    ✗ The company directors receive very high wages.
    ✓ **The company directors receive very high salaries.**
    See note at SALARY

wait 1

    ✗ I'm waiting a letter from my boyfriend.
    ✓ **I'm expecting a letter from my boyfriend.**
    ✗ Anyway, I'll wait for you next weekend.
    ✓ **Anyway, I'll expect you next weekend.**

> **wait** = stay somewhere until someone or something comes: 'I'll wait here until you get back.' 'It's quicker to walk than wait for a bus.'
> **expect** = believe that someone or something is going to come: 'The train is expected to arrive in the next five minutes.' 'I can't leave the house - - I'm expecting visitors.'

2

    ✗ I stopped and waited the truck to pass.
    ✓ **I stopped and waited for the truck to pass.**
    ✗ I'll wait you outside.
    ✓ **I'll wait for you outside.**

> **wait for sb/sth**: 'I'll wait for you outside the post office.' 'What can I do while I'm waiting for the paint to dry?'

3

    ✗ I'm waiting to see the photographs with great impatience.
    ✓ **I can't wait to see the photographs.**

> In informal styles, to show that you are really looking forward to something, use **I (just) can't wait** or **I can hardly wait**: 'I can't wait to see you again.' 'I can hardly wait for the holidays to begin.'

wanna

    ✗ We didn't wanna miss the train.
    ✓ **We didn't want to miss the train.**
    See note at GONNA

want 1

    ✗ My parents wanted that I should go to a different university.
    ✓ **My parents wanted me to go to a different university.**
    ✗ 'Do you want I take you to his house?' she asked
    ✓ **'Do you want me to take you to his house?' she asked.**

> **want sb to do sth**: 'The doctor wants me to go for another check-up in two weeks' time.'

2
? I want you to send me the coat if you find it.
✓ **I'd like you to send me the coat if you find it.**
> For polite requests, use **would like** (NOT **want**): 'If you're not too busy, I'd like you to have a look at my homework.'

was
? Everybody looked at him as if he was from another planet.
✓ **Everybody looked at him as if he were from another planet.**
> In formal styles, when you are talking about an unreal situation, use **were** (NOT **was**): 'If the motorway were extended, farming would be severely disrupted.'

wash
✗ I wash my body and then get dressed.
✓ **I have a bath/shower and then get dressed.**
✗ He's gone upstairs to wash.
✓ **He's gone upstairs to have a wash.**
> When you talk about someone washing themselves, you usually use **have a wash/bath/shower**: 'I always feel better after I've had a good wash.'
> See also Language Note at MYSELF

waste
✗ The report deals with the problem of nuclear wastes.
✓ **The report deals with the problem of nuclear waste.**
> See Language Note at INFORMATION

way 1
✗ He explained the ways how we can help to protect the sea.
✓ **He explained how we can help to protect the sea.**
> **describe/explain/examine (etc) how ...** (WITHOUT **the way/s**): 'You have to know how their minds work.' 'In this morning's talk I'll be looking at how smaller companies are dealing with these problems.'
> Note the alternative: 'He explained the ways in which we can help to protect the sea.'

2
✗ She loves the farm and refuses to change her way of living.
✓ **She loves the farm and refuses to change her way of life.**
> See note at LIFE 2

wear
✗ Then I wore some clothes and went downstairs.
✓ **Then I put on some clothes and went downstairs.**
> See Language Note on next page

weather
✗ We had a miserable weather while on holiday.
✓ **We had miserable weather while on holiday.**
> See Language Note at INFORMATION

week 1
✗ We knew that a four weeks holiday would bring us closer together.
✓ **We knew that a four-week holiday would bring us closer together.**
> See Language Note at HUNDRED

2
See Language Note AT TIME

GET DRESSED • DRESS ONESELF • PUT ON • TAKE OFF • DRESS • DRESS UP • WEAR • HAVE ON • BE + ADV + DRESSED

ACTIONS	
get dressed	When you **get dressed** you put on your clothes or a different set of clothes: 'I had a shower, got dressed and went downstairs.' 'I was still getting dressed for the party when the taxi arrived.'
dress oneself	**Dress oneself** is not common. It is mainly used when you are thinking about the special skill or ability that is required to put on clothes: 'Sally isn't old enough to dress herself yet.' See Language Note at MYSELF
put on	When you **put on** a piece of clothing or a watch, necklace etc, you put it into position on your body: 'Wait a minute! I haven't put my coat on yet.' 'Put your gloves on or your hands will get cold.'
take off	**Take off** is the opposite of **put on**: 'I can't wait to take off these new shoes.' 'Why don't you take your coat off and come and sit down?'
dress	If you **dress** someone, you put clothes on them: 'The nurses have to wash and dress the patients before the doctor sees them.'
dress up	When you **dress up** you put on: (1) a special costume: 'When the children were young, George used to dress up as Father Christmas.' (2) formal or smart clothes: 'We won't be going to an expensive restaurant so there's no need to dress up.'
STATES	
wear	When you **wear** something, it is on a part of your body: 'Did you notice the jacket she was wearing at Alan's party?' 'He always wears smart clothes.'
have on	If you **have** something **on**, you are wearing it: 'The trousers he had on were too big for him.' 'You won't get cold as long as you have a coat on.'
be dressed in/be in	If you **are dressed in** or **are in** something, you are wearing it: 'She arrived at the theatre dressed in a long white gown.' 'Everyone was in their best clothes, but Alex turned up in an old T-shirt and jeans.'
be + adverb + **dressed**	When you are talking about someone's appearance, you can say that they **are smartly/neatly/well etc dressed**: 'Make sure you're smartly dressed for the interview.' 'He's always very well dressed - smart jackets, silk ties and so on.'

weekend 1   ✗ I seldom stay at home on weekend.
         ✓ **I seldom stay at home at the weekend.**
         ✗ At weekend we go to the sports club.
         ✓ **At the weekend we go to the sports club.**
         ✗ During the weekend we usually go to a Chinese restaurant.
         ✓ **At the weekend we usually go to a Chinese restaurant.**

         See Language Note at TIME

2   ✗ During this weekend there is a squash tournament.
    ✓ **This weekend there is a squash tournament.**

    See Language Note at TIME

welcome   ✗ You can bring as many friends to the party as you like.
         Everyone is welcomed.
         ✓ **You can bring as many friends to the party as you like.**
         Everyone is welcome.

> **welcome** (verb) = greet a guest or visitor in a friendly way when they arrive: 'Her Royal Highness was welcomed at the airport by a party of Cabinet Ministers.'
> If you are pleased when someone comes to stay at your house or comes to your party, they are **welcome** (adjective), (WITHOUT **d**): 'You're always welcome to stay here, you know.' 'Aunt Edna always makes us feel welcome.'

well 1   ✗ Everything was well until somebody came and sat in the seat next to mine.
         ✓ **Everything was fine until somebody came and sat in the seat next to mine.**
         ✗ His table manners were not very well.
         ✓ **His table manners were not very good.**

> **Well** is usually used as an adverb: 'The team played well on Saturday.' As an adjective, **well** usually means 'in good health': 'George can't come because he's not very well.' 'He always looks well after a holiday.'

2   See KNOW 4

West   See NORTH

wet   ✗ It started pouring with rain and we all got completely wet.
         ✓ **It started pouring with rain and we all got soaked.**

> **soaked** or **soaking wet** = extremely wet: 'Don't leave the cushions in the garden. If it rains, they'll get soaking wet.'

what 1   ✗ A woman can do everything what a man can do.
         ✓ **A woman can do everything (that) a man can do.**
         ✗ I'll do all what I can to help you.
         ✓ **I'll do all (that) I can to help you.**

> **What** is not used as a relative pronoun. After **all, everything, anything** etc, use **that** or nothing: 'You can have anything (that) you like.' 'I have everything (that) I need for the time being.'

2   ✗ She told him that she didn't want to marry him, what in my opinion was very silly of her.

✓ **She told him that she didn't want to marry him, which in my opinion was very silly of her.**

What is not used as a relative pronoun. When you comment on a previous statement, use **which**: 'Lizzie ate the whole box of chocolates, which was very greedy.'

3 ✗ Please tell me what would you like for a wedding present.
✓ **Please tell me what you would like for a wedding present.**

When a **wh-** clause is part of a sentence (e.g. the subject or the object), the subject and verb in the **wh-** clause do not change places. Compare: 'Why did she leave so soon?' 'Do you know why she left so soon?'

when 1 ✗ When hearing that the child had been found, she burst into tears.
✓ **On hearing that the child had been found, she burst into tears.**

To show that two things happen at the same time or that one thing happens immediately after the other, use **on/upon doing sth** (NOT **when**): 'On examining the suitcase, he noticed that the locks had been tampered with.'

2 ✗ When I'll return home, I'll look for a better job.
✓ **When I return home, I'll look for a better job.**

See Language Note at WILL

3 ✗ I don't know when is she coming.
✓ **I don't know when she is coming.**

See note at WHAT 3

whenever ✗ Whenever you'll hear about this place, you'll want to come back.
✓ **Whenever you hear about this place, you'll want to come back.**

See Language Note at WILL

where 1 ✗ He wanted to get to Paris, where his uncle lived there.
✓ **He wanted to get to Paris, where his uncle lived.**

When **where** is used to begin a relative clause, it is not followed by **there**. Compare: 'Every weekend she drives down to London. Her parents live there.' 'Every weekend she drives down to London, where her parents live.'

2 ✗ The box where she kept her jewellery in had disappeared.
✓ **The box where she kept her jewellery had disappeared.**

When **where** begins a relative clause, it is not followed by **in, at, for, etc**: 'We went to see the house where Shakespeare lived.'
Compare: 'The box that/which she kept her jewellery in had disappeared.'

3 See note at WHAT 3

which 1 ✗ Students which fail the exam have to take the course again.
✓ **Students who/that fail the exam have to take the course again.**

Which is used to refer to things (NOT people): 'I like music which/that helps me to relax.'

| | 2 | See note at WHAT 3 |

while 1   ✗ The Japanese have a tendency to keep silent while meetings.
✓ **The Japanese have a tendency to keep silent during meetings.**

> **While** (conjunction) introduces a clause: 'While we were on holiday, we did a lot of walking.'
> **During** (preposition) introduces a noun phrase: 'During the holiday we did a lot of walking.'

2   ✗ While I drove to the airport, my car broke down.
✓ **While I was driving to the airport, my car broke down.**

> To refer to a 'background action', use the past progressive tense (**was /were doing**): 'While I was having a bath, the telephone rang.'

3   ✗ Who will look after the children while you will be at work?
✓ **Who will look after the children while you are at work?**

> See Language Note at WILL

whole   ✗ As a whole, I am very happy here.
✓ **On the whole, I am very happy here.**

> **as a whole** = considered as a single body or unit: 'The country as a whole is not ready for another election.'
> **on the whole** = generally speaking: 'On the whole, I can see no reason why you shouldn't apply.'

whom 1   ? Most of the people whom I met were very kind.
✓ **Most of the people (that) I met were very kind.**

> **Whom** is used only in formal styles: 'Those applicants whom the selection committee recommends for interview should be contacted without delay.' 'The police officer to whom the crime was first reported has been transferred to another unit.'
> In non-formal styles, use **that/who** or nothing: 'The man (that) she intends to marry comes from Stockport.' 'The girl (that) you were speaking to is a friend of mine.' In non-identifying clauses, however, only **who** is possible: 'Both girls - who you may remember from Helen's party - have got places at Oxford.'

2   ✗ She is one of the few people whom I think might be good at the job.
✓ **She is one of the few people who/that I think might be good at the job.**

> When you need a subject relative pronoun, use **who/that** (NOT **whom**): 'He was the one who/that came to meet me at the station.'

why   See note at WHAT 3

wide   ✗ My education has given me a wide view of life.
✓ **My education has given me a broad view of life.**
✗ The magazine gives wide descriptions of market trends.
✓ **The magazine gives broad descriptions of market trends.**

> **broad view/picture/description/outline (of sth)**, NOT **wide**: 'Can you give me a broad outline of what the speech was about?'

will 1   ✗ When capital punishment was abolished, people thought that murders will become more numerous.

✓ **When capital punishment was abolished, people thought that murders would become more numerous.**

> A reporting verb in the past tense (e.g. 'thought') is usually followed by **would/could** (NOT **will/can**). Compare: 'I think she will accept any job that comes along.' 'I thought she would accept any job that came along.'

2   ✗ If a developing country will become a developed country, it has to attract foreign investors.

✓ **If a developing country is to become a developed country, it has to attract foreign investors.**

> When you are talking about what must happen in order to make something possible, use **if ... am/is/are to do sth** (NOT **will**): 'If we are to get there by six o'clock, we'll have to get a taxi.'

3   See Language Note below

Talking about the future

- When you talk about something happening in the future, you often use one of the following conjuctions:

TIME	**after, as soon as, before, immediately, once, the moment, until, when, whenever, while**
CONDITION	**if, whether, as long as, in case, unless**

- To refer to the future after these conjunctions, use the present simple tense (NOT **will/shall**):

> I'll phone you as soon as I <u>arrive</u> at the airport.
> The plane should be taking off shortly, as long as there <u>aren't</u> any delays.

Note:
1 Sometimes it is possible to use the present perfect tense instead of the present simple. The present perfect expresses a sense of completion:

> She doesn't want to buy a car until she's <u>passed</u> her driving test.
> Once you'<u>ve made</u> a few friends, you won't feel so lonely.

2 When the clause beginning with **if, whether, when,** etc is the object of the sentence, **will** may be used:

> I doubt <u>whether David will still recognize me.</u>
> I don't know <u>when they'll be back.</u>

Also, **if ... will** is possible when **will** expresses the idea of willingness:

> What are you going to do if she won't help you?
> If you'll take a seat for a moment, I'll tell Mr Fox you're here.

win   ✗   We have never won the American team.
✓   **We have never beaten the American team.**

> **win** a game, match, race, competition, election, etc: 'United have won four of their last five matches.' 'Who won the FA Cup last year?'
> **beat** a person, team or group (in a game, match, race, competition, election etc): 'They're a good side but I'm sure we can beat them.' '

wish 1   ✗   I wish you have a wonderful holiday.
✓   **I hope you have a wonderful holiday.**
✗   I wish you will enjoy your stay here.
✓   **I hope you will enjoy your stay here.**

> Use **wish that** (+ past/past perfect tense) for things that cannot happen or will probably not happen: 'I wish I hadn't told them my address.' 'I wish you could stay here longer.' (= this will probably not happen)
> Use **hope that** (+ present/present perfect tense) for things that may easily happen or may easily have happened: 'I hope you've had a successful trip.' 'We hope you all have a very merry Christmas.'
> When **wish** is used for this meaning, the object is a noun phrase (NOT a **that** clause): 'I wish you a safe journey.' 'We'd like to wish you all a very merry Christmas.'

2   ?   I wish to send you a wedding present.
✓   **I'd like to send you a wedding present.**
?   I wish to stay until the end of July but I can't.
✓   **I'd like to stay until the end of July but I can't.**

> When you tell someone what you want (to do), or ask someone what they want (to do), use **would like** or (especially in informal styles) **want**: 'I'd like to buy a few postcards.' 'What would you like to do tonight?'
> **Wish** is used with this meaning only in formal styles: 'We wish to apologize for the late arrival of this train.'

3   ✗   I wish that they will stop killing each other.
✓   **I wish that they would stop killing each other.**
✗   He wishes he can drive a car; taxis are so expensive.
✓   **He wishes he could drive a car; taxis are so expensive.**

> When you are thinking about the present or the future, use **wish (that)** + **would /could/had** etc. (NOT **will/can/have** etc.) 'I wish I knew his telephone number.' 'I wish I didn't have to go to school tomorrow.'

with 1   ✗   I finally opened the can with using a screwdriver.
✓   **I finally opened the can by using a screwdriver.**

> To explain 'how' something is achieved, use **by doing sth** (NOT **with**): 'The thieves got into the house by climbing through the kitchen window.'
> Compare: 'I finally opened the can with a screwdriver.'

2   See CAR 2, TAXI

within   ✗   She is getting married within a few hours and she feels a bit nervous.
✓   **She is getting married in a few hours and she feels a bit nervous.**
✗   My examinations are within two weeks' time.
✓   **My examinations are in two weeks' time.**

> **within** = before the end of the stated period: 'The parcel should be

arriving within the next five days.' 'Within six years of joining the company he was Managing Director.'
in = at the end of the stated period: 'The doctor wants to see me again in a week's time.' 'Don't go away. I'll be back in a few minutes.'

wood

✗ The coat has a leather belt and three brown wood buttons.
✓ **The coat has a leather belt and three brown wooden buttons.**

The adjective meaning 'made of wood' is usually **wooden** (NOT **wood**): 'Stir the mixture gently with a wooden spoon.'

work 1

✗ Without a full-time work, some people think it's not worth living.
✓ **Without a full-time job, some people think it's not worth living.**
✓ **Without full-time work, some people think it's not worth living.**
✗ I've come to England to do a research work in civil engineering.
✓ **I've come to England to do research work in civil engineering.**

See Language Note at OCCUPATION

2

✗ I got up and got ready to go to my work.
✓ **I got up and got ready to go to work.**

See Language Note at OCCUPATION

3

✗ These days a lot of women go to work outside.
✓ **These days a lot of women go out to work.**
✗ My wife goes to work outside the house.
✓ **My wife goes out to work.**

See Language Note at OCCUPATION

4

✗ I would like to work at an international organization.
✓ **I would like to work for an international organization.**
✗ My mother works in a large insurance company.
✓ **My mother works for a large insurance company.**

See Language Note at OCCUPATION

world 1

✗ Nepal has one of the highest mountains in all over the world.
✓ **Nepal has one of the highest mountains in the world.**
✗ The sewing machine is one of the most widely used products of the world.
✓ **The sewing machine is one of the most widely used products in the world.**

superlative + noun + **in the world**: 'At that time China was the richest and most powerful country in the world.'

2

✗ Pollution is a serious problem in all of the world.
✓ **Pollution is a serious problem all over the world.**
✗ Their music is played in every part of the world.
✓ **Their music is played all over the world.**

all over the world = everywhere in the world: 'Since joining the newspaper, she's travelled all over the world.' 'There will be teams from all over the world.'

worse
- ✗ It was the worse journey I had ever made.
- ✓ **It was the worst journey I had ever made.**
- ✗ People's lack of responsibility makes the problem even more worse.
- ✓ **People's lack of responsibility makes the problem even worse.**

  bad, worse, (the) worst: 'The medicine just made me feel worse.' 'It's the worst film I've ever seen.'

worst
- ✗ The next time I saw her she looked even worst.
- ✓ **The next time I saw her she looked even worse.**
- ✗ The day finished worst than it began.
- ✓ **The day finished worse than it began.**

  See note at WORSE

worth 1
- ✗ The ring has great sentimental worth.
- ✓ **The ring has great sentimental value.**
- ✗ They do not appreciate the worth of life.
- ✓ **They do not appreciate the value of life.**

  Worth is usually used as a preposition: 'A four-bedroomed house in the middle of town is probably worth about £200,000.'
  The noun related to **worth** is **value**: 'The current value of property is very low compared with this time last year.'
  Compare: 'That watch is worth fifty pounds.' 'That watch has a value of fifty pounds.'

2
- ✗ The missing ring worths about two thousand pounds.
- ✓ **The missing ring is worth about two thousand pounds.**
- ✗ A holiday doesn't worth all the effort it takes preparing for it.
- ✓ **A holiday isn't worth all the effort it takes preparing for it.**

  be worth £20/very little/a fortune etc: 'These old computers aren't worth much nowadays.'

3
- ✗ It's also worth to visit the north of England if you have time.
- ✓ **It's also worth visiting the north of England if you have time.**
- ✗ The museum was certainly worth to see.
- ✓ **The museum was certainly worth seeing.**

  it's worth doing sth; sth is worth doing (NOT to do): 'It's worth remembering that these old cars can be very expensive to run.'

worthwhile
- ✗ The film reviews are always worthwhile looking at.
- ✓ **The film reviews are always worth looking at.**

  it's worth/worthwhile doing sth: 'It might be worth having one or two copies made.' 'Is it worthwhile talking about it now, or shall we leave it until our next meeting?'
  sth is worth doing (NOT worthwhile): 'Some of these so-called professional teams aren't worth watching.'
  Compare: 'Was the long drive up to Scotland really worthwhile?'

worthy
- ✗ It's not worthy taking your own car.
- ✓ **It's not worth taking your own car.**
- ✗ The cathedral is certainly worthy to be visited.
- ✓ **The cathedral is certainly worth visiting.**

it's worth doing sth; sth is worth doing (NOT **worthy**): 'Do you think it's worth having the engine tuned?' 'The letter isn't worth worrying about.'

would 1   ✗ If I would live in the countryside, I would be much healthier.
   ✓ **If I lived in the countryside, I would be much healthier.**

When you are talking about the present or the future and you imagine something that is untrue or unlikely, use the past tense ('lived') in the **if** clause (NOT **would**): 'If I knew her address, I'd send her a postcard.' 'If I won a lot of money, I'd buy a new car.'

2   ✗ If you would have caught the earlier train, we could have travelled together.
   ✓ **If you had caught the earlier train, we could have travelled together.**

When you are talking about the past and you imagine something that is impossible, use the past perfect tense ('had caught') in the **if** clause (NOT **would have**): 'If he hadn't got on the plane, he would still be alive.'

3   ✗ If you would have any more questions, I'll do my best to answer them.
   ✓ **If you should have any more questions, I'll do my best to answer them.**

When you are talking about the present or the future and you imagine something that is possible but unlikely, use **if ... should** (NOT **if ... would**): 'If anyone should need me, I'll be back in half an hour.'

wound   ✗ Only the driver was wounded in the accident.
   ✓ **Only the driver was injured/hurt in the accident.**
See note at DAMAGE 1

wrapping   ✗ Manufacturers should dispense with all unnecessary wrapping.
   ✓ **Manufacturers should dispense with all unnecessary packaging.**

wrapping (also **wrappings**) = paper or paper-like material that is put round something: 'I wanted to tear off the wrapping and see what was inside.'
packaging = the container or material that something is placed in by a manufacturer, especially to protect it or make it look attractive: 'Packaging should be biodegradable and kept to a minimum.'
Note that both **wrapping** and **packaging** are used in connection with food: 'Somewhere on the packaging/wrapping there should be a date stamp.'

write 1   ✗ I'd like to apologize for not having written you before.
   ✓ **I'd like to apologize for not having written to you before.**

In British English you **write to** a person or place (WITH **to**): 'Wingate wrote to his father, asking for more money.'
In American English **to** is optional: 'I'll write (to) you and give you all the latest news.'

2   ✗ Dear ... I write to you to ask for your advice.
   ✓ **Dear ... I am writing to you to ask for your advice.**

For actions which are happening at the time when they are mentioned, use the present progressive tense (NOT the present simple): 'I'm writing to tell you that I'll be coming to London next Thursday.'

wrong

✗ The belief that Spanish is easy to learn is wrong.
✓ **The belief that Spanish is easy to learn is mistaken.**

To describe a belief or idea that is wrong although people do not know it is wrong, use **mistaken**: 'Some people have the mistaken idea that cats need to drink milk.' 'I'm afraid you must be mistaken.'

Yy

year 1
    ✗ I've been playing the piano since I was seven years.
    ✓ **I've been playing the piano since I was seven.**
    ✓ **I've been playing the piano since I was seven years old.**
    ✓ **I've been playing the piano since I was seven years of age.**

> When stating someone's age, use just a number on its own OR a number + **years old/years of age** (NOT **years**): 'I'm almost eighteen.' 'My sister is fifteen years old.'

2
    ✗ Robert was a little boy of ten years.
    ✓ **Robert was a little boy of ten.**

> **a boy/girl/son etc** + **of** + number (WITHOUT **years**): 'a child of six', 'a man of fifty'

3   See AGE 2, 6, 7

4   See OLD 1, 2

5   See Language Note at TIME

6   See RECENT

yearly
    ✗ More houses are built yearly.
    ✓ **More houses are built every year.**
    ✗ Thousands of people die from cancer yearly.
    ✓ **Thousands of people die from cancer every year.**

> **Yearly** usually means that something is done or takes place once a year: 'The interest is paid yearly or, if you prefer, every six months.' 'The front of the house was getting its yearly coat of white paint.'
> **Yearly** is also used to connect a total number or amount with a period of one year: 'We were manufacturing and selling about 20,000 tonnes yearly.' 'The yearly catch rose to a peak of 52,000 tonnes.'
> When you simply want to say that something happens 'all the time', use **every year** or **each year** (NOT **yearly**): 'The country's tourist industry is growing every year.'

yet 1
    ✗ He left the house at five in the morning, when the family was yet asleep.
    ✓ **He left the house at five in the morning, when the family was still asleep.**
    ✗ I've only been here two weeks and everything is strange yet.
    ✓ **I've only been here two weeks and everything is still strange.**

> **Yet** means 'up to the moment of speaking' and is used mainly in ques-

tions and negative sentences: 'Do you feel any better yet?' 'The post office isn't open yet.'
When you want to say that an earlier state or situation has not changed, use **still**: 'I've taken the medicine but I still feel terrible.' 'Does Hilary still go to the same school?'

2 ✗ I didn't finish my thesis yet.
✓ **I haven't finished my thesis yet.**

Yet (= up to the moment of speaking) is usually used with the present or present perfect tense (NOT the past tense): 'Has the taxi arrived yet?' 'Is the taxi here yet?'

3 See note at BUT

yours 1 ✗ Dear Mary ... Yours faithfully ...
✓ **Dear Mary ... Yours/With love/With best wishes ...**
✗ Dear John, ... Yours sincerely ...
✓ **Dear John, ... Yours/With love/With best wishes ...**

Yours faithfully and **Yours sincerely** are used only in formal letters. At the end of a letter to a friend or relative, use **Yours, With love, With best wishes, etc.**

2 ✗ Dear Sir, ... Yours,
✓ **Dear Sir, ... Yours faithfully,**

When a formal letter begins with **Dear Sir** or **Dear Madam**, it usually ends with **Yours faithfully**.

youth ✗ There'll be a lot of youths at the party and so you should be able to enjoy yourself.
✓ **There'll be a lot of young people at the party and so you should be able to enjoy yourself.**
✗ Life in a city is more interesting for the youth because there are more things to do.
✓ **Life in a city is more interesting for young people because there are more things to do.**

Youth (countable) is used, often in a disapproving way, to refer to a boy/young man between the ages of about fifteen and twenty: 'He was attacked and robbed by a gang of youths.'
Youth (uncountable) is used mainly in formal styles to refer to all young people considered as a group in society: 'The youth of industrialized nations need to be made aware of global problems.'
The usual phrase for 'people between the ages of about fifteen and twenty' is **young people**: 'These holidays are designed for young people like yourselves.'

Spelling Error	Correction	Spelling Error	Correction
absent (for noun)	absence	fourty	forty
accomodation	accommodation	freind	friend
acheive	achieve	futur	future
acheivement	achievement	garantee	guarantee
adress	address	goverment	government
advance (for adj)	advanced	greatful	grateful
advertisment	advertisement	habitant	inhabitant
air port/air-port	airport	influencial	influential
allready	already	immediatly	immediately
allready	all ready	independant	independent
allways	always	independance	independence
anymore	any more	laught	laughed
anytime	any time	license (n, AmE)	licence (n, BrE)
apologise (for noun)	apologies	lightening	lightning
appartment	apartment	mathematic	mathematics
appeerence	appearance	mean	means (method)
approch	approach	medecine	medicine
approximatly	approximately	misterious	mysterious
begining	beginning	mistery	mystery
beleive	believe	neclear	nuclear
cancell	cancel	nowaday	nowadays
carreer	career	nowdays	nowadays
carrer	career	occured	occurred
comittee	committee	offerred	offered
completly	completely	old fashion	old-fashioned
curiousity	curiosity	old fashioned	old-fashioned
definitly	definitely	oposite	opposite
dependant (for adj)	dependent	ourself/s	ourselves
descendent	descendant	payed	paid
desperatly	desperately	physic	physics
develope	develop	prefered	preferred
diner (for meal)	dinner	principle	principal (college)
dinning room	dining room	pronounciation	pronunciation
disapear	disappear	promblem	problem
disapointed	disappointed	proplem	problem
discribe	describe	realy	really
downstair	downstairs	recieve	receive
ect	etc	refered	referred
embarass/-ed/-ing	embarrass/-ed/-ing	responsability	responsibility
exite	excite	responsable	responsible
exited	excited	resturant	restaurant
exiting	exciting	seperate	separate
exitment	excitement	shinning	shining
fondamental	fundamental	sincerly	sincerely
forsee	foresee	sometime	sometimes
forth	fourth	specialy	specially
fortunatly	fortunately	stoped	stopped

Spelling

Error	Correction
strenght	strength
succesful	successful
surprise	surprised (adj)
teaher	teacher
technic	technique
theif	thief
theirself/s	themselves
themself	themselves
thier/ther	their
ther	there
therefor	therefore
throught	through
tittle	title
transfered	transferred
truely	truly
tryed	tried
uncurable	incurable
undoubtly	undoubtedly
unfortunatly	unfortunately
unpolite	impolite
untill	until
weeding	wedding
wellcome	welcome
wether	weather
wether	whether
wich	which
wifes	wives
wolfs	wolves
wonderfull	wonderful
writting	writing
yourselfs	yourselves

Word division

Error	Correction
allready	all ready
allright	all right
an other	another
any body	anybody
anymore	any more
anytime	any time
back ground	background
base ball	baseball
basket ball	basketball
boy friend	boyfriend
boy-friend	boyfriend
business man	businessman
business woman	businesswoman
can not	cannot, can't
country side	countryside
eventhough	even though
foot-ball	football
further more	furthermore
girl friend	girlfriend
girl-friend	girlfriend
grand father	grandfather
grand-father	grandfather
grand mother	grandmother
grand-mother	grandmother
grand parent	grandparent
grand-parent	grandparent
head quarters	headquarters
home land	homeland
home sick	homesick
infact	in fact
inspite of	in spite of
more over	moreover
no body	nobody
rain coat	raincoat
soft ball	softball
some body	somebody
some thing	something
some times	sometimes
thankyou	thank you
there fore	therefore
under ground	underground
under stand	understand
where as	whereas
wild life	wildlife
work force	workforce
worth while	worthwhile

The list below shows those verbs that have irregular past tense, PAST PARTICIPLE, or PRESENT PARTICIPLE forms. The INFINITIVE form is shown first, e.g. **begin**.
2 = past tense, e.g. *As I was walking home it* **began** *to rain.*
3 = past participle, e.g. *It had already* **begun** *to rain before I left home.*
4 = present participle, e.g. *It is just* **beginning** *to rain now.*
The number **2/3** means that the past tense and past participle are the same form.

abide[1] **2/3** abided **4** abiding
abide[2] **2** abode **3** abided **4** abiding
arise 2 arose **3** arisen **4** arising
awake 2 awoke or awaked **3** awaked or awoken **4** awaking
be - see BE
bear 2 bore **3** borne **4** bearing
beat 2 beat **3** beaten or beat **4** beating
become 2 became **3** become **4** becoming
befall 2 befell **3** befallen **4** befalling
begin 2 began **3** begun **4** beginning
behold 2/3 beheld **4** beholding
bend 2/3 bent **4** bending
bereave 3 bereaved or bereft **4** bereaving
beseech 2/3 besought or beseeched **4** beseeching
beset 2/3 beset **4** besetting
bet 2/3 bet or betted **4** betting
bid[1] **2/3** bid **4** bidding
bid[3] **2** bade or bid **3** bidden or bid **4** bidding
bide 2 bode or bided **3** bided **4** biding
bind 2/3 bound **4** binding
bite 2 bit **3** bitten **4** biting
bleed 2/3 bled **4** bleeding
bless 2/3 blessed or blest **4** blessing
blow 2 blew **3** blown **4** blowing
break 2 broke **3** broken **4** breaking
breed 2/3 bred **4** breeding
bring 2/3 brought **4** bringing
broadcast 2/3 broadcast || *also* broadcasted *AmE* **4** broadcasting
build 3 built **4** building
burn 3 burnt or burned **4** burning
burst 3 burst **4** bursting
buy 3 bought **4** buying
cast 2/3 cast **4** casting
catch 2/3 caught **4** catching
chide 2 chided or chid **3** chid or chidden || *also* chidded *AmE* **4** chiding
choose 2 chose **3** chosen **4** choosing
cleave 2 cleaved or cleft or clove **3** cleaved or cleft or cloven **4** cleaving
cling 2/3 clung **4** clinging
clothe 2 clothed || *also* clad *AmE* **3** clad || *also* clothed *AmE* **4** clothing
come 2 came **3** come **4** coming
cost 2/3 cost **4** costing
creep 2/3 crept **4** creeping
cut 2/3 cut **4** cutting
dare 2/3 dared **4** daring
deal 2/3 dealt **4** dealing
dig 2/3 dug **4** digging
dive 2 dived || *also* dove *AmE* **3** dived **4** diving
do - see DO
draw 2 drew **3** drawn **4** drawing
dream 2/3 dreamed or dreamt **4** dreaming
drink 2 drank **3** drunk **4** drinking
drive 2 drove **3** driven **4** driving
dwell 2/3 dwelt or dwelled **4** dwelling

eat 2 ate **3** eaten **4** eating
fall 2 fell **3** fallen **4** falling
feed 2/3 fed **4** feeding
feel 2/3 felt **4** feeling
fight 2/3 fought **4** fighting
find 2/3 found **4** finding
flee 2/3 fled **4** fleeing
fling 2/3 flung **4** flinging
fly 2 flew **3** flown **4** flying
forbear 2 forbore **3** forborne **4** forbearing
forbid 2 forbade or forbad **3** forbidden or forbid **4** forbidding
forecast 2/3 forecast or forecasted **4** forecasting
foresee 2 foresaw **3** foreseen **4** foreseeing
foretell 2/3 foretold **4** foretelling
forget 2 forgot **3** forgotten **4** forgetting
forgive 2 forgave **3** forgiven **4** forgiving
forsake 2 forsook **3** forsaken **4** forsaking
foreswear 2 forswore **3** forsworn **4** forswearing
freeze 2 froze **3** frozen **4** freezing
get 2 got **3** got *esp. BrE* || gotten *AmE* **4** getting
gild 2/3 gilded or gilt **4** gilding
give 2 gave **3** given **4** giving
go 2 went **3** gone **4** going
grind 2/3 ground **4** grinding
grow 2 grew **3** grown **4** growing
hang[1] **2/3** hung **4** hanging
hang[2] **2/3** hanged **4** hanging
have - see HAVE
hear 2/3 heard **4** hearing
heave[1] **2/3** heaved **4** heaving
heave[2] **2/3** hove **4** heaving
hew 2 hewed **3** hewed or hewn **4** hewing
hide 2 hid **3** hidden **4** hiding
hit 2/3 hit **4** hitting
hold 2/3 held **4** holding
hurt 2/3 hurt **4** hurting
keep 2/3 kept **4** keeping
kneel 2/3 knelt || *also* kneeled *AmE* **4** kneeling
knit 2/3 knit or knitted **4** knitting
know 2 knew **3** known **4** knowing
lay 2/3 laid **4** laying
lead 2/3 led **4** leading
lean 2/3 leant *esp. BrE* || leaned *esp. AmE* **4** leaning
leap 2/3 leapt *esp. BrE* || leaped *esp. AmE* **4** leaping
learn 2/3 learned or learnt **4** learning
leave 2/3 left **4** leaving
lend 2/3 lent **4** lending
let 2/3 let **4** letting
lie[1] **2** lay **3** lain **4** lying
lie[2] **2/3** lied **4** lying
light 2/3 lit or lighted **4** lighting
lose 2/3 lost **4** losing
make 2/3 made **4** making
mean 2/3 meant **4** meaning
meet 2/3 met **4** meeting
mislay 2/3 mislaid **4** mislaying
mislead 2/3 misled **4** misleading

misspell 2/3 misspelt or misspelled **4** misspelling
misspend 2/3 misspent **4** misspending
mistake 2 mistook 3 mistaken **4** mistaking
misunderstand 2/3 misunderstood **4** misunderstanding
mow 2 mowed 3 mown or mowed **4** mowing
outbid 2 outbid 3 outbid || *also* outbidden *AmE*
　4 outbidding
outdo 2 outdid 3 outdone **4** outdoing
outshine 2/3 outshone **4** outshining
overcome 2 overcame 3 overcome **4** overcoming
overdo 2 overdid 3 overdone **4** overdoing
overhang 2/3 overhung **4** overhanging
overhear 2/3 overheard **4** overhearing
override 2 overrode 3 overridden **4** overriding
overrun 2 overran 3 overrun **4** overrunning
oversee 2 oversaw 3 overseen **4** overseeing
overshoot 2/3 overshot **4** overshooting
oversleep 2/3 overslept **4** oversleeping
overtake 2 overtook 3 overtaken **4** overtaking
overthrow 2 overthrew 3 overthrown **4** overthrowing
partake 2 partook 3 partaken **4** partaking
pay 2/3 paid **4** paying
prove 2 proved 3 proved or proven **4** proving
put 2/3 put **4** putting
quit 2/3 quit 3 quit or quitted **4** quitting
read 2/3 read **4** reading
rebuild 2/3 rebuilt **4** rebuilding
redo 2 redid 3 redone **4** redoing
relay 2/3 relayed **4** relaying
remake 2/3 remade **4** remaking
rend 2/3 rent || *also* rended *AmE* **4** rending
repay 2/3 repaid **4** repaying
rewrite 2 rewrote 3 rewritten **4** rewriting
rid 2 rid or ridded 3 rid **4** ridding
ride 2 rode 3 ridden **4** riding
ring 2/3 ringed **4** ringing
ring 2 rang 3 rung **4** ringing
rise 2 rose 3 risen **4** rising
run 2 ran 3 run **4** running
saw 2 sawed 3 sawn || *also* sawed *AmE* **4** sawing
say 2/3 said **4** saying
see 2 saw 3 seen **4** seeing
seek 2/3 sought **4** seeking
sell 2/3 sold **4** selling
send 2/3 sent **4** sending
set 2/3 set **4** setting
sew 2 sewed 3 sewn || *also* sewed *AmE* **4** sewing
shake 2 shook 3 shaken **4** shaking
shave 2/3 shaved **4** shaving
shear 2 sheared 3 sheared or shorn **4** shearing
shed 2/3 shed **4** shedding
shine 2/3 shone **4** shining
shine 2/3 shined **4** shining
shoot 2/3 shot **4** shooting
show 2 showed 3 shown || *also* showed *AmE* **4** showing
shrink 2 shrank or shrunk 3 shrunk or shrunken
　4 shrinking
shut 2/3 shut **4** shutting
sing 2 sang 3 sung **4** singing
sink 2 sank || *also* sunk *AmE* 3 sunk || *also* sunken *AmE*
　4 sinking
sit 2/3 sat **4** sitting
slay 2 slew 3 slain **4** slaying
sleep 2/3 slept **4** sleeping
slide 2/3 slid **4** sliding
sling 2/3 slung **4** slinging

slink 2/3 slunk **4** slinking
slit 2/3 slit **4** slitting
smell 2/3 smelt *esp. BrE* || smelled *esp. AmE* **4** smelling
smite 2 smote 3 smitten || *also* smote *AmE* **4** smiting
sow 2 sowed 3 sown or sowed **4** sowing
speak 2 spoke 3 spoken **4** speaking
speed 2/3 sped || *also* speeded *AmE* **4** speeding
spell 2/3 spelt *esp. BrE* || spelled *esp. AmE* **4** spelling
spend 2/3 spent **4** spending
spill 2/3 spilled or spilt **4** spilling
spin 2/3 spun **4** spinning
spit 2/3 spat || *also* spit *AmE* **4** spitting
split 2/3 split **4** splitting
spoil 2/3 spoiled or spoilt **4** spoiling
spread 2/3 spread **4** spreading
spring 2 sprang || *also* sprung *AmE* 3 sprung
　4 springing
stand 2/3 stood **4** standing
steal 2 stole 3 stolen **4** stealing
stick 2/3 stuck **4** sticking
sting 2/3 stung **4** stinging
stink 2 stank or stunk 3 stunk **4** stinking
strew 2 strewed 3 strewn or strewed **4** strewing
stride 2 strode 3 stridden **4** striding
strike 2 struck 3 struck || *also* stricken *AmE* **4** striking
string 2/3 strung **4** stringing
strive 2 strove 3 striven || *also* strived *AmE* **4** striving
swear 2 swore 3 sworn **4** swearing
sweep 2/3 swept **4** sweeping
swell 2 swelled 3 swollen or swelled **4** swelling
swim 2 swam 3 swum **4** swimming
swing 2/3 swung **4** swinging
take 2 took 3 taken **4** taking
teach 2/3 taught **4** teaching
tear 2 tore 3 torn **4** tearing
tell 2/3 told **4** telling
think 2/3 thought **4** thinking
thrive 2 throve or thrived 3 thrived or thriven **4** thriving
throw 2 threw 3 thrown **4** throwing
thrust 2/3 thrust **4** thrusting
tread 2 trod 3 trodden or trod **4** treading
unbend 2/3 unbent **4** unbending
undergo 2 underwent 3 undergone **4** undergoing
understand 2/3 understood **4** understanding
undertake 2 undertook 3 undertaken **4** undertaking
undo 2 undid 3 undone **4** undoing
unwind 2/3 unwound **4** unwinding
uphold 2/3 upheld **4** upholding
upset 2/3 upset **4** upsetting
wake 2 woke or waked 3 woken or waked **4** waking
waylay 2/3 waylaid **4** waylaying
wear 2 wore 3 worn **4** wearing
weave[1] 2 wove 3 woven **4** weaving
weave[2] 2/3 weaved **4** weaving
wed 2/3 wedded or wed **4** wedding
weep 2/3 wept **4** weeping
wet 2/3 wet or wetted **4** wetting
win 2/3 won **4** winning
wind[2] 2/3 winded **4** winding
wind[3] 2/3 wound **4** winding
withdraw 2 withdrew 3 withdrawn **4** withdrawing
withhold 2/3 withheld **4** withholding
withstand 2/3 withstood **4** withstanding
wring 2/3 wrung **4** wringing
write 2 wrote 3 written **4** writing

Glossary

abstract noun a word used to refer to an idea or feeling (not something that you can actually see or touch): e.g. danger, jealousy, luck, peace, success.

active See PASSIVE

adjective a word which describes someone or something: 'In his new grey suit, he looked very smart.'

adverb 1 a word which tells us 'how', 'when', 'how often', 'where', etc: 'Drink it slowly.' 'She usually arrives late.'

2 a word like very, quite, too, slightly, which says something about degree or extent: 'very cold', 'rather suddenly', 'completely destroyed'.

3 a word like probably, definitely, fortunately, surprisingly, which says something about the speaker's attitude or degree of certainty: 'Perhaps she's changed her mind.' 'Unfortunately, the car wouldn't start.'

4 a word like however, therefore, also, furthermore, which shows how two points or ideas are related: 'Both hotels are very expensive. Also, they are a long way from the city centre.'

affirmative See NEGATIVE

agree See NUMBER

auxiliary verb See MAIN VERB

bare infinitive See INFINITIVE

clause a string of words, usually with a subject and verb, which forms either a sentence by itself ('We're going out tonight.') or a major part of a sentence ('if it doesn't rain'). See also MAIN CLAUSE, SUBORDINATE CLAUSE

colloquial A colloquial word or expression is used mainly in everyday conversation, and is not appropriate in formal styles.

comparative the form of an adjective or adverb that is used to express a greater or smaller degree. Most comparatives end in -er or begin with more/less: 'The new cameras are easier to use but the old ones are more reliable.' See also SUPERLATIVE

compound a word which is made up of two or more parts: e.g. boyfriend, headache, washing machine, air travel, 'a five-minute wait'.

conditional 1 a clause beginning with a word such as if or unless, or a sentence containing such a clause

2	a verb form beginning with would/should: 'They would like to see a copy of the report.' 'Would you like a drink?'
conjunction	a word like and, but, because, since, when, as soon as, if, which joins two points or ideas together or shows how they are related to each other: 'We had some cheese and a few biscuits.' 'I'll phone you when I get back.' 'Although he was late, he made no attempt to apologize.'
context 1	the word or words which come immediately before and/or after a particular word or phrase
2	the social situation in which language is used
countable	A countable noun (also 'count noun') is one which has both singular and plural forms: e.g. 'apple' - 'apples', 'child' - 'children'. See also UNCOUNTABLE
determiner	a word like a/an, the, this, my, some, every, which comes in front of a noun: 'an apple', 'her new car', 'most people'.
direct object	See OBJECT
direct speech	speech that is written down in the exact words of the original speaker. The words are usually enclosed within inverted commas: "My purse has been stolen." Indirect speech (also called 'reported speech') is speech that is written down in the words of the reporter, with changes to tenses, pronouns, adverbs etc: She said that her purse had been stolen.
double negative	the incorrect use of two negative words instead of one, e.g. 'Nobody never ...' instead of 'Nobody ever ...'
emphasis	the special force that is sometimes given to a word or phrase to draw it to the listener's or reader's attention: 'I do hope you feel better soon.' 'They themselves have never been to Italy.'
finite	A finite verb is one which has a subject and a tense: e.g. 'takes', 'took', 'has taken', 'was being taken'.
first person	See PERSON
fixed phrase	two or more words which are always used together and cannot be changed in any way: e.g. 'as a matter of fact', 'on the contrary' (NOT 'on a contrary', 'on the contraries', etc)
formal	Formal styles are those in which words and structures are chosen with care, as in business letters, official reports, academic textbooks, news broadcasts, public ceremonies, etc. See also INFORMAL
identifying relative clause	See RELATIVE CLAUSE
indirect object	See OBJECT
indirect speech	See DIERCT SPEECH
infinitive	the form of a verb that you look up in a dictionary. There are two types of infinitive, the 'bare infinitive' (e.g. 'come', 'take', 'send') and the 'to-infinitive' (e.g. 'to come', 'to take', 'to send'), sometimes shown in this book as 'to-v'.

informal	Informal styles are those in which language is used in a casual, spontaneous way, as in everyday conversation and letters to friends. See also FORMAL
-ing form	the form of a verb which ends in '-ing', e.g. 'coming', 'taking', 'sending', sometimes shown in this book as 'v-ing'.
	When an -ing form is used as a noun, it is sometimes called a 'gerund': e.g. 'I like reading.' When an -ing form is used as a verb, it is sometimes called a present participle: 'I saw her talking to Dr Edwards this morning.'
intransitive	An intransitive verb is one that is used without an object, e.g. 'Wait here until I come back.' See also TRANSITIVE
main clause	(also 'independent clause') a string of words containing a subject and verb, which can stand alone as a sentence: e.g. 'I'm going out tonight.' See also SUBORDINATE CLAUSE
main verb	a verb like 'speak', 'take' or 'go' which can be used as the only verb in a sentence: 'She speaks German and Russian.' 'He took her to the airport.' A main verb is often preceded by one or more auxiliary verbs such as 'be', 'do', 'have', 'will', 'may', 'must': 'She is learning French.' 'He must have taken her to the airport.' 'Do you know their address?'
modify	(also 'qualify') A word is often used with one or more other words which provide additional information about it or limit its meaning. In such cases, the word is said to be 'modified'. For example, in 'Japanese cars are quite expensive', 'cars' is modified by 'Japanese', and 'expensive' is modified by 'quite'. The words 'Japanese' and 'quite' are used as modifiers. In 'a luxury hotel', the first noun ('luxury') modifies the second noun ('hotel').
negative	A verb is negative when it is used with not, never, rarely, etc: 'She never answers my questions.' A clause or sentence containing a negative verb is also negative. Compare: He wanted to go to bed.' (affirmative verb/sentence); 'He didn't want to go to bed.' (negative verb/sentence)
non-identifying relative clause	See RELATIVE CLAUSE
noun	a word used to refer to a person, animal, place, thing, etc: 'Each visitor received a small gift.'
noun phrase	a group of words in which the main word is a noun or pronoun: 'Each visitor received a small gift.' 'Have you finished reading the book I lent you?'
number	the contrast between words which are singular (e.g. 'child') and words which are plural ('children'). Two words are said to 'agree in number' when they are both singular or both plural. Compare: 'The child was playing in the garden' (singular); 'The children were playing in the garden' (plural).
object	The object (also 'direct object') of a sentence is the person or thing that is directly affected by the action of the verb: 'She bought a packet of envelopes'; 'I'd already seen the film'. An 'indirect object' is usually the person or thing that receives the

direct object: 'She sent my mother a postcard.' 'He gave her a diamond ring.' 'We told them the news.'

participle See PAST PARTICIPLE, -ING FORM

passive When the subject of a sentence 'performs' the action expressed by the verb, the verb and the sentence are said to be 'active': 'Someone has stolen my watch.' 'The government spends a lot of money on cancer research.' Sometimes the subject of a sentence does not perform the action expressed by the verb but 'receives' it: 'My watch has been stolen.' 'A lot of money is spent on cancer research.' In these cases, the verb and the sentence are said to be 'passive'.

past participle the verb form that is used to make the present perfect and past perfect, and all passive structures: 'She's lost her address book.' 'I hadn't seen her before.' 'Have the letters been posted yet?'

past perfect the verb form that is made with had and the past participle: 'After everyone had gone, we began to tidy up.' 'If I'd known your address, I would've come to see you.' See also PROGRESSIVE

past progressive See PROGRESSIVE

past tense The past tense of a regular verb ends in -ed and has the same form as the past participle: 'cooked', 'thanked', 'opened'. The past tense of an irregular verb is formed in many different ways: 'went', 'saw', 'thought', 'found', 'took', 'spoke'. See also PROGRESSIVE

person the contrast between words which refer to ourselves (e.g. I, we = 'first person'), words which refer to the person we are talking to (e.g. you = 'second person'), and words which refer to someone or something else (e.g. he, she, Mrs Robinson, the apple trees = 'third person').

phrase 1 a group of words whose main word is a noun ('many people'), main verb ('has been written'), adjective ('quite difficult') or adverb ('fairly soon'), or which begins with a preposition: ('at six o'clock', 'in the garden', 'for political reasons')

2 two or more words which are often used together: 'have a bath', 'make a mistake', 'it is obvious that' See also FIXED PHRASE

plural See NUMBER

plural noun a noun which is always plural and does not have a singular form, e.g. trousers, scissors, goods, surroundings

possessive A possessive form or meaning is one which expresses ownership or close connection: 'Is this your handbag?' 'Have you met her husband?' 'It's Bob's birthday tomorrow.' 'We had lunch at Rosemary's.'

preparatory subject Instead of using a clause as the subject of a sentence, it is often more natural to begin the sentence with it and put the clause later: 'It's amazing that nobody was injured.' 'It will be good to see you all again.' When used in this way, it is called a preparatory subject.

preposition a word like at, from, for, during, into, in spite of which is used before a noun, pronoun, etc: 'We went to the airport in a taxi.'

present perfect   the verb form that is made with have and the past participle: 'My watch has stopped.' 'Have you seen Alex this morning?' See also PROGRESSIVE

present
progressive   See PROGRESSIVE

present simple   the verb form which has no endings apart from -s/-es with subjects such as 'he', 'she', 'it', 'Mrs Robinson' etc: 'I play a lot of tennis.' 'The sun rises in the east and sets in the west.' See also PROGRESSIVE

progressive   (also 'continuous') a verb form made with be + -ing: 'It was raining this morning.' (past progressive); 'Are you coming tonight?' (present progressive); 'I've been waiting here for over an hour.' (present perfect progressive); 'Before coming to London, she had been working in Paris.' (past perfect progressive). See also SIMPLE

pronoun   a word like he, her, mine, themselves, some, who, which is used in place of a noun or noun phrase: 'Ann was very upset when she heard the news.' ('she' is the pronoun for 'Ann'); 'If Alex needs a red pen, there's one in the drawer.' ('one' is the pronoun for 'a red pen')

reflexive pronoun   a word like myself or ourselves that ends with -self or -selves: 'I found myself a seat and sat down.'

reflexive verb   a verb that is used with myself, herself, themselves etc: 'You mustn't blame yourself for the accident.'

relative clause   a descriptive clause usually beginning with that, who, which, whose or whom. An 'identifying' relative clause answers the question 'which?' and identifies or defines the preceding noun: 'The man who was carrying a torch showed us to our seats.' A 'non-identifying' relative clause simply adds further information about the preceding noun: 'The man, who was carrying a torch, showed us to our seats.'

relative pronoun   a word like that, who, which, used at the beginning of a relative clause. See also RELATIVE CLAUSE

reporting verb   a verb like say, answer, ask, complain which is used when reporting what someone has said, asked, etc: 'She complained that she needed more time.' ' "I can't afford a new car," he replied.'

second person   See PERSON

simple   A simple verb form does not have an -ing ending: e.g. 'It rained all day.' (past simple); 'What time does the train arrive?' (present simple); 'He's bought a new bicycle.' (present perfect); 'One of the books had fallen on the floor.' (past perfect). See also PROGRESSIVE

singular   See NUMBER

subject   The subject of a sentence is the person, thing or idea that the sentence is about. In statements, the subject usually comes at the beginning and is followed by a verb: 'These old newspapers should be thrown away.' 'The house they intend to buy is in

Kensington.' 'Looking after a young child can be very tiring.' See also PREPARATORY SUBJECT

subordinate clause
(also 'dependent clause') a string of words that cannot be used on its own as a sentence, but usually forms a major part of a sentence: 'As soon as my exams are over, I'm going on holiday.' 'Driving on the wrong side of the road is dangerous.' See also MAIN CLAUSE

superlative
the form of an adjective or adverb that is used to express the greatest or smallest degree. Most superlative forms end in -est or begin with most/least: 'It was the longest and most boring film I'd ever seen.' See also COMPARATIVE

syllable
A syllable is one or more speech sounds pronounced as one unit. For example, hat has one syllable, jacket has two syllables, and cardigan has three.

that-clause
a subordinate clause beginning with that which does the job of a noun, pronoun, etc: 'She told me that you don't like her.' 'It's amazing that nobody was injured.' Sometimes, especially in informal styles, the word that may be left out: 'She says (that) she's looking for a new job.' 'It's a pity (that) you won't be coming.'

third person
See PERSON

to-infinitive
See INFINITIVE

to-v
See INFINITIVE

transitive
A transitive verb is one that is used with an object, e.g. 'She opened the drawer and took out a knife.' See also INTRANSITIVE

uncountable
An uncountable noun is one which has no plural form and is not used with a/an: e.g. 'We need some new furniture.' 'She needs advice.' 'Poverty can lead to unhappiness and despair.'

verb
a word which refers to an action or a state: 'She said that she felt ill.'

v-ing
See -ING FORM

vowel
(also 'vowel sound') a speech sound made when the breath escapes freely, without being blocked or restricted in the mouth or throat, such as /iː/ as in 'key' /kiː/, or /aː/ as in 'car' /kaː/.

wh-clause
a subordinate clause beginning with a wh-word, e.g. what, why, how, where, who: 'Do you know where she lives?' 'What we need is a faster printer.'

wh-word
See WH-CLAUSE